Territories of Poverty

Territories of Poverty

RETHINKING NORTH AND SOUTH

EDITED BY
ANANYA ROY
EMMA SHAW CRANE

THE UNIVERSITY OF GEORGIA PRESS
Athens and London

Most University of Georgia Press titles are
available from popular e-book vendors.

Printed digitally

Library of Congress Cataloging-in-Publication Data
Territories of poverty : rethinking North and South /
edited by Ananya Roy and Emma Shaw Crane.
     pages cm. — (Geographies of justice and social transformation ; 24)
Includes bibliographical references and index.
ISBN 978-0-8203-4842-1 (hardcover : alk. paper) —
ISBN 978-0-8203-4843-8 (pbk. : alk. paper) — ISBN 978-0-8203-4844-5 (ebook)
1. Poverty. 2. Equality. 3. Poor—Political activity. 4. Public welfare.
5. Economic assistance, Domestic. 6. Economic assistance.
I. Roy, Ananya. II. Crane, Emma Shaw.
    HC79.P6T46 2015
    339.4'6—dc23
                                                                2015005761

British Library Cataloging-in-Publication Data available

In memory of the life and work of
our beloved colleague
Michael B. Katz.

CONTENTS

Why *Territories of Poverty* Now?

Our interest in questions of poverty and inequality has been directed by the numerous places and histories that have shaped our lives, from Kolkata, India, to Chiapas, Mexico; from Oakland, California, to Beirut, Lebanon. Convening and curating a joint project of scholarship, we were both inspired by two genres of research, critical ethnographies of development and social histories of welfare and penality, which have allowed us to make sense of these places and histories. We were also keenly aware that these genres remained divided and separated, rarely in conversation across academic borders. Yet in our academic and political lives, we each drew extensively on both, crossing these forbidden borders out of necessity. From the very start, *Territories of Poverty* was meant to occupy this transgressive space.

But there was something else that mattered to us: the work of theory. This project is unapologetically concerned with theory—theory as an argument about the world, theory as a concern with the epistemology of power, and theory as a collective imagination. Bound together by the classroom of the public university where we first met—Emma as student and Ananya as teacher—we have participated in the scarcely voiced and yet ever-present task of rethinking our inheritances of authoritative knowledge. Theory for us—as those initial roles of student and teacher have been dramatically revised and reversed—remains a crucial site of politics. And theories of poverty have been especially important. Following Alice O'Connor's work, we are interested in the encounter between the social sciences and the problematic of poverty. As Emma notes in the conclusion of this book, "how we think and act on poverty informs how we imagine what is possible, and what is just." To remake theories of poverty is thus an effort to consider what this book series foregrounds as key themes: geographies of justice and social transformation.

But to remake theory is also an effort to remake the institutional context within which we undertake the work of representation. Theory, as Emma notes, must ride the bus! To do so we engage not only in interdisciplinary collaborations but also in intergenerational ones. It is in the interstices of disciplines and generations that new possibilities of representation and transformation can be forged. With this in mind, *Territories of Poverty* gathers not only the scholarship of multiple disciplines but also that of multiple generations. Thus, in conversation with the full-length chapters are short essays by undergraduate and graduate students at the University of California, Berkeley, who participated in organizing and documenting the conference that resulted in this book. We wanted them—Anh-Thi Le, Christina Gossmann, Luis Flores Jr., Rebecca Peters, Somaya Abdelgany, and Stephanie Ullrich—to not only organize but also curate, to not only document but also theorize. Their reflections provide an important glimpse of the intergenerational task of remaking theory, and indicate how young scholars inhabit their disciplines and professions.

Finally, for this project, we have sought to enact an analytical shift from thinking about places of poverty to territories of poverty. This is why the cover of the book is the provocative artwork of Chris Johanson. Eschewing the usual images of places of poverty, whether apocalyptic or humanized, we were drawn to an image that, for us, suggests subjectivity, relationality, and multiplicity. Johanson's art is part of the Mission School Arts Movement, which emerged in San Francisco in the 1990s. We find the repertoire of this movement to be an important prompt for us to think about the politics of difference and representation across North–South divides.

We agreed easily and immediately upon the term "territory," for all of the reasons outlined in Ananya's introduction and throughout the book. As we considered more fully the mandate of collaboration, we made territory the organizing concept of our joint research. Using the occasion of this project, we immersed ourselves in an investigation of two fields of power that we each continue to inhabit and hope to transform: the city of Oakland and the discipline of urban planning. Seeking to understand how community development emerged as a dominant paradigm of progressive urban planning, and how Oakland was the laboratory for such an emergence, we tried to make sense of the territories of our own existence: city and discipline.

As we complete this book, the full meaning of territory is very much on our minds. During the preparation of our first draft of the manuscript, Janet Napolitano, then Secretary of the Department of Homeland Security, was appointed the first woman president of the University of California, what we believe to be the world's premier public university, and of which we are both alumna and now at which we are each educator and researcher. If *Territories of Poverty* attempts to dismantle entrenched academic borders, then our academic lives are also enmeshed in the crude consolidation of "homeland" borders. Our beloved public university, we realize, is fully implicated in the practices of securitization through which territories are constituted and policed. To cast the "homeland," securitized through Napolitano's deportation machinery, as territory, is to recognize, as does Alyosha Goldstein in his essay in this book, the "afterlives" of colonialism, continental conquest, and slavery.

As we wrote and revised our chapters in 2013, a jury in Sanford, Florida, acquitted George Zimmerman of the murder of Trayvon Martin, an unarmed black teenager, whom Zimmerman shot and killed in 2012. Trayvon Martin, rendered bare life, was put on trial and found to be guilty for his own death. Institutionalized through the American justice system, this is a reminder of the brutal territorializations of race that constitute the present history of America. Enacted through the rituals of "neighborhood watch" and defended through the device of "stand your ground" laws, that gated townhouse community of Sanford, Florida, is territory. It is the territory where Trayvon Martin's embodied presence could not be permitted or tolerated. Theory cannot grant Trayvon Martin permission to pass, unassaulted by the vigilant neighborhood watch citizen. But it can give us permission to undertake critical and sustained scrutiny of one of the key discourses through which social relations of inequality are organized: poverty. At a moment marked by the deportation of undocumented migrants and the legally sanctioned murder of young black men, we must engage theory to more deeply understand territories of poverty, and strategically challenge this politics of disappearance and death.

Territories of Poverty is made possible through the effort and support of many. At the University of California, Berkeley, the project found a home at the Blum Center for Developing Economies. The Distinguished Chair in Global Poverty and Practice held by Ananya, and underwritten by an anonymous donor, provided the funds for a conference held at Berkeley in fall 2012. The conference was generously cosponsored by the Department of City and Regional Planning, the Center for Middle Eastern Studies, the Center for South Asia Studies, and the Institute for the Study of Societal Issues. At the conference, Teresa Caldeira, Gillian Hart, Aihwa Ong, and Jennifer Wolch chaired sessions, moderated discussion, and provoked debate. We are grateful for their roles in shaping this project. As we have already mentioned, two Blum Center student writers, Luis Flores Jr. and Christina Gossmann, along with five students belonging to the Undergraduate Research Apprenticeship Program, Somaya Abdelgany, Anh-Thi Le, Aviya McGuire, Rebecca Peters, and Stephanie Ullrich, provided assistance with the organization of the conference and conducted research.

We are delighted that *Territories of Poverty* is a part of the University of Georgia Press's book series on Geographies of Justice and Social Transformation. We thank the series editors, Deb Cowen, Nik Heynen, and Melissa Wright, as well as Mick Gusinde-Duffy, editor-in-chief, and John Joerschke, project editor, at UGA Press, for their interest in the project and constant support. We are grateful to Chris Johanson for generously allowing us to use his art for the book cover.

This book is dedicated to our beloved author and collaborator, Michael B. Katz. A towering figure in the critical scholarship of poverty and welfare, the inspiration for this project came from him and his work. When Ananya discovered that he was teaching her book, *Poverty Capital* (concerned with the politics of international development) in his graduate seminar at the University of Pennsylvania on the social history of poverty in America, she was intrigued. His explanation for why passage across such scholarly divides is necessary lies at the heart of this book and the alliances it hopes to make possible.

Ananya Roy and Emma Shaw Crane
Oakland, July 2014

Territories of Poverty

INTRODUCTION

The Aporias of Poverty

ANANYA ROY

> This discourse on death also contains, among so many other things, *a rhetoric of borders*, a lesson in wisdom concerning the lines that delimit the right of absolute property, the right of property to our own life, the proper of our existence, in sum, a treatise about the tracing of traits as the borderly edges of what in sum *belongs to us [nous revient]*, belonging as much to us as we properly belong to it.
>
> —JACQUES DERRIDA, *Aporias* (1993: 3, emphasis in original)

Territories

In the summer of 2013 the *New York Times Magazine* ran a cover story by Ben Austen titled "The Death and Life of Chicago" (Austen 2013). The essay and its photographs delineated a divided city: on the one hand, a "global city," "a tourist destination for the world, a player with derivatives and trade shows, a city of big transportation hubs," characterized by the "downtown renaissance" that is a familiar formula in such cities; and on the other hand, a city of "derelict communities of resources," neighborhoods with abandoned homes and schools facing closure. One of the urban planners interviewed for the article described Chicago as resembling "London or Jakarta, with a hyperdense core—a zone of affluence—and something else beyond."

The urban divides Austen sketches are neither novel nor unique, although some aspects of this sociospatial inequality indicate a distinctive historical conjuncture. For example, the face of urban poverty, as depicted in this essay, is not the inner-city ghetto. Instead, it is the southernmost edge of Chicago, a zone that is an example of what, in the American context, has come to be called the "suburbanization of poverty." Indeed, during the last decade, the American metropolis has witnessed the rapid increase of suburban poverty, a process that has now outpaced the increase of urban poverty (Garr and Kneebone 2010). Austen describes this geography as a "moneyed elite residing within the glow

1

of that jewel-like core and the largely ethnic poor and working-class relegated to the peripheries, the *banlieues*."

Such metropolitan reconfigurations are shaped by complex processes, of which the housing crisis is one. If in the past dilapidated public housing towers and the hollowed-out ghetto were the stereotypical images of American urban poverty, then today neighborhoods with foreclosed homes and abandoned properties are the image of poverty. These are the new geographies of poverty in America, thoroughly imbricated in global circuits of financialization. As the work of Wyly and colleagues (2012), Newman (2009), and most recently Chakravartty and Ferreira da Silva (2012), has shown, such circuits of finance mobilize and deepen histories of racial difference and social exclusion. The American foreclosed suburb is thus not simply an evacuated space but rather a territory, the normalized place where racialized and financialized impoverishment is enacted. To undertake an analysis of such territories of poverty is to call into question this normalization.

But there is more to the story of the southernmost edge of Chicago. Austen's purpose was not only to depict wealth and poverty in Chicago but also to analyze "how the epidemic of empty, foreclosed homes in Chicago's poorest neighborhoods has ignited a new form of guerilla activism." Foregrounding a movement called the Chicago Anti-Eviction Campaign, the essay explores how such activism is reclaiming space. The Chicago Anti-Eviction Campaign can be understood, Austen argues, as a "radical urban homesteader" movement that claims foreclosed homes. It is a movement keenly attuned to finance capital and its predations, and thus it is an example of how urban social movements are organized around global, indeed multiscalar, imaginations of crisis and dispossession. In particular, the movement in Chicago takes its cue from the Western Cape Anti-Eviction Campaign, which was formed in 2000 in South Africa with the aim of fighting evictions, water cut-offs, and poor health services; obtaining free electricity; securing decent housing; and opposing police brutality. Thus has a poor people's movement in the global South become the template for housing takeovers in Chicago's fringe.

I have opened *Territories of Poverty* with the foreclosed zones of the American metropolis, and specifically the case of the Chicago Anti-Eviction Campaign and the Southern templates on which it relies, because such spaces and processes exemplify the global historical context within which a new agenda of poverty scholarship must be forged. This historical conjuncture requires a reconsideration not only of familiar territories of poverty but also of the modalities of global North and global South through which poverty research and expertise are structured. It is no longer the twentieth century, and the new century portends a dramatically rearranged world, one in which shifting territorializations of power and poverty demand new analytical practices and new imaginations of politics. Urban social movements, often connected in networks of transnational solidarity such as those that extend from the Western Cape of Africa to the southern periphery of Chicago, already know this. But does critical theory? This volume seeks to curate the new modalities of analysis through which critical theory can inhabit the global historical context and respond to the persistent, yet rearranged, territorializations of poverty.

This opening anecdote is meant to evoke three key elements of the agenda of poverty scholarship in the essays included in this book: an analytical shift from places of poverty to territories of poverty; attention to poor people's movements not simply as grassroots mobilization but as processes that exist in relation to ideologies of power and bureaucracies of poverty; and a global historical approach to poverty, welfare, and development that eschews multinational comparison and instead holds in simultaneous view the uneven geographies, and temporalities, of global North and global South. These are more fully elucidated in this opening essay as well as in those that follow, but let me say a few words about each analytical point at the outset.

Territories of Poverty is concerned with how the problematic of poverty is closely linked to the question of territory. In the simplest sense, we are interested in old and new geographies of poverty and poverty management: border, hyperghetto, Third World, periphery, community, suburb, slum. The story of the Chicago Anti-Eviction Campaign signals new geographies of poverty and more broadly the spatial character of racialized poverty and its regulation. But what is at stake in this story is territory, not place. As Elden (2013: 5) argues, the question of territory is not the problem of terrain, as the question of population is not the problem of people. Territory, according to Elden (2010: 760), and following Foucault, is a "political technology" through which the "spatial order of things" comes to be normalized and perpetuated. Elden (2013: 16) notes that such a political technology involves techniques in the narrower sense (think maps, land surveys, population controls) as well as the broader notion of *techne* as a "way of grasping and conceiving of the world" (think literature, legal systems, political debates).

A territorial understanding of poverty has several implications. It marks a rupture with what Wacquant (2008: 1) has described as the "topographic lexicon" of poverty studies. In his essay in this volume, "Class, Ethnicity, and State in the Making of Marginality: Revisiting Territories of Urban Relegation," Wacquant cautions that territories of poverty must be understood not as low-income communities or districts of dispossession but instead as relations of "urban relegation." The ghetto, he thus notes, is not "a zone of social disintegration" but a "*spatial implement of ethnoracial closure and control*" (emphasis in original). "The proper object of inquiry," Wacquant concludes, "is not the place itself and its residents but the multilevel structural processes," including the process and mechanisms of relegation, or what he identifies as "territorial stigma."

In conceptualizing poverty in relation to territory, we are specifically interested in programs of government, or in how poverty is governed as a problem. We follow Wacquant (2008: 6) in arguing that what seems to be "'effects of place' turn out to be essentially effects of state projected on to the city." But in keeping with the Foucauldian turn, we also follow Rose and Miller (1992) in studying political power beyond the state. As they note, "government is a domain of strategies, techniques and procedures through which different forces seek to render programmes operable, and by means of which a multitude of connections are established between the aspirations of authorities and the activities of individuals and groups" (Rose and Miller 1992: 281). To understand how poverty is governed as a problem, and above all produced and normalized as a territory, we accordingly pay close attention to programs of government. But as Painter notes (2010), this does not mean that territory—as statespace—is neatly fixed, bounded, and stable. Instead, he sees territory as something that has to be brought into being, effectuated, and that is thus "never complete, but always becoming . . . a promise the state cannot fulfil" (2010: 1094). In other words, territory might very well mark the limits—or as I will argue later in this essay, the aporia—of government.

Finally, in its emphasis on territories of poverty, this book delves into the relationship between government and security, one indicated in Foucault's 1977–78 lectures, *Security, Territory, Population*, but that is not fully explored in the scholarship on poverty. In his essay in this volume, "Is Poverty a Global Security Threat?," Akhil Gupta provides a much-needed genealogy of the idea of security as it comes to be entangled with another idea, that of global poverty. As Gupta notes, in a post-9/11 era, global poverty itself has been conceptualized as a national security threat by "defense intellectuals" in the "global North." Gupta's genealogical analysis of security asks who is the "human" of "human security"? He argues that "the securitization of poverty creates the elites in the global North as the new subjects of security, the people most threatened by poverty in the global South." Gupta's careful attention to the imperial histories at work in the geopolitics of poverty discourse is of course missing from Foucault's analysis of security. But it is useful to turn to Foucault to consider the relationship between territory and poverty. Foucault (2007: 20, 23) states that "discipline structures a space and addresses the essential problem of a hierarchical and functional distribution of elements," but security plans a "milieu," and thus requires the sovereign to intervene by "acting on the milieu." The problem of sovereignty,

Foucault (2007: 64–65) argues, is no longer how territory can be "demarcated, fixed, protected, or enlarged," but instead that of "allowing circulations to take place" to ensure the "security of the population," not just the "safety of the Prince." *Territories of Poverty* uses this framework of security to consider how the government of poverty requires not only practices of discipline but also the planning of a milieu. In our essay on U.S. poverty programs in the 1960s, "Gray Areas: The War on Poverty at Home and Abroad," Stuart Schrader, Emma Shaw Crane, and I foreground one such milieu: community. Miller and Rose (2008: 85, 88) describe this meaning of community as the "territory of government," one that is a "new plane or surface upon which micro-moral relations among persons are conceptualized and administered." Following Cowen and Siciliano (2011: 107), we are thus concerned with how practices of security seek to turn "surplus subjects" into "productive" lives.

While the Foucauldian framework lends itself to an analysis of territory as a form of government, government is also the locus of politics, and of dissent. Mbembe (2000: 261) asks that we view territory as "a set of possibilities that historically situated actors constantly resist or realize." At the southernmost edge of Chicago, the work of the Anti-Eviction Campaign is one example of such contestation. It must be understood as a poor people's movement, a phrase I borrow from the classic text by Piven and Cloward (1977). Recent poverty scholarship, especially in the American context, has paid new attention to the role of poor people's movements, for example in the important edited collection by Orleck and Hazirjian (2011) on the grassroots history of the War on Poverty. And of course, critical ethnographies of development have long focused on the "cramped spaces" (Li 2007) from within which subaltern classes stage resistance and rebellion against programs of government. But *Territories of Poverty* approaches poor people's movements in a very specific way. Instead of positioning them as grassroots mobilization, we seek to uncover the contradictory articulation of poor people's movements and bureaucracies of poverty, between practices of dissent and ideologies of power. I deliberately use the term "articulation" to reference the work of Stuart Hall, Chantal Mouffe, and others on articulation as a cultural practice crafted in the interstices of hegemony. It is thus instructive to consider that as a "radical urban homesteader" movement, the Chicago Anti-Eviction Campaign at once contests and deploys notions of property. Their work deploys a simple, elegant, and provocative motto: "Homeless people in people-less homes." But the movement must use the symbolic frame of homesteading, in this case justifying occupation through a legal clause in the Illinois trespass statute focused on the beautification of property. In previous work, I have argued that such tactics simultaneously challenge and consolidate "paradigms of propertied citizenship" (Roy 2003). Thus, Piven and Cloward (1977: x) call for a "dialectical analysis" of poor people's movements, one in which they are understood to be "both formed by and directed against institutional arrangements."

One way of considering the relationship between government and the poor is through the influential concept of political society advanced by Chatterjee. Concerned with the "deepening and widening of the apparatuses of governmentality," Chatterjee (2012: 46) foregrounds "tussles" over "governmental services." In the global South, these welfare entitlements, he notes, "do not flow from the universal rights of citizenship—as in the post-war welfare state in Western Europe or North America" (Chatterjee 2011: 88) but instead emerge from the popular demands of political society. Other scholars, such as Caldeira and Holston (2014), view such mobilizations as bearing the potential for new forms of insurgent citizenship as well as the reform and even democratization of programs of government itself. In aligning with such scholarship on politics, we break with apocalyptic accounts of the poor as marginalized humanity—for example, Standing's (2011: 41) framing of the global precariat as "a new dangerous class" shaped by "anger, anomie, anxiety, and alienation." Instead, we take our cue from poor people's movements to reconsider the global historical context of poverty, welfare, and development. While quite a bit of poverty scholarship is concerned with multinational comparisons—poverty here versus poverty elsewhere—*Territories of Poverty* is concerned with a relational approach that holds in simultaneous view the global North and global South. In doing so, we seek to learn from poor people's movements. For example, Chicago's dilapidated zones must be seen not simply as an example of a new geography of poverty in America but rather as a node in a global political economy of urbanism and in a global network of housing rights movements. The Chicago Anti-Eviction Campaign is thus an example of "seeing from the South." I borrow the phrase from Watson (2009), who argues that dominant modes of planning, produced in the context of the global South, cannot make sense of the "globe's central urban issues." In fact, it is in the cities of the global South that collective action by the urban poor has become an important platform of social justice. Appadurai (2002) has labeled such poor people's movements "deep democracy," and drawn attention to the horizontal ties of solidarity through which they constitute global formations of protest, knowledge, and mobilization.

I was reminded of this recently in Johannesburg where young artists and hip-hop musicians from the township of Diepsloot presented "arts in action" in a public performance that was an instantiation of such global formations. It is tempting to read such performances as the aestheticization of poverty, and indeed in past work I have been critical of the portrayal of the slum or ghetto as spaces of cultural creativity (Roy 2011b). But what if we were to understand this as cultural politics, one that seeks to reinscribe the meaning of poverty? What if we were to understand this as the collective imagination that Teddy Cruz, in his manifesto for this volume, "Spatializing Citizenship and the Informal Public," deems so important? Diepsloot Arts in Action produces complex narratives of territories of poverty and their attendant subjectifications. This is most evident in its spoken word genre, for example the "Dear Diepsloot" performances:

DEAR DIEPSLOOT,
From Monday to Wednesday, you make me love you like a butterfly, that comes out of its cocoon.
I can only have a good time then, like a cat drinking its milk, like a rabbit eating its carrots.
When its Thursday, my feelings change about you.
You turn into a pack of angry dogs.
You make me angry like a chicken whose chicks have been taken away.
When it's Thursday Diepsloot, you act like a bunch of baboons.
You forget I need to hunt like an owl, searching for knowledge, working at night.
When it's Thursday Diepsloot, you let my prey escape me.
DEAR DIEPSLOOT, I LOVE YOU, BUT YOU BREAK MY HEART."
(See "Diepsloot Public Art 2012—Process," *Sticky Situations*, May 2, 2012, http://www.stickysituations.org/2012/05/02/diepsloot-public-art-2012-process/)

I do not want to suggest that such forms of cultural politics constitute an autonomous and alternative public sphere produced by poor people's movements. The Diepsloot Arts in Action performance was curated and mediated by Sticky Situations, a community capacity building organization, and Global Studio, a planning and design studio involving Columbia University and University of Witwatersrand. Such infrastructures of mediation must be understood as uneasy alliances rather than as platforms of subaltern representation. The Diepsloot Arts in Action performance took place not in the township but in Maboneng, a new arts district in Johannesburg where Global Studio has exhibition space. A site of gentrification, this strip of Maboneng is buzzing with creative energy, all within a hypersecuritized cordon that separates this zone of cultural consumption from the territory of poverty around it.

But what is irrefutable is the global imagination of poor people's movements, and this is not new. For example, during the 1960s, social mobilizations in the inner cities of America not only called into question the long history of marginalization and racialization but also explicitly cast this history as an example of "domestic colonialism" and a world order of dependency and underdevelopment (Katz 1989: 58). In cities like Oakland the Black Panther Party claimed territories of poverty as sites of political community. Huey Newton, along with other Black Panther leaders, saw "community to exist not just in the local contexts of

Oakland or Chicago" but instead as "collectives of people living in colonized ghettos" around the world (Heynen 2009: 416). Such imaginations remind us of the importance of a relational understanding of North and South. This is the prompt that we take seriously in seeking to advance a new agenda of poverty scholarship attentive to a history of the present.

In his philosophical treatise *Aporias*, Jacques Derrida (1993: 8) presents aporia as "the difficult or the impracticable . . . the impossible, passage, the refused, denied, or prohibited passage, indeed the nonpassage." Of course, the term aporia is a statement of doubt. But Derrida takes us further by having us consider aporia as a nonpassage or impasse. Derrida (1993: 20–21) uses the plural term "aporias" to indicate a multiplicity of meaning. There is aporia as impermeability, "the opaque existence of an uncrossable border." In the second type, aporia is an impasse because there is "not yet or there is no longer a border to cross . . . the limit is too porous, permeable, and indeterminate." In the third type, aporia is "the impossible": the "nonpassage" because "there is no more path."

But an impasse or nonpassage in and across what territory? Derrida (1993: 1, 5) poses the question of aporia in relation to a set of limits or borders, the "finis" of territory. He thus notes the "limits of truth," of how truth is "precisely limited, *finite*, and confined within its borders." In particular, Derrida (1993: 23) wants to consider three types of limits: those that separate countries, nations, cultures; the "separations and sharings" between disciplines of research and domains of discourse; and the borders that demarcate concepts or terms. The point of Derrida's analysis is not to find safe passage across such borders and limits but instead to consider the aporias that haunt the attempt to pass and trespass. Put another way, Derrida (1993: 9) is keenly attuned to what he describes as the "essential incompleteness of translating."

I present this opening essay of *Territories of Poverty* in the spirit of Derrida's reflection on aporias as prohibited or impossible passage. The aporias of poverty indicate the limits or borders that this book attempts to cross and that yet are passages that remain prohibited, impossible, refused, undecidable. These include the limits of truth, the threshold of normal science that must be negotiated each time an agenda of scholarship is crafted. In particular, *Territories of Poverty* is interested in broaching and breaching what Derrida (1993: 41) calls the "problematic closure," that which "assigns a domain, a territory, or a field to an inquiry, a research, or a knowledge." What is the passage between social histories of the North Atlantic welfare state and critical ethnographies of development in the global South? What is the *finis*, the border, that demarcates global North and global South and that must be exceeded in order for such a passage to exist? In what ways is this passage an aporia, an impossible passage?

Aporia haunts not only this agenda of scholarship but also the very processes and movements from which this book takes its cue. On the one hand, a rearranged world order connotes new territorial relations of development and underdevelopment, sovereignty and dependence, prosperity and poverty. On the other hand, these recalibrated borders must be seen as prohibited, difficult, refused. In particular, the category of the global South—including that which animates the analytical modality of seeing from the South—is an aporia. To view poverty territorially is to take on this aporetic impulse, to disrupt the limits of which Derrida (1993: 41) warns: the "single braid" of problematic closure, anthropological border, and conceptual demarcation. Such is the single braid of well-worn topographic designations of poverty—slum, ghetto—each securely located in its hemisphere of difference—South, North.

It is worth reflecting that Derrida explores the question of aporias in tandem with the question of death. It is the discourse of death that initiates for him the "rhetoric of borders," including the "borders of truth and borders of property." After all, death, he argues, implicates the "right of property to one's own life," what can also be understood as the "proper of our existence" (Derrida 1993: 3). While this topic exceeds the scope of this book, poverty necessarily involves the work of death, or what Mbembe (2003: 13) has termed necropolitics, "where becoming subject therefore supposes upholding the work of death." Akhil Gupta (2012: 5) thus presents extreme poverty in India "as a direct and culpable form of killing made possible by state policies and practices." What are the limits of truth at these limits of life?

For a moment let us return to Chicago. Ben Austen's (2013) essay narrates an incident involving Joe Peery, a key figure in the Chicago chapter of the National Union of the Homeless, and a resident of the infamous Cabrini-Green public housing project, which until its demolition was located just blocks from Chicago's zone of affluence: "Peery remembered a homeless man freezing to death in a cardboard box just 100 feet from one of the Cabrini towers—a building filled with vacant units, central heat pumping ceaselessly into each of them." The incident became an impetus for the homeless union to begin takeovers of vacant government-owned housing, to transform the politics of life and death.

And for a moment let us return to Maboneng, that hypersecuritized zone of creative energy and cultural consumption in Johannesburg. Here, the work of death becomes the cultural politics of gentrification. An art installation on the sidewalk features a guard booth, an uncanny mimicry of the security borders—visible and invisible—that mark the limits of Maboneng. "The guard sat on my cactus, now my cactus is dead," reads the epigraph (figures 1 and 2). Reconstituted as aesthetic object, the territory of poverty thus becomes the site of a

FIGURE 1.
Maboneng,
Johannesburg.
Photo by author.

FIGURE 2.
Maboneng,
Johannesburg.
Photo by author.

parody of death. At once passage and impasse, such parody is one of the many aporias of poverty.

THE REARRANGEMENT OF THE WORLD

In a modest and preliminary way, my purpose is to investigate more closely what makes *one single braid* of these three forms of limits, to which I have given the somewhat arbitrary names of *problematic closure, anthropological border,* and *conceptual demarcation.*

—JACQUES DERRIDA, *Aporias* (1993: 41, emphasis in original)

The start of the twenty-first century is marked by a new world order of development and underdevelopment, the rearrangement of prosperity and growth across global North and global South. On the one hand, the economies of the North Atlantic are in turmoil. From the American Great Recession to what has been dubbed the existential crisis of the Eurozone, hitherto prosperous liberal democracies are on shaky ground. If the 1980s was billed as the lost development decade in Africa and Latin America because of structural adjustment, then today the Bush era of neoliberal redistribution is being billed as the lost decade for the American middle class (Pew Research Center 2012). On the other hand, in the economic powerhouses of the global South, such as India and China, new hegemonic models of capital accumulation are being put into place. And there is fast and furious experimentation with welfare programs and human development, be it the building of the world's largest development NGO in Bangladesh, or the crafting of a "new deal" for India's slum dwellers, or the institutionalization of "right to the city" policies in Brazil, or vigorous debate about a guaranteed minimum income in South Africa. These exist in relationship with, and also at odds with, what Wacquant (2009: xi) has billed as "the neoliberal government of social insecurity," or "America as the living laboratory of the neoliberal future." They reveal the intense reinventions of development that are taking place in the global South, practices and imaginations that seem foreclosed in the North Atlantic. They also bring into view the multiplicity and heterogeneity of capitalism's futures. It is in this context that we attempt to rethink territories of poverty—beyond the categories of slum and ghetto, beyond urban underclass and heroic informal entrepreneur, beyond North and South.

Poverty is no longer where it once was. In the North American metropolis, familiar geographies of ghetto poverty now exist alongside large swaths of suburban poverty. In the global South, the "new bottom billion" lives not in low-income, fragile states but in middle-income countries (Sumner 2012). In his essay in this volume, Akhil Gupta thus asks us to consider the various reterritorializations of space that are at work in a rearranged world. Not only are territories of poverty changing, he notes, but processes of dramatic stratification and segregation are unfolding in both the global North and global South. Alongside this "new geography of global poverty" (Sumner 2012) is possibly a new architecture of sovereignty. While President Barack Obama recently toured Africa with the familiar script of American leadership and Third World poverty—trade not aid, has been his motto—the story of development in Africa has a quite different lead character: China. In order to "decentre the North" in the study of development, as Mohan and Power (2009: 27) put it, it is necessary to reinscribe new and heterogenous cartographies of power and poverty. From China's drive to secure farmland and mineral resources in Africa to the U.S. quest for homeland security, to South Korea's transformation from an aid-receiving nation to a replicable model of Asian success, to ambitious experiments with social democracy in Latin America, to the remaking of popular politics in the Middle East, this is a world of multiple polarities and shifting alliances. This is clearly not the world order established at Bretton Woods.

It is tempting to interpret a rearranged world as the entrenchment of neoliberalism and austerity politics in the North Atlantic contrasted with the reinvention of New Deal social democracy in the global South. But it is instead more useful to consider how, as Ferguson (2009) notes, new rationalities of poverty alleviation are emerging from within, and not just against, neoliberalism. Thus, in their ongoing work on neoliberalization, including in this book ("Paying for Good Behavior: Cash Transfer Policies in the Wild"), Jamie Peck and Nik Theodore highlight a set of globally circulating models of poverty interventions that are simultaneously pro-poor and pro-market. This is a new logic of social assistance, and it is also a new spatio-temporality of welfare and development: the uneven global geographies of fast policy that cut across hemispheres and continents. Or, Bill Maurer, in his contribution "Data-Mining for Development? Poverty, Payment and Platform," by studying what he calls "poverty payment," the vast sprawl of mobile payments through which the poor increasingly participate in global capitalism, highlights the limits of a laissez-faire approach. The means of value transfer, Maurer notes, are seen not only as transactional data and opportunities for profit, but also as public good. Needless to say, I use the word "new" with the caution it deserves. For example, in her essay in this book, "Funding the Other California: An Anatomy of Consensus and Consent," Erica Kohl-Arenas traces neoliberal consensus politics all the way back to the height of farmworker organizing in California and to César Chávez's faith in ideologies of "mutual prosperity." Her work reminds us of the contradictory articulation of poor people's movements and the bureaucracy of poverty, the uneasy suturing of radical practices of self-determination and ideologies of self-help. In our essay "Gray Areas," Stuart Schrader, Emma Shaw Crane, and I explore such contradictions in the context of community development in the United States during the turbulent 1960s. We demonstrate how community action was rapidly transformed into programs of community development, especially those animated by the ethos of self-help rather than self-determination. But also in cities like Oakland, the bureaucracy of poverty became the platform for radical visions and practices of self-determination, notably by the Black Panther Party. Such poor people's movements, as I have already suggested, had a global imagination, linking ghetto and colony, the battlefields of Vietnam and the inner cities of America. Today's neoliberalism has been indelibly shaped by such movements, their institutionalization in community development, as well as their militant disavowal of liberal government.

In their recent manifesto "After Neoliberalism," Stuart Hall, Doreen Massey, and Michael Rustin (2013: 10) analyze the "global character of neoliberalism," its "financial imperialism," and "its planetary search for new assets in which to speculate." But, as they note, "neoliberalism never conquered everything. It operated within, and created, a world of great diversity and unevenness." It is this uncertain and incomplete character of neoliberalism, these diverse and uneven geographies, that are the object of interest for *Territories of Poverty*. In fact, we do not necessarily privilege the analytical framework of neoliberalism in our investigations. Instead, our wager is that the problematic of poverty provides unique insights into the global present. As Alyosha Goldstein states in the opening line of his essay for this volume ("The Duration of Inequality: Limits, Liability, and the Historical Specificity of Poverty"), "the 'persistence of poverty' is a constitutive dilemma for the idea of historical progress." It is also our wager that the regulation and management of poverty entails practices of state, civil society, and market that often exceed and even disrupt the templates of crude austerity. From conditional cash transfers to philanthrocapitalism to microfinance and mobile money, a proliferation of programs and rationalities recalibrate market fundamentalism. Reflecting on Bill Maurer's essay in this volume on payment platforms, Christina Gossmann, in "Representation: Fast Policy in a Mobile World," thus notes that the privatization of mobile banking may not be so easily accomplished.

The single braid of neoliberalism is particularly limited when we turn our attention to poverty, welfare, and development in the global South. Take for example the case of the BRICS, the formation comprising Brazil, Russia, India, China, and South Africa. On the one hand, this alignment of economic hegemony may be understood as what Prashad (2012: 145) has called "Neoliberalism with Southern Characteristics." On the other hand, it is a refusal of the northern formula of structural adjustment. Thus, consider the bold 1989 declaration of Manmohan Singh, later to become prime minister of India, that "new locomotive forces have to be found within the South" (Prashad 2012: 9). Thus, consider the distinctive framing of North–South geographies formulated by Maite Nkoana-Mashabane, South Africa's minister of international relations, in preparation for the 2013 Durban summit of the BRICS. For her, the BRICS present an opportunity to challenge "North–South disparities in knowledge production" and to recognize "multiple centres of human civilization" (Nkoana-Mashabane 2013: 6). She draws her inspiration not only from Frantz Fanon and Paulo Freire but from a 1915 essay by W. E. B. Du Bois that identifies the "accumulation of wealth by the North while the South was being underdeveloped" (Nkoana-Mashabane 2013: 9). Celebrating that "since then China has risen and Africa is rising," Nkoana-Mashabane (2013: 9) distinguishes the "emerging global players of the South" from "the traditional powers." Hers is a vision of a rearranged world that relies at once on new formations of economic hegemony and the long history of anti-imperialist struggle.

Such regimes of global liberalism demand analytical attention on their own terms, and not simply as instantiations of a predictable and universal script of neoliberalism. And they demand, as Hall, Massey, and Rustin (2013: 11) suggest, an account of the "tectonic shift of economic power," from the North Atlantic, "to China and the other BRIC countries." For a while now, scholars of global political economy have foreshadowed this shift of economic hegemony. Arrighi (2009) thus narrates the history of the present as "the new Asian Age," an "Asian renaissance," that marks the end of an age of American supremacy. Territories of Poverty does not conceptualize this rearranged world as a unidirectional shift in economic hegemony from the North Atlantic to the global South. Arrighi, I would argue, gets it wrong in suggesting that the neoconservative Project for the New American Century is over, eclipsed by the New Asian Age. American imperialism remains a vital part of the present historical conjuncture. The terminal crisis of American economic hegemony remains integrally connected to new vectors and frontiers of militarization, both at home and abroad. Territories of Poverty, by keeping in simultaneous view the multiple cartographies of development and welfare, performs a genealogy that is attentive to a rearranged world and its multiple histories.

Inspired by the current historical moment, Territories of Poverty thus seeks to move beyond the North–South geographies that have shaped the study of capitalism and its social regulation, notably Euro-American welfare states versus Third World development. That such a divide has persisted is in and of itself surprising, since, as Goldstein (2012: 3) notes in his recent book, Poverty in Common, "early Cold War doctrines of international development and modernization . . . were intimately and increasingly associated with U.S. policy on domestic poverty during the thirty years following the Second World War." Despite this long history of geopolitical entanglements, American poverty scholarship and Third World poverty scholarship have grown up apart. The important shift in American poverty scholarship—from the causes and symptoms of poverty to the analysis of how poverty is managed and regulated as a social problem—led by scholars such as Frances Fox Piven, Michael B. Katz, Alice O'Connor, and Loïc Wacquant, has been staged in near complete separation from critical ethnographies of development. This latter body of work, led by Julia Elyachar, James Ferguson, Michael Goldman, Akhil Gupta, Gillian Hart, Tania Murray Li, Timothy Mitchell, Anna Tsing, and Michael Watts, among many others, has sought to understand international development as a distinctive project, instantiated and negotiated through competing practices, rationalities, and hegemonies. It is rather obvious that these two separated worlds of analysis have much to say to one another. It is perhaps less obvious that a multinational comparison may not necessarily accomplish such a task. Comparative efforts, as in the classic 1996 text, *Urban Poverty and the Underclass: A Reader*, edited by Enzo Mingione, are important but usually leave untouched the geohistorical categories of the urban industrial North and its others. *Territories of Poverty* is an effort in relational analysis, one that brings critical ethnographies of development in relation with social histories of the welfare state, and one that inevitably positions the West and the rest in relation to one another in a rearranged world. One inspiration comes from Vincanne Adams (2013). In keeping with the genre of critical ethnographies of development, Adams reframes the analysis of American neoliberalism by uncovering its articulations with disaster recovery, faith-based charity, and humanitarian reason. Her essay in this volume, "Disaster Markets and the Poverty Factory," continues such lines of analysis.

Needless to say, *Territories of Poverty* is not unique in its efforts to rethink the relational categories of North and South. In particular, it builds on key approaches in postcolonial theory, notably Chakrabarty's (2000) call to "provincialize" Europe "in global times." Chakrabarty demonstrates the parochial character of seemingly universal thought, thereby revealing the narrowly European origins of canonical histories of capital and modernity. This is not, as he notes, an argument against the idea of universals but instead an argument "that the universal was a highly unstable figure." In asking how thought is related to place, Chakrabarty is thus able to suggest that a renewal of thought may come "from and for the margins" (2007: 16). But, as he notes, "the margins are as plural and diverse as the centers." Thus it is that in the place of the universal history of capital, Chakrabarty (2007: xvii) calls for "heterotemporal horizons" of "innumerable" histories. Such an approach, I believe, is invaluable for an agenda of poverty scholarship and its universals.

Closely related to the ambitious task of rethinking capitalism and its fu-

tures is the ongoing endeavor to craft a Southern theory of the present historical conjuncture. Following Sparke (2007: 117), I mean the global South as a
"concept-metaphor" that interrupts the "flat world" conceits of globalization.
Sparke (2007: 117) notes that "the Global South is everywhere, but it is also
always somewhere, and that somewhere, located at the intersection of entangled political geographies of dispossession and repossession, has to be mapped
with persistent geographical responsibility." I take this to mean that the global
South cannot be mapped as a single and stable location. And in particular, the
global South cannot be understood as a stable ontological category symbolizing
subalternity from which we can produce theory. In their recent treatise *Theory
from the South*, Comaroff and Comaroff (2012: 47) thus argue that the "the south
cannot be defined, *a priori*, in substantive terms. The label bespeaks a *relation*,
not a thing in or for itself." They define the task of Southern theory in a manner
that is attentive to the historical conjuncture I have already outlined: that it is in
the global South that "radically new assemblages of capital and labor are taking
shape" and that these "prefigure the future of the global north" (Comaroff and
Comaroff 2012: 12). Theory from the South, they argue, is not about narrating
modernity from its "undersides," but rather revealing the "history of the present"
from the "distinctive vantage point" that are these frontiers of accumulation
(Comaroff and Comaroff 2012: 7). Such is the case with the southernmost edge of
Chicago, which must be understood not simply as the (post)industrial North but
instead as the territory of the dispossessions and activisms that are prefigured in
the global South and which have always been a part of the making of the global
North. In keeping with Alyosha Goldstein's essay in this volume, "The Duration
of Inequality: Limits, Liability, and the Historical Specificity of Poverty," this
means attending to the long histories of colonialism and continental conquest
in North America, to "slavery and its afterlives."

For a while now in urban studies, scholars have called for "new geographies
of theory" (Roy 2009). In keeping with Chakrabarty's mandate, this has been
an effort to consider the relationship between thought and place. To see from
the South is not to replace one location of theory with another but instead to
rethink the territory of thought itself. As Comaroff and Comaroff (2012: 1) note,
the West has been the privileged location of "universal learning" while the "non-
West—variously known as the ancient world, the orient, the primitive world,
the third world, the underdeveloped world, the developing world, and now the
global south" has been seen "primarily as a place of parochial wisdom, of an-
tiquarian traditions, of exotic ways and means . . . above all, of unprocessed
data." To rethink the territory of thought is to also rethink this divide, one that
I interpret as also the divide between Theory—capital and capitalized—and
ethnography—diminutive and modest. *Territories of Poverty* thus holds in si-

multaneous view the rearrangement of the global North and global South as well as the methodologies of ethnography and history.

Here it is worth turning to James Clifford's (1989: 179) "Notes on Theory and Travel." Clifford writes: "'Theory' is a product of displacement, comparison, a certain distance. To theorize, one leaves home. But like any act of travel, theory begins and ends somewhere." For Clifford, "every center or home" is today "someone else's periphery or diaspora." Theory, he thus argues, "is no longer naturally 'at home' in the West," because the West is no longer "a privileged place" to "collect, sift, translate, and generalize." Clifford "challenges the propensity of theory to seek a stable place, to float above historical conjunctures." If the condition of no longer being "at home in the West" is understood as the present historical disjuncture, then it may mark a useful, albeit unstable, (dis)location for a theory from the South or a provincialized Northern theory. Put another way, this understanding of the global South is an aporetic formulation, one that insists on the South not as stable geographical location but instead, following Sparke (2007: 119), as a "form of reterritorialization." The South is "everywhere but always somewhere" is also an analytical modality, allowing us to rethink the territory of thought that is the analysis of poverty.

Poverty as a Social Problem

> "I keep the word *problem* for another reason: so as to put this word in tension with another Greek word, *aporia*. . . . There, in sum, in this place of aporia, *there is no longer any problem*. Not that, alas or unfortunately, the solutions have been given, but because one could no longer even find a problem that would constitute itself and that one would keep in front of oneself, as a presentable object or project, as a protective representative or a prosthetic substitute, as some kind of border still to cross or behind which to protect oneself."
>
> —JACQUES DERRIDA, *Aporias* (1993: 12, emphasis in original)

The turn of the century is marked by the reemergence of poverty as a public concern. In particular, poverty has been reconstituted as a global issue. Global poverty is now a dominant and ubiquitous area of discourse, with a bold imagination of poverty action and social change. In his essay in this book, Akhil Gupta argues that "global poverty" is a discourse that seeks universal explanations and universal solutions, often defining a relationship between "wealthy nation-states and peoples in the global North" and the "unfortunate poor in the global South." Connecting unusual constellations of multilateral development institutions, global poverty campaigns, transnational nongovernmental organizations and social movements, powerful philanthropic foundations with international reach, and multinational corporations, global poverty is an emergent field of practice and intervention. It is also a field of knowledge, with new methodologies of assessment and evaluation integrally connected to human development. As Jamie Peck and Nik Theodore outline in their essay in this book, the present historical conjuncture involves new regimes of fast policy, what they call "model power," "orchestrated from global centers of persuasion, enacted through expert networks, sustained by narratives of best practice, and mediated by the rationalistic lore of experimental evaluation." These are no longer simply the "money doctors" of the 1980s and 1990s but a new group of poverty experts. Poverty knowledge is also being produced in the crucible of volunteerism, charity, aid advocacy, and humanitarian engagement. In and through such intimate encounters with poverty, "millennials"—college students and young professionals in both the global North and global South—are defining a global sense of self, articulating an ethics of global citizenship, and making and unmaking their own class ontologies.

Territories of Poverty is premised on the wager that the problematic of poverty, especially poverty as a global issue, provides unique analytical purchase in the investigation of capitalism's multiple futures. Inspired by social histories of the North Atlantic welfare state and critical ethnographies of development, its focus is not on the lived experience of poverty or on the causes and symptoms of poverty, but instead on the management and regulation of poverty as a social problem. Put another way, *Territories of Poverty* is concerned with how "the history of government might well be written as a history of problematizations" (Rose and Miller 1992: 279). To pursue such a line of analysis, we have to ask, as does Michael B. Katz in the first essay of this collection: "What kind of a problem is poverty?"

The global present is marked by a dizzying proliferation of programs of government organized around poverty as a social problem. Unfolding in a rearranged world order, these programs indicate the renewal and reinvention of welfare and development in the global South. As I have suggested earlier in this essay, it would be a mistake to limit the analysis of such programs to the common denominator of neoliberalism, even if we were to take neoliberalism as an inevitably incomplete and hybrid formation. Instead of positioning contemporary programs of welfare and development in relation to neoliberalization, we follow Ferguson's (2013: 260) important mandate to consider how "social assistance has long been a challenging site for liberal thought."

Of course, many of the most visible programs of the global poverty era are those that rely on market solutions. In my previous work, I have designated this composition of ideas and practices "poverty capitalism," that which seeks to integrate the world's bottom billion into market rule (Roy 2010). Yet, as Bill Maurer argues, in his essay in this book, there are many projects of liberal government that defy the format of poverty capitalism. His own focus on payment platforms, notably the mobility of money, presents one such instance. More broadly, it is necessary to consider the heterotemporal horizons of welfare and development and to thus provincialize the universal and singular history of neoliberalism. As Molyneux (2008) notes, the "new social policy" mandates in Latin America cast doubt on "totalizing conceptions of neoliberalism" and instead indicate the need to consider regional histories and their distinctive formations of democratic politics.

Put another way, the problem of poverty may require a complexity of rule that cannot be limited to the repertoire of neoliberal techniques of government. Thus, in her essay "From Poor Peripheries to Sectarian Frontiers: Planning, Development, and the Spatial Production of Sectarianism in Beirut," Hiba Bou Akar shows how entities like Hezbollah—those that are both inside and outside the state—can simultaneously deploy military power, humanitarian reason, urban planning, and global financialization. Erica Kohl-Arenas's essay in this volume, on powerful foundations in California's Central Valley, reminds us of organized philanthropy as a well-established technology of governing in America but also shows the entanglement of farmworker social movements, infrastructures of nonprofit service delivery, and corporate philanthropy.

Nor is the designation "postneoliberalism" particularly satisfying. We temper the prevailing optimism about poverty programs as "a southern challenge to the aid and development industry" (Hanlon, Barrientos, and Hulme 2010: 11). Instead, we follow Ballard (2013: 1) who argues that what is at work in these experiments with welfare in the global South is "an increasingly heterodox approach which combines an enduring emphasis on liberalized economic growth with bolder biopolitical interventions for the poor." Perhaps the best known of these programs of government is conditional cash transfers, what Jamie Peck and Nik Theodore in their essay describe as the "vanguard" of a "new hegemonic front in the field of social-assistance policy." As Peck and Theodore argue, such programs have broken down the divides between "mainstream" economics (in the global North) and "development" economics (in the global South), as well as those between "different welfare worlds," albeit those that "invoke, hail, and work upon an ostensibly universal economic subject, a rational actor duly enabled to act on her own to escape poverty" with the appropriate "patterning of incentives." It is this (prohibited) passage across South and North that is of interest to us. In *Territories of Poverty*, we thus frame programs of government that regulate the problem of poverty as aporetic formulations, the impossible formations of social citizenship in a rearranged world.

To pay attention to the problem of poverty is to take seriously the analytical task of telling the history of government as the history of problematizations, in our case, as a provincialized rather than universal history. As Rabinow (2004: 43) discusses, Foucault's concept of problematization requires understanding not only how an object of thought comes to exist but also "how there are always several possible ways of responding to the same ensemble of difficulties." *Territories of Poverty* seeks to advance precisely the shift that Rabinow calls for in his analytics of problematization: from the singular to the multiple, from the necessary to the contingent. We find this in Katz's magisterial work on the American welfare state. As he notes "relief or welfare policy has never been inevitable . . . always, policies and practices have emerged from a choice among alternative possibilities" (Katz 1986: xii). In his essay in this volume, Bill Maurer thus notes that if we think of territories of poverty as political technologies, then we recognize that "they are contested within themselves, from within their own structuring logics or in terms of the conglomerations of people, capital, infrastructure, and space making them up." Following this provocation, *Territories of Poverty* charts how new poverty interventions incite uncharted cooptations and collaborations. Thus, in our essay on early American experiments with community development, I join Stuart Schrader and Emma Shaw Crane to foreground how the Ford Foundation's Gray Areas program and later the Great Society's Model Cities program were appropriated by Black Power movements, ultimately becoming platforms for the rise of a black political class in "laboratory cities," such as Oakland. Or as another example, Jamie Peck and Nik Theodore demonstrate how Brazil's Bolsa Familia, and now Namibia's Basic Income Guarantee, are unruly mutations of the global script of development, eluding the authoritative consensus on poverty alleviation programs, their conditionalities, and their methodologies of evaluation.

Here it is useful to turn to Derrida's reminder that the concept of "problem" must always be placed in tension with the concept of "aporia." Derrida (1993: 12) notes that a problem is constituted as a "presentable object or project," often as a "protective representative or a prosthetic substitute" for what is complex and undecidable. Aporia, by contrast, suggests doubt in the place of project, dilemma in the place of representation, impasse in the place of solution. One example of this aporia comes in the form of what I call the Polanyi puzzle. In his masterful depiction of the rise of a market economy in England, Polanyi (2001) charts the double movement of capitalism. In doing so, he notes that pauperism, political economy, and the discovery of society were closely interwoven (Polanyi 2001: 89). Such an insight anchors *Territories of Poverty* and its engagement with the global present. Polanyi's analysis, including his theory of fictitious commodities, and his vision of socialism, are now part of the canon of political economy.

Less known is Polanyi's detailed analysis of the welfare regimes of the Industrial Revolution, specifically England's Speenhamland Law.

Polanyi devotes a significant portion of *The Great Transformation* to the Speenhamland Law, which lasted in England from 1795 to 1834. A system of public subsidies to the poor in aid of wages, Speenhamland was based on the idea of the "right to live." Polanyi (2001: 82) recognizes it as a "social and economic innovation," a minimum income policy for its times, but argues that it created paupers out of the poor. Polanyi's critique of Speenhamland is threefold. First, "it effectively prevented the establishment of a competitive labor market" (Polanyi 2001: 82) and thus stalled the formation of a working class able to organize on the basis of class interest. Second, since Speenhamland assured subsidies to the poor "*irrespective of their earnings*," it could not serve as a check against either the declining productivity of labor or the decline of wages. Workers, Polanyi (2001: 82) laments, could now make a living "by doing nothing (or not much more than nothing)." Third, Polanyi (2001: 86) views the Speenhamland Law as "an act of mercy" but "not of justice," destroying the "self-respect of the common man," and pauperizing the masses, "who almost lost their human shape in the process." Polanyi thus concludes that the Poor Law Reform of 1834, while marked by "scientific cruelty," freed the poor from such pauperization. Abolishing the "right to live," it also abolished the "snug misery of degradation" (2001: 87). For the working classes, Polanyi prefers "death through exposure"—the fate of the proletariat in a "free labor market"—than the "rot of immobility" that the Speenhamland Law had created in its thoroughly localized regime of welfare.

Polanyi's critique of the Speenhamland Law bears uncanny resemblance to contemporary discourses of dependency, of how the "right to live" can bind public funds to a subsidy of wages and install systems of paternalism. At key historical moments in the making and unmaking of the U.S. welfare state, Polanyi's interpretation of the Speenhamland Law has been resurrected. For example, Block and Somers (2003: 314) conclude that Polanyi's critique of the Speenhamland Law lacks "historical foundation," that "poor relief did not hurt the poor; it helped to protect them from structural changes in the economy that had made it far more difficult for people to earn a living." But they also detail how, during the Nixon administration, the Family Assistance Plan put forward by Daniel Patrick Moynihan was compared to the Speenhamland Law and its immiseration of the poor (Block and Somers 2003: 284). As Katz (1989: 102) has argued, the Family Assistance Plan was "the first major attempt to overhaul the social welfare structure erected in the 1930s" and a departure from "the service-based programs of the War on Poverty." In their critiques of the proposal, Nixon's policy advisors relied heavily on Polanyi's interpretation of poor relief (Block and Somers 2003: 284). Similarly, in the 1980s, conservative critics of welfare used Polanyi's account of Speenhamland "at length to argue against both income guarantees and programs like AFDC" (Block and Somers 2003: 285).

An important issue raised by Polanyi's interpretation of the Speenhamland Law is the matter of historical archives. Block and Somers (2003: 297) argue that the archives remain silent on the lives and experiences of the recipients of poor relief. "Only parish officers," they note, "could be counted on to give the kinds of answers that commissioners or parliamentary investigators were seeking." In fact, Elder (1964: 264) notes that critics of poor relief often "came from the struggling lower-middle class which bore an unjust share of poor-relief costs" and drew much of their information "from the 1834 report of the Royal Commission of Poor Law, rather than from firsthand experience." Needless to say, we cannot uncover the authentic voices of the poor governed by the Speenhamland system. But following the argument laid out by Luis Flores Jr. in his essay in this volume, "Representation: An Archeology of Poverty for the Present," we can pay attention to the "concrete work" enabled by these ideas of poverty. Flores concludes: "Necessary in this task are both the historian's purposeful chisel and the ethnographer's critical field notes, not to unearth buried ideas, but to map the dynamic ways in which they live through deliberate and eventful rearrangements in the present."

I present the Polanyi puzzle—the fierce opposition of this advocate of municipal socialism to welfare—as an example of the present history of poverty and its aporias. It demonstrates how social assistance is a not only "a challenging site for liberal thought," as argued by Ferguson (2013: 26), but also an impasse for the philosophers of capitalism's ravages. It is thus that in his treatise on the "global precariat," Standing (2011: 55) echoes Polanyi's critique of Speenhamland and evokes the "subsidy state as the bane of the precariat." Put bluntly, welfare policies, human development programs, and antipoverty interventions—and their attendant "declarations of dependence," to use Ferguson's (2013) felicitous phrase—seem to confound the teleology of class struggle and in turn notions of personhood premised on the idea of the worker.

But if we are to take seriously the task of provincializing the North Atlantic, then the seemingly universal history of capital narrated by Polanyi must be understood as a parochial story, one embedded in the distinctive history of the Industrial Revolution in England and its politics of social class. *Territories of Poverty* does not seek to replace this history but instead holds it in view, in genealogical fashion, alongside numerous other histories, including those that require a nonlaborist analysis of welfare. In contrast to Polanyi's unrelenting emphasis on the economic freedom enabled by proletarianization, it brings into view other economies, including those that Ferguson (2007: 83) identifies as the "striking vision of the future," where waged work is "a receding, twentieth century relic." It is in this sense that the global South can be seen as a prefiguration of North Atlantic futures.

Does such a global present force a refashioning of the concerns about human degradation wrought by welfare? Take for example the contemporary debates about basic income. In a distinctively nonlaborist analysis, Pateman (2004: 92) presents basic income as providing the *"freedom not to be employed"* (emphasis in original). Pateman (2004: 89) argues that basic income must be understood as a "democratic right," one that can help break the "mutual reinforcement of the institutions of marriage, employment, and citizenship." In a reflection on her father's legacy, Polanyi Levitt (2013: 114) argues that Karl Polanyi would have lent his support to the idea of "a share in the social product as a citizen right." Can such views only be advanced in the global South, where "the baggage of 20th century social security is light" and "the industrial labour model clearly does not apply"? (Standing 2008: 23). Could it be that the "desocialization of wage labor," Wacquant's (2008: 246) description of the precariat, this time in the North Atlantic but always already elsewhere, inaugurates new lines of political thought about social assistance?

If we think of the global present in these terms—this time in the North Atlantic but always already elsewhere—then we are required to return to the question of heterotemporality posed by Chakrabarty and other postcolonial theorists. *Territories of Poverty* is concerned with the historical conjuncture that is the "now." But I rely on Derrida (1993: 1) to think about the now as "a time that is out of joint." This "radical untimeliness" (Derrida 1993: 29) has no dialectical resolution but instead persists as an anachrony, a disjointedness with the past and present. In his essay in this volume, Alyosha Goldstein examines juridical scripts of settlement and reconciliation that seek to resolve past injustice. As a "constitutive dilemma for the idea of historical progress," the "persistence of poverty" is thus managed through "moments of apparent incremental resolution and institutional mechanisms that enact periodization." But despite such forms of "compensatory closure," poverty remains as an "unseemly presence in the present."

I am arguing, then, that such a disjunctive understanding of temporality is especially useful in understanding a rearranged world of South and North, not simply as different geographies but as multiple futures. I also turn to Derrida's notion of untimeliness as an autocritique. After all, I first conceptualized the intellectual project that became *Territories of Poverty* as the ethical task of the critical theorist. Inspired by Fraser (2009: 158), I saw myself as reflecting on "the historical situation" I inhabit, asking "what do the times demand?" But Derrida (1993) casts doubt on this comfortable habitation and thus on the timeliness of our ethical aspirations. Through anachrony, Derrida forces a reconceptualization of justice from "calculable equality" to "incalculability" in a world where responsibility exceeds the "living present." To step out of the living present is deeply disconcerting. It renders us out of joint. But, as I have been arguing all through this essay, it allows us to understand the elsewhere that has already always been outside, or rendered outside, of the living present. In this way, radical untimeliness might indeed be what Cornell (2005), in her homage to Derrida, has called the "gift of the future."

The Ethics of Encounter

No justice . . . seems possible or thinkable without the principle of some responsibility, beyond all living present, within that which disjoins the living present.
—JACQUES DERRIDA, *Specters of Marx: The State of the Debt, the Work of Mourning, and the New International* (1994: xviii)

In *Fragments of an Anarchist Anthropology*, Graeber (2004: 6) seeks to advance an "ethical discourse about revolutionary practice." Inspired by Kropotkin, he imagines an anarchism that is "society without government," a society constituted through "free agreements concluded between the various groups, territorial and professional." One of Graeber's (2004: 82) examples is the "new global uprising"—"the autonomous municipalities of Chiapas . . . the asambleas barriales of Buenos Aires . . . an international network (People's Global Action) . . . days of action against the WTO (in Seattle)." Celebrating the "unprecedented tactics" of this uprising, Graeber (2004: 84, 77) argues that it is "increasingly anarchist in inspiration." *Territories of Poverty* has been conceptualized and written in the global present of a world rearranged by such social forces. And of course, other social movements have appeared on the world stage since Graeber's treatise. The Occupy Movement, in which Graeber was an important interlocutor, created a new common sense, in cities from New York to Oakland, about poverty and inequality. Not only did it enact occupations of space but it also sought to disrupt the temporality of financialized futures. In November 2011 I wrote thus of the movement:

Yesterday was a day of action in Berkeley, to defend public education and to protest the police brutality that had been unleashed against Occupy Cal student protesters just a few days ago. (Not surprisingly, alongside the democratic experiments of the Occupy movement has unfolded a set of experiments in penality). Two years ago, the public education movement at Cal had stalled over the territorialization of protest. A string of building occupations—and fierce police action against them—had effectively served as a clamp. But now thousands marched—as their signs read, to occupy, to occupy the future (no reference to Chomsky intended).

As I walked alongside some of my undergraduate students (barely twenty) in a rally that shut down city streets, they recounted how two weeks ago they had joined a general strike to blockade the port of Oakland. Euphoric about collective action, they nevertheless registered ambivalence—because the referents of protest, from the site of the port to the very term "strike," seemed alien to their generation, one with neither memory nor anticipation of such landscapes of labor. Encampments, barricades, rent strikes, picket lines, were all of interest to them, but what mattered most they said was the moment. What did that entail, I asked? Refusing futures of student debt, resisting systematic disinvestment in our collective futures, remanding the foreclosure of politics, they replied. For this global generation of austerity, occupations may indeed be predictable, from Tahrir Square to Zuccotti Park to Sproul Plaza, but there is nothing predictable about a creativity that seeks to occupy the Great Recession itself.

Could it be that such spatializations are a détournement not just of the establishments of capitalism but equally of established geographies of resistance? (Roy 2011a)

Since then, spectacular and sweeping mass-political uprisings have transformed the Arab world, challenging authoritarian regimes from Tunisia to Egypt to Turkey. As we must rethink capitalism and its futures, so we must rethink the established geographies and vocabularies of resistance. In many ways, these diverse movements are bound together in a common global imagination of collective action. Yet they bear fundamentally different purpose and meaning and cannot be read as parts of a singular and coherent global uprising. In particular, they cannot be understood as poor people's movements arrayed against the machinations of global capitalism. While speaking the language of social justice, they are often haunted by indeterminacy, an aporia if you will. It is with this indeterminacy that they seek to negotiate the "gift of the future."

If it is not possible to sustain the framework of a singular and coherent global uprising, then how can an ethical discourse about practice be imagined and approached? *Territories of Poverty* locates this question in programs of government, those that seek to manage and regulate poverty as a social problem. Following Lawson and Elwood (2013), I conceptualize such programs as "zones of encounter," those in which "middle class people come into close contact with 'poor others,'" and "where class difference is troubled and reworked." While Graeber (2004: 9) argues that "policy is the negation of politics . . . something concocted by some form of elite," an instantiation of the "state or governing apparatus which imposes its will on others," I see policy, or more broadly liberal government, to be the terrain of politics. This politics includes the complex and contradictory entanglement of poor people's movements and bureaucracies of poverty. But it is also the intimate relationalities through which an ethics of the (middle class) self is crafted through encounters with poverty. In contrast to Graeber's understanding of an ethical discourse of revolutionary action as an anarchist disavowal of government, I understand ethics in the Foucauldian sense, as the "constitution of oneself as a moral subject," "as a care of the self" that includes "a general attitude with respect to oneself, to others, and to the world" (Davidson 2007: xxiii–xxiv). As zones of encounter, programs of government are one of the sites at which such practices of the self are enacted. Following Foucault, such practices of the self can be understood as the "deliberative practice of freedom," a "freedom of conduct" (Davidson 2007), which is a quite different understanding of power than the imposition of will concocted by an elite that Graeber advances. With this in mind, *Territories of Poverty* undertakes what Povinelli (2011: x), following Clifford, terms a "sociography," "a way of writing the social from the point of view of social projects."

The most ambitious of these social projects is poverty action. As an idea and practice, poverty action is inchoate and indeterminate, but like the diverse mass-political uprisings of the past two decades, it is a key marker of the present historical conjuncture. Indeed, the new millennium can be understood as the age of poverty, one in which poverty has been constituted as a global issue but also as an ethical issue. In this sense, poverty action has become an important mode of subjectivation, a way of defining a sense of self, relations with "poor others," and thus a place in the world. Today, sites of poverty action abound: from the rituals of volunteerism and church missions to rock concerts with sideshows of antipoverty campaigns. If Jeffrey Sachs (2005) has boldly hailed "the end of poverty," then such an imagination is being enacted not only in the offices of the World Bank and USAID or the campaigns and projects of international NGOs such as Oxfam and World Vision, but also in the countless moments of charity, philanthropy, and advocacy through which middle-class actors seek to act upon, and mitigate, the poverty of others. *Territories of Poverty* seeks to uncover emergent formats of encounters with poverty, as well as the formations of poverty knowledge thus engendered. Our wager is that this type of poverty knowledge must be taken seriously, that it permeates and transforms the official worlds of welfare and development and articulates, in uneasy fashion, with poor people's movements. As territory must be understood as political technology, so too must such practices of the self.

In this sense, poverty is not just a global social problem, but rather an ethical discourse in and through which social class is being crafted. Writing about the

Industrial Revolution, its welfare regimes and poor reforms, Polanyi (2001: 89) reminds us that "it was in relation to the problem of poverty that people began to explore the meaning of life in a complex society." So is it the case today. My own research and teaching has been concerned with the relationship between global poverty and "millennials," college students and young professionals in both the global North and global South who are making and unmaking their class position through encounters with poverty and engagements with poverty action. This book thus includes short essays by such millennials as they craft their own relationships to poverty knowledge and critical theory. Today's millennials and their poverty action are reminiscent of historical accounts of Progressive Era social reformers in America, many of them middle-class women with college degrees, who were residing in settlement houses, producing social surveys, occasionally allying with the labor movement, and serving as advocates for the poor (Katz 1986). Yet, they are also part of a global present with its own distinctive histories. Take the account of Anh-Thi Le in this book, "Representation: Moving Beyond the Geography of Privilege," which charts the "geography of privilege" that has marked her various endeavors of volunteerism and philanthropy. But as Anh-Thi notes, these "principles of service and volunteerism" are rooted in a specific immigrant experience, her "parents' struggles as refugees during the Vietnam War, and the political, financial, and communal support that they received when they first arrived to the United States." These are the global, territorial, and imperial histories through which the problem of poverty is today mediated.

Territories of Poverty thus attempts to study the intimacies and ontologies of poverty action. In her essay for this book, Vincanne Adams links such social ontologies of poverty action to the apparatus of disaster capitalism. Writing in the context of post-Katrina New Orleans, she shows how a vast flow of volunteers into the city sustains an "affect economy," which not only generates an affect of sympathy and aid but also becomes an unwitting accomplice to privatization. Adams analyzes affect as a purposive ethics, mediated by emotional urgency and translated into injunctions to action. In his essays on Foucault, Gilles Deleuze (1986: 71) notes that "an exercise of power shows up as an affect"—it incites, it invokes, it produces. It is in this sense that Adams's exposition of affect must be taken up as a methodology of power, one that in turn serves as an important methodology of poverty studies. Let me elaborate how a focus on the ethics of encounter advances this type of methodology.

At the conference at the University of California, Berkeley, which led to this book, Loïc Wacquant suggested that the *Territories of Poverty* project be reconceptualized to include territories of wealth. After all, this is a historical conjuncture of obscene income inequality in America and of new hegemonic formations of capital accumulation in the global South. I agree with Wacquant's caution that we do not study poverty as an isolated phenomenon, somehow separate from the production of wealth. There is much more analytical work to be done on this front, for example, by following Teddy Cruz's call here in "Spatializing Citizenship and the Informal Public" to study how the condition of "economic excess" has dramatically shaped entire professions. He notes that the "the world's architecture intelligentsia" has "flocked en masse to the United Arab Emirates and China to help build the dream castles that would catapult these enclaves of wealth as global epicenters of urban development."

In this collection we adopt a relational approach to wealth and poverty, not by studying territories of poverty *and* territories of wealth, or programs of government that manage poverty *and* those that enable wealth, but instead by situating relations of inequality at the site of poverty constituted as a social problem. In 1958 John Kenneth Galbraith did the converse, analyzing poverty and social policy in the context of "the affluent society." To consider affluence, he argued, meant to study the "line which divides our area of wealth from our area of poverty" (Galbraith 1984: 190). *Territories of Poverty* suggests that zones of encounter, their social ontologies, and their modes of subjectivation, are an important analytical framework for the study of the relations of wealth and poverty. In her essay in this book, Erica Kohl-Arenas thus foregrounds one of the most significant institutions mediating such relations: private foundations and their philanthropic investments. Desai and Kharas (2008: 156) describe this regime of "private development aid" the "California consensus." Ostensibly meant to be distinguished from the Washington consensus, its institutions, and its ideology of austerity, the California consensus is fueled by Silicon Valley wealth and "an abiding faith in the capacity of innovation, technology and modern management methods to solve problems of extreme poverty" (Desai and Kharas 2008: 158). In previous work (Roy 2012), I have described such formations of development and philanthropy as "the ethicalization of market rule," one that defies the simple label of neoliberalism. Tracing this strange conjunction also requires paying attention to the complex and contradictory entanglement of social mobilization and global capitalism. Thus, Sparke (n.d.) shows how, in 1999, globally oriented activists remade Seattle as a site of dissent, but that in its wake, Seattle was revisioned as a "world class center of global health philanthropy," home to the powerful Gates Foundation and its "private sector treatments for the mismatch between global markets and global justice."

Such forms of power can possibly be understood as pastoral, what Foucault (2007: 192, 165) describes as the "conduct of souls" rather than the "methods used to subject men to a law or to a sovereign." For Foucault (2007: 184–85), pastoral power is the "prelude to governmentality," and is thus a "decisive moment" in the "constitution of a specific subject." While Foucault sees this subject as a "modern Western subject," in a rearranged world, it is worth considering the various territories of pastoral power, in the West and beyond. I use the term "territories" deliberately, because Foucault argues that pastoral power is "exercised on a multiplicity rather than on a territory." And yet, the essays by Han and Adams demonstrate how the affect economy—if we are to understand it as an example of pastoral power—is fully implicated in the constitution and governance of territory. And this making and unmaking of territory inevitably entails the long histories of colonialism and imperialism in which Foucault remains disinterested as he explores the constitution of the modern Western subject. In her essay in this book, "Our Past, Your Future: Evangelical Missionaries and the Script of Prosperity," Ju Hui Judy Han shows how young South Korean missionaries seek to act upon poverty in Africa but in doing so find their place in the world, and more important, find South Korea's place in the history of development. In Han's words, such poverty missions are "spatiotemporal projects of purpose-driven mobility, and they produce a geography of aspirations." Han's essay reminds us of the heterotemporal horizons of a rearranged world. It is South Korea's ascendancy from aid recipient to donor country that sets the context for church missions to Africa. What thus unfolds in these missions is not only the work of saving poor others in Africa but also "a triumphant script" of South Korea's victory over poverty, a script that is, as Han notes, one of "racial difference and geographical distance."

And yet the politics engendered by the problem of poverty is not predictable. Poverty action rests on an unsurpassable paradox or impasse, what Erica Kohl-Arenas, in her work on California's foundations, describes as that of "funding working-class organizing through the surplus of capital." And while poverty action is an injunction to action, the action is indeterminate, undecidable, and often a nonpassage across the borders of social class. Lawson and Elwood (2013) thus ask if the interactions between middle-class actors and poor others in zones of encounter challenge dominant representations of poverty to create a politics of solidarity. They conclude that such negotiations are marked by a persistent ambiguity.

It is also worth considering how poverty action implicates what is the "incalculable," a word I borrow from Derrida's (1993) reflections on aporia. If calculation has been seen as central to liberal government—its programs and its territories—then Vincanne Adams's work on affect urges us to consider that which is beyond calculation. Rose (2000: 1398) notes that a "new politics of behavior" is in the making, a way of governing that creates affective and ethical fields, what he calls "ethopolitics." Social government, he argues, has been replaced by ethopolitics, where social problems are recast as ethical problems.

Territories of Poverty does not chart the death of the social, as does Rose. But it is keenly attuned to how poverty as a social problem is also the terrain of ethopolitics. Here feminist attention to the category of intimacy (Pratt and Rosner 2012) is important, for I would argue it is intimacy rather than calculation that must be understood as the basis for ethopolitics, and its injunction to action. And here poverty action must be held in view alongside other "dense sites" at which the social relations of class are mediated and negotiated. Ray and Qayum (2009: 18), for example, foreground domestic servitude as one such dense site, a space of domestic intimacy and yet where the "Indian middle classes distinguish themselves from classes below . . . by boundary-maintaining labor." Such forms of incalculable intimacies contrast and coexist with the technologies of law that Alyosha Goldstein analyzes in his essay for this book. He notes how the Claims Resolution Act utilizes monetary compensation as a form of "juridical closure," seeking to transform "racialized logics of dehumanization, property, and dispossession" into legible and timebound acts of discrimination.

Finally, *Territories of Poverty* is concerned with how ethopolitics unfolds in the disciplines and professions of academic knowledge and spatial transformation. Put another way, we are interested in how the problem of poverty shapes particular domains of inquiry and practice and their forms of "epistemic privilege," a phrase that Luis Flores Jr. uses in his essay. Is it possible for "theory to ride the bus"? asks Emma Shaw Crane, then, in her concluding essay. In his manifesto for this book, Teddy Cruz envisions architects and artists as the "designers of political processes, alternative economic models, and collaborations across institutions and jurisdictions to ensure accessibility and socioeconomic justice." But where do these designs come from? The informal practices and protocols of the border neighborhood, Cruz asserts. It is in such territories of poverty, Cruz argues, that it is both necessary and possible to craft a new public, including new arrangements of profit and property. There is an unusual resonance between Cruz's manifesto and Maurer's analysis of poverty platforms as potential public goods. What does it mean to generate a vision of the public from the very sites of spatial segregation and digital capitalism?

Precisely such struggles animate the ethical lives of millennials in the age of global poverty. Acutely aware of territorialized exclusion, they nevertheless want to craft a politics of change. Thus, Stephanie Ullrich ("Representation: Poverty Action in Neighborhoods of Relegation"), immersed in service work and community organizing in post-Katrina New Orleans, wants to forge "critical understandings of neighborhoods of relegation" but also wants to understand how such critical understandings can "help shape the creative and collective imaginations of poverty actors, organizers, activists, and scholars." Millennials like Stephanie grapple with such questions by participating in poor people's movements—from the southern edge of Chicago to the Western Cape of South Africa. Others do so in the affect economy of disaster volunteerism and overseas church missions. Yet others seek out frontiers of capitalism, in Silicon Valley and in the New Asia, but seek to forge lines of ethical engagement across such frontiers. From microfinance to social enterprises, they have an unwavering faith in the ethicalization of market rule. In the most radical of these imaginations, young professionals speak back to their professions and seek to enact what Somaya Abdelgany in her reflection piece for this book ("Representation: The Bridge between Design and Poverty Action") describes as knowledge redistribution. Challenging the design studio and its disavowal of both human problems and human aspiration, Somaya insists on rethinking her disciplinary and professional home, architecture. A new agenda of poverty scholarship, of which *Territories of Poverty* is one instantiation, must take serious account of such aspirations and visions as well as of their impossible contradictions. We have jointly authored this book with the hope that it will allow Rebecca Peters ("Representation: The Privatization of Everything?") and others like her, "hopeful millennial scholar[s] skeptical of the beneficence of the free market," to continue their refusal to turn "political processes into technical solutions."

REFERENCES

Adams, Vincanne. 2013. *Markets of Sorrow, Labors of Faith: New Orleans in the Wake of Katrina*. Durham: Duke University Press.

Appadurai, Arjun. 2002. "Deep Democracy: Urban Governmentality and the Horizon of Politics." *Public Culture* 14:1, 21–47.

Arrighi, Giovanni. 2009. *Adam Smith in Beijing: Lineages of the 21st Century*. New York: Verso.

Austen, Ben. 2013. "The Death and Life of Chicago." *New York Times Magazine*, May 29, http://www.nytimes.com/2013/06/02/magazine/how-chicagos-housing-crisis-ignited-a-new-form-of-activism.html?pagewanted=all&_r=0.

Ballard, Richard. 2013. "Geographies of Development II: Cash Transfers and the Reinvention of Development for the Poor." *Progress in Human Geography* 37:6, 811–21.

Block, Fred, and Margaret Somers. 2003. "In the Shadow of Speenhamland: Social Policy and the Old Poor Law." *Politics and Society* 2003 31:2, 283–323.

Caldeira, Teresa, and James Holston. 2014. "Participatory Urban Planning in Brazil." *Urban Studies*, http://usj.sagepub.com/content/early/2014/03/04/0042098014524461.full.

Chakrabarty, Dipesh. 2000. *Provincializing Europe: Postcolonial Thought and Historical Difference*. Princeton: Princeton University Press.

Chakravartty, Paula, and Denise Ferreira da Silva. 2012. "Accumulation, Dispossession, and Debt: The Racial Logic of Global Capitalism: An Introduction." *American Quarterly* 64:3, 361–85.

Chatterjee, Partha. 2011. *Lineages of Political Society: Studies in Postcolonial Democracy*. New York: Columbia University Press.

Chatterjee, Partha. 2012. "After Subaltern Studies." *Economic and Political Weekly* 47:35, 44–49.

Clifford, James. 1989. "Notes on Theory and Travel." *Inscriptions* 5, http://cultural studies.ucsc.edu/PUBS/Inscriptions/vol_5/v5_top.html.

Comaroff, J., and J. Comaroff. 2012. *Theory from the South: Or, How Euro-America Is Evolving toward Africa*. Boulder, Colo.: Paradigm Publishers.

Cornell, Drucilla. 2005. ""Derrida" The Gift of the Future" differences: A Journal of Feminist Cultural Studies 16:3, 68–75.

Cowen, Deborah, and Amy Siciliano. 2011. "Schooled In/Security: Surplus Subjects, Racialized Masculinities, and Citizenship." In *Accumulating Insecurity: Violence and Dispossession in the Making of Everyday Life*, ed. Shelley Feldman, Charles Geisler, and Gayatri Menon, 104–21. Athens: University of Georgia Press.

Davidson, Arnold. 2007. "Introduction." In Michel Foucault, *Security, Territory, Population: Lectures at the College de France, 1977–78*. Translated by Graham Burchell. New York: Picador.

Deleuze, Gilles. 1986. *Foucault*. Translated by Sean Hand. Minneapolis: University of Minnesota Press.

Derrida, Jacques. 1993. *Aporias*. Translated by Thomas Dutoit. Stanford: Stanford University Press.

Derrida, Jacques. 1994. *Specters of Marx: The State of the Debt, the Work of Mourning, and the New International*. Translated by Peggy Kamuf. New York: Routledge.

Desai, Raj and Homi Kharas. 2008. "The California Consensus: Can Private Aid End Global Poverty?" *Survival* 50:4, 155–68.

Elden, Stuart. 2010. "Thinking Territory Historically." *Geopolitics* 15:4, 757–61.

Elden, Stuart. 2013. "How Should We Do the History of Territory?" *Territory, Politics, Governance* 1:1, 1–16.

Elder, Walter. 1964. "Speenhamland Revisited." *Social Service Review* 38:3, 294–302.

Ferguson, James. 2007. "Formalities of Poverty: Thinking about Social Assistance in Neoliberal South Africa." *African Studies Review* 50:2, 71–86.

Ferguson, James. 2009. "The Uses of Neoliberalism." *Antipode* 41:1, 166–84.

Ferguson, James 2013. "Declarations of Dependence: Labour, Personhood and Welfare in Southern Africa." *Journal of the Royal Anthropological Institute* 19:2, 223–42.

Foucault, Michel. 2007. *Security, Territory, Population: Lectures at the College de France, 1977–78*. Translated by Graham Burchell. New York: Picador.

Fraser, Nancy. 2009. *Scales of Justice: Reimagining Political Space in a Globalizing World*. New York: Columbia University Press.

Galbraith, John Kenneth. 1984. *The Affluent Society*. Boston: Houghton Mifflin. (Orig. pub. 1958.)

Garr, Emily, and Elizabeth Kneebone. 2013. *The Suburbanization of Poverty: Trends in Metropolitan America, 2000–2008*. Metropolitan Opportunity Series, Report 2. Washington, D.C.: Brookings Institution.

Goldstein, Alyosha. 2012. *Poverty in Common: The Politics of Community Action during the American Century*. Durham: Duke University Press.

Graeber, David. 2004. *Fragments of an Anarchist Anthropology*. New York: Prickly Paradigm Press.

Gupta, Akhil. 2012. *Red Tape: Bureaucracy, Structural Violence, and Poverty in India*. Durham: Duke University Press.

Hall, Stuart, Doreen Massey, and Michael Rustin. 2013. "After Neoliberalism: Analyzing the Present." *Soundings: A Journal of Politics and Culture* 53, 8–22.

Hanlon, Joseph, Armando Barrientos, and David Hulme. 2010. *Just Give Money to the Poor: The Development Revolution from the Global South*. Sterling, Va.: Kumarian Press.

Heynen, Nik. 2009. "Bending the Bars of Empire from Every Ghetto for Survival: The Black Panther Party's Radical Antihunger Politics of Social Reproduction and Scale." *Annals of the Association of American Geographers* 99:2, 406–22.

Katz, Michael. 1986. *In the Shadow of the Poorhouse: A Social History of Welfare in America*. New York: Basic Books.

Katz, Michael. 1989. *The Undeserving Poor: From the War on Poverty to the War on Welfare*. New York: Pantheon Books.

Lawson, Victoria, and Sarah Elwood. 2013. "Encountering Poverty: Space, Class, and Poverty Politics." *Antipode* 46:1, 209–28.

Li, Tania Murray. 2007. *The Will to Improve: Governmentality, Development, and the Practice of Politics*. Durham: Duke University Press.

Mbembe, Achille. 2000. "At the Edge of the World: Boundaries, Territoriality, and Sovereignty in Africa." Translated by Steven Rendall. *Public Culture* 12:1, 259–84.

Mbembe, Achille. 2003. "Necropolitics." *Public Culture* 15, 11–40.

Miller, Peter, and Nik Rose. 2008. *Governing the Present*. Malden: Polity Press.

Mingione, Enzo, ed. 1996. *Urban Poverty and the Underclass: A Reader*. Cambridge: Blackwell Publishers.

Mohan, Giles and Marcus Power. 2009. "Africa, China, and the 'New' Economic Geography of Development." *Singapore Journal of Tropical Geography* 30, 24–28.

Molyneux, Maxine. 2008. "The 'Neoliberal Turn' and the New Social Policy in Latin America: How Neoliberal, How New?" *Development and Change* 39:5, 775–97.

Newman, Kathe. 2009. "Post-Industrial Widgets: Capital Flows and the Production of the Urban." *International Journal of Urban and Regional Research* 33:2, 314–31.

Nkoana-Mashabane, Maite. 2013. "The Brics Come to Durban." In *BRICS in Africa: Anti-Imperialist, Sub-Imperialist or In Between? A Reader for the Durban Summit*, ed. Patrick Bond. Center for Civil Society, Durban, South Africa.

Orleck, Annelise, and Lisa Gayle Hazirjian, eds. 2012. *The War on Poverty: A New Grassroots History, 1964–1980*. Athens: University of Georgia Press.

Painter, Joe. 2010. "Rethinking Territory." *Antipode* 42:5, 1090–118.

Pateman, Carole. 2004. "Democratizing Citizenship: Some Advantages of a Basic Income." *Politics and Society* 32, 89–105.

Pew Research Center. 2012. *Fewer, Poorer, Gloomier: The Lost Decade of the American*

Middle Class. http://www.pewsocialtrends.org/2012/08/22/the-lost-decade-of-the -middle-class/.

Piven, Frances Fox, and Richard Cloward. 1977. *Poor People's Movements: Why They Succeed, How They Fail.* New York: Pantheon Books.

Polanyi, Karl. 2001. *The Great Transformation: The Political and Economic Origins of Our Time.* Boston: Beacon Press. (Orig. pub. 1944.)

Polanyi Levitt, Kari. 2013. *From the Great Transformation to the Great Financialization: On Karl Polanyi and Other Essays.* New York: Zed Books.

Povinelli, Elizabeth. 2011. *Economies of Abandonment: Social Belonging and Endurance in Late Liberalism.* Durham: Duke University Press.

Prashad, Vijay. 2012. *The Poorer Nations: A Possible History of the Global South.* New York: Verso.

Pratt, Geraldine, and Victoria Rosner, eds. 2012. *The Global and the Intimate: Feminism in Our Time.* New York: Columbia University Press.

Rabinow, Paul. 2004. "Midst Anthropology's Problems." In *Global Assemblages: Technology, Politics, and Ethics as Anthropological Problems,* ed. Aihwa Ong and Stephen Collier, 40–54. Malden, Mass.: Wiley-Blackwell.

Ray, Raka, and Seemin Qayum. 2009. *Cultures of Servitude: Modernity, Domesticity, and Class in India.* Stanford: Stanford University Press.

Rose, Nik. 2000. "Community, Citizenship, and the Third Way." *American Behavioral Scientist* 43:9, 1395–411.

Rose, Nik, and Peter Miller. 1992. "Political Power Beyond the State: Problematics of Government." *British Journal of Sociology* 43:2, 173–205.

Roy, Ananya. 2003. "Paradigms of Propertied Citizenship: Transnational Techniques of Analysis." *Urban Affairs Review* 38:4, 463–91.

Roy, Ananya. 2009. "The 21st Century Metropolis: New Geographies of Theory." *Regional Studies* 43:6, 819–30.

Roy, Ananya. 2010. *Poverty Capital: Microfinance and the Making of Development.* New York: Routledge.

Roy, Ananya. 2011a. "Occupy the Future." Society and Space Open Site: Forum on the Occupy Movement. November 18. http://societyandspace.com/material/discussion -forum/forum-on-the-occupy-movement/ananya-roy-occupy-the-future/.

Roy, Ananya. 2011b. "Slumdog Cities: Rethinking Subaltern Urbanism." *International Journal of Urban and Regional Research* 35:2, 223–38.

Roy, Ananya. 2012. "Ethical Subjects: Market Rule in an Age of Poverty." *Public Culture* 24:1, 105–8.

Sachs, Jeffrey. 2005. *The End of Poverty: Economic Possibilities for Our Time.* New York: Penguin Press.

Sparke, Matthew. n.d. "Global Seattle: The City, Citizenship and the Meaning of World Class." Unpublished paper.

Sparke, Matthew. 2007. "Everywhere But Always Somewhere: Critical Geographies of the Global South." *The Global South* 1:1&2, 117–26.

Standing, Guy. 2008. "How Cash Transfers Promote the Case for Basic Income." *Basic Income Studies* 3:1.

Standing, Guy. 2011. *The Precariat: The New Dangerous Class*. New York: Bloomsburg Academic.

Sumner, Andy. 2012. *Where Will the World's Poor Live? An Update on Global Poverty and the Bottom Billion*. CGD Working Paper 305. Washington D.C.: Center for Global Development.

Wacquant, Loïc. 2008. *Urban Outcasts: A Comparative Sociology of Advanced Marginality*. New York: Polity Press.

Wacquant, Loïc. 2009. *Punishing the Poor: The Neoliberal Government of Social Insecurity*. Durham: Duke University Press.

Watson, Vanessa. 2009. "Seeing from the South: Refocusing Urban Planning on the Globe's Central Urban Issues." *Urban Studies* 46:11, 2259–75.

Wyly, Elvin, C. S. Ponder, Pierson Nettling, Bosco Ho, Sophie Ellen Fung, Zachary Liebowitz, and Dan Hammel. 2012. "New Racial Meanings of Housing in America." *American Quarterly* 64:3, 570–604.

Programs of Government

We understand poverty programs—from welfare in the North Atlantic to development projects in the global South—as political technologies that act both to problematize poverty and to govern the poor. Charting an analytical shift from thinking about spaces of poverty, bounded and bordered (a neighborhood or a village or a slum), to territories of poverty, we pay particular attention to how we know poverty. In tracing genealogies of poverty knowledge, this section seeks to situate ways of knowing and acting upon poverty in historically specific forms of political organization. In doing so, these chapters and essays interrogate how authoritative poverty knowledges are produced, and how they travel and transform across the reconfigured geographies of millennial development.

ESC

What Kind of a Problem Is Poverty?
The Archeology of an Idea

MICHAEL B. KATZ

Lilian Brandt Explains the Causes of Poverty

In the early twentieth century, no one wrote about poverty with more authority
and insight than Lilian Brandt. Born in Indianapolis in 1873, Brandt followed her
1895 graduation from Wellesley College with a stint teaching history and classical
languages at various colleges before returning to Wellesley, where she earned her
master's degree in economics and history in 1901 with a thesis, "The Negroes of
St. Louis: A Statistical Study." Her return marked a career shift from the humanities to practical social science and social reform, which in the summer of 1902
brought her to the New York Charity Organization Society's Summer School of
Philanthropy, the precursor of Columbia University's School of Social Work. Her
talent for statistical analysis led Edward T. Devine, president of the Charity Organization Society, to appoint her secretary of the organization's Bureau of Labor
Statistics in 1902. From 1902 to 1904, she served as the statistician to the cos's
Committee on the Prevention of Tuberculosis, a position that forced her into
intimate contact with the poverty with which the disease was closely correlated.
In 1905 she became secretary of the cos Committee on Social Research and a
member of the National Conference of Charities and Corrections Committee
on Statistics. In 1907 she authored the remarkable twenty-fifth-anniversary history of the Charity Organization Society. She also worked as Devine's research
assistant, analyzing the five thousand cases on which he based his 1909 Kennedy
lectures at the School of Philanthropy, subsequently published as *Misery and Its
Causes* (Devine 1911: ix). Brandt continued in a distinguished career in social
research until her death in 1951.[1]

In the December 1908 issue of *Political Science Quarterly*, Brandt published
one of the first articles on poverty in an academic journal. "The Causes of Poverty" (Brandt 1908) offered a devastating critique of experts' analyses of poverty
in the late nineteenth and early twentieth century. Her criticism drew on the
emerging revolution in social science that was transforming both the causal

analysis of social problems and the practical work of social amelioration. The article is worth sustained attention because it reveals assumptions that underlie enduring differences in explanations of poverty, the consequences of different theoretical orientations, and the emergence of an aborted progressive program as relevant today as when it was formulated a century ago.

Brandt (1908: 637) began by highlighting a "new view of poverty—that it not only is not desirable and not inevitable, but is actually unnatural and intolerable and has no legitimate place on our diagram of social conditions." Following up this insight "involves logically an inquiry into the reasons for the existence of poverty, but as a matter of experience this step seems to be omitted" because reformers wanted to jump straight to the attack. However, to grasp "how . . . poverty may be diminished and prevented . . . we are again driven to hunt for its causes" (Brandt 1908: 637). This is why she wrote her article.

Brandt damned the prevailing individual-centered approach to studying poverty. Her critique reflected the emergence of new forms of causal attribution throughout the social sciences that replaced single-factor explanations with a much more sophisticated understanding of the multiple, interacting factors producing social problems like poverty (Haskell 1977). The individual-centered, single-cause "method consists in studying a large number of individual cases of poverty, indicating in each case what is considered to be the cause, then adding up the number of cases ascribed to each cause and finding what proportion they form of the number of cases studied" (Brandt 1908: 638). Some research-ers refined the method by differentiating between "principal" and "subsidiary" causes, and one expert ranked them on a scale of one to ten in importance. Practical weaknesses undermined this method because charity investigators reporting on individual cases or coding case histories varied wildly in their assessment of causation. The assumptions on which the method rested—"(1) that in every case of poverty there is one chief or principal cause, and (2) that this cause will readily be recognized by the person who is told to find it" (Brandt 1908: 638)—were anything but scientific and, in fact, both a theoretical and practical dead end.

The first attempt by the National Conference of Charities and Corrections to classify the causes of poverty, Brandt points out, consisted of twenty-two items held together by no theory and focused mainly on individuals and families. In 1899 dissatisfaction with the list led to a revision dividing items into "causes within the family" and "causes outside the family" (Brandt 1908: 642). In the nine years between the revision and her article, Brandt observed, the causes in the first group generally were moved into the second. Poverty had become less an in-ternal problem—a problem of persons—and more a problem of conditions—a problem of place and, to the most acute students, political economy. "Behind

'intemperance,'" for instance, "we see poor food, congested living, lack of opportunities for wholesome recreation and the power of the liquor trust" (Brandt
1908: 642). Rather than "'licentiousness, dishonesty, and other moral defects,'"
students of poverty now emphasized "ineffectual penal methods and, again,
defective education, and, again, unwholesome conditions of modern city life"
(Brandt 1908: 643).

Older explanations of poverty missed the symptoms for the causes: "In short,
the recognized causes of poverty are . . . largely symptoms or results of poverty"
(Brandt 1908: 643). To be sure, they produce poverty, but they are not its "'underlying' causes." Even the most sacrosanct tenet of nineteenth-century scientific
charity embodied in the work and advocacy of the Charity Organization Society
crumbled under the weight of the new understanding. The notion that overly
generous and unsystematic relief bred dependence and deeper poverty proved
shallow: "If we were now to pick out a family whose dependence is due to the
unwise administration of relief, we should be apt to select a widow broken down
by over-exertion in supporting her children because we had not been generous
enough in our help" (Brandt 1908: 644). Brandt (1908: 649) also pointed astutely
to the prolonged dependence of children and the aged—the intersection of demography and political economy—to underscore the intensification of modern
poverty: "Both of these periods during which dependence is the normal state, are
lengthening at the expense of the working period." Children started to work at
a later age, and older workers left the workforce earlier and lived longer: "Until
wages have fully responded by an increase that will enable the average man not
only to support his children for a longer time, but also to provide in a shorter
working period for a longer old age, or until the effective working period has
been materially lengthened, this adverse condition will persist. In it we find the
reason why the problem of old-age pensions has become acute; from it comes
much of the misery which gives point to radical socialistic proposals" (Brandt
1908: 649).

In fact, Brandt (1908: 644) observed, in the last two or three years the heretical
idea that "poorly paid employment" constituted one of the prime causes of poverty had taken root among some researchers: "And we are coming, therefore, to
think of 'insufficient income,' when it means inadequate compensation, not as a
joke, but as one of the authentic causes of dependence." In the end, most poverty,
Brandt (1908: 644) concluded, resulted from "some form of exploitation or . . .
some defect in governmental efficiency." Poverty, in short, was at heart a problem of political economy: exploitation without, in modern terms, an adequate
safety net. To be sure, some "natural depravity" and "moral defects" resulted in
dependence, but they "may not be large enough to constitute a serious problem"
(Brandt 1908: 645)

Knowing the causes of poverty, Brandt (1908: 645) asserted, held value in two ways: "It is equally important in helping the individual family that needs assistance and in planning movements for the improvement of social conditions." Recent antipoverty efforts left Brandt optimistic—she cited the emergence of a successful "social movement" to conquer tuberculosis and its impact on families and communities and the successful campaigns against child labor—as evidence that something less than an attack on ancient underlying causes would ameliorate the poverty of individuals: "The existing conditions are what we have to deal with, and our practice has been to deal with them more hopefully than our theories would warrant. The results have justified the hopefulness; and a new theory is now emerging, namely that there is in human nature recuperative power of such strength that the removal of the existing visible effects of the 'underlying causes' will do almost as well, as far as the individual case is concerned, as the removal of the causes themselves; or, in other words, that poverty is itself one of the most potent causes of poverty and one of those most responsive to treatment" (1908: 647). Brandt cited with approval George Bernard Shaw's observation "that the whole trouble with the poor was their poverty, and that this could be made all right by dividing among them the money contributed for charity without any intermediate waste in salaries" (1908: 647). Poverty, in other words, was at root a problem of resources; what made people poor was a lack of money—a simple insight never wholly absent from poverty talk but submerged, rarely able to gain traction in mainstream policy. Poverty, however, was very much also a product of place: "Even in normal times there are adverse conditions in every American city. There are insanitary houses, over-crowded apartments, ill-ventilated factories, germ-laden dust in the streets and germ-laden water in the mains" (Brandt 1908: 650).

Poverty did not appear only in hard times. Rather, it resulted from the routine operation of the political economy: "Little children are in glass-works or selling papers, when they should be in school or in bed. Men and women are working over-long hours in disease-breeding surroundings . . . Men are exploiting, for their own profit, the weaknesses of their fellows, both as employees and consumers" (1908: 650). The study of poverty, therefore, "need not wait for hard times or times of great calamity, but may proceed at all times, under the most favorable conditions yet known in any community" (Brandt 1908: 650–51).

Brandt had contradicted herself, or at least backed into an inconsistency. She had started by arguing that the essential precondition for ameliorating poverty lay in grasping its deep causes, and she criticized the theoretical weakness of existing causal models that inhibited their practical effectiveness. By the end of her article, however, she had retreated. Some mechanisms for reducing poverty were well known. They could be applied with success even in the absence of a developed theory of poverty's underlying causes. Reformers should place their efforts on what worked. She was, of course, right on both counts. Understanding the deep causes of poverty remains essential to the development of coherent antipoverty programs. But some things just work, and they should not be dismissed or overlooked because they do not result from theory. This inconsistency has bedeviled every practically minded reformer who harbors an appreciation of theory.

In the last analysis, Brandt (1908: 651) considered her article less a contribution to theory than a call to action, a plea for evidence-based application of the known levers of poverty alleviation, even when they elided its fundamental causes: "In the language of current philosophical discussion, pragmatism affords our best working program." Nonetheless, Brandt had contributed to theory by implicitly laying out most—although not quite all—of the definitions of poverty that have reverberated during the century since she wrote.

Let us step back, then, and ask what answers to the question—what kind of a problem is poverty?—emerge from Brandt's article and which ones are missing.

What kind of a problem is poverty? The literature on poverty gives six answers. Certainly, there is overlap among them, but each can be teased out of the record to stand on its own. Brandt identified the first four. What they give us is not just a historical taxonomy but an archeology—a progressive discovery of the layers of meaning in poverty discourse.

- Persons. Poverty is the outcome of the failings of individuals or families.
- Places. Poverty results from toxic conditions within geographic spaces.
- Resources. Poverty is the absence of money and other key resources.
- Political economy. Poverty is the by-product of capitalist economies.
- Power. Poverty is a consequence of political powerlessness.
- Markets. Poverty reflects the absence of functioning markets or the failure to use the potential of markets to improve individual lives.

How one bundles these answers carries consequences because, as Brandt realized, they lead straight to what one does, or tries to do, about poverty. In the rest of this essay, I will expand briefly on each of these answers, pointing out their origins and trajectories and their implications for the present moment. My examples will come mainly from U.S. history because that is what I know best. However, I am well aware that these definitions of poverty are international in their scope and that the interplay between the international and domestic constitutes one of the most promising and important areas for poverty research and theory.

Persons

The idea that poverty results from personal inadequacy has dominated the history of poverty for more than two centuries. Before the twentieth century, the idea that poverty is a problem of persons—whether deserving or undeserving—remained intertwined with the biblical idea that poverty is always with us. With production limited and population pressing on resources, poverty appeared ingrained within the human condition (D. Fox 1967: 88). When this fatalistic idea of poverty as a result of universal scarcity began to crumble in the early twentieth century under Progressive Era economists' "discovery of abundance," a wholly new dilemma emerged. If poverty was unnecessary, then what accounted for its stubborn persistence? Why were so many people poor? The most straightforward answer unbundled the two strands: scarcity and individual deficiency. With scarcity off the table, individual failings marked persons as all the more undeserving in a world of possibility where poverty was unnecessary. This idea—we might call it the irony of optimism—carved a hard edge of inferiority into ideas about poor people. That is one reason why the idea that poverty as a problem of persons persists with such tenacity, despite whatever evidence social scientists produce. The idea is so ubiquitous that there is no need to belabor its march through the twentieth and twenty-first centuries or its role in keeping poverty off the political agenda during the Great Recession.

The idea of poverty as a problem of persons comes in both hard and soft versions. The soft version portrays poverty as the result of laziness, immoral behavior, inadequate skills, and dysfunctional families. The hard version views poverty as the result of inherited deficiencies that limit intellectual potential, trigger harmful and immoral behavior, and circumscribe economic achievement. The soft view, which is the older of the two, holds out the possibility of individual escape from poverty. In America the primary antipoverty mechanism supported by the soft side has been education in one form or another. The hard side burst onto the policy scene in the 1860s to explain institutional failure. Its pessimistic implications fixated on containing and managing dependence at the least possible cost. Neither the soft nor hard side resulted in much sympathy for poor persons other than children, widows, and a few others whose lack of responsibility for their condition could not be denied. These were the deserving poor. Today they are most often referred to as the working poor, and in recent years they have elicited sympathy and support from public programs. The others have been thought to have brought their poverty on themselves; they are the undeserving poor.

In one form of another, this distinction between the deserving and undeserving poor has dominated discussions of poverty for more than two hundred years, but the identity of the undeserving poor, constructed by time and circumstance, has varied. In the late nineteenth and early twentieth centuries, for instance, they were mainly men—shiftless, out-of-work, intemperate tramps whose behavior disqualified them from the limited bounty of public and private charity. In the 1920s, as Cybelle Fox shows in her remarkable recent book *Three Worlds of Relief*, social workers led a campaign to brand Mexicans as the undeserving poor. They advocated restricting Mexicans' entry to the United States and deporting those already here (C. Fox 2012: 73–94). In the 1960s, women of color dependent on public assistance became the face of the undeserving poor and the primary object of punitive policies, which culminated in the 1996 "welfare reform" act. Today, out-of-work black men and undocumented immigrants dominate the ranks of the undeserving poor.

A methodological point: identifying the undeserving poor, it is crucial to remember, needs to extend beyond reading what is said about individuals or groups. Equally, if not more, important is how they are treated in legislation, administrative regulations, and on-the-ground practices. The key is discovering who is excluded from public and private relief and charity.

Not all persons in need ever could be helped. In the eighteenth as well as the twenty-first century, making distinctions has proved essential, and identifying and administering the grounds for exclusion has remained the quintessential act of policy. Where to draw the line has persisted as the fundamental dilemma. The earliest distinctions separated the "able-bodied" from the "impotent" poor and "paupers" from the rest of the poor. The distinction between the able-bodied and impotent poor divided the needy by factors beyond their control—those who could work and those who because of reasons such as illness, infirmity, or widowhood could not. In practice, this distinction remained blurred at the boundaries, as it has ever since. The distinction between paupers and the rest of the poor separated those dependent on charity for survival from the rest who managed to stay alive through their own efforts. The emergence of the distinction between the deserving and undeserving poor in the late eighteenth and early nineteenth centuries signaled the moralization of the older language of the able-bodied and impotent poor. In 1827 the Philadelphia Guardians of the Poor claimed, "The poor in consequence of vice, constitute here and everywhere, by far the greater part of the poor. . . . From three-fourth to nine-tenths of the paupers in all parts of our country, may attribute their degradation to the vice of intemperance" (Katz 2013: 8). As the Guardians' bold assertion implied, efforts to retain distinctions between categories of poor people eroded in the early nineteenth century. Writing in 1843 the Unitarian minister Walter Channing observed that in the "popular mind" poverty "is looked to solely as the product of him or her who has entered its dreadful, because dishonored, uncared for, or unwisely cared for, service. Let me repeat it, the causes of poverty are looked for, and found in him or her who suffers it" (Katz 2013: 8).

Despite the pessimistic ring to Channing's observation, in the early nineteenth century a belief in the plasticity of human nature fueled the creation of mental hospitals, penitentiaries, and reform schools built on the optimistic assumption that removal from pathological settings coupled with a supportive environment—"moral therapy"—would cure or rehabilitate the mentally ill, criminal, and delinquent. Other than widows, adult supplicants for charity or relief—the undeserving poor—remained the exception, beyond the reach of moral therapy or hope of rehabilitation. For them, public authorities also created a new institution: the poorhouse. But poorhouses rested on the idea of "less eligibility"—conditions in them had to be worse than the worst conditions outside. The point was to deter people from claiming poor relief. Poorhouses were founded on the optimistic but faulty belief that they would cut the cost of pauper support and terrify potential claimants for outdoor relief—in today's terms, welfare outside institutions—by forcing all paupers into miserable institutions (Katz 1996: 3–36).

Most of all, from the nineteenth century onward hope has rested in children. Education promised to prevent dependence, delinquency, and adult crime. By counteracting the baneful influence of families, education promised to redeem America and secure its future. This messianic belief underlay the origins of American public educational systems in the second quarter of the nineteenth century and runs through the writing of the great founding generation of school reformers. In his twelfth annual report as secretary of the Massachusetts State Board of Education, the most famous of them, Horace Mann, explained that "if education be equally diffused, it will draw property after it, by the strongest of all attractions; for such a thing never did happen, and never can happen, as that an intelligent and practical body of men can be permanently poor. . . . Education, then, beyond all other devices of human origin, is the great equalizer of the conditions of men—the balance-wheel of the social machinery. . . . It does better than to disarm the poor of their hostility towards the rich; it prevents being poor" (Mann 1849).

This soft-side view—poverty is a problem of persons best addressed through education—has remained an article of faith throughout American history—a staple of Progressive Era thought in the work of John Dewey and many others. It underpinned the 1960s educational literature on the "culturally deprived" child (Riessman 1962) and was one of the influences on the War on Poverty, which stressed job training over job creation (Aguiar 2012). It endures, today, in the rhetoric of education reform.[2] Its record is mixed. Education by itself never proved sufficient to counteract poverty. Job training has emerged from the War on Poverty and Great Society with a disappointing record.[3]

What happens when education manifestly does not work? When environmentally based therapies fail to change behavior? This is the question that confronted policy makers by the 1860s. The issue arose with all of the new institutions—reform schools, prisons, mental hospitals, and even poorhouses. As optimism that they could reach their goals faded, administrators and public officials turned to hard new explanations. In 1866 the Massachusetts Board of State Charities, which had oversight of the state's public institutions, wrote: "The causes of the evil ['the existence of such a large proportion of dependent and destructive members in our community'] are manifold, but among the immediate ones, the chief cause is inherited organic imperfection,—vitiated constitution, or *poor stock*" (Katz 1981: 181). The hard-side view of poverty as a problem of persons arose as a response to institutional failure, not from new theory. Darwinism soon gave it an intellectual anchor. Race theory, intelligence testing, and sociobiology have kept it alive and healthy. But the balance between soft- and hard-side views has shifted over time, with optimistic or environmentally based views accompanying periods of reform and pessimistic, hereditarian views surging in response to perceived failures of reform. Two examples are Arthur Jensen's controversial 1969 *Harvard Educational Review* article arguing for the inheritance of cognitive ability and Richard L. Herrnstein's and Charles Murray's 1996 *Bell Curve*, which also promoted the hereditary basis of intelligence (Jensen 1969: 1–123, Herrenstein and Murray 1996).

Followed to their extreme, hard-side views of poverty as a problem of persons lead to mean, custodial, punitive, nihilistic approaches to policy. Policies based on soft-side views appear more promising. But they also have severe limitations. Their track record as antipoverty strategies does not inspire confidence. Today, the new, rapidly growing field of epigenetics claims to bridge the distance between soft- and hard-side advocates. It purports to show, for instance, that environmental influences associated with poverty can trigger lasting genetic changes that handicap children throughout their lives. These claims demand dispassionate evaluation by independent experts. While it is crucial not to deny or hide from the findings and implications of science, it cannot be forgotten the best "science" of the day has been invoked to support every race, gender, and nationality based program of racial discrimination and violence since the nineteenth century.[4]

Whether anchored in the soft or hard side, or the new epigenetic center, the relentless individual focus of poverty defined as a problem of persons too often obscures its other dimensions. One of these is place.

Place

The great service of Michael Harrington's (1962) *The Other America* was to render poverty visible. Harrington, Harold Meyerson (2012: 68) points out, saw "what almost everyone else had missed: that 40 million Americans in a nation of 176 million were poor":

> The new middle-class majority that had moved to suburbia bypassed the decaying inner cities on the recently built interstates, kept their distance from the African American ghettos, never encountered the migrant farmworkers, and failed to see (at least in aggregate) the millions of impoverished elderly. None of these groups had political power or a visible collective presence; they had not found a way to announce their existence. So Harrington did.

Territories of poverty often remain invisible. That is why so much writing about poverty has taken the form of discovery and exposure, or what Michele Dauber (2012: 87–88) in *The Sympathetic State* labels *aggregation* and *iconization*, subsuming individual heterogeneity into a mass whose suffering results from a "single, overarching cause" and "rendering individuals as representatives of a type—victims of circumstance—rather than as individuals with personal biographies." Think about the role of Charles Dickens, Henry Mayhew, and Charles Booth in Britain, or Jacob Riis, Robert Hunter, Dorothea Lange, John Steinbeck, Michael Harrington, or Barbara Ehrenreich in America. Their key contribution was moral: the exposure of mass poverty and the framing of classes of poor people as blameless or victims. Why has poverty proved so hard to see when it has been so pervasive? One reason is geographic. Often it has concentrated in urban slums and rural backwaters, easy to miss on a day-to-day basis. That situation persists today, accentuated by increased economic and racial segregation, and by the poverty hidden behind the façades of outwardly comfortable-looking suburban housing whose residents, laid off from work, struggle just to get by. Willful ignorance is a second reason territories of poverty are invisible. Evasion offers the easy way out. The consequences of recognizing mass poverty pose painful and difficult challenges to consciences and politics. In America, poverty also has proved hard to see because its recognition contradicts the country's image as a land of boundless opportunity and a ubiquitous middle class. This is the "paradox" that motivated much mid-twentieth century writing on poverty (O'Connor 2001: 3). But "paradox" is the ultimate liberal evasion, for it turns poverty into an aberration, extrinsic to the political economy of capitalism, not a condition that calls for serious and divisive structural reforms.

Although a long tradition of social criticism presents poverty as a problem of place, no one has written a history of "territories of poverty," and the subject remains ripe—full of potential both for reorienting social history and informing social policy. Poverty as a problem of place, as well as of persons, exhibits two sides. On one side, which has dominated discussions, conditions *in* places— most notably, substandard housing—produce, reinforce, or augment poverty. On the other side, poverty is a product of place itself, reproduced independent of the individuals who pass through it. The first version holds out the hope of improvement; its paradigmatic strategy is housing reform, which has come in many guises. The implications of the other side are gloomy. There is no paradigmatic strategy. Attempts to engineer change do not have an outstanding record of success. What follows are examples of each side, not a history of territories of poverty. Indeed, I could just as well have used rural poverty—the South after the Civil War and Appalachia, where poverty sparked the War on Poverty, to make the same point.

The famous late nineteenth-century journalist and social reformer Jacob Riis, writes historian Max Page (1999: 79), "believed that people's behavior would improve exactly as much as did their living conditions. Tenement dwellers 'are shiftless, destructive and stupid,' wrote Riis. 'In a word, they are what the tenements have made them.'" Since the mid-nineteenth century, New York City reformers had identified a package of pathologies—crime, moral depravity, disease, poverty—with the city's emergent slums, most notoriously the Five Points district, and later, Riis saw as its epicenter Mulberry Bend. For Riis, the only way to fix Mulberry Bend was to destroy it. Slum clearance offered the main road out of poverty. "When he was asked if the result of destroying Mulberry Bend was simply to scatter poverty," reports Page (1999: 82), "Riis insisted that 'the greater and by far the worst part of it [poverty] is destroyed with the slum.'" What to do about the tenements that epitomized New York's slums proved contentious; tenement house reform split into camps "at odds with one another over the purpose and effectiveness of tenement destruction and creation" (Page 1999: 88). All reformers, however, treated tenements as incubators of sickness, epidemics, and social pathologies (Bates 1992; Rosenberg 1987). In nineteenth-century social thought, crime, poverty, ignorance, and disease did not constitute separate problems. Instead, they were bundled together, an unholy package with origins in the pathogenic environments of cities and manufacturing districts, nourished by population density and crowded, unwholesome housing.[5]

A detailed history of tenement house reform in New York City, let alone a broader history of housing reform in the twentieth century, would distract from the point of this essay. But a few observations are relevant to the point of this section. As the housing reform project became increasingly technical, the early language of moral outrage and social fear was subordinated to concerns with sponsorship (public versus private), building codes, location (frequently a racial issue), costs, and other factors. But the older concerns with the intersection of housing and social outcomes never disappeared. In fact, they surfaced dramatically in the federal government's Moving to Opportunity Program, which moved people out of high poverty neighborhoods (Briggs, Popkin, and Goering, 2010), and in the transformation of high-rise public housing from its initial function as a temporary home for aspiring working families to badly maintained, dangerous reservations for the urban poor. The language of fear and loathing about high-rise public housing eerily echoed Jacob Riis and other nineteenth-century reformers, and the eventual solution proved one that Riis would have approved. Late twentieth-century reformers found Chicago's Robert Taylor Homes, and its counterparts around the country, as irredeemable as Riis had found Mulberry Bend. With more decisive force than Riis could muster, they blew them up (see, for example, Brown 2009). It is interesting that the one major city where high-rise public housing has remained relatively successful is New York City (Bloom 2009). Unfortunately, whatever its other beneficial effects, the demolition of public housing has not reduced poverty.

Nineteenth-century reformers assumed the importance of place. No one doubted what came to be called, in the language of late twentieth-century social science, "neighborhood effects." Many reformers responded to the consequences of pathogenic places by advocating "silver bullet" solutions. Education promoters, for instance, described with passion and detail rampant crime, immorality, and poverty in crowded city and manufacturing districts. Their solutions, however, by and large evaded the difficult questions of political economy to which their observations might have led and focused instead on the promise of educational expansion and reform. The same can be said of many housing reformers, like Riis, whose wide indictment narrowed to a single solution. In the first two decades of the twentieth century, other reformers, labeled "positive environmentalists" by the historian Paul Boyer, took a broader view. Positive environmentalists believed that social disorder, rampant immorality, illness, and poverty all stemmed from poisonous urban environments. But the most effective strategy of social control did not lie, as it did for many nineteenth-century social critics, in "repression . . . . but [in] a more subtle and complex process of influencing behavior and molding character through a transformed, consciously planned urban environment" (Boyer 1978: 221). To housing reform, positive environmentalists added advocacy of parks and playgrounds and city planning, which became "the culminating expression of the positive environmentalists' efforts to achieve moral and social ends through environmental means" (Boyer 1978: 268). Although positive environmentalists also by and large avoided difficult questions of political economy, they remained optimistic that place could be fixed, that pathogenic qualities could be identified and excised, and social problems like poverty reduced. Other writers on place left readers less hopeful.

In his 1929 classic, *The Gold Coast and the Slum*, Chicago school sociologist Harvey Warren Zorbaugh observed: "It is apparent that the slum is more than an economic phenomenon. The slum is a sociological phenomenon. Based upon a segregation within the economic process, it nevertheless displays characteristic social patterns which differentiate it from adjoining areas. . . . The slum sets its mark upon those who dwell in it, gives them attitudes and behavior problems peculiar to itself" (151). The Chicago school originated a powerful current in American urban studies that stresses the independent influence of place on the production of poverty. Subsequent scholarship has modified or rejected the Chicago school's ecological model of succession and concentric circles. But its larger emphasis on the role of place in the patterning of social experience—on the need for the close study of neighborhoods as wholes and the intersection of context with lived experience—has endured, despite serious challenge from the a-spatial turn in American social science after World War II embodied in the rise of survey research based on national samples detached from context.[6] From a global perspective, recent work on Third World urbanization, as in Mike Davis's (2007) *Planet of Slums*, powerfully reinforces the spatial tradition in writing about poverty.[7] Nonetheless, in the 1980s social scientists began to question whether neighborhoods had independent impacts on individual behavior. Indeed, a review of the complex literature on the subject by Christopher Jencks and Susan Mayer (1990) concluded that the emphasis on neighborhood effects was misplaced. Nonetheless, the older emphasis on the importance of place resurfaced, also in the late 1980s, in writing about the "underclass"—in the identification of areas of concentrated urban poverty that produced an array of social pathologies.

The most famous book was sociologist William Julius Wilson's (1987) *The Truly Disadvantaged*. "It is the growth of the high- and extreme-poverty areas that epitomizes the social transformation of the inner city," wrote Wilson (1987: 55). Further: "If I had to use one term to capture the differences in the experiences of low-income families who live in inner-cities from the experiences of those who live in other areas of the central city today, that term would be *concentration effects*." From this concentration flowed "massive joblessness, flagrant and open lawlessness, and low achieving schools." With these areas shunned by outsiders, the residents, "whether women and children of welfare families or aggressive street criminals, have become increasingly socially isolated from mainstream patterns of behavior" (Wilson 1987: 58). Sociologists Douglas Massey and Nancy Denton (1993: 118) in their *American Apartheid* explained the reproduction and intensification of inner city poverty with a model grounded in racial segregation:

> Geographically concentrated poverty is built into the experience of urban places by racial segregation. Segregation, not middle-class out-migration, is the key factor responsible for the creation of communities characterized by persistent and spatially concentrated poverty. Concentrated poverty is created by the pernicious interaction between a group's overall rate of poverty and its degree of segregation in society. When a highly segregated group experiences a high or rising rate of poverty, geographically concentrated poverty is the inevitable result, and from this geographic concentration of poverty follows a variety of other deleterious conditions.

In their emphasis on the independent role of racial segregation, Massey and Denton differed from Wilson, who stressed the role of middle-class out-migration and joblessness in the production of spatially concentrated poverty. For purposes of this essay, however, the main point is that together they rekindled an understanding of poverty as a problem of place—an understanding powerfully reinforced by Robert Sampson's (2012) recent magisterial *Great American City: Chicago and the Enduring Neighborhood Effect* (with a foreword by William Julius Wilson). In the "broadest sense," writes Sampson (2012: 22), "the present study is an effort to show that neighborhoods are not merely settings in which individuals act out the dramas produced by autonomous and preset scripts, or empty vessels determined by 'bigger' external forces, but are important determinants of the quantity and quality of human behavior in their own right." As for poverty, "neighborhood social disadvantage has durable properties and tends to repeat itself, and because of racial segregation is most pronounced in the black community" (Sampson 2012: 99).

Does poverty as a problem of place lead in more promising directions than poverty as a problem of persons? For Wilson (1996), it directs attention to work, notably to the chronic joblessness within inner city ghettos; for Massey and Denton (1993) it points to the necessity of combatting racial segregation through fair housing legislation and other means; for Sampson (2012) it necessitates dramatic public action. "The 'poverty trap' cycle can be broken only with structural interventions of the sort that government or other large organizational units (e.g., foundations) are equipped to carry out" (Sampson 2012: 99). What, precisely, are those interventions, and what is necessary for them to succeed? In the 1990s, foundations sponsored massive comprehensive community initiatives premised on the need to attack housing, jobs, and other problems simultaneously. Their outcomes disappointed. Can a new generation work better? Geoffrey Canada's Harlem Children's Zone, the most famous recent comprehensive initiative, depends on massive philanthropic funding and on his charismatic leadership, which are hard to imagine outside New York City, and its results, Canada makes clear, will be not be evident until a generation has passed through its programs. As part of his campaign for the presidency, Barack Obama promised to combat urban poverty in part by replicating the Harlem Children's Zone, and his Promise Neighborhoods Initiative intends to replicate the HCZ in twenty cities across the country (Croft and Whitehurst 2010). The resurgence of poverty as a problem of place represents a welcome move away from the relentless individualism of poverty as a problem of persons. But it still excludes other lenses that focus on even less comfortable and more challenging questions. One of these is poverty as a problem of resources.

Resources

Recall the surprising conclusion to Lilian Brandt's article on the causes of poverty: forget for a moment about poverty's underlying causes and just give poor people money. This was the point of her paraphrase of George Bernard Shaw, "that the whole trouble with the poor was their poverty, and that this could be made all right by dividing among them the money contributed for charity without any intermediate waste in salaries" (1908: 647). In the history of writing about poverty, this simple view is a radical idea, more often evaded or contested than accepted. But it has never lacked advocates. Some have focused on the poverty that resulted from low wages—the impossibility of escaping at least intermittent poverty through work. Others concentrated on those who lacked wages—call them the nonworking or dependent poor. In the 1960s, bureaucratic necessity forced the federal government to officially define poverty as a problem of resources, that is, income below a fixed standard.

In 1831 the Philadelphia printer and editor Mathew Carey documented the prevalence of poverty among the city's workers. A combination of seasonal work and low wages left most of the "numerous . . . laborers on canals and turnpikes" (Carey 1833: 8) as well as women seamstresses without enough money to survive. Carey drove home his point with careful comparisons of annual wages to expenses. Contrary to public opinion, he stressed, most of the city's poverty did not result from laziness or immorality. "I am most fully satisfied that the worthless of both sexes bear but a small proportion to those who are industrious and meritorious. Unfortunately, the worthless occupy a more prominent space in the public eye, and with many are unceasing objects of animadversion and reprobation—their numbers and their follies and vices are magnified; whereas the industrious are always in the background out of view" (Carey 1833: 12). Carey hoped his analysis showed "that there are classes of people, male and female, whose dependence is on their hands for support, and whose wages, when fully employed, are not more than sufficient for that purpose; that when unemployed, they must be reduced to penury and want; and that there are classes of females, whose wages are inadequate for their support, even when constantly employed" (Carey 1833: 19). Carey wanted to rouse sympathy among the wealthy and to overcome their opposition to taxation for poor relief. With only a few exceptions, what the city's poor needed was higher wages or, in its absence, cash relief. Carey was one of the earliest American writers to cut through the moralism of most discussions of poverty. His proved, however, a lonely voice. Poverty remained ubiquitous in the land of opportunity.

Dependence—the need for support in order to survive—was in fact an ancient problem in America, and colonists responded to it with relief practices copied from the Elizabethan Poor Laws. Welfare may be the oldest American public policy, as American as Thanksgiving. But it has always been disliked (Katz 1996: 37–59). Called outdoor relief, later welfare, it has earned the distinction as the most unpopular public policy in American history. Frequently attacked, sometimes temporarily abolished, it never has totally disappeared—testament to the enduring need to which it responds. The 1996 welfare reform legislation testifies to the permanent war on outdoor relief, and the failure of federal welfare policy to respond adequately to the Great Recession highlights why attempts to do away with outdoor relief—as in the August 2012 abolition of General Relief in Pennsylvania—invariably increase hardship (Abramsky 2012: 62–64; Gaestel 2012, A01; Gilens 1999).

Outdoor relief and its successors were responses to destitution, but never antipoverty measures. They aimed to keep persons alive at the lowest possible cost. The opprobrium that surrounded them—the incorrect belief that they increased dependence—showed the reluctance to recognize poverty as a problem of resources. The lengths to which public officials and private charity representatives went to deny the simple truth that what claimants needed most was cash often appear astonishing. One function served by the idea of the demoralizing consequences of cash relief (now often theorized as moral hazard) has been to reinforce mean, punitive, or, at best, paternalistic policies.

Critics of cash relief never entirely submerged the view that what the poor need most is money. Mothers' pensions, introduced in most states in the early decades of the twentieth century, for instance, recognized that widows and deserted women required cash income. In the Social Security Act of 1935, the federal government federalized mothers' pensions as Aid to Dependent Children (later Aid to Families with Dependent Children or AFDC, abolished in 1996 and replaced by Temporary Assistance to Needy Families, or TANF). In 1938 the Fair Labor and Standards Act introduced a federal minimum wage and regulated hours of work. In the 1960s the conservative economist Milton Friedman advocated a negative income tax (Friedman 1962, chap. 12), and in the 1970s the federal government mounted a social experiment to test the idea (Haveman 1987: 175–88). President Richard Nixon unsuccessfully proposed in effect a national minimum income in his Family Assistance Plan (Steensland 1962). Today, an international organization keeps advocacy of a guaranteed income alive, while the Living Wage Movement counts victories in a host of cities.[8] At the same time, material poverty appears as a violation of human rights in the international human rights movement, which has arced back to the United States, fostering new and vibrant national organizations and invading law school curricula with astonishing speed.[9]

Within the federal government, the idea of poverty as a problem of money gained traction in the 1960s with the launch of the War on Poverty when the administration needed a benchmark—a standard against which to measure the impact of its programs. The work of a young government economist, Mollie Orshansky, became the basis of the federal poverty line. Despite its grave deficiencies this measurement has endured to this day, though it is finally being edged toward replacement.[10] America at last had an official poverty rate. For administrative reasons, poverty became a problem of money.

With money as the standard, the history of the poverty rate shows that the federal government has enjoyed spectacular successes in reducing poverty, although the downward trend has been neither straight nor irreversible. When the poverty line was first formulated in 1960, Americans age sixty-five and over suffered the highest poverty rate of any age group; they were three times as likely to be poor as others. Today, their poverty rate is the lowest among age groups, the direct result of using money to combat poverty through Social Security. The high rate of child poverty results in part from the absence of a child allowance, a feature of social policy in most other Western democracies. The Earned Income Tax Credit was greatly increased by President Clinton, with bipartisan support, to resolve the contradiction between falling wages and the demand that everyone work—the slogan was "make work pay"—and has lifted large numbers of people out of poverty, even though the real value of the minimum wage has eroded.

Comparing the amount of poverty before and after government transfers (what has been called pre- and post-transfer poverty) provides the best way to gauge the effect of money and other resources like food in lifting people out of poverty. Pre-transfer poverty has remained high, with reductions in poverty resulting to a large extent from government transfer programs. In 2009, with market wages and salaries the measure of income, 23.7 percent of the population lived in poverty; with all government benefits added, the proportion dropped to 10.1 percent (Gould and Edwards 2011). In 2012 the *New York Times* produced an analysis that showed the proportion of individual income resulting from government transfer programs. Nationally, the amount increased from 8 percent in 1969 to 18 percent in 2012 (New York Times 2012).

The idea that poverty is a problem of money does not receive the intellectual and popular respect it deserves. The success of cash-based antipoverty programs do not register nearly enough in the extensive sociological literature on poverty or in public responses to poverty. Even successful cash-based programs, however, by and large slide over the question of why so much poverty exists in the first place. For answers to that question, it is necessary to turn to the literature on poverty as a problem of political economy.

Political Economy

Poverty does not result solely from the deficiencies of persons, the pathology of places, or the absence of resources, or from a toxic mix of all three. Modern poverty—and by modern I mean since the late eighteenth century—emerges from the routine intersection of politics with economics. This is what Lilian Brandt (1908: 643) meant when she observed that "the recognized causes of poverty are in fact largely symptoms or results of poverty. . . . [T]hey are not the 'underlying' causes." Modern poverty, in a nutshell, and at the risk of oversimplification, has been produced by capitalist economics serviced by conservative politics. For more than two centuries, an impressive body of theory has for the most part masked or subordinated this core idea.

In his brilliant *An End to Poverty?* historian Gareth Stedman Jones (2004) excavates the origins of this story. The "moment of convergence between the late Enlightenment and the ideals of a republican and democratic revolution," writes Stedman Jones, "was a fundamental historical turning point. However brief its appearance, however vigorously it was thereafter repressed, it marks the beginning of all modern thought about *poverty*" (Stedman Jones 2004: 9, emphasis in original). The "first practicable proposals to end poverty," found in the writings of Condorcet and Thomas Paine, "date back to the 1790s, and were a direct product of the American and French Revolutions" (Stedman Jones 2004: 224). In their aftermath, attacks on the institutions of state and church in Britain and France provoked a fierce reaction fueled by Paine's wild popularity in Britain. "The effort to thwart this revolutionary subversion of beliefs demanded the mobilization of unprecedented numbers of the population and engaged the energies of every organ of church and state in every locality" (Stedman Jones 2004: 226). The result "stamped upon the still protean features of political economy . . . a deeply anti-utopian cast of mind, transforming future enquiry in the area into a gloomy and tirelessly repeated catechism" (Stedman Jones 2004:

226). The "ambition to combat poverty," writes Stedman Jones (2004: 226), "was henceforward conceived as a bleakly individual battle against the temptations of the flesh."

The oldest and most coherent tradition in the political economy of poverty in the United States as well as Britain is a product of this history. The poor constitute the unfortunate casualties of a dynamic, competitive economy in which they fail to grasp or hold onto the levers of opportunity. The widowed, the sick, and a few others remain exceptions, but for the most part the poor are losers, too incompetent or badly disciplined to reap the bounty of increasing productivity. Aiding them with charity or relief only interferes with the natural working of markets, retards growth, and, in the end, does more harm than good. From the Social Darwinists of the nineteenth century through the work of contemporary political economists on the right, this idea, dressed often with quantitative sophistication and theoretical skill, has retained an amazing purchase on popular thought and on politics as well.[11]

Consider two examples. In her superb *Poverty Knowledge*, historian Alice O'Connor (2001) narrates the formulation of an antipoverty agenda in the Kennedy administration as a competition between growth-based and structural models. The victory of the growth model—the vehicle, as Alan Wolfe (1981: 143) has shown, for combining capitalist expansion with social justice in the post–World War II era—signaled the triumph of what came to be known as the "new economics":

> The impact on the subsequent trajectory of poverty knowledge was immense. First and foremost, the new economics made the struggle against poverty compatible with lightly managed, if not free-market, capitalist growth. The new economics also provided a central theoretical framework—neoclassical labor market theory—from which economists and, later, sociologists, began in the mid-1960s to generate 'testable hypotheses' and to build an expanding program of poverty research. The ubiquity of the neoclassical model as a way of explaining the causes and consequences of poverty—alternately labeled human capital, social capital, or cultural capital—indicates the extent to which that central theoretical framework still prevails. So, too, does the overwhelming emphasis on individual-level attributes as 'causes' of poverty, an emphasis that avoids recognition of politics, institutions, or structural inequality.

In his powerful essay, "The State, the Movement, and the Poor," historian Thomas Jackson (1993) criticizes the neglect of history and politics in writing about the "underclass." Like O'Connor, Jackson (1993: 404) identifies a tradition of political economy of poverty conservative in its implications and shared by liberal and conservative writers. Experts and policymakers, he argues, are concerned "with how to frame policies benefiting the poor in the context of the current political structure, which favors the middle class and the wealthy, local elites, and powerful economic interests." In his discussion of the "underclass debate," Jackson (1993: 404) observes that "authors [had] wholly neglected questions of national and local political structures as they may have contributed to urban poverty." It has been conservatives, however, who have followed the implications of free-market theory to its most logical conclusions, with devastating effects for antipoverty policy: "More than anyone else, recent conservative critics of welfare policy have argued that the state contributed to the current underclass problem" (Jackson 1993: 404). Their explanation of the persistence of poverty during an era of "unprecedented economic growth. . . . downplays the performance of the economy and blames the state." For the two leading conservative writers on poverty and social policy, Charles Murray and Lawrence Mead, "poverty increased not in spite but *because* of the expansion of social policy expenditures in the 1960s and 1970s, which eroded poor people's work ethic, family values, and sense of social obligation" (Jackson 1993: 404, emphasis in original).

Conservatives, of course, have not held a monopoly on the political economy of poverty. Nonetheless, even left-leaning social science has not shaken loose from a tradition that obscures the production of poverty in the routine working of politics and economy and focuses instead on what Lilian Brandt (1908: 643) called "largely symptoms or results of poverty."

Among the myriad critics of poverty on the American left, undoubtedly the most famous was Michael Harrington, whose 1962 *The Other America* is said, with some exaggeration, to have touched off the War on Poverty through its impact on President John F. Kennedy. Harrington did touch the conscience of Americans, unmasking the poverty that a self-congratulatory politics and social theory, not to mention willful ignorance, kept hidden. But even Harrington could not sustain Americans' interest in poverty, and his subsequent book, the excellent *The New American Poverty* (1984), enjoyed nothing like the same influence when it appeared in Reagan-era America. In fact, throughout the massive rise in economic inequality and the Great Recession poverty has remained off the political agenda. In the 2008 presidential election, only candidate John Edwards made poverty the focal point of his campaign, which went nowhere and eventually imploded. So thoroughly has the centuries-old conservative political economy permeated American ideas about how society and government work that poverty has become the newest "third rail" in American politics (Tough 2012).

There is, of course, a long tradition of writing about the political economy of poverty from the perspective of the political left. The consequences of the Industrial Revolution—inescapable immiseration, the pathogenic slums of Manchester, England, and other early industrial cities, early death, rampant disease, stunted childhoods—in short, the "social question," provoked a radical political economics, notably in the work of Marx and writers in the Marxian tradition. In the United States, the poverty and inequality that resulted from naked capitalist greed in the first Gilded Age laid bare the opposition of capital and labor with a clarity that dropped from sight in the twentieth century. Mainstream writers and newspapers routinely referred to the division of America into two great camps—capital and labor—with a frankness that today would be denied and dismissed as "class warfare" (Katz, Doucet, and Stern 1982: 14–63). But class warfare did exist in the great railway strike of 1877, the Homestead strike of 1892, the Pullman strike 1894, and the Colorado coal strike of 1913–14. As never before or since, radical political-economic explanations for poverty and inequality went mainstream, or nearly mainstream. In 1886 Henry George, who grounded his interpretation in the immiseration that followed the monopoly of land (see George 1880), nearly won the mayoralty of New York City. In the presidential election of 1896, William Jennings Bryan, with his fiery condemnation of the gold standard as the root of misery, ran for the White House on the Democratic ticket, winning 6.5 million votes or 46.7 percent of the total cast. In 1912 Eugene Debs led the Socialist Party to its best showing in presidential politics in American history, winning about 900,000 votes or 6 percent of the total.

All three men acquired huge followings. Their messages resonated across America, reaching ordinary workers searching for explanations of why they received so little in the land of plenty and what could be done to turn the situation around. Yet none of the three men captured power; none founded an important and lasting school of political economy.[12] Progressive Era reformers achieved more, taming Gilded Age capitalism with antitrust legislation, mothers' pensions, early social insurance plans, regulation of hours of work, and other measures.[13] But they stopped short of confronting the deeper political economy itself. The Marxian tradition never gained traction even before it was discredited by the founding and subsequent history of the Soviet Union. The radicalism that flourished briefly in the Great Depression of the 1930s proved evanescent, blunted by the New Deal, pushed offstage by World War II with its full employment and by the Cold War and McCarthyism. The trade unions that emerged in the postwar years proved effective at winning higher wages and a private welfare state but paid a high price, giving up the oppositional stance of early unions, like the IWW, and drawing back from the early radicalism of the CIO.

The New Deal, the War on Poverty, the Great Society: all could point with pride to stunning achievements moderating the unmediated impacts of free-market capitalism and putting into place a welfare state. But none of them grounded their reforms in a theory of political economy that linked wealth and poverty to the routine operations of modern capitalism. That, in fact, was the point. American liberalism could not deny the paradox of poverty—the persistence of poverty in the land of abundance. But it could tame its political implications by defining poverty as outside the routine workings of the political economy—the exception rather than the rule. As Alyosha Goldstein (2012: 10) writes, "Since poverty was understood as an aberration or anomaly rather than as a requisite for capitalism, mainstream research on poverty held that mitigating or even eliminating poverty was possible within the framework of capitalism."

In the 1960s and 1970s, in fact, antipoverty scholarship turned toward race and gender. The major left exception has been the work of Frances Fox Piven and Richard Cloward who in a series of trenchant and powerful works beginning with *Regulating the Poor* linked the production of poverty and the deployment of relief to the routine functioning of a capitalist political economy (Piven and Cloward 1993). Black poverty became part of the Civil Rights agenda, although, as Thomas Jackson (2006) has shown, throughout his career Martin Luther King Jr. grasped the links between racial oppression and discrimination and broader questions of economic inequality. It is intriguing to wonder if King could have built a powerful transracial poor people's movement grounded in a radical political economy had he not been assassinated. The most powerful alternative political economics, in fact, emerged from black scholars who developed a short-lived school of thought that rooted black disadvantage and inequality in what they termed "internal colonialism"—a theory that analogized the American urban ghetto to Third World colonies (Katz 2013: 73). Feminist scholars highlighted what they termed the "feminization of poverty," finding poverty's origins in a long history of patriarchy and gender discrimination (Stallard, Ehrenrich, and Sklar 1983). Close to the ground, poor women activists in the National Welfare Rights Movement and its offshoots anchored their protests in homegrown understandings of the intersection of politics and economics. Despite impressive victories, as in the story told by Annelise Orleck (1996) in *Storming Caesar's Palace*, when they seemed headed for real power, the forces they threatened closed them down (Kornbluh 2007).

There is, of course, a great deal more that can be written about both conservative and left political economies of poverty. This little sketch—almost a caricature—has two main points. One is to highlight the persistence of a reasonably coherent and powerful conservative political economy of poverty that has lasted for more than two centuries. The other is to point out the absence of a comparable intellectual tradition on the political left where a coherent, persuasive political economy of poverty has failed to coalesce. (The most significant attempt to construct a contemporary political economy of urban poverty is the work of Loïc Wacquant [2008]). If my observation is correct, the question is obvious. What accounts for the intellectual fragmentation of the left? Even more, what does it matter? Suppose we identify and disseminate a political economy of poverty, what happens next? As the political right has known all along, the gap between theory and implementation is filled by power. Poverty is more than a problem of political economy; it is also a problem of power.

Power

In theory, in a democracy poor people should be able to gain purchase on the levers of power by electing representatives who champion their interests. In America, this has happened briefly and occasionally, as with the New Deal in the 1930s, the War on Poverty and Great Society in the 1960s, and the occasional state and local election. But for the most part electoral politics has not proved an effective route to power for poor Americans or those who hope to serve their interests. With the unchecked influence of wealth on politics, this may be truer today than at any point since the first Gilded Age. The trade union movement, of course, emerged as a counterweight to the power of capital in the nineteenth century. Not directly an antipoverty movement, it nonetheless addressed the miserable wages that were one of its primary sources. Relatively unsuccessful in their nineteenth- and early twentieth-century battles with capital, which remained free to harness the power of the state in the interests of repression, in the 1930s trade unions joined with other organizations to compose a potent and broad-based social movement. They acquired power during the Great Depression thanks to the 1935 Wagner Act. It is probably impossible to quantify how many people the trade union movement has kept out of poverty since the 1930s, and how many fewer people would be in poverty today had the rate of unionization not plummeted. But the number, if indefinable, surely is huge.

Periodic "poor people's movements" also have tilted the balance of power. They are the subject of Frances Fox Piven and Richard A. Cloward's (1977) *Poor People's Movements: Why They Succeed, How They Fail*. Piven and Cloward remind readers that protests remain unusual events. They do not erupt "during ordinary periods" but when "large-scale changes undermine political stability. . . . It is this context that makes political leaders somewhat vulnerable to protests by the poor" (Piven and Cloward (1977: 28). During these moments of vulnerability, insurgencies mounted by poor people have wrung concessions from public authorities. Power, they emphasize, derives from the insurgency itself, not leadership or organization. This is their most challenging and controversial point: "Whatever influence lower-class groups occasionally exert in American politics does not result from organization but from mass protest and the disruptive consequences of protest" (Piven and Cloward 1977: 36).

When protest ebbs, politicians withdraw some concessions: "Since the poor no longer pose the threat of disruption, they no longer exert leverage on political leaders; there is no need for conciliation" (Piven and Cloward 1977: 35). But some important concessions and institutional changes remain, such as the right to join unions or the extension of the franchise to Southern blacks. Because the retreat from protests' initial passion is inevitable, all organizers and leaders can do is to seize the moment: "They can only try to win whatever can be won while it can be won" (Piven and Cloward 1977: 37). After protest dies out, organizers find themselves incorporated into "stable institutional roles" that coalesce into new institutions that themselves become part of the established order, not sources through which poor people can continue to leverage power on their own behalf (Piven and Cloward 1977: 33, 34–35, 37). In the Great Depression of the 1930s, for instance, a number of worker protest organizations coalesced into the Workers Alliance, which, according to Piven and Cloward, failed to seize the moment "during the brief and tumultuous period when people were ready to act against the authorities and against the norms that ordinarily bind them. Instead of exploiting the possibilities of the time by pushing turbulence to its outer limits, the leaders of the unemployed set about to build organization and to press for legislation, and in so doing, they virtually echoed the credo of officialdom itself" (Piven and Cloward 1993: 91).

The recognition that whatever power poor people can muster on their own behalf derives from mobilization and protest also has led down a second road— one that, in contrast to Piven and Cloward, points to organization, leadership, and institution building. The main destination is community organizing. The great founding figure of community organizing was Saul Alinsky, who began in Chicago's Back of the Yards neighborhood in the 1930s. Alinsky "recruited local leaders from the churches, block clubs, sports leagues, and unions that formed the Back of the Yards Neighborhood Council, the first of what Alinsky would call the People's Organization. Alinsky guided them to identify common interests that brought together into a large organization previously hostile ethnic groups of Serbs and Croatians, Czechs and Slovaks, Poles and Lithuanians. The council pressured, demanded, and negotiated with government officials and businesses on bread-and-butter issues such as better garbage collection, improved schools, fresh milk for children, and more jobs" (Atlas 2010: 20). The organizing tradition Alinsky inspired stresses concrete, local grievances, not abstract causes. Only the role of the organizer is central. Organizers bring together local people, help them define their grievances, and plan militant strategies, often called "actions," to pressure authorities. In 1940 Alinsky founded the Industrial Areas Foundation to train organizers. Through its work, the IAF turned organizing into a profession whose members have mobilized poor people to win local, and even not so local, victories. However, when organizers threaten entrenched interests, they provoke ferocious and devastating reactions. This is what the history of one of the most effective community organizing networks, ACORN, illustrates. Subject for years to vicious attacks by right-wing media, ACORN, which won important national and state, as well as local, victories, finally was brought to its knees by a carefully orchestrated scam designed to discredit its integrity (Atlas 2010).

Its opponents killed ACORN as a national organization, but they did not destroy community organizing. The remarkable PICO provides the best example. Like ACORN, PICO organizes at neighborhood, state, and national levels. It even has established a policy office in Washington. Founded in 1972 by Father John Bauman, a Jesuit priest, PICO originated as a regional training institute to assist neighborhood community organizing in California. PICO works through a congregational-community model it pioneered. Its networks embrace congregations of all denominations and faiths, and in 2012 it counted 44 affiliated federations as well as 8 statewide networks working in 150 towns and cities and 17 states. More than one million families belonged to the one thousand congregations in its networks. PICO's website describes its many achievements in health care access and reform, immigration policy, housing, school improvement, rural development and other areas (PICO 2012).

Another story about community organizing could be told by focusing on the history of community action in the War on Poverty whose founding legislation, the Economic Opportunity Act, required federally funded programs to include the "maximum feasible participation" of the people they served. This provision proved the most radical and controversial strand within the poverty war. Predictably, it elicited fierce opposition, which diluted its potential (Goldstein 2012; O'Connor 2001: 167–73). History and historians have not treated the community-action strand in the poverty war kindly. They have portrayed it as ineffective and patronage-ridden, subject to cooptation, accomplishing little, and diverting resources and attention from more promising strategies for change (see Matusow 1984). Scholars too often have viewed the local programs through the eyes of their critics. Skeptical of the capacity of poor people to organize effectively on their own behalf, even liberal scholars have neglected close-grained studies of local programs. Liberal social policy remains more comfortable with social and policy change engineered by elites and applied from the top down. Liberal elites find it hard to appreciate the often-messy process through which reform originates at the grassroots. In this, they unwittingly reinforce the power relations that need rearranging if poverty is to be effectively addressed. In fact, an exciting new body of historical writing has begun to reevaluate the community action component of the War on Poverty (Aguiar 2012; Korstadt and Leloudis

2010; Orleck and Hazirjian 2011). It finds all over the country promising grass-roots programs stifled by the interests they threatened. Nevertheless, community action's institutional legacy remains in a host of programs (Orleck and Hazir-jian 2011: 440–41) and in a commitment to grassroots politics that occasionally bubbles to the surface, as in the Chicago School Reform movement, which in 1989 through an act of the Illinois Legislature wrested control of the city's public school system from the central office and turned it over to local school councils (Katz 1995: 99–143; Katz, Fine and Simon 1997: 117–57).

Since the Civil Rights Movement of the 1970s, organizing rather than mobilization has dominated strategies for leveraging power by and on behalf of poor Americans. That suddenly and unexpectedly changed with the eruption of the Occupy movement in fall 2011. Occupy was not a poor people's movement. It focused more on inequality, and initially, on the depredations of banks and the financial industry. Protestors primarily were white and well educated. The movement deliberately lacked a platform; it was diffuse. But it erupted all across the country, and it resulted in an upsurge of writing about inequality in the press. President Barack Obama for the first time spoke powerfully and directly about inequality as a national problem (Alternet 2011; Knefel 2012; Younge 2012).

Not surprisingly, the political right attacked Occupy, focusing a vicious assault, including a death threat, on Frances Fox Piven, who was an early strong supporter (Dreier 2011). Where the Occupy movement will go, whether it will direct its energies to specific issues, what tactics it will employ, whether it can sustain its energy and draw in more demographically and economically diverse participants: all these remain unclear. Clearly, as of this writing it is too soon to assess its potential or significance other than to marvel at the speed and scope of its eruption and its capacity for rekindling hope for democratic social change and reorienting the discussion of power.

This excursion into the question of power leads to a few central points. The first is that the political economy of poverty needs a theory of power. The playing field never is level. The second point is that effective responses to poverty have originated outside the electoral system. Ultimately, the redress of poverty requires legislation and policy. But the engine of change starts beyond the formal political arena. Third, significant changes will not come about as a result of elite good will. Real change requires countervailing centers of power. The trade union movement, decimated by decades of attack, still remains vital, if weakened. Community organizing networks provide the second center. Building from the grassroots to players on the national policy scene, they have mounted some of the most effective challenges to entrenched interests and institutions. Fourth, attempts to leverage countervailing power—from trade unions through community action agencies in the War on Poverty to ACORN—provoke powerful backlash. There is no question that any meaningful assault on poverty will not happen easily or quietly, or without great skill and effort.

There is, however, a different sort of response to the persistence of poverty that does not threaten existing arrangements of power or pose uncomfortable questions about capitalism. It is, in fact, of a piece with the hegemony of markets as models for American public policy. And in a short span of time it has become the cutting-edge technology of antipoverty work.

Markets

Beginning in the 1980s, market-oriented models reshaped public policy in housing, health care, education, welfare, and elsewhere. They also reconfigured ideas about poor people and antipoverty policy. No longer an underclass, poor people became entrepreneurs. In the new market-based approach to poverty policy, initiative passed from a reduced state to the private sector, which offered innovations at once less demeaning and more effective—as well as less expensive. Advocates of market-based antipoverty policies rejected pathological descriptions of poor people. Instead, in the writing of market theorists poor people emerged as rational actors—consumers, savers, and entrepreneurs. Four overlapping but distinct strategies dominated what I have elsewhere called new technologies of poverty work: place-based approaches intended to rebuild markets in inner cities; microfinance programs to transform poor people into entrepreneurs; asset-building strategies designed to give poor people the means to accumulate capital; and conditional cash transfers that deployed monetary incentives to encourage poor people to change their behavior (Katz 2012: 101–50).

Zones of concentrated poverty at the core of older American cities drifted outside legitimate markets. Prices plummeted so low, and supply so outstripped demand, that no housing market remained (Bartelt 1993: 118–57) Supermarkets and banks, as well as manufacturing and other institutions of commerce had fled. In this situation, urban planners reasonably concluded that inner-city revitalization required the recreation of markets. Two widely heralded policies—Ronald Reagan's Enterprise Zones and Bill Clinton's Empowerment Zones—proved disappointments, falling short of expectations. Enterprise and Empowerment Zones started with deficit models. They intended to supply poor inner-city neighborhoods with missing assets. In his famous 1995 *Harvard Business Review* article, "The Competitive Advantage of the Inner City," Harvard Business School professor Michael Porter took a radically different tack, portraying inner cities as full of untapped strengths that capitalism, free of the clumsy and bureaucratic interference of governments, could tap to revitalize cities and reduce poverty. Porter influenced both the federal Small Business Administration and

President Bill Clinton's New Markets Initiative, which attempted to mobilize tax incentives and private capital to revitalize poor urban and rural areas. On its website, the Initiative for a Competitive Inner City, Porter's national nonprofit, highlights successes in mobilizing money with which to support the creation of small businesses and tens of thousands of jobs. Impressive as the numbers are, nowhere on its website does the ICIC assess the bottom line: poverty and employment rates in inner cities and joblessness among African American men. Will its efforts prove isolated instances of success or transformative? The jury remains out.[14]

Of the four market-based antipoverty strategies, only the first, rebuilding markets in inner cities, concentrated on regenerating places. The other three focused on individuals. Microfinance, the most famous of these, started in Bangladesh and spread with breathtaking speed around the world, to developed as well as developing countries. Microfinance began in January 1977 when Muhammed Yunus, an economics professor in Bangladesh, started to lend poor women small amounts of money with which to start their own businesses. In 1993 he founded the Grameen bank (*grameen* means village). The Grameen program offered poor women, unable to tap the formal banking system, an alternative to the informal economy of exploitative loan sharks and moneylenders. Yunus lent money to women rather than men because he believed women were more likely to use it for the well-being of their families and because he hoped it would empower them. Borrowers repaid their loans in one year at an interest rate of 20 percent. Yunus claimed a repayment rate of 98 percent. Conventional poverty programs, which assumed poor people lacked the skills with which to find and hold paid work, began with training programs. Yunus turned this idea on its head by starting with cash. What the poor lacked, he believed, was access to credit—a fundamental right. Inspired by Grameen, a great many organizations around the world developed microcredit programs. The number of organizations affiliated with Grameen exploded. In 2008, throughout the world, 112 million people participated in microcredit programs. In 2006 Muhammed Yunus received the Nobel Peace Prize (Counts 2008; Yunus 1999, 2007).

Grameen reached even the United States—the first antipoverty program to spread from an Asian country to the developed West, with Grameen America opening its first branch in the New York City borough of Queens in January 2008. The second opened in Omaha, Nebraska, in 2009. Experienced managers were imported from Bangladesh to run them. Even the U.S. federal government adopted microfinance programs. With its own national organization, the Association for Enterprise Opportunity, microlending in fact became an industry. Eventually, sharp philosophical differences divided microlenders into two camps. To Yunus, the purpose of microlending was poverty alleviation.

To the Consultative Group to Assist the Poor (CGAP), sponsored by the World Bank, the first priority was economic development. In practice, this resulted in the entrance of for-profit firms into microlending. Appalled at this transformation of microfinance, Yunus told listeners at the United Nations, "We didn't create microcredit to encourage loan sharks. . . . Microcredit should be seen as an opportunity to help people get out of poverty in a business way, but not as an opportunity to make money out of poor people" (MacFarquhar 2010). Microfinance has not lacked for critics, and in recent years scandals have rocked programs (Polgreen and Bajaj 2010; Radhakrishna 2010).[15] There is in fact much more to be said about microfinance, for which I direct readers first to Ananya Roy's (2010) spectacular *Poverty Capital: Microfinance and the Making of Development*. In the end, the bottom line about the results of microfinance remains unclear. Defining a metric of success, designing research programs, agreeing on a methodology for evaluation: all remain elusive. What is clear is that Muhammad Yunus and Grameen have replaced pathological stereotypes of the poor with images of competent entrepreneurs. In the history of poverty policy, this is a signal achievement.

In its second phase, Yunus and other leaders of the microfinance movement began to recognize the importance of financial services to poor people and the importance of savings (Dowla and Barua 2006). Reframed as asset building, saving became the core of an asset-building movement started in the United States—stimulated notably by Michael Sherraden's (1991) *Assets and the Poor*. Asset building quickly became an antipoverty strategy of choice throughout the world of social policy. A 2010 report by the New America Foundation (Cramer et al. 2010), one of the principal advocates of asset building as social policy, explained: "Asset building refers to public policy and private sector efforts to enable individuals to accumulate and preserve long-term, productive assets—savings, investments, a home, post-secondary education and training, a small business, and a nest-egg for retirement" (Cramer et al 2010: 1). Like Yunus, the asset-based movement rejects pathological, moral, or culturally based theories of poverty. In the United States the federal, state, and local governments have promoted the importance of individual assets. Through the tax code, for example, the federal government has supported home ownership and retirement savings. Almost all federal asset-based policy, however, goes to steadily employed homeowners, not the poor. According to one authoritative analysis, in 2005 less than 3 percent of tax-based subsidies went to the three-fifths of families with the lowest incomes. The situation is especially bleak among African Americans. The gap separating black from white wealth is much greater than the income gap. Between 1984 and 2009, report Thomas Shapiro and his colleagues (2012), the gap between black and white assets skyrocketed from $84,000 to $236,500. At $265,000, median white household assets dwarfed the $28,500 figure among blacks (Cramer et al. 2010; Shapiro, Meschede, and Orso 2012).

To direct asset building toward helping poor people leave poverty Michael Sherraden proposed Individual Development Accounts (IDAS). These are subsidized savings accounts targeted at poor people through matching grants rather than tax breaks. Sherraden sees IDAS as the vanguard of a revolution that will shift the emphasis of social policy from income support to asset accumulation. In fact, hundreds of IDA programs are spread across the country. Most states have some sort of IDA-enabling policy while "federal legislation . . . provided a legal structure and funding mechanism for IDAS" (Schreiner and Sherraden 2007: 3). Many community-based organizations implemented IDAS in the 1990s, most often with foundation funds. Major sponsorship has come from the Ford Foundation, the New American Foundation, the Bill and Melinda Gates Foundation, and several others. The Assets@21 conference sponsored by the New America Foundation in May 2012 clearly illustrated how asset building has become a national social movement. Two major research projects—the American Dream Demonstration (ADD) and Savings for Education, Entrepreneurship, and Downpayment (SEED)—have tested asset building as policy. The results, however, although pointing to useful directions for future policy, fell short of unequivocal evidence of success. Research on IDA programs raises many questions, as the researchers themselves admit. Some are practical; others are more philosophical. Indeed, the reorientation of the welfare state around asset building would hasten its redesign on market principles. Still, it is undeniable that the lack of assets traps people in poverty and that many promising asset-building programs are underway throughout the country (Bill and Melinda Gates Foundation 2010; Cramer 2009; Ford Foundation 2002; Schreiner and Sherraden 2007).

In New York City, Mayor Michael Bloomberg launched an ambitious antipoverty program that also rejected pathological images of the poor. The program included Conditional Cash Transfers (CCTs)—the fourth new strategy of antipoverty work—which Bloomberg imported from Mexico. CCTs did not constitute the most important part of his antipoverty agenda, but they became the most controversial. After eighteen months, they proved the most visible failure. Conditional Cash Transfer programs transfer cash to poor households on the condition that they make specific investments in the human capital of their children: for instance, periodic medical checkups, growth monitoring, vaccinations, prenatal care for mothers, mothers' attendance at periodic health information talks, and school-related behavior, including enrollment, regular attendance, and sometime academic achievement. Most CCT programs transfer money directly to mothers or, in some circumstances, to students. Details of CCT programs vary—there are huge programs in Brazil and Mexico—but all of them, a World Bank specialist points out, provide poor families with cash "on the condition that they make investments in human capital such as sending children to school or bringing them to health centers on a regular basis" (Rawlings 2005: 1). CCTs represent a "new generation of social programmes" that rely "on market principles" (Fizbein and Schady 2009; New York City Commission for Economic Opportunity 2006; Rawlings 2005: 134).

Bloomberg, who traveled with staff to Mexico to observe its Oportunidades program, formed a public–private partnership, Opportunity NYC, to implement the first full CCT program in the United States. A cross section of elite American philanthropy put up $50 million to fund a three-year trial. After eighteen months, a midcourse evaluation by the firm MDRC, hired to design and evaluate the program, turned in a mixed report, and Bloomberg announced the abrupt termination of the program, although not the evaluation. Neither the political left nor right liked Opportunity NYC. To the right, it rewarded the undeserving poor—why reward parents who had failed to send their children to school regularly or take them for medical checkups? The left found CCTs paternalistic and offensive. Lacking a solid constituency, Bloomberg could not scale up CCTs with city funds. Perhaps it was less embarrassing to pull the plug than to lose a bruising fight with city council. The other components of Bloomberg's antipoverty program appeared more promising, although the program failed to stop the rise in the city's poverty rate, which reached 21 percent in 2010. In fact, Bloomberg deserves great credit for mounting a major antipoverty program with poverty off the national political agenda. No other mayor within memory had tried anything remotely similar (Bosman 2010; MDRC 2013; Riccio et al. 2010; Roberts 2012).

Bloomberg created the perfect antipoverty program for a twenty-first-century American city because it did not rely on federal initiatives or funding, it combined public and private resources, it reflected market-based principles, and it was resolutely pragmatic and non-ideological. It also fit the twenty-first century because it focused on the deserving or working poor, eschewed redistribution, and paid no attention to the dependent poor. In this, Bloomberg's antipoverty initiative tracked national policy, which since the 1990s has developed an array of programs to help the working poor while neglecting the nonworking poor, whose situation stagnated or deteriorated.

Market-based technologies of poverty work do not assault the rigidities of social structure or the citadels of power. They ignore the political economy of power. They propose to solve poverty on the cheap, with relatively little public money, and without growing the size of government very much. They reduce the role of government to impresario organizing, partially funding, and coordinating a new show rather than creating and managing new programs. That said, these initiatives have the potential to improve the lives of a great many people while smoothing the rough edges of capitalism. Is this the best we can hope for?

What kind of a problem is poverty? Not one single kind of problem. This essay has pointed, in fact, to six kinds of problems implied in discussions of poverty over more than two hundred years. They are not mutually exclusive; nor do they represent a simple taxonomy. Rather, they are more of an archeology, each taking us deeper into the meaning of poverty, with markets, the last and newest addition, moving in an orthogonal direction, away from the main line of poverty discourse. None of them is incorrect; all of them can point poverty policy in useful directions, although the policies that flow from them differ radically. One problem with American poverty discourse is that it tends to get stuck at the first or second level, poverty as a problem of persons or of places. The tendency to shy away from resources distracts attention from direct, redistributive policies needed especially by the nonworking poor, who never have fared well in America's modern welfare state or its precursor regimes. The reluctance to admit that poverty is a problem of power inhibits poverty policy from focusing on the most powerful levers of change. The new market-based antipoverty technologies provide a way of eliding these topics—resources, political economy, power—and refocusing attention elsewhere, usefully, for sure, but not with anything like the force needed to confront the massive and growing economic deprivation in twenty-first-century America.

Each interpretive tradition suffers from a "blind spot." The idea that poverty is a problem of persons turns a blind eye to the myriad sources of poverty outside individual control. Interpretations that treat poverty as a spatial problem run the risk of overemphasizing the causal power of concentrated poverty or residential segregation and missing the political-economic forces that produce uneven geographies. Theories that view poverty as a problem of market failure or absence fail to grasp how market-based societies produce poverty. Definitions of poverty as a lack of resources often stop short of focusing on the sources of unequal income distribution.[16] Interpretations that present poverty as a problem of political economy or power reveal their own blind spots when they stop short of the difficult task of translating their insights into realistic and potentially effective strategies.

Despite their differences, one strand runs through all these problem definitions: the question of work. Indeed, so central have concerns about work remained to poverty discourse over the centuries that I considered highlighting work as a seventh definition. But in one way or another, work runs through all the others. In the eighteenth century the capacity to work defined the boundary between types of poor people—the able-bodied and the impotent. Today, it polices the border of social policy, separating the working and nonworking poor and rewarding only the former with anything approaching adequate benefits, although for how long remains uncertain given the conservative assault on unemployment insurance and workers' compensation (Katz 2008: 195–231, 382–86). Chronic joblessness marks the areas of concentrated poverty in America's cities where the lack of work distinguishes the territories of poverty. At the same time, another way to talk about the political economy of poverty is through the unemployment produced by the routine workings of capitalism. This was true in the nineteenth and early twentieth centuries when work remained irregular and seasonal. It remains the case today when so many have been laid off on account of deindustrialization followed by the contraction of service-sector jobs, especially in the public sector. The rewards of work, moreover, have depended on power, notably on the capacity of organized workers to extract a living wage, without which work becomes exploitation, not the means to a decent life. Work, of course, also has been tied closely to labor markets. Tight labor markets always have proved effective antipoverty strategies, as in World War II or during the early 1990s.

In practical terms, where does that take us? At the risk of intellectual incoherence, we should support whatever works, taking advantage of successful ideas and programs that flow from each definition of poverty. But we need to pay special attention to those strands that mainstream poverty policy treats most lightly: resources, political economy, and power. Giving people money, it should not be forgotten, is a tried and true successful way to reduce poverty. Mobilizing and organizing have proved the only way to move the levers of power so that they work on behalf of poor people. Without a coherent progressive political economy of poverty, it will not prove possible to fully refute the mystifications and canards of the right.

This means we need to risk inconsistency. Inconsistency is the price progressives have to pay in a world marked by contradiction. Recall the article by Lilian Brandt with which this essay opened. Brandt began by arguing that an understanding of the deep causes of poverty was essential to the development of effective policy. She ended by saying that effective measures for combatting policy had become well known, even when theory lagged behind, and that the sensible thing to do was to use whatever worked. Pragmatism, she said, was, in the end, the only guide. We are more or less in the same place, except that Brandt had one advantage. She wrote at a moment when poverty suddenly appeared unnecessary and the possibility of its near disappearance was a sustaining faith. Her boss, Edward T. Devine (1911: 12), wrote that misery, including poverty, "is economic, accidental, and transfigured by the abiding presence of hope." For Brandt and Devine, poverty was also a seventh kind of problem—a problem of pessimism, which she and her Progressive Era reformer colleagues were determined to overcome. To make real progress, we need to recapture their energy and their faith.

NOTES

For detailed, fast, and exceptionally helpful readings of a previous draft of this essay, I am indebted to Daniel Amsterdam, Merlin Chowkwanyun, Adam Goodman, Mark J. Stern, and Viviana Zelizer. Their comments have improved the essay in many ways. I of course remain responsible for the final product.

1. "Lilian Brandt 1873–1951," http://tigger.uic.edu/depts/hist/hull-maxwell/vicinity/nws1/documents/html/brandt-introduction.htm; obituary, *New York Times*, July 6, 1951; Brandt 1901: 100. At Wellesley, courses on applied economics and sociology were taught by future Nobel laureate Emily Green Balch, who was later fired from the college because of her objection to America's entry into World War I. For an article-length version of her thesis, see Brandt 1903. Brandt's thesis was influenced by and to an extent modeled on W. E. B. DuBois's famous study, *The Philadelphia Negro*. On the history of scientific charity, see Katz 1996, 60–87; Furner 1975. At the time of her death, Brandt lived with her sister, Genevieve Brandt, at 410 W. 24th St., New York.

2. The most sophisticated recent statement is Goldin and Katz 2008. I have written an extensive critique of the book; see Katz 2009. See also the excellent Kantor and Lowe 2011; and Katz and Rose 2013.

3. Still, important examples of successful job training programs do exist today, for example, the Wisconsin Regional Training Partnership and Austin's Capital Idea. These are described in the special *American Prospect* issue on poverty, July/August 2012, 36, 44–49.

4. For a popular discussion of epigenetics and its astonishing rise, see Shulevitz 2012.

5. On the bundling of social problems, see Katz 1983: 138–55.

6. Igo (2007) contrasts the place-based character of the first major survey research, Lynd's study of Middletown, with the a-spatial national samples of Kinsey and Gallup.

7. The power of Davis's book comes at the cost of homogenizing the many differences among the places about which he writes, downplaying their internal variety, ignoring the energy and agency of their residents, and missing promising movements for change within them.

8. See the U.S. Basic Income Guarantee Network—http://www.usbig.net/index.php. A good overview of the living wage movement is Bernstein 2002.

9. See the U.S. Human Rights Network at http://www.ushrnetwork.org; and Martha F. Davis 2007. Thanks to Karen Tani for pointing me to the Davis article.

10. For a brief, lucid overview of the poverty line, see Levinson 2012. There is an extensive literature on the topic.

11. This point is made well in Reich 2012.

12. This is partly qualified in the case of Henry George, whose single-tax theory finds contemporary advocates and an institutional home in the Henry George Institute (http://www.henrygeorge.org/hgi.htm). But it is not a large or powerful movement.

13. For a succinct statement of the Progressive Era antipoverty agenda see Hunter 1904: 338–39.

14. See Porter 1995; Initiative for a Competitive Inner City online, http://www.icic .org/site/c.fnj; Initiative for a Competitive Inner City 2005; Rubin and Staniewicz 2005.

15. For the operations of Grameen in the United States, see the Grameen America website: http://www.grameenamerica.com. For more background, see Shevory 2010.

16. For the insight that the interpretive traditions have "blind spots", I am indebted to Merlin Chowkwanyun, personal communication to author, August 12, 2012.

REFERENCES

Abramsky, Sasha. 2012. "Creating a Countercyclical Welfare System." *American Prospect,* July/August, 62–64.

Aguiar, Gretchen. 2012. "Operation Headstart at the Grassroots." PhD diss., University of Pennsylvania.

Alternet, Eds. 2011. *The 99%: How the Occupy Wall Street Movement Is Changing America.* San Francisco: Alternet Books.

Atlas, John. 2010. *Seeds of Change: The Story of ACORN, America's Most Controversial Antipoverty Community Organizing Group.* Nashville: Vanderbilt University Press.

Bartelt, David W. 1993. "Housing the 'underclass.'" In *The Underclass Debate: Views from History,* ed. Michael B. Katz, 118–59. Princeton: Princeton University Press:

Bates, Barbara. 1992. *Bargaining for Life: A Social History of Tuberculosis, 1876–1938.* Philadelphia: University of Pennsylvania Press.

Bernstein, Jared. 2002. "The Living Wage Movement—Viewpoints." Economic Policy Institute. http://www.epi.org/publication/webfeatures_viewpoints_lw_movement/

Bill and Melinda Gates Foundation. 2010. "Financial Services for the Poor: Strategy Overview." http://www.gatesfoundation.org/financialservicesforthepoor/Pages /session-briefs-2010-global-savings-forum.aspx.

Bloom, Nicholas Dagen. 2009. *Public Housing That Worked: New York In the Twentieth Century.* Philadelphia: University of Pennsylvania Press.

Bosman, Julie. 2010. "Disappointed, City Will Stop Paying Poor for Good Behavior." *New York Times.* March 31.

Boyer, Paul. 1978. *Urban Masses and Moral Order, 1820–1920.* Cambridge, Mass.: Harvard University Press.

Brandt, Lilian. 1901. "The Charity Organization Society of the City of New York, 1882–1907, History: Account of Present Activities. Twenty-fifth Annual Report for the Year Ending September Thirtieth, Nineteen Hundred and Seven." *Calendar Wellesley College.* http://www.archive.org/stream/charityorganizationoocharich _dju.txt.

Brandt, Lilian. 1903. "The Negroes of St. Louis." *Publications of the American Statistical Association,* viii: 61: 203–68. Boston: American Statistical Association.

Brandt, Lilian. 1908. "The Causes of Poverty." *Political Science Quarterly* 23:4, 637–51.

Briggs, Xavier de Souza, Susan J. Popkin, and John Goering. 2010. *Moving to Oppor-*

tunity: The Story of an American Experiment to Fight Ghetto Poverty. New York: Oxford University Press.

Brown, Robbie. 2009. "Atlanta Is Making Way for New Public Housing." *New York Times*, June 20.

Carey, Mathew. 1833. "Address to the Wealthy of the Land, Ladies as Well as Gentlemen, on the Character, Conduct, Situation, and Prospects of Those Whose Sole Dependence for Subsistence, is on the Labour of Their Hands." Philadelphia: Wm. F. Geddes.

Counts, Alex. 2008. *Small Loans, Big Dreams: How Nobel Prize Winner Muhammad Yunus and Microfinance Are Changing the World*. Hoboken, N.J.: Wiley.

Cramer, Reid. 2009. "The Big Lift: Federal Policy Efforts to Create Child Development Accounts." CSD Working Paper 09-43. St. Louis: Center for Social Development, George Warren Brown School of Social Work, Washington University.

Cramer, Reid, Mark Huelsman, Justin King, Alejandra Lopez-Fernandini, and David Newill. 2010. "The Assets Report 2010: An Assessment of President Obama's Budget and the Changing Policy Landscape for Asset Building Opportunities." New America Foundation. http://newamerica.net/publications/policy/the_assets_report _2010

Croft, Michelle, and Grover J. Whitehurst. 2010. "The Harlem Children's Zone, Promise Neighborhoods, and the Broader, Bolder Approach to Education." *Brookings Institution*, July 20, http://www.brookings.edu/research/reports/2010/07/20-hcz -whitehurst.

Dauber, Michele. 2012. *The Sympathetic State*. Chicago: University of Chicago Press.

Davis, Martha F. 2007. "The Pendulum Swings Back: Poverty Law in the Old and New Curriculum." *Fordham Urban Law Journal*. 34, 1390–415.

Davis, Mike. 2007. *Planet of Slums*. London: Verso.

Devine, Edward T. 1911. *Misery and Its Causes*. New York: MacMillan Co.

Dowla, Asif, and Dipal Barua. 2006. *The Poor Always Pay Back: The Grameen II Story*. Bloomfield, Conn.: Kumarian Press.

Dreier, Peter. 2011. "Glen Beck's Attacks on Frances Fox Piven Trigger Death Threats." *Huff Post Media*, January 23, http://www.huffingtonpost.com/peter-dreier/glenn -becks-attacks-on-fr_b_812690.html.

Fizbein, Ariel, and Norbert Schady. 2009. *Conditional Cash Transfers: Reducing Present and Future Poverty*. Washington, D.C.: World Bank.

Ford Foundation. 2002. "Building Assets to Reduce Poverty and Injustice." http://www .fordfoundation.org/pdfs/library/building_assets.pdf.

Fox, Cybelle. 2012. *Three Worlds of Relief: Race, Immigration, and the American Welfare State from the Progressive Era to the New Deal*. Princeton: Princeton University Press.

Fox, Daniel M. 1967. *The Discovery of Abundance: Simon N. Patten and the Transformation of Social Theory*. Ithaca: Cornell University Press.

Friedman, Milton, with the assistance of Rose D. Friedman. 1962. *Capitalism and Freedom*. Chicago: University of Chicago Press.

Furner, Mary O. 1975. *Advocacy and Objectivity: A Crisis in the Professionalization of Social Science, 1865–1905*. Lexington: University of Kentucky Press.

Gaestel, Allyn. 2012. "Loss of Pennsylvania Aid Worries Drug-Recovery Homes and their Neighbors." *Philadelphia Inquirer*, August 20.

George, Henry. 1880. *Progress and Poverty: An Increase into the Cause of Industrial Depressions and of Increasing Want with Increase of Wealth. The Remedy*. New York: D. Appleton and Co.

Gilens, Martin. 1999. *Why Americans Hate Welfare*. Chicago: University of Chicago Press.

Goldin, Claudia, and Lawrence Katz. 2008. *The Race between Education and Technology*. Cambridge, Mass.: Harvard University Press.

Goldstein, Alyosha. 2012. *Poverty in Common: The Politics of Community Action during the American Century*. Durham: Duke University Press.

Gould, Elise, and Kathryn Anne Edwards. 2011. "Another Look at Poverty in the Great Recession." *Economic Policy Institute*, January 5, http://www.epi.org/publication/ib293/.

Harrington, Michael. 1962. *The Other America: Poverty in the United States*. New York: Macmillan.

Harrington, Michael. 1984. *The New American Poverty*. New York: Holt, Rinehart, and Winston.

Haskell, Thomas O. 1977. *The Emergence of Professional Social Science: The American Social Science Association and the Nineteenth-Century Crisis of Authority*. Urbana: University of Illinois Press.

Haveman, Robert H. 1987. *Poverty Policy and Poverty Research: The Great Society and the Social Sciences*. Madison: University of Wisconsin Press.

Herrenstein, Richard L., and Charles Murray. 1996. *Bell Curve: Intelligence and Class Structure in American Life*. New York: Free Press.

Hunter, Robert. 1904. *Poverty*. New York: Macmillan.

Igo, Sarah. 2007. *The Averaged American: Surveys, Citizens, and the Making of a Mass Public*. Cambridge, Mass.: Harvard University Press.

Initiative for a Competitive Inner City. 2005. "State of the Inner City Economies: Small Businesses in the Inner City." *Small Business Research Summary* 260: October, 1–2.

Jackson, Thomas F. 1993. "The State, the Movement, and the Urban Poor: The War on Poverty and Political Mobilization in the 1960s." In *The "Underclass" Debate: Views from History*, ed. Michael B. Katz, 403–39. Princeton: Princeton University Press.

Jackson, Thomas F. 2006. *From Civil Rights to Human Rights: Martin Luther King, Jr., and the Struggle for Economic Justice*. Philadelphia: University of Pennsylvania Press.

Jencks, Christopher, and Susan E. Mayer. 1990. "The Social Consequences of Growing Up in a Poor Neighborhood." In *Inner City Poverty in the United States*, ed. L. Lynn and M. McGreary, 111–86. Washington, D.C.: National Academy Press.

Jensen, Arthur R. 1969. "How Much Can We Boost IQ and Scholastic Achievement." *Harvard Educational Review* 39, 1–123.

Kantor, Harvey, and Robert Lowe. 2011. "The Price of Human Capital." *Dissent*, http://www.dissentmagazine.org/article/the-price-of-human-capital.

Katz, Michael B. 1981. *The Irony of Early School Reform: Educational Innovation in Mid-Nineteenth Century Massachusetts*. Cambridge, Mass.: Harvard University Press. (Orig. pub. 1968.)

Katz, Michael B. 1983. *Poverty and Policy in American History*. New York: Academic Press.

Katz, Michael B. 1995. *Improving Poor People: The Welfare State, the "Underclass," and Urban Schools as History*. Princeton: Princeton University Press.

Katz, Michael B. 1996. *In the Shadow of the Poorhouse: A Social History of Welfare in America*. New York: Basic Books. (Orig. pub. 1986.)

Katz, Michael B. 2008. *The Price of Citizenship: Redefining the American Welfare State*. Rev. ed. Philadelphia: University of Pennsylvania Press.

Katz, Michael B. 2009. "Can America Educate Itself Out of Inequality?" *Journal of Social History* 43:1: 183–93.

Katz, Michael B. 2012. *Why Don't American Cities Burn?* Philadelphia: University of Pennsylvania Press.

Katz, Michael B. 2013. *The Undeserving Poor: America's Enduring Confrontation with Poverty*. New York: Oxford University Press.

Katz, Michael B., Michael J. Doucet, and Mark J. Stern. 1982. *The Social Organization of Early Industrial Capitalism*. Cambridge, Mass.: Harvard University Press.

Katz, Michael B., Michelle Fine, and Elaine Simon. 1997. "Poking Around: Outsiders View Chicago School Reform." *Teachers College Record* 99:1, 117–57.

Katz, Michael B., and Mike Rose. 2013. *Public Education under Siege*. Philadelphia: University of Pennsylvania Press.

Knefel, John. 2012. "Media Get Bored with Occupy and Inequality." *Common Dreams*, July 14, http://www.commondreams.org/headline/2012/05/03-3.

Kornbluh, Felicia Ann. 2007. *The Battle for Welfare Rights: Politics and Poverty in Modern America*. Philadelphia: University of Pennsylvania Press.

Korstadt, Robert, and James Leloudis. 2010. *To Right These Wrongs: The North Carolina Fund and the Battle to End Poverty and Inequality in 1960s America*. Chapel Hill: University of North Carolina Press.

Levinson, Mark. 2012. "Mismeasuring—and Its Consequences." *American Prospect*, July/August, 42–43.

MacFarquhar, Neil. 2010. "Banks Making Big Profits from Tiny Loans." *New York Times*, April 13.

Mann, Horace. 1849. *Twelfth Annual Report of the Secretary of the Massachusetts State Board of Education*. Boston: Dutton and Wentworth State Printers.

Massey, Douglas S., and Nancy A. Denton. 1993. *American Apartheid: Segregation and the Making of the Underclass*. Cambridge, Mass.: Harvard University Press.

Matusow, Allen J. 1984. *The Unraveling of Liberalism in the 1960s*. New York: Harper and Row.

Meyerson, Harold. 2012. "Seeing What No One Else Could See." *American Prospect*, July/August.

MDRC. 2013. "Opportunity NYC Demonstrations: Project Overview." http://www.mdrc .org/project_16_88.html.

New York City Commission for Economic Opportunity. 2006. "Increasing Opportunity and Reducing Poverty in New York City." Report to Mayor Michael R. Bloomberg. http://www.nyc.gov/html/om/pdf/ceo_report2006.pdf

New York Times. 2012. "The Geography of Government Benefits." February 11. http:// www.nytimes.com/interactive/2012/02/12/us/entitlement-map.html?_r=0.

O'Connor, Alice. 2001. *Poverty Knowledge: Social Science, Social Policy, and the Poor in Twentieth-Century U.S. History*. Princeton: Princeton University Press.

Orleck, Annelise. 1996. *Storming Caesar's Palace: How Black Mothers Fought Their Own War on Poverty*. Boston: Beacon Press.

Orleck, Annelise, and Lisa Gayle Hazirjian, eds. 2011. *The War on Poverty: A New Grassroots History*. Athens: University of Georgia Press.

Page, Max. 1999. *The Creative Destruction of Manhattan, 1900–1940*. Chicago: University of Chicago Press.

PICO National Network. 2013. http://www.piconetwork.org/.

Piven, Frances Fox, and Richard A. Cloward. 1977. *Poor People's Movements: Why They Succeed, How They Fail*. New York: Pantheon Books.

Piven, Frances Fox, and Richard A. Cloward. 1993. *Regulating the Poor: The Functions of Public Welfare*. New York: Vintage Books.

Polgreen, Linda, and Vikas Bajaj. 2010. "India Microcredit Sector Faces Collapse from Defaults." *New York Times*, November 17.

Porter, Michael E. 1995. "The Competitive Advantage of the Inner City." *Harvard Business Review* 73:3, 55–71.

Radhakrishna, G. S. 2010. "Suicide Shock for Loan Sharks," *Telegraph* (Calcutta, India), November 23, http://www.telegraphindia.com/11/1123/jsp/nation/story _13210331.jsp.

Rawlings, Laura B. 2005. "A New Approach to Social Assistance: Latin America's Experience with Conditional Cash Transfer Programmes." *International Social Security Review* 58:2–3, 133–61.

Reich, Robert B. 2012. "Mitt Romney and the New Gilded Age." *The Nation*, June 16–23, http://www.thenation.com/article/168623/mitt-romney-and-new-gilded-age.

Riccio, James A., Nadine DeChuasay, David Greenberg, Cynthia Miller, Zawadi Rucks, and Nandita Verma. 2010. *Toward Reduced Poverty across Generations: Early Findings from New York City's Conditional Cash Transfer Program*. New York: MDRC.

Riessman, Frank. 1962. *The Culturally Deprived Child*. New York: Harper.

Roberts, Sam. 2012. "New York's Poverty Rate Rises, Study Finds." *New York Times*, April 17.

Rosenberg, Charles E. 1987. *The Cholera Years: The United States in 1832, 1849, and 1866*. Chicago: University of Chicago Press.

Roy, Ananya. 2010. *Poverty Capital: Microfinance and the Making of Development*. New York: Routledge.

Rubin, Julia Sass, and Gregory M. Staniewicz. 2005. "The New Markets Tax Credit Program: A Midcourse Assessment." *Community Development Investment Review* 1:1, 1–11.

Sampson, Robert J. 2012. *Great American City: Chicago and the Enduring Neighborhood Effect*. Chicago: University of Chicago Press.

Schreiner, Mark, and Michael Sherraden. 2007. *Can the Poor Save? Saving and Asset Building in Individual Development Accounts*. New Brunswick, N.J.: Transaction.

Shapiro, Thomas, Tatjana Meschede, and Sam Orso. 2012. "Why the Racial Wealth Gap Is Increasing and How to Close It." Draft Working Paper. Boston: The Institute on Assets and Social Policy, Heller School for Social Policy and Management, Brandeis University.

Sherraden, Michael. 1991. *Assets and the Poor: A New American Welfare Policy*. Armonk, N.Y.: Sharpe.

Shevory, Kristina. 2010. "With the Squeeze on Credit, Microlending Blossoms." *New York Times*, July 28.

Shulevitz, Judith. 2012. "Why Fathers Really Matter." *New York Times*, September 8.

Stallard, Karin, Barbara Ehrenreich, and Holly Sklar. 1983. *Poverty in the American Dream: Women and Children First*. Boston: Institute for New Communications, South End Press.

Stedman Jones, Gareth. 2004. *An End to Poverty? A Historical Debate*. London: Profile Books.

Steensland, Brian. 1962. *The Failed Welfare Revolution: America's Struggle Over Guaranteed Income Policy*. Princeton: Princeton University Press.

Tough, Paul. 2012. "Roseland, Where Obama the Politician Was Born." *New York Times Sunday Magazine*, August 18.

Wacquant, Loïc. 2008. *Urban Outcasts: A Comparative Sociology of Marginality*. Cambridge: Polity Press.

Wilson, William Julius. 1987. *The Truly Disadvantaged: The Inner City, the Underclass, and Public Policy*. Chicago: University of Chicago Press.

Wilson, William Julius. 1996. *When Work Disappears: The World of the New Urban Poor*. New York: Knopf.

Wolfe, Alan. 1981. *America at an Impasse: The Rise and Fall of the Politics of Growth*. New York: Pantheon Books.

Younge, Gary. 2012. "State of the Union: President Obama Addresses Inequality." *The Guardian*, January 20, http://www.guardian.co.uk/commentisfree/cifamerica/2012/jan/25/state-of-the-union-president-obama.

Yunus, Muhammad. 1999. *Banker to the Poor: Micro-Lending and the Battle Against World Poverty*. New York: Public Affairs.

Yunus, Muhammad. 2007. *Creating a World without Poverty*. New York: Public Affairs.

Zorbaugh, Harvey Warren. 1929. *The Gold Coast and the Slum: A Sociological Study of Chicago's Near North Side*. Chicago: University of Chicago Press.

REPRESENTATION

An Archeology of Poverty for the Present

LUIS FLORES JR.

> Ideas are not "out there" waiting to be discovered, but are tools—like forks
> and knives and microchips—that people devise to cope with the world in
> which they find themselves.
> —LOUIS MENAND, *The Metaphysical Club* (2001: xi)

The value of an artifact to an archeologist derives overwhelmingly from the information about the craftsman or user of the artifact that its study reveals. Similarly, Michael B. Katz's archeology as history allows us to study progressive reformers, market capitalists, bureaucrats, and advocates from the middle class through their ideas of poverty. Wielding a critical shovel, Katz digs back through U.S. history to suggest that ideas of poverty are layered with six explanations: poverty as a problem of persons, places, resources, political economy, power, and markets. "How one bundles these answers carries consequences," warns Katz (this volume). "They lead straight to what one does, or tries to do, about poverty." But Katz's dissection of poverty paradigms, while historically illuminating, runs the risk of promoting an approach to handling these types of explanations as discrete layers. The archeological method through which Katz takes us "deeper into the meaning of poverty, with the last and newest addition, markets moving in an orthogonal direction, away from the mainline of poverty discourse," could lead us on a search for epistemic soil samples.

I will build on Katz's archeology below with the aim of informing the broader agenda for critical poverty research. I propose that approaching the rearrangement of poverty knowledge with the concepts of "articulation" and "epistemic privilege" at hand can allow us to escape a layered interpretation of poverty knowledge and develop a relational approach. This approach reveals that rearrangements of poverty knowledge are more than "programs of government," and are enabled not by the layering of explanation but by the dynamic rearrangement of existing explanations and social relationships to mediate newly visible social problems or market conundrums. After a summary of this amended approach,

I will offer an example that points to contemporary articulations of poverty knowledge and potential agendas for poverty research.

Instrumental in mapping out the dynamic rearrangements behind selectively layered explanations of poverty should be an anchoring of poverty logics to the "concrete work" they enable. In this effort, Stuart Hall's analysis of contemporary racism is instructive. Hall (1980: 338) stresses an analytical focus on the "concrete historical 'work' which racism accomplishes under specific historical conditions—as a set of economic, political and ideological practices of a specific kind, concretely articulated with other practices in a social formation." Hall suggests that modern racism is not strictly a historical holdover or artifact, but rather a dynamic modality, constantly rearticulated to achieve concrete work. Katz's (this volume) characterization of the current logic of poverty as at "peace with the hegemony of markets, . . . [which] does not assault the rigidities of social structure or the citadels of power," is precise but can understate how both the logics of poverty and of the market system itself are mutually reinforcing, not just passively coexisting.

Attention to *articulation* as being simultaneously the meaningful and practical "joining together" and "giving expression to" (Hart 2014: 17) raises the four following considerations: What epistemological (and institutional) "tools" are historically available in the form of past explanations and practices addressing poverty? Who are the individuals and institutions with the authority to reorganize poverty paradigms (and where does this authority come from)? Which are the arenas on which competing ideas battle and spread? And, importantly, what historical conjunctures, or crises (social, political, and economic) warrant a re-articulation of poverty knowledge?

Beginning with that last consideration is perhaps most illuminating, as any historical study of crisis will almost immediately run into competing interpretations of the crisis by different groups, in different arenas, and employing different epistemological (often historical and ideological) tools. A study of these contestations is key to understanding what gives particular ideas and articulations "epistemic privilege," meaning social receptiveness to an idea or method of generating ideas (Block and Somers 2005: 265). The battle for epistemic privilege seems to involve the molding of a convincing "shape" of a crisis, then the public proposal that a particular articulation of poverty knowledge precisely *fits the shape of the crisis.* Of course, shape and fit are molded by power but with historic tools, as shape and fit match due to the "transposability" of historically or ideologically familiar crisis shapes, (Bourdieu 1977: 83; elaborated in Sewell 2005: 124). This attention to articulation and the crafting of epistemic privilege suggests a relational and more dynamic process of knowledge production.

In keeping with this volume's intergenerational mandate, I want to briefly illuminate one example derived from my upbringing along the U.S.–Mexico border in order to explore this approach to critical poverty studies.

In my native desert Southwest, the last two decades have seen the peculiar and related rise of two industries that must be interpreted as domestic technologies of poverty: the for-profit college industry (whose contemporary origins lie in the University of Phoenix) and the direct-sales marketing industry (which many know through popular companies such as Herbalife, Tupperware, and Avon that rest on "pay as you go" labor models). By 2013, 13 percent of the entire higher education student body was enrolled in a for-profit institution, while the sales force of direct-sales companies stood at nearly 16 million people—a staggering number comparable to 10 percent of the formal domestic labor force. Both industries cater to a similar subset of the population. For-profit colleges, whose profits rest on Federal Pell Grants and private loans to students, recruit overwhelmingly low-income students, often of color. A controversial 2010 revelation of recruitment at homeless shelters exposed the predatory tactics of the industry (Golden 2010).

For the $30-billion direct-sales industry, which once relied on women's social networks and provided small amounts of supplementary income, the 2008 recession resulted in a dramatic expansion toward attracting the young under- and unemployed seeking primary incomes, with one popular public-traded energy drink company welcoming its "flexible" sales force into a "young people revolution," or #YPR. Sparked by the recession, this social revolution is being launched from suburban living-room recruitment meetings and led by self-proclaimed entrepreneurs.

While these industries most often fall short of their promises by burdening students with private debt, or by leading sales representatives into prolonged engagements that yield a pittance in income, they remain surprisingly popular in the suburban desert Southwest.

These highly profitable technologies of poverty rely on a particular articulation of poverty that casts the problem in terms of a lack of individual human capital (best accumulated through self-investment in the form of student debt or entrepreneurial self-employment), thus tapping into deeply symbolic practices, like schooling. Ethnographic evidence suggests that key to the spread of this articulation is the popularity of staunchly apolitical self-help literature, and the practical "10-step" lifestyle changes they prescribe. This literature, English-language publishers claim, will surpass celebrity biographies in sales in 2014. Flattening histories of racism, gender marginalization, economic opportunism, and structural inequality, this apolitical articulation is not merely subjective, as it relies on streams of federal grant aid, federal protection of private student debt (rendering it unforgivable), and the stock market—as both these industries channel revenue into the financial system.

Yet to uncover the "concrete work" that this articulation of poverty enables, this brief epistemic autopsy must be contextualized in a critical analysis of the historical moment that is producing this poverty, which I can merely summarize here. Significant is the post-1970s shift to rely increasingly on speculative profitability and wealth generation's relative liberation from the constraints of labor and time. The resulting decline in not only real wages, but also in the number of workers needed to generate massive wealth, can be characterized as the spread of "wageless life" (Denning 2012). Soaring speculative profits can be generated by a small group of workers in Silicon Valley or Wall Street, massively devaluing labor that is disconnected from key sectors. In short, through their dependency on high youth unemployment, student debt financing, and flexible arrangements of labor, both of the industries mentioned here are connected to financialization, or the increased dependence on financial and speculative profits in the national economy (Krippner 2011).

With this context in mind, it seems insufficient to categorize this articulation under "problems of persons." The practical and historical work that this definition enables should instead be our analytical entry point. Working backward, the articulation under which these industries thrive serves to moralize and normalize the credit-dependence that buttresses consumption in a low-wage economy—shifting attention away from declining wages, the precarious and uneven nature of financial accumulation, and state disinvestment from education. It neutralizes histories of racial and gender marginalization by translating the "underclass to entrepreneur" (Katz 2012: 101) in a controlled movement to address these histories of marginalization in which the state is understood as an accomplice by fueling dependency and stifling self-improvement. Finally, this articulation is given "epistemic privilege" by the profitability it enables, the extent to which it quells (extra-partisan) political unrest in poverty-stricken suburbs, the manner in which it taps into deeply symbolic practices (like property ownership, entrepreneurialism, and schooling), and by its ability to institutionalize flexible labor experiments that capture superfluous labor in a financialized economy.

Critical poverty scholarship should engage with the legitimization of poverty prescriptions and the social arrangements their credibility depends on, while always striving to understand these ideas in relation to "concrete work," often in enabling profits or quelling social unrest. Necessary in this task are both the historian's purposeful shovel and the ethnographer's critical field notes, not for unearthing buried ideas, but for mapping the dynamic ways in which they live through deliberate and eventful rearrangements in the present.

WORKS CITED

Block, Fred, and Margaret R. Somers. 2005. "From Poverty to Perversity: Ideas, Markets, and Institutions over 200 years of Welfare Debate." *American Sociological Review* 70:2, 260–87.

Bourdieu, Pierre. 1977. *Outline of a Theory of Practice*. Cambridge: Cambridge University Press.

Denning, Michael. 2012. "Wageless Life." *New Left Review* 66, 79–97.

Golden, Daniel. 2010. "The Homeless at College." *Bloomberg BusinessWeek Magazine*, April 30, http://www.businessweek.com/magazine/content/10_19/b4177064219731.htm#p1.

Hall, Stuart. 1980. "Race, Articulation and Societies Structured in Dominance." In *Sociological Theories: Race and Colonialism*, 305–45. Paris: UNESCO.

Hart, Gillian. 2014. *Rethinking the South African Crisis: Nationalism, Population, Hegemony*. Athens: University of Georgia Press.

Katz, Michael B. 2012. *Why Don't American Cities Burn?* Philadelphia: University of Pennsylvania Press.

Krippner, Greta. 2011. *Capitalizing on Crisis: The Political Origins of the Rise of Finance*. Cambridge, Mass.: Harvard University Press.

Menand, Louis. 2001. *The Metaphysical Club: Story of Ideas in America*. New York: Farrar, Straus and Giroux.

Sewell, William H., Jr. 2005. *The Logics of History: Social Theory and Social Transformation*. Chicago: University of Chicago Press.

Is Poverty a Global Security Threat?

AKHIL GUPTA

This essay, which sets out to rethink the territorialization of poverty, emphasizes four ideas. First, that the relationship between poverty and security has a long genealogy, and that this history is largely ignored in contemporary formulations of the problem. Second, I argue that poverty as a problem for security, crystallized in the discourse of "human security," arose before September 11, 2001, and not, as we might be inclined to think, after that tragic event. Third, 9/11 gave a fillip to the already existing idea that poverty was a problem for the citizens of the global North because globalization was bringing people closer together, increasing contact, contagion, and friction between rich people in the global North and poor people in the global South. Finally, I argue that the reterritorialization of space following the uneven geographies of global capitalism require us to think beyond the problematic of "global North" and "global South." The territories of poverty are changing, and may no longer be representable in the logic of units that resemble the nation-state (see Roy's introduction to this volume).

Contrary to what one might expect, the discourse of "poverty as a problem of security," or the "securitization of poverty" did not begin after September 11, 2001, although the relation between poverty and security may have been given a different inflection after that date. Well before 9/11, what we see is the convergence of two trends that come from very different discourses and literatures. One of these trends came from security studies, and the other from poverty studies. Within security studies, the orbit of security was widened after the fall of the Berlin Wall from a focus on national security and the state to "the security of the population."[1] The second trend has been the movement of poverty ideas from "basic needs" and "human development" to "human security." These two ideas converged to produce the idea of poverty as a threat to human security. This convergence was historically contingent—I am not arguing that it was inevitable, the result of inexorable processes whose unfolding finally gave us the idea that poverty was a major threat to human security. I am interested in how the idea that poverty is a threat to security was produced, but even more in what effects it might have in the world, particularly for acutely poor people throughout the globe.

I argue that we need to interrogate who the "human" is in "human security." Exactly who is being threatened by global poverty? The securitization of poverty creates the elites in the global North as the new subjects of security, the people most threatened by poverty in the global South. Poor people in the global North have always been a source of insecurity for elites in their own societies, and the problem posed by the poor has been "solved" by increasing the force of disciplinary mechanisms and by implementing carceral regimes (Wacquant, this volume; Roy, introduction to this volume). The security concerns of poor people in the global South have been displaced by the more pressing concerns of the elite population of nation-states first in the global North, and now including elites in the global South as well. Human security remains an enduring concern in the different literatures, but the "subject" of security who is under threat by global poverty is mainly the elite citizen of the global North.

Having given an overview of the main argument, I will now step back and briefly map the precursors of the idea that poverty is a problem of security. Without attempting to survey the large and rich anthropological literature on how acutely poor people dealt with uncertain weather conditions and risky livelihood strategies, I will introduce some key ideas from this literature, and ask why the importance of those ideas has not been recognized. The second part will then trace the metamorphosis of "national security" to "human security" after the end of the Cold War, and the convergence of security studies discourse with that of the human development paradigm. Human security as it emerges from the human development paradigm is itself an outgrowth of the idea of "basic needs" and represents a critique of mainstream development institutions and approaches. The third part will connect these developments to global poverty and the post-9/11 political configuration. The conclusion will interrogate received ideas of "global North" and "global South" as new representations of poverty arise partly in response to transformations in global capitalism.

Has Poverty Always Concerned Security?

The problem of security has always loomed large in the study of peasants in the global South. Peasant production—characterized by small-scale holdings; rainfed, subsistence agriculture; and production for one's own household—faced perpetual insecurity due to drought, pestilence, unseasonal weather, political conflict, and so forth. Those households that specialized in commercial crops, like cotton or coffee, or sold excess food grains on the market, were subject to the vicissitudes of price fluctuations and to the depredations of usurious merchant classes in the towns.[2]

Faced with these uncertainties, there were three major forms of insurance practiced by peasant households. First, peasants typically grew a wide variety of crops, so that even if one crop was blighted and failed, others would still yield something for household consumption. Production risks could also be spread by cultivating plots in different areas rather than in just one place. Geographic dispersion, even when it pertained to different plots in one village, provided safeguards against spatially localized incidents, such as the flooding of one side of the village. This is probably why one finds a particularly interesting method of dividing land in coparcenary systems of inheritance in north India. If a family owns three plots of roughly the same size and the land is to be inherited by three brothers, then instead of allocating one plot to each brother, each plot is subdivided into three. Thus, each brother gets a small share of land in three different parcels, rather than a larger piece of land in one parcel. The problem with such a division is that each brother then owns plots of land in different locations, and all the plots individually are too small to benefit from lumpy investments such as tubewells or tractors. Such "nonrational" economic behavior appears puzzling until one understands it primarily as a risk-aversion strategy. Having even suboptimal sizes of land in different places is preferable to having a larger parcel in one place because one can spread the risk of crop failure better in different plots, even if one consolidated plot would allow for higher returns during a normal crop season.

A second form of insurance is to invest in kinship relations, both inside and outside the village, so that one can request the aid of relatives in hard times. In peasant communities, therefore, one often finds strong mechanisms of mutual aid and support to kin connected through descent or marriage. In periods of drought or flooding, such relations are very important, particularly those that connect people to other villagers outside one's area of residence. The practice of exogamy, which is long-established in most peasant communities in north India, enables people to forge relations with other communities through marriage.

Third, even in elaborately stratified peasant societies, there were often community-level forms of insurance so that the pain of a downturn—such as a bad harvest—was shared by the whole community. For example, tenancy contracts or labor contracts that were calculated as a share of the output automatically adjusted rents and wages to the size of the harvest. In good times, the tenant had to pay the landlord more in nominal terms, and landlords had to pay laborers more by way of wages; in the case of a poor harvest, the reverse was true.

Finally, for poor households that do not earn enough to store food for the whole year, insurance against seasonal fluctuations in the demand for labor (and, therefore, food) can lead to various types of labor-tying arrangements. This can take the form of labor contracts that last one year or more, and may even shade into forms of indenture and bondage (Bardhan 1980, 1983).

As Scott (1976: 17) argued in *The Moral Economy of the Peasant*, peasant communities' preoccupation with survival drove them to "safety first" principles. Beyond the argument that Scott makes, the fragility and insecurity of peasant life more generally has played a critical explanatory role in peasant studies. The need to provide security against downside risks has been the basis of many functional explanations that purport to explain the nature of rural institutions, patron–client relations, inheritance systems, family types, reciprocity networks, moral structures, and subject formations. Poor people could increase their own security, or decrease their insecurity, by employing a whole host of institutional and familial strategies to mitigate downward shocks.

I bring up the literature on insecurity in peasant communities to ask why so little of this body of work finds its way into contemporary discussions of human security. In countries like India, the majority of the population is still rural and continues to be critically dependent on agriculture, even when agricultural income is not the primary source of income for the household. The literature on peasant communities that links insecurity to risk and provides models of communitarian social arrangements that mitigate against the insecurity of livelihoods might offer us some templates to deal with dilemmas about poverty in the present.

Post–Cold War Security Discourse and Alternative Approaches to Development

There have been many efforts to redefine "security" after the Cold War, particularly in the field of security studies. Having lost the enemy who supplied them their reason for existence, "defense intellectuals" and military personnel and thinkers, who had been preoccupied by national security, began to search for alternative ways to conceptualize security threats. At the same time, there arose an initiative from peace studies and allied intellectual fields that proposed thinking of security not just in terms of harm to the territorial state, but in terms of the threats to which its people—citizens and populations—were exposed. Not equating the security of people and nation-states also allowed for the possibility that the national state could be harming some of its own citizens and residents, and therefore, that the security of people could not be guaranteed by the securing of the nation-state. One scholar has called this trend "the broadening and deepening of the idea of security"—a good example is Jessica Tuchman Mathews's 1989 article on environmental security, which was one of the earliest efforts to redefine security (Krause and Williams 1996).

This move in security studies toward human security was paralleled by a shift in poverty discourse toward human security. The landmark here is the 1994 United Nations Development Program (UNDP) Human Development Report, whose vision came from its charismatic head, Mahbub ul Haq. "The concept of security has for too long been interpreted narrowly: as security of territory from external aggression, or as protection of national interests in foreign policy or as global security from the threat of nuclear holocaust. It has been related more to nation-states than to people. . . . Forgotten were the legitimate concerns of ordinary people who sought security in their daily lives" (1994: 22). The report goes on to say that for most people feelings of insecurity arise from worries of daily life having to do with getting enough to eat, job security, safe neighborhoods, repressive states, gendered violence, or religious and ethnic intolerance (United Nations Development Program 1994: 22). It goes on to identify seven major components of human security: economic security, food security, health security, environmental security, personal security, community security, and political security (United Nations Development Program 1994: 24–33). The move from "human development" to "human security" puzzled many followers of Mahbub ul Haq, who was clearly the chief force behind both concepts.

In reading the 1994 Human Development Report, it becomes clear that the agenda in moving to the concept of "human security" was to seize the peace dividend in the period after the Cold War (United Nations Development Program 1994: 5). Other arguments that have been made as to why "human security" is a better umbrella for the developmental agenda than "human development" are the following:

1. Human development is too diffuse a concept, and it fails to prioritize its components. In stressing the expansion of human capabilities, human development does not help determine whether the provision of food is more important than the provision of medical services or educational services, or other needs. Human security narrows the scope of the human development concept by focusing on that which is essential for human security (Gasper 2005: 226–7).

2. Human security draws attention not just to the provision of goods and services necessary for human development, but to the regularity of their provisioning. Thus, if access to food is, on the average, adequate, but seasonally variable or unstable, then human security better captures this element of unreliability or unpredictability (Gasper 2005: 226). "Human security" is a minimal program to safeguard the vulnerable against downside risks rather than a maximal program to develop human potential.

3. The term "security" is preferable because it "conveys urgency, demands public attention, and commands governmental resources" (Paris 2001: 95). Governments are more likely to act in the name of human security than for general purposes of development.

4. "Human security" brings a human rights agenda into the developmental discussion of basic needs, blending the worlds of social movements and humanitarian intervention with those of social and economic policy and aid (Gasper 2005: 232). In particular, it places at par people who have suffered physical and structural violence at the hands of their own nation-states with those whose suffering is due to the military threats of other nation-states.

Once the idea was introduced, the reaction to human security was surprisingly positive: it was taken up by many different actors and was quickly institutionalized. Here is a partial list, taken from Büger (2008: 15), of some of the important institutions and global assemblies where this term was adopted: the 1995 Copenhagen World Summit on Social Development[3]; the 1997 Ottawa Treaty, which came out of the International Campaign to Ban Landmines; the UN Trust Fund for Human Security in 1999 (part of the UN Office for the Coordination of Humanitarian Affairs [OCHA]); the Human Security Network in 1998[4]; the Ogata and Sen (2003) report, *Human Security Now*, for the UN Commission on Human Security; and in several think tanks and research centers on human security in different parts of the world, especially in Canada, the UK, and Germany.

A great deal has already been written on explaining *why* the concept of "human security" caught on in the way that it did, but that is not my concern here (see, e.g., Büger 2008; Gasper 2005; Paris 2001). I wish to ask a different question. Taking the widespread adoption of "human security" as a social fact, I ask what its effects have been on our understanding of poverty. In particular, I wish to raise the question of the articulation of the idea of human security with another idea that gained prominence at the same time, that of "global poverty."

Forms of globalization pushed by dominant powers that centered on integrating markets in the global South with those in the global North helped produce the conditions that led to a discourse of global poverty. "Global poverty" references a depoliticized, context-light concern with acute poverty whose "solutions" involve integrating the poor more tightly into global commodity markets (see Gupta 2011).

In previous work (Gupta 2009, 2011), I have argued that "global poverty" arose as an important concept after 1999. If we chart the number of publications in which the term "global poverty" is employed, we find a clear pattern that demonstrates that there is almost a 500 percent increase in references to the term in the six years between 1999 and 2005. It appears that a new consensus on global poverty took shape in the late 1990s, culminating in the UN Millennium Declaration in September 2000. The year 1999 is also significant because it inaugurated a new approach to poverty by the World Bank and the IMF. It was in that year that the World Bank and the IMF adopted the Poverty Reduction Strategy Paper (PRSP) approach to poverty. By 2005 the calls for reducing global poverty had become a tidal wave. *Time* magazine made "global poverty" its cover story and prominently featured the work of Jeffrey Sachs. That same year, the G-8 summit made global poverty its main focus; the Millennium Development Goals Report was also released in 2005 (United Nations 2005). Tony Blair's Commission for Africa released a high-profile report in March 2005 entitled *Our Common Interest*, which focused on poverty reduction strategies for Africa (Commission for Africa 2005). Global poverty even made it to the top of the agenda at the high-profile economic summit in Davos in 2005, the World Economic Forum (WEF). This was not entirely an elite-driven agenda. The year 2005 also launched the Global Call to Action against Poverty (GCAP) in Porto Alegre, Brazil, by the World Social Forum (WSF). The same year saw the introduction of two highly visible campaigns to eradicate global poverty: the White Band campaign and the Power of One, sponsored by corporations and NGOs.

In tracking the rise of the term "global poverty" in this manner, and of "human security" before that, I do not wish to claim that poverty was not present as a severe problem for large parts of the population of the world before 2000, or that security was not a problem for poor people before the release of the Human Development Report of 1994. The underlying problems of poverty and human insecurity did not change dramatically after these ways of conceptualizing poverty and security became dominant. What did change was how these problems were seen, how they were understood and perceived, and, as a result of the new optics, how "solutions" to the problems of poverty and insecurity were devised. When "global poverty" became an important global idea, the problem of poverty as human insecurity was already well established. How did these two concepts articulate with each other? In the next section, I will track their intersections and transmutations.

From Human Security to Global Poverty

In chronological terms, the development of the discourse of "human security" precedes the rise of the concept of "global poverty." The question I wish to ask is whether these two discourses on poverty are related, and if so, how? Did "human security" discourse and its corresponding institutions create the conditions for the rise of "global poverty" discourse and its institutionalization? Or, was it just a coincidence that these two ways of thinking about poverty emerged one after the other? And how did 9/11 intervene in shaping these two discourses, one of which originated largely before 9/11 (human security) and one which really took off only after 2001 (global poverty)? For the moment, I offer some tentative hypotheses, which may be rejected or refined by further research and argumentation.

First, let me note that the analytical trajectory would have been much neater had we first seen the UN, scholarly institutions, NGOs and civil society organizations react to the interest in globalization in the early 1990s with the invention of something like "global poverty." When globalization became part of the vocabulary of rule, then it seems that "global poverty" as an idea could not be far behind. And then when 9/11 occurred, it would not be at all surprising to witness the securitization of poverty and the replacement of the concept of "global poverty" by "human security" as the currency of the poverty industry.

Unfortunately, it makes my argument more convoluted that things actually unfolded in the reverse order. I have already mentioned that "human security" emerged in the aftermath of the Cold War to capture the peace dividend by injecting a sense of urgency and focus, and perhaps inspiration, to development programs. "Human security" brought together scholars and practitioners from security studies, development studies, and human rights, and it succeeded in capturing the attention of many different actors in states, multilateral institutions, and NGOs. The basic argument held that poverty was a security issue in that the lives of the poor were insecure along multiple dimensions, and the eradication of all those risks was necessary in antipoverty efforts. However, at that point, poverty was still largely conceptualized as national, and the risks it posed were largely to poor people themselves, and, secondarily, to national economies and states. Although the concept of human security left it open whose security was in question, and potentially included poor people in the global North, it was clear that the primary concern of human security discourse was with poor people in the global South—they were the ones whose security mattered because they were the ones at risk. Certainly, Mahbub ul Haq's formulation of human security was largely in these terms.

The rapid rise of the discourse of "global poverty" did not displace human security from the developmental agenda but complemented it in certain critical respects. Human security has been severely criticized by some security studies scholars for its lack of specificity and measurability, and the more traditional branch of security studies has largely ignored it for this reason. However, others have argued that this lack of precision is exactly what makes it useful, as it can be differently employed in diverse contexts, depending on what the greatest risks are in those contexts: lack of physical security in one context, and lack of food security in another.[5] It can, therefore, simultaneously serve as an umbrella term and be fine-tuned to fit local circumstances. By contrast, "global poverty" frames poverty in such a manner that local context does not matter (Gupta 2011). "Global poverty" offers a contextually thin understanding of poverty that seeks universal explanations and universal solutions. Moreover, the discourse of global poverty arose in a context in which the key concern was what the wealthy nation-states and peoples in the global North could do for the unfortunate poor in the global South. The depoliticization of poverty occurs by seeing it as not being created by global inequalities or by structural inequalities in a global system (Sachs 2005).[6]

The referent of "global poverty" was almost never poor people in the global North. It was understood that the globally poor were the poor people in the global South, and aggregating them under the umbrella category of those "who lived under $1/day" made it possible to put people who were desperately poor into the same statistical and analytical framework. If the dominant mode of relating to the poor was that of charity or aid, it made sense to lump them together in this way. However, if one wanted to think of cultural context and structural location, and especially if one wanted to link poverty to relational inequalities between the global North and South, it made little sense to lump the poor in Africa with the poor in India. In the work of thinkers such as Sachs (2005), Singer (2010), and Collier (2008), it is precisely this lack of analysis of systematic, structural inequality in a globally interconnected world that enables the construction of the global poor as abject objects of sympathy and aid.

As Roy points out in the introduction to this volume, the relationship between poverty "at home" and poverty "abroad" can never be grasped without a global historical approach that keeps in "simultaneous view the uneven geographies of global North and global South." What is at stake here is not just the existence of such uneven geographies, but their reproduction. Martin Luther King Jr., in his famous antiwar speech, made this connection clearly:

> A few years ago there was a shining moment in that struggle. It seemed as if there was a real promise of hope for the poor, both black and white, through the poverty program. There were experiments, hopes, new beginnings. Then came the buildup in Vietnam, and I watched this program broken and eviscerated as if it were some idle political plaything on a society gone mad on war. And I knew that America would never invest the necessary funds or energies in rehabilitation of its poor so long as adventures like Vietnam continued to draw men and skills and money like some demonic, destructive suction tube. So I was increasingly compelled to see the war as an enemy of the poor and to attack it as such.
>
> Perhaps a more tragic recognition of reality took place when it became clear to me that the war was doing far more than devastating the hopes of the poor at home. It was sending their sons and their brothers and their husbands to fight and to die in extraordinarily high proportions relative to the rest of the population. We were taking the black young men who had been crippled by our society and

sending them eight thousand miles away to guarantee liberties in Southeast Asia which they had not found in southwest Georgia and East Harlem. So we have been repeatedly faced with the cruel irony of watching Negro and white boys on TV screens as they kill and die together for a nation that has been unable to seat them together in the same schools. So we watch them in brutal solidarity burning the huts of a poor village, but we realize that they would hardly live on the same block in Chicago. I could not be silent in the face of such cruel manipulation of the poor. (King 1967)

There could be no clearer example of the relationship between violence on the poor at home and abroad. Poor, minority men, subjects of structural and police violence at home, are recruited to wage war and perpetuate violence on poor people in Vietnam in the name of the U.S. state. Martin Luther King Jr. was aware that the "problem" of minority youth was being solved by sending them to wage war on poor people abroad, that the two modes of violence on the poor were integrally interconnected (see Roy, Schrader, and Crane, this volume).

Another, perhaps equally important reason why the discourse of global poverty was not seen as a challenge to the idea of human security was because the referent of human security shifted after 9/11. In Mahbub ul Haq's formulation, and in the UN documents in which "human security" was first developed, the idea was that the insecurity of the poor was the problem on which one needed to focus. After 9/11, the *subject* of security changed, so that poverty became a problem for "human security": the poverty of the global South became a problem for the security of the elite citizens of the global North. Sachs (2005: 330–31) argues, for example, that terrorist bases are established in "unstable societies beset by poverty, unemployment, rapid population growth, hunger, and lack of hope. . . . Poverty abroad can indeed hurt us at home, and has repeatedly done so." Defense intellectuals discovered in this idea of "human security" something they could finally recognize.

There is a long history of the idea that poverty in the Third World is a security problem for the West, although the fear earlier concerned the nation-state much more than it did citizens.[7] One widely shared belief among American policymakers promoting development in the Third World after decolonization was that poverty was a fertile breeding ground for communism.[8] Apart from its implications for the Cold War, revolutionary movements were to be feared because they created political instability that, in turn, affected the business climate negatively. American corporations were of course negatively affected by any political instability, but so were domestic businesses that were needed for a country to advance to the next stage of growth (Rostow 1991). Huntington worried that without a strong government, political instability would be created because mass republican mobilization, even if it was noncommunist, would outrun institution building (Huntington 2006).

Persistent poverty would lead to Third World states becoming communist, and growing communist influence, in turn, threatened the security of the Free World. This was clearly one of the most important lessons that Robert Mc-Namara, as secretary of defense during the Vietnam War, took from his experience advising two presidents on the war in Vietnam. On being appointed president of the World Bank immediately afterward, McNamara turned the World Bank's focus to "basic needs." In the words of the World Bank's archives, "McNamara believed that there was a direct link between concerns about military security and economic development. For McNamara the threat of warfare was a consequence of the widening income gap between the industrial and developing countries."[9] As Roy, Schrader, and Crane demonstrate in their essay in this volume, McNamara was to extend this insight from the battlefields of Vietnam to potentially insurgent minorities within the United States.

Since the Vietnam War, security concerns in the global North have shifted from a fear of an attack by another nation-state to a concern with the damage that might be inflicted by terrorist groups. Defense intellectuals theorize that terrorists thrive in settings that uncannily resemble the conditions that were said to give rise to communism. Poverty is the underlying cause, and if on top of that, one overlays failed states, the paucity of job prospects, and extremist ideology, then one gets ideal breeding grounds for recruitment to terrorist organizations (Sachs 2005: 215, 330). Sachs's predilection for eloquently recycling modernization theory makes him especially prone to restate its tenets about security as freshly minted insights into terrorism. But Sachs is scarcely alone in extending the insights about security gained during the Cold War to the brave new world of nonstate threats to elite citizens in the global North.

Global capitalism has altered existing class structures and modified the old geographies of "West" versus "Third World." Day by day, it increasingly makes the new imaginaries of "global North" and "global South" less tenable as well. The whole problematic of security, ensconced in the geographies of the Cold War, has to be constantly reconceived. What is really being retheorized in these debates is how to define the subject whose insecurity is to be addressed. The Cold War definition of security was national, but the vision of the nation-state was such that it already excluded its minority citizens from civil rights and substantive equality. Global capitalism is creating a new, transnational elite spread across the world, whose geographical location is increasingly escaping the territoriality implicit in the term "global North," however that is envisioned. In such a world, definitions of security are caught between the old nation-state formulations familiar to security analysts embedded in the military-industrial complex, and new ideas seeking to theorize modes of security that would be adequate to protect the life and well-being of this elite.

The ideas of security presented by Sachs are no doubt a theory of human security and not about national security in the narrow sense. But the insecurity that defense intellectuals worry about is not that of poor people across the globe. The subject of security here is the elite citizen of the nation-states of the global North who is under threat due to poverty in the global South.[10] The argument that poverty abroad should be eradicated because it ultimately undermines "our" security may be a strategic essentialism to make the poor less remote and poverty as an issue that needs to be tackled urgently. After all, the argument goes, appealing to people's selfish interests is always more effective than engaging their humanitarian intentions. But the problem is that such arguments effect a critical shift in the subject of insecurity—from the poor person in the global South to the elites in the global North. After all, whose security is being threatened by poverty? Who is the "we" and the "our" who are the subjects of sentences like the one constructed by Sachs? Almost certainly, it is not the poor people in the global South and it is not even the poor people in the global North. Elites in the global North cannot be secure at home without eradicating poverty abroad. The poor subject who was proposed as the center of the human security concept by Mahbub ul Haq has been erased and became instead an instrument toward an end, which is the security of elite subjects mostly in the global North but increasingly spread across the world.

Poverty in the global South threatens elites in the global North not only because it breeds frustration and thereby political extremism, but for a host of other reasons. The argument begins by acknowledging that globalization has resulted in tightly interconnecting the lives of people all over the world. For this reason, poverty in any part of the world ("Africa") will, sooner or later, threaten "our" security: through disease vectors such as AIDS, tuberculosis, bird flu, and Ebola; through bioterrorism; through environmental destruction of rainforests and other important global resources; through the threat to biodiversity posed by the nonsustainable use of genetic resources; through financial volatility that creates new layers of poverty and results in social crises; and through unchecked migration and human trafficking (Chen and Fukuda-Parr 2003). A very similar line of argument was used by New Labour and Prime Minister Tony Blair's government when, soon after 9/11, Blair called Africa "a scar on the conscience of the world" (Abrahamsen 2005: 55). The argument made by New Labour was that in an increasingly interconnected world, poverty and conflict in other places can, and will, spill over and affect the global North. That is why Africa's failed states needed to be helped, and chronic poverty in the continent addressed (Abrahamsen 2005). Abrahamsen (2005: 68) asks what the price is for framing Africa's problems less as a development/humanitarian issue and more as a security issue. When one moves from development to security, what is lost in shifting the emphasis from the poor person in the global South, who was the subject of development, to the elite citizen of the global North, who is the subject of security and whose life is threatened by new kinds of risks in an increasingly interconnected world?

In the kinds of arguments marshaled by New Labour, the division between "inside" and "outside" is maintained. The geographies of nationalism in which the domestic sphere is separated from foreign policy and foreign relations, the implicit bulwark of security studies thinking, is replicated in these "progressive" statements (Walker 1992). Globalization is a promise but also a threat because it brings the "outside" in and threatens to breach the border fences of the nation-state. In the logic of such arguments about security, "we" should do something about poverty "outside," that is, about "global poverty," not because there is something morally compelling about it, not because it makes us, the comfortable classes, complicit in killing the poor (Gupta 2012), but because it will eventually make our own lives worse, because it will make our comfortable, ecocidical, consumerist, narcissistic, existence slightly less tolerable. If such an argument strikes one as being "reasonable" and "pragmatic," then how far are we from acknowledging the pain of those who are losing their lives due to acute poverty?

Beyond "Global North" and "Global South"?

As Roy notes in her introduction to this volume, poverty is being reterritorialized in the world today: moving from inner cities to suburbs in the global North and South, and from rural areas to peri-urban slums. Poverty is also being produced and reproduced in novel ways. We have to study the production of poverty, which means that we need to pay attention to new forms of accumulation and distribution in the global economy. These produce not only poverty, but privilege; the "global poor" and the "global elite" are produced by the same processes of accumulation and dispossession, and by the production of inequality. Although acute poverty is often defined in absolute terms, poverty is relational, and any argument such as the one made here about poverty being a threat to the security of global elites begs the question of the relationship—physical, geographical, transactional, legal—between the rich and the poor. It is this relationship that is creating new geographies, new cartographies, of poverty, new forms of the territorialization, deterritorialization, and reterritorialization of poverty.

The rise of the BRICS (the economic association of Brazil, Russia, India,

China, and South Africa) is only one large trend in the reterritorialization of wealth and accumulation in the global economy today. The larger picture of a move of the center of the global economy toward Asia signifies an important shift in the geography of capitalist accumulation. However, what matters for poverty is not such aggregate movements, but whether such macro shifts indicate also a qualitative difference in the lives of the poor. If high growth is accompanied by growing rates of inequality, then it may do little to help the acutely poor. And, indeed, the evidence does seem to point to the fact that change in the lives of the poorest people in South Asia, particularly in India, is occurring marginally, despite two decades of fast growth. India seems to be producing billionaires faster than any other country, but it also appears to have more difficulty in using its newfound resources to get more people out of poverty.

The larger point here about patterns of neoliberal accumulation is that inequality seems to be growing in every region of the world. The implications of this fact for a reterritorialization of poverty need to be worked out. In the global North, the middle-class is being squeezed out as the distribution of wealth becomes more bimodal. At the same time, the real wages of the working classes are either stagnant or falling. The disciplinary mechanisms being used against immigrants are making their lives and livelihoods even more precarious, and the threat of deportations and illegality is forcing their wages down below the minimum wage. The result is that the existence of larger groups of people, including those formerly in the middle class, is becoming increasingly precarious. Allison (2012, 2013) documents this precariousness for the lives of young, middle-class Japanese men and women, but the phenomenon is not confined to the downwardly mobile middle classes. It affects all non-elite people in the global North (Standing 2011).

A very similar process of stratification is occurring in the fast-growing economies of the global South. New elites are being constituted as incomes rise to "global" levels for the upper segments of the income bracket, whereas those without skills or education find themselves unable to find employment or participate in the benefits of growth. The elite are increasingly insulating themselves from the hordes outside their gated communities. Children of elites in India, for example, go from air-conditioned homes to air-conditioned schools without any exposure to the lives of their poorer compatriots. Most rural children, for example, have never been in an air-conditioned space and may not even have electricity to power lightbulbs to do homework in the evenings (if they are lucky enough to be able to go to school).

The old territorial logic held that elites in a country occupy "the same space" as their fellow citizens, the space of the nation-state. I want to argue that, although the space of the nation-state has not completely been reterritorialized, the experience of elites in a global economy has seen the substantial reterritori-alization of space. Increasingly, elites in both the global North and global South no longer share the "same experience" of spatiality as their poorer geographical neighbors. Their experiences of work, travel, shopping, leisure, and consumption are cut off from their geographically contiguous poorer neighbors, and they are conducted in enclave economies and gated spaces that they share with other transnational elites. Obviously, this is not true of all such activities, but it is increasingly becoming the norm, especially with the rise of such things as social media and Internet shopping. In such a situation, we need to rethink whether the categories of "global North" and "global South" are adequate to the territories of poverty being produced by new regimes of accumulation in the global capitalist system.

Poor people's movements that are global in scope have also arisen in the new territories of poverty. The paradigms of poverty inside the nation-state and outside it, implicit in domestic policy and foreign aid respectively, assumed the territoriality of the nation-state and raised the question about the relationship between poverty "at home" and poverty "abroad." As Roy points out so elo-quently in her introduction, such a formulation opens up the question of the relationship between the two, between domestic treatment of poverty here and the foreign policy interventions into poverty abroad. Roy underlines the sur-prising convergences between formulations of the problem of poverty at home and the destabilizing effects of poverty abroad, convergences that were missed because of the academic division between those who study domestic poverty and those who study poverty in the global South.

Such a critique makes possible a broader retheorizing of the territories of poverty that goes beyond the boundary-making processes of the nation-state. Poverty is being produced both in the global South and in the global North by similar patterns of accumulation that are concentrating wealth in the hands of fewer and fewer people, and producing precariousness for the vast majority. Poor people all over the world are finding it harder to get out of poverty, even when they are lucky enough to find employment, because their wages are shrinking or stagnant. The middle-class in the global North is being depopulated, while the middle-class in the global South is growing. Thus, the geographies where wealth is being accumulated are shifting, and a completely different set of people are becoming wealthy. In this landscape, the subjects whose lives are to be secured against poverty are not the poor themselves, but elites in both the global North and the global South who fear that their quality of life will be compromised by poverty outside their insulated environments. The perceived threats are every-where the same: disease vectors, militant uprisings, environmental destruction, and unchecked migration. The solutions to these threats are also the same: increased insulation from poor people in urban environments through security barriers; the abandonment of public schooling, housing, medical facilities, transportation, and public spaces; and the pressure on public policy and politicians to provide special facilities where the poor will not be welcome.

Conclusion

In this essay, I have made four related arguments. First, that there is much to be learned from the forgotten history of the relationship between security and poverty from the rich literature on peasant economies. How to secure one's life and livelihood in the face of risk and uncertainty was a central theme in this literature and, in neglecting it, the new body of work on human security misses out on some important reflections on the role of communitarian social arrangements in mitigating insecurity in social life. Beyond the two options of the state and the individual facing the market, lie myriad other forms of social organization, and this was recognized in the literature well before Putnam employed the term "social capital" to describe it. For example, Gandhi's notion of self-sufficient village communities was one such idea; workers' cooperatives in different parts of the world mobilized other such visions of combating insecurity.

I next argued that the history of the securitization of poverty precedes 9/11 by some time, although both are connected to the Cold War.[11] The end of the Cold War raised high hopes of a so-called peace dividend, and the move to "human security" was intended to take advantage of that fact. The concept of "human security" gained a great degree of traction because it was vague enough that different actors could mobilize projects in its name without agreeing on a meaning. Human security also mobilized constituents from the fields of security, human rights, and development, and thus increased its sphere of influence.

Third, I noted that what changed after 9/11 was that the human whose security was being protected was no longer the poor in the global South beset by uncertainties in the supply of food, housing, clothing, medical aid, and education. Instead, poverty in the global South itself became a threat to the security not only of states in the global North, but also to its elite citizens. In a world increasingly well connected globally, poverty in the global South was a real threat to the existence of populations in the global North because of the fears of disease vectors, bioterrorism, unchecked immigration, refugees, collapsed states, trafficking in illegal substances, and so forth—the list of potential threats is quite long.

Finally, I argued that the reterritorialization of poverty being effected by the changed geographies of capitalist accumulation in the world today threaten the established geographies of "global North" and "global South" as elites in both contexts seek to secure themselves against the poor around them. Rising inequality both produces poverty and also creates the threat to the well-being of global elites by poverty. Poverty studies, which has yet to make the leap to connect "domestic" poverty to poverty abroad, lags far behind in the attempt to rethink the territories of poverty.

If poverty is seen primarily as a security threat to global elites, then what needs to be done to combat it is quite different from what needs to be done if poverty is seen mainly as a problem of basic needs and human development. If poverty is seen through the depoliticized lens of "global poverty" discourse and is combined with discourses of "human security" in which the security of elites in the global North is primary, it makes it less likely that any interventions into poverty will make a positive difference to the lives of the poor. The new territories of poverty require a fundamental rethinking of politics, including poor peoples' collective politics, and forms of policy intervention that are feasible and desirable.

NOTES

1. The phrase "security of the population" evokes Foucault (2007: 87–114), who argues that, in Western Europe, state concerns moved from securing territory to population in the eighteenth century. Despite Foucault's claims, the "national security apparatus," consisting of defense intellectuals and others closely allied with the military, continued to think of national security primarily in territorial terms. Approaches to security based on territory, and those based on the welfare of the population, continue to coexist. Examples of this are found in the increased militarization of the U.S.–Mexico border, the continual increases in military spending, and, at the same time, the expansion of food aid to poor families after the recession of 2008 to reach more people than ever before.

2. This is one reason there is a long-established antagonism between the city and the country in most agrarian contexts.

3. The 1994 Human Development Report was explicitly addressed to the World Summit on Social Development in Copenhagen.

4. The HSN (http://www.humansecuritynetwork.org/) now comprises Austria, Canada, Chile, Costa Rica, Greece, Ireland, Jordan, Mali, the Netherlands, Norway, Slovenia, South Africa (observer), Switzerland, and Thailand.

5. Büger (2008) calls it a "boundary object" that allows different discourses to be mobilized around it.

6. Sachs's (2005) discussion of poverty, and his solutions to poverty, emphasizes foreign aid but manages to sidestep the connection between growing global inequality and extreme poverty.

7. I am deliberately using the terms "Third World" and "West" here because I am referring to historical trends. The terms "global South" and "global North" are of relatively recent origin.

8. It is not surprising that Walt Rostow's (1960) *The Stages of Economic Growth* is

subtitled *A Non-Communist Manifesto*. Sachs (2005: 215–22) restates this position in an almost identical fashion in *The End of Poverty*.

9. Full details are to be found here: "Robert Strange McNamara," The World Bank: Archives, 2013, http://go.worldbank.org/44V9497H50.

10. The tension between the geographical imagination implicit in the protection of citizens of the global North, not all of whom are elite, and the changing geographies of capitalism in which elites in the global South are becoming increasingly central has created difficulties for the discourse on security.

11. The connection between 9/11 and the Cold War is often "forgotten" by defense intellectuals and mainstream media outlets. The cynical use of "jihadis" against the Soviet Union in Afghanistan trained an entire generation of fundamentalist young men to use sophisticated weapons, and they were always clear that they regarded the United States to be as much of an enemy as the Soviet Union. As has happened so often in the past, to achieve a short-term objective, the United States compromised its long-term security.

REFERENCES

Abrahamsen, Rita. 2005. "Blair's Africa: The Politics of Securitization and Fear." *Alternatives* 30, 55–80.

Allison, Anne. 2012. "Ordinary Refugees: Social Precarity and Soul in 21st-Century Japan." *Anthropological Quarterly* 85:2, 345–70.

Allison, Anne. 2013. *Precarious Japan*. Durham: Duke University Press.

Bardhan, Pranab K. 1980. "Interlocking Factor Markets and Agrarian Development: A Review of Issues." *Oxford Economic Papers*, n.s., 32:1, 82–98.

Bardhan, Pranab K. 1983. "Labor-Tying in a Poor Agrarian Economy: A Theoretical and Empirical Analysis." *Quarterly Journal of Economics* 98:3, 501–14.

Büger, Christian. 2008. "Human Security—What's the Use of it? On Boundary Objects and the Constitution of New Global Spaces." Paper presented at 49th Annual Conference of the International Studies Association, San Francisco, Calif., March.

Chen, Lincoln, and Sakiko Fukuda-Parr. 2003. "Editor's Introduction: Special Issue on New Insecurities." *Journal of Human Development* 4:2, 163–66.

Collier, Paul. 2008. *The Bottom Billion: Why the Poorest Countries are Failing and What Can Be Done About It*. New York: Oxford University Press.

Commission for Africa. 2005. *Our Common Interest*. Glasgow: Commission for Africa.

Foucault, Michel. 2007. *Security, Territory, Population: Lectures at the College de France, 1975–76*. Translated by Graham Burchell. New York: Palgrave Macmillan.

Gasper, Des. 2005. "Securing Humanity: Situating 'Human Security' as Concept and Discourse." *Journal of Human Development* 6:2, 221–45.

Gupta, Akhil. 2009. "Nationale Armut, globale Armut und Neoliberalismus: eine anthropologische Kritik." *Entwicklungswelten. Globalgeschichte der Entwicklungszusammenarbeit*, ed. Hubertus Büschel and Daniel Speich, 113–39. Frankfurt am Main: Campus Verlag.

Gupta, Akhil. 2011. "National Poverty and Global Poverty in the Age of Neoliberalism."
 Cahiers d'Études Africaines 51:2–3, 415–26.

Gupta, Akhil. 2012. *Red Tape: Bureaucracy, Structural Violence, and Poverty in India.*
 Durham: Duke University Press.

Huntington, Samuel P. 2006. *Political Order in Changing Societies.* New Haven: Yale
 University Press.

King, Martin Luther, Jr. 1967. "Beyond Vietnam." Speech delivered in New York
 City at Riverside Church, April 4. Available at Martin Luther King, Jr., and the
 Global Freedom Struggle, http://mlk-kpp01.stanford.edu/index.php/encyclopedia
 /documentsentry/doc_beyond_vietnam/.

Krause, Keith, and Michael C. Williams. 1996. "Broadening the Agenda of Security
 Studies: Politics and Methods." *Mershon International Studies Review* 40:2, 229–54.

Mathews, Jessica Tuchman. 1989. "Redefining Security." *Foreign Affairs* 68:2, 162–77.

Ogata, Sadako and Amartya Sen. 2003. *Human Security Now.* New York: Commission
 on Human Security.

Paris, Roland. 2001. "Human Security: Paradigm Shift or Hot Air?" *International
 Security* 26:2, 87–102.

Rostow, Walt W. 1960. *The Stages of Economic Growth: A Non-Communist Manifesto.*
 New York: Cambridge University Press.

Sachs, Jeffrey D. 2005. *The End of Poverty: Economic Possibilities for Our Time.* New
 York: Penguin Books.

Scott, James C. 1976. *The Moral Economy of the Peasant: Rebellion and Subsistence in
 Southeast Asia.* New Haven: Yale University Press.

Singer, Peter. 2010. *The Life You Can Save: How to Do Your Part to End World Poverty.*
 New York: Random House.

Standing, Guy. 2011. *The Precariat: The New Dangerous Class.* London: Bloomsbury.

United Nations. 2005. *The Millennium Development Goals Report.* New York: United
 Nations Department of Public Information.

United Nations Development Program. 1994. *Human Development Report 1994.* New
 York: Oxford University Press.

Walker, R. B. J. 1992. *Inside/Outside: International Relations as Political Theory.* New
 York: Cambridge University Press.

Paying for Good Behavior:
Cash Transfer Policies in the Wild

JAMIE PECK AND NIK THEODORE

Introduction. From Money Doctors to Model Peddlers

The period since the declaration of the Millennium Development Goals has been marked by an unprecedented attempt to build, advance, and consolidate a new hegemonic front in the globalizing field of social-assistance policy. Conditional cash transfer (CCT) programs have been in the vanguard of this effort. Often styled as a Latin American "invention," the operational principles and programming practices of CCTs have been actively coproduced, almost since their inception, by the multilateral development agencies and their roving representatives. They have since spread throughout South America, and indeed to every continent, at a prolific rate. In less than a decade, what began as a pair of geographically isolated experiments (in Mexico and Brazil) has become established, in effect, as the default setting for antipoverty reform: "The international development community has clearly defined CCTs as the new norm" (Sugiyama 2011: 264).

But what Lawrence Aber and Laura Rawlings (2011: 1) describe, writing for the World Bank, as the "remarkable global expansion" of CCTs has not been achieved by way of heavy-handed coercion; these widely emulated programs have been subject to a distinctive form of best-practice contagion, fueled by evaluation evidence and guided by expert networks: "CCTs have been closely studied and well evaluated, creating both a strong evidence base from which to inform policy decisions and an active global community of practice." Classically modeled on Progresa-Oportunidades in Mexico, CCTs provide modest cash assistance to low-income families that play by the rules, "conditioning" payments on a matrix of human-capital building behaviors in education, health care, and labor-force attachment. Now found in approaching fifty countries, CCTs have been trumpeted by the *Economist* (2010: 10) as "the world's favourite anti-poverty device," while for Nancy Birdsall, president of the Center for Global

Development, they are "as close as you can come to a magic bullet" (quoted in Dugger 2004: A1).

The CCT model encapsulates a new logic of social assistance, transnational in reach and quite different from the welfare-state rationalities of needs-based entitlement and universal coverage, most of which were anchored in national citizenship regimes and nation-state delivery systems: it emphasizes socioeconomic promotion over social protection and long-term human-capital investment over temporary relief; it advances notions like reciprocal obligation and "co-responsibility" over universal human rights or top-down forms of social responsibility; and it inculcates active engagement over passive benefit receipt, an approach captured in the phrase "paying for good behavior." CCTs seek to be both pro-poor and pro-market by incentivizing those human-capital building behaviors, like regular school attendance and preventive health care, determined to benefit the *children* of low-income households. In this regard, CCTs not only share, but have helped to realize, a programmatic philosophy for globalizing social-assistance initiatives, privileging market "solutions" to entrenched problems of uneven development, economic dislocation, and social disadvantage (see Roy 2010, and introduction to this volume). As such, they borrow concepts from behavioral economics and motivational psychology, melding these with the pragmatic, best-practice style characteristic of the "new" Washington Consensus, in service of building a postwelfare rationale for "safety net" spending. *Conditioning* cash transfers is the crucial maneuver here, for this transforms what might be seen as an ameliorative handout into an instrumentalist hand up, while enabling a form of social targeting actively linked to human-capital investment. According to the World Bank's logic, "by supporting minimum levels of consumption, helping credit-constrained poor people to be productive, and providing incentives for long-term investments in human capital, safety nets have a potentially important role in compensating for the market failures that help perpetuate poverty, particularly in high inequality settings" (Aber and Rawlings 2011: 4).

The global CCT wave has been enabled, bankrolled, and steered by the World Bank and its allies in the multilateral community (in concert with a small army of policy entrepreneurs, consultants, evaluation scientists, and practitioner-advocates), both through established channels like policy-based lending and, no less consequentially, through the increasingly isomorphic fields of expert knowledge and technocratic practice. The World Bank, the Inter-American Development Bank (IABD), and other multilateral development agencies often underwrite the operating costs of CCT programs—this having become, in effect, their authorized mode of social-policy intervention—but they have also actively fostered an experimental ethos around these programs, supporting the deployment of randomized control trials and the extensive dissemination of impact-evaluation studies. Echoing the way in which CCT programs incentivize "appropriate" behaviors among poor families, the multilateral development agencies have been "paying for good behavior" in policymaking communities themselves, insisting that elaborate evaluation strategies must accompany all new interventions, and that the policy development process must be rigorously evidence based. The macro logic of this evidence-based approach is one that favors incrementalist mutation and technocratic tinkering in the shadow of preferred "models."

The rapid ascendancy and transnational diffusion of CCTs call attention to a historically distinctive form of "model power," orchestrated from global centers of persuasion, enacted through expert networks, sustained by narratives of best practice, and mediated by the rationalistic lore of experimental evaluation. If the structural adjustment efforts of the multilateral agencies during the 1980s and 1990s were notable for spawning a new actor-class of money doctors, the subsequent rise of "knowledge bank" functions seems to have given rise to a emergent class of model peddlers. In the structural-adjustment era, "conditionalities" referred to those notoriously blunt financial instruments that compelled debt-stricken countries to follow the neoliberal macroeconomic policy advice of the Washington Consensus agencies; today, this same term, endowed with new microsocial meanings, is more likely to be invoked as an ostensibly benign principle of social-policy design. The rise of CCTs, in this sense, may reflect a shift to new registers of transnational power and influence—favoring technocratic persuasion over financial coercion, and evidence-based learning and experimental incrementalism over systemic reform and "shock treatment."

But there are continuities here as well. Both structural adjustment and the emergent modalities of model power can be seen as expressions of policymaking hubris, and both have their limits. The structural adjustment programs pursued by the IMF and World Bank were undeniably associated with transformative social, economic, and institutional effects, but they did not simply remake the world in their own image (see Mosley, Harrigan, and Toye 1995; Stiglitz 2002); multilaterally sanctioned policy models may likewise display a global reach, shaping the coordinates (and sometimes providing the currency) for policy debates in contexts far and wide, but this should not be taken to mean that they are drivers of some quasi-automated form of policymaking predetermination and unilateral global convergence. Despite appearances to the contrary, this is most certainly not a realm of technocratic certainty. The reach of global policy models continues to exceed their grasp; "in the wild" they have mutated in some surprising ways, speaking to the limits of multilateral power as well as its potency. Furthermore, the fact that they are often incubated and propagated under crisis conditions means that dreams of friction-free, paradigm-affirming evolution-ary reproduction are routinely frustrated, while unruly and paradigm-bending mutations are also commonplace. The ascendancy of global policy models, like CCTs, should therefore not be read as a prelude to the establishment of a social-policy monoculture on a planetary scale, but it arguably does call at-tention to new terrains and registers of policy formation, transformation, and contestation.

In this respect, the CCT phenomenon also indexes emerging spatialities of (social) policymaking, which are being shaped simultaneously by multilateral agencies and cosmopolitan networks, by national reformers (re)positioning their (globally self-conscious) interventions on the shifting terrain of "experi-mentality," and by a host of local agencies, activists, and advocates, mobilizing around (and against) what have become proving grounds and testbeds for sys-tem change (Peck and Theodore 2015). With reference to the transnational trav-els and translations of CCT models, this chapter explores some of the theoretical implications of these emergent forms of fast-policy mobility and mutation. It begins with a consideration of the nature of model power in this fast-moving field of policy development, examining how the CCT model was made and mo-bilized, before turning to the question of the less-than-ruly mutations of this model "in the wild," across and beyond Latin America.

Model Power

What makes a policy model a *model*, as opposed to a promising experiment or indeed a humble case? The word "model" is itself appropriately polysemic, but in a manner that directs attention to some of the ways in which policy models are understood, how they function, and what effects they (are assumed to) have. The *Oxford English Dictionary* lists several definitions of "model," a number of which can be considered apt.[1] First, in its most elemental sense, a model is a "represen-tation of structure," sometimes a "set of designs (plans, elevations, sections, etc.) for a projected building or other structure." It refers, in this respect, to a set of constituent relations of a functioning system, which by implication possesses a certain mutual coherence or internal logic (as a potentially free-standing struc-ture). The thing "holds up." But it is also a *projection*, a design, a plan. The word denotes not only some original construction (structure); it explicitly signals the potential (indeed desire for) *re*construction on another site. And it is here that the notion of a model as a physical structure comprising interlocking compo-nents blends with the more abstract meaning of the term. In the *OED*'s words, a model can also be "a simplified or idealized description or conception of a partic-ular system, situation, or process . . . that is put forward as a basis for theoretical or empirical understanding, or for calculations, predictions, etc.; a conceptual or mental representation of something." (Here, the model takes the form of a *theoretical* projection, a rendering of an idealized vision, or more formally, an axiomatic system.) Policy models echo these meanings in their invocation of coherent, functional designs, designs that are readily stylized and systematized, but often also idealized. They stand in as codified representations of working models, comprising logically interrelated components and usually resting on some proof of concept in an original form or location.

Second, it follows that a model is not only a logically coherent system, but an aspirational projection of that system. Received models combine an *in situ* logic with a claim to *ex situ* salience. Models, in other words, are jointly constituted through internal features and external referents; their inside presumes and indeed works on an outside: the presence of a model implies a hinterland of influence, a following audience, a field of reception. And here, the term abuts an additional set of meanings, where "model" designates "an object of [or pattern for] imitation," which for the *OED* signifies "a person, or a work, that is proposed or adopted for imitation." This definition, of course, implies worth (indeed positive valuation), in the sense of "a person or thing eminently worthy of imitation; a perfect exemplar of some excellence." Often the object of a distant, admiring gaze, a model will seek and find attention, but rather like in its catwalk manifestations may display qualities beyond the realistic reach of the onlooking population. (The "person employed to wear clothes for display" is of course hired, presented, and paraded for this express purpose.) The model, in other words, should be without flaws; it should be close to perfection. Policy models, too, are objects of desire, and they are fundamentally *relational* constructions in the sense that the path to *recognized* model status implies the enrollment of an (approving and aspirational) audience and the designation of a space of projection. The policy model not only demands attention but commands admiration; it is looked (up) to as a source of inspiration, even if absolute replication is understood to be practically unattainable.

Finally, the word "model" is associated with more specialized meanings that also resonate with the notion of a policy model. In evolutionary biology, "model" denotes a condition of "mimetic resemblance," referring to similarities in behavior, scent, or appearance between species—usually acquired for self-defense or mutual protection—on the part of inhabitants of similar locations. These forms of mimicry can be defensive (as in the case of camouflage), or in some instances more aggressive (where the imitative deception reflects ulterior motives). For model followers, there is some safety in the policymaking crowd, as well, in the sense that a degree of (political) risk often attends to the status of an outlier; support and sustenance derives from being part of a fashionable "movement," especially one with the imprimatur of experts, which is deemed to be a "best" practice or an intervention located at the leading edge of reform. It is typical for "original" policy models to be celebrated for their convention-challenging boldness (as institutional first movers), while following such a model actually attenuates the degree of risk and uncertainty for downstream adopters (who can learn lessons, borrow legitimacy, and maybe even share the limelight). A second more technical meaning of model originates from social psychology, where it refers to a particular form of "imitative behavior," particularly where the model in question is associated with rewards, which experimental studies have linked to the adoption of patterns of *desired* imitative behavior. Those policies that seek to govern provident and desired forms of conduct, especially in potentially unruly populations, may indeed *model* that conduct through signaling, sanctions, or incentives, pairing an idealized design with a strategy for engineering behavioral modification.

The "behavioral turn" in antipoverty policymaking, epitomized by CCTs, self-consciously operates in this spirit (Aber and Rawlings 2011); sharing with behavioral economics and motivational psychology a predilection for experimental program designs, the rigorous testing of stimulus-response relationships, and the deployment of quasi-clinical trials.[2] There is a corresponding deference to the most pristine of experiments and meticulously documented test cases, the integrity of which is taken as a prerequisite for "scaling up" social-protection programs (see Moreno-Dodson 2005; Steele, Fernando, and Weddikkara 2008). The aura of scientism that pervades these performative expressions of evidence-based policymaking reciprocally secures the expert status of model architects, advocates, and evaluators, underpinning those knowledge claims that are made on the basis of (measurable) efficiency, effectiveness, impact, and reproducibility. But first a model must be stabilized, and conditions appropriate not only for its (local) existence *but for its extralocal salience* must be secured. Here, the story of the origins and spread of CCTs itself stands as something of a model.

It is no exaggeration to say that Mexico's CCT program (Progresa, as it was originally called) was born as a model. But the "iconic" status that it would eventually achieve, to borrow the World Bank's munificent phrase (Fiszbein et al. 2009: 36), would need to be secured through a combination of astute technocratic design and enduring political will. The case for radical reform of the Mexican social-assistance system was pressed in the midst of the peso crisis of 1994–95, when it was championed by Santiago Levy (a U.S.-trained economist and senior official in the ministry of finance, previously a World Bank consultant on poverty issues) and José Gómez de León (a demographer, director of the National Population Council, and confidant of then-president Ernesto Zedillo).

Fulsome reconstructions of the rationale, justification, and decisive steps that were taken to build and secure Mexico's pioneering CCT program have since been published by Levy. *Progress against Poverty*, Levy's (2006) book, is effectively presented as a model-making manual. Here, three (pre)conditions are held to have been decisive: first, the entire approach was (presented as) rooted in a reading of recent "analytical advances" concerning the multidimensional determinants of poverty that had been achieved by economists, sociologists, and nutritionists, which provided the "analytical backbone" for Progresa, including the management of risk aversion, the containment of dependency, and the active engagement of beneficiaries—all rendered in technical terms; second, deliberate attention was paid to the "lessons" from previous Mexican experiences, most of which were deemed to be negative (inadequate targeting of extreme poverty, inefficiencies associated with the use of food subsidies, proneness to bureaucratic corruption and political manipulation, even though evidence for the latter was not only unscientific but "subjective"); and third, those involved knowingly "use[d] the crisis as a motivation for change," as an opportunity for systemic reform, sold as a single, bold leap to world best practice, and designed to bring costs under control in anticipation of long-run budgetary pressure (Levy 2006: 10, 14, 15).

On Levy's (2006: 13–14) telling, the refinement of a rigorous *conceptual* definition of the CCT model preceded not only practical but even political considerations:

> [The] challenge . . . was to bring academic researchers' analytical insights and [an] individual nation's best practices together in a unified conceptual framework in order to incorporate that knowledge systematically in the design of the poverty program . . . While the economic crisis created the immediate motivation for change—and the beginning of a new administration naturally created a political climate that facilitated change—the accumulation of empirical evidence, administrative experience, and analytical arguments was fundamental in gradually persuading the members of the Cabinet to make substantive adjustments to the existing food subsidy and related poverty programs.

This amounted to an extreme form of technocratic policymaking, prosecuted in the teeth of opposition not only from civil-society groups but also from the leadership of the government's own social-policy ministry (Teichman 2008, 2009). Exaggerated faith was placed in the kind of economistic technoscience favored by the World Bank, for whom Levy had worked as a professional economist-cum-policy analyst, an organization later credited for "generously provid[ing] technical advice" during the design, piloting, and startup phases of the program (Levy 2006: 114). Crucially, however, the involvement of the multilateral development agencies (in particular, the World Bank and the IADB), while formative, was not to be rendered politically legible in the form of a large-scale loan, notwithstanding the severe financial pressures under which the Mexican government was operating at the time. In an instance of mandarin-class bureaucratic understatement, Levy (2006: 114) would later explain that "it was not deemed convenient to obtain international funding for the program [in] 1996–97 [because] such financing would have added yet one more controversial aspect to what was already a fairly significant change in poverty policy, perhaps giving the impression that the program was the result of a mandate or an adjustment program agreed upon with international financial institutions" (see also Teichman 2007; Dion 2010).

This said, Progresa was in many respects a World Bank/IADB–style project in all but name, since in its rationale and design the program reflected ascendant currents in expert opinion across the multilateral agencies, albeit mostly at the level of conceptual principle rather than actually existing practice. In as far as Progresa really was a bold experiment, this was because it sought to capture, and then to act decisively on, a still-emergent expert consensus—what might be called "pre-best practice." Retrospective accounts, however, continue to position the experiment out in front of global best practice, which not coincidentally confers leadership status on an inner circle of elite decision-makers in Mexico City. According to one of those closely involved,

> [The Progresa] proposal was received with great skepticism and opposition by some Mexican policy makers as well as by international agencies. In Mexico, some policy makers saw the proposal as a "neo-liberal attempt to eliminate subsidies for the poor" and as "an imposition by international agencies." Political parties were concerned about a federal program that would "give out money," presumably with electoral and political motives. International agencies thought it operationally and politically unfeasible. (Rodriguez 2008: 288)

The international agencies, one can perhaps conclude, did not, however, find the Progresa proposal to be *conceptually* incoherent. Its model-like rationality would not have been questioned by policy experts in Washington, D.C., and indeed, the robustness of this rationality—that "analytical backbone"—was the basis on which the audacious experiment was defended during the protracted debate in Mexico City around the program's rationale (Levy 2006; Rodriguez 2008).

A key strategy of those championing Progresa had been to focus "discussions as much as possible on objective and technical elements," bringing in "well-known national and international experts" to bolster the case for controversial aspects of the plan, in order to technocratically settle matters "where there had been differences of opinion" (Rodriguez 2008: 297). Decisively, it would later transpire, a state-of-the-art evaluation was built into the program at the design stage, based on a randomized control-group methodology and managed by the well-regarded Washington, D.C., evaluation house the International Food Policy Research Institute, or IFPRI (see Adato and Hoddinott 2010). Program-design components, such as the development of an index of marginality and the specification of targeting and (random) assignment procedures were designed and enacted with nothing short of scientific rigor, even as "critics, particularly leaders of civil society organizations, expressed moral revulsion at a program evaluation process that involved the use of a control group (10 million Mexicans) who received no Progresa support [on the basis of a purely statistical rationale, so that their] progress could be compared with those who did" (Teichman 2009: 79). The denial of aid to millions of the rural poor in the midst of a macroeconomic crisis, whose extreme poverty had been meticulously verified as a prelude to assignment to the off-program control group, was deemed a price worth paying, evidently, "to test whether the design hypothesis was correct . . . to quantify the impacts of the programme [and] to determine whether design guidelines were being followed and identify if observed outcomes were attributable to implementation or design aspects" (Rodriguez 2008: 293). However, this apparent violation of the principle of equipoise—the axiom that populations should not be denied access to beneficial interventions for the purposes of research, an ethical litmus test for approving randomized trials on populations in need (see Kukla 2007)—seems to have raised few, if any, red flags from the multilateral development agencies, which began vigorously promoting this approach to the evaluation (and de facto authorization) of social-protection programs.

Some would no doubt argue that the greater good was in fact served, since the first results of the IFPRI evaluation—which were interpreted in largely positive terms—became available on the eve of the transition from the presidency of Zedillo to that of Vicente Fox in 2000. The newly elected President Fox was persuaded (by Santiago Levy, whose services he was to retain) not only to preserve the program, but to expand it. Rebranded as Oportunidades, what would become the country's flagship social program was extended to cities and other rural regions, eventually reaching one-fourth of the Mexican population and becoming a celebrated test case-cum-lesson for "scaling up success" (Cohen and Easterly, 2009; UNDP, 2011). The IADB initiated large-scale funding for the expanded program in 2001, which was soon the object of lavish praise in nearly every quarter of the multilateral policy community:

> [I]n July 2003 an important event took place in Mexico City. In the presence of President Fox, the media, and policymakers from Latin America, the president of the Inter-American Development Bank, the vice president for Latin America of the

World Bank, and the Secretary General of the United Nations Economic Commission for Latin America [all] recognized the importance of Progresa-Oportunidades in alleviating poverty in Mexico and called the program a valuable model for other countries. (Levy 2006: 113)

When James Wolfensohn finished his term as president of the World Bank, in July 2006, one of his first acts as eponymous head of the Brookings Institution's new Wolfensohn Center for Development was to commission Santiago Levy to write the definitive account of the Progresa/Oportunidades story. In the foreword to Levy's book, Wolfensohn (2006: vii) rather generously—but certainly not innocently—chose to characterize the Mexican CCT as a "home-grown [program], based on solid economic and social analysis," indeed one based on an arrestingly "simple idea," magnanimously (but again not innocently) credited to Levy himself. Wolfensohn's (2006: ix–x) hope was that "this volume can serve . . . as a model of effective design of large-scale sustainable poverty reduction programs," since the Progresa/Oportunidades story amply demonstrated that "*in addition to the technical aspects of a poverty program*, institutional elements that can ensure adequate scale and continuity are equally indispensable for effective poverty alleviation" (emphasis added). As an experiment that worked, the Mexican experience stood as a shining example of rigorous model building, with a purpose. The scientific rationales and rigorous evaluations that had defined this experiment, and which have since sustained it through several transfers of presidential power, were the means to an end of a form of technocratic (re)production effectively "insulated" from politics (see Teichman 2008). At the same time, such models enact a form of high politics. As Paul Romer (2009: 127) has bluntly stated, the "motivation for the [Progresa] evaluation was political, not scientific."

Unruly Mutations

"The widespread distribution of published reports of PROGRESA's outcomes," Sugiyama (2011: 254) notes, "furthered the notion that Mexico had developed a model social program." The model had apparently found its moment. But nothing about this was accidental, of course. The IABD had discreetly funded IFPRI's evaluation work on Progresa, further cementing close relationships between the project's technocratic leadership and the bank (Teichman 2007), and the evaluation itself had been addressed as much to external audiences as to internal policymaking constituencies. Even though the IFPRI team relocated to Mexico for three years to manage the project (which far from a third-party evaluation entailed the co-manangement of the design and rollout of the program, in order to satisfy the randomized-control methodology), the first presentation of the evaluation results took place not in Mexico City, but in Washington, D.C.

Little wonder, then, that Aber and Rawlings (2011) call attention to the ascendancy of evaluation-driven and evidence-based policymaking—especially involving randomized trials—as one of three decisive factors behind the globalization of CCTs. Long maligned as "gray" literature, destined for the back drawers of ministry filing cabinets, evaluation research has propelled from the shadows to the spotlight, emerging as a significant model-building arena in its own right. Positive evaluation results, especially where these meet the stern tests of statistical validity, have become an international currency of sorts for model builders and peddlers. A model "story" articulated only through (often self-interested) narratives is easily dismissed as merely anecdotal or a form of special pleading; if a compelling story can be combined with the hard science of randomized-trial evidence, it has a chance of gaining real credibility and traction. Progresa's state-of-the-art evaluation not only preserved the program's longevity (especially at the vulnerable moment when the incoming Fox administration had both a clear mandate and a presentational need to break with the Zedillo inheritance), it effectively secured international-model status for the rebadged Oportunidades program, which was (re)born as a *validated* best practice.

Randomized-control trials have rapidly become the "gold standard" of program evaluation in the field of social protection. By randomizing participation, evaluators seek to minimize selection bias within a target population, allowing causal variables and their effects to be isolated and measured. As IFPRI and World Bank researchers explain, "Program evaluation of this kind serves several functions: it determines with confidence the effectiveness of program design and the efficiency of the investment, it identifies design and implementation issues requiring change or improvement, and it illuminates how people understand and react to the program, including, for example why beneficiaries do or do not respond to program incentives" (Maluccio, Adato, and Skoufias 2010: 26). Randomized control trials, in other words, are thought to be especially well suited for evaluating programs aimed at achieving behavioral modifications among a target population. Through randomized experiments, the "nudge" that CCT programs provide to the poor through the enforcement of conditionalities can be precisely quantified, allowing these technocratic instruments of persuasion to be fine-tuned, and the return on social-protection "investments" to be closely calculated.

This kind of experimental design was literally embedded into Progresa-Oportunidades, initially as a way to insulate the program from the threat of political "interference." (Note that this maneuver positions the imperatives of social-policy technoscience "above" domestic politics.) Its longer-term impact, though, has been to propel the program into the center of international debates over social protection, while also contributing to the "culture of evaluation" that has enveloped the design and implementation of CCTs worldwide (Fiszbein et al. 2009: 94–5). Aber and Rawlings (2011: 7, 10) state that CCTs "are now arguably the best evaluated development initiative in the Global South," their rapid global spread having been

> fueled by [the] compelling design features [of the paradigmatic programs], their promising evaluation results and the emphasis on knowledge sharing within the CCT and welfare reform community. This experience provides an example of the speed with which innovation can be adopted and scaled up, following a dynamic demonstration effect, with a solid grounding in evidence.

However, even as it has served to accelerate the rate of adoption of CCT programs by low- and moderate-income countries, the use of randomized-control trials in the real-world "laboratory" of antipoverty policymaking imposes both direction *and limits* on the nature and scope of policy experimentation.

The ethics of constituting a control group in the context of an antipoverty development initiative aside, experimental evaluation design is an exceedingly costly approach to program assessment. As randomized-control trials have become the common currency in international policy debates, their high implementation costs impose implicit entry barriers for participation in the global social-protection debate. Since it costs, in effect, several million dollars to ask a question using a randomized control trial methodology, only the institutions with the deepest pockets get to determine the questions. This creates a macro selection bias in favor of orthodox lines of policy development. Evaluations without a significant experimental-design component are also prone to be treated as "softer" and "less scientific," being seen as subject to political manipulation or overselling, and suspect in terms of innate evaluative rigor. Those programs that have been evaluated using randomized-control procedures, on the other hand, are enthusiastically promoted to external audiences by the multilateral development agencies and leading evaluation houses, as best-practice models *with papers*. This establishes, populates, and incentivizes a field of immutable social-policy models, accredited traveling truths, the most potent of which cut path-dependent trajectories through emerging hinterlands of emulation.

Through these means, local experiments are transformed into models capable of acting on the world. Such processes of expert isomorphism, realized in this case largely through the medium of randomized trials, has dynamized, structured, and circumscribed the debate over cash-transfer program models. Experimental evaluation designs seek to measure the efficacy of specific programmatic components, literally testing the properties of the model, in laboratory-like or near closed-system conditions, where these effects can be (supposedly) isolated from exogenous factors. This creates incentives for policymakers to focus instrumentally on those program-design elements that are suitable for experimental manipulation, such as targeting formulas, delivery mechanisms, treatment dosages, outreach methods, and the like, channeling policy development along pathways of incremental adjustment within a "design universe" (pre)structured by first-mover models. Not only does this tend to naturalize certain forms (and directions) of technocratic reproduction, it further contributes to the sense that the "big questions" concerning the philosophy and design of CCT programs are firmly settled. Searching questions regarding the efficacy and ethics of conditionality, for example, as a central and necessary feature of social-protection programs, are systemically bracketed out. Failing that, they can become effectively smothered (or forgotten) in relation to what can rapidly become dominant patterns of global practice. This very much describes the way in which CCTs made their rapid transition from local model to global norm, with evaluation results accrediting their "success," and their defining components (means testing, social targeting, and strict conditionality) rendered amenable for replication.

If the rise of evaluation science is the first driver of transformation in social-welfare policy identified by Aber and Rawlings (2011), the second concerns the use of incentives in program design, a trend that reflects both the behavioral turn in economic thinking and the political embrace of approaches that "responsibilize" the poor. And just as the behavioral turn has played a part in unifying economic theory, breaking down—in tandem with neoliberalization—some of the old distinctions between a "mainstream" economics ostensibly applicable in the global North and "development" economics for the South (Naím 2000), so too have the policymaking boundaries between different "welfare worlds" (cf. Esping-Andersen 1990) become increasingly porous, as policy discourses and debates associated with the global North and South have become increasingly interrelated, combined, and mutually referential. So it has become increasingly common to position developments in, say, U.S. social and labor-market policy (like the transition to the Temporary Assistance for Needy Families program or the rise of Earned Income Tax Credits) as part of the same "movement" as CCTs, with the Latin American experiments assuming the vanguard, as a moderately disruptive technology. The unifying "focus on a 'hand-up and not a hand-out' has broad political appeal," note Aber and Rawlings (2011: 5), one that has "crossed traditional party lines and is reflected in political discussions and popular debate in both the North and South calling for an emphasis on work, on investing in human capital, on temporary assistance and on co-responsibility between the state and its citizens."

Not coincidentally, such interventions also invoke, hail, and work on an ostensibly universal economic subject, a rational actor duly enabled to act on her own to escape poverty once appropriate adjustments have been made to the structure of opportunity costs, the patterning of incentives, and the calibration of risks and rewards. Among the notable features of the rise of CCTs, in this context, has been a certain leveling of the experimental playing field, as the global South is reimagined as a potential site of positive programming lessons and not simply as a location of wicked problems or a "receiving region" for made-in-Washington solutions. The agencies of the Washington Consensus remain deeply involved, of course, but in a situation in which the hubris of unilateral imposition has given way to a more facilitative posture, one that emphasizes the coproduction of expertise with governmental and nongovernmental actors in the South, the enabling of "horizontal" learning across sites and policy fields, and studied deference to well-documented impact evaluations and evidence of "what works." In this era of (supposedly) "pro-poor" policymaking, moreover, the language of the incentives paradigm yields obvious presentational advantages: what defines incentive-based programs like CCTs is that they *pay* for *good* behavior, in contrast to the negative undertones of workfare-style programs (with their penalties or "sanctions" for "noncompliance"). This said, both negative sanctions and positive incentives work on a behavioralist "deficiency model" of the poor, since both seek to adjust inappropriate behaviors (dependency, underinvestment in schooling, poor hygiene, etc.) in order to mold more productive and more responsible subjects. CCTs, though, represent the positive face of this process.

The third driver of transformation in globalizing social policy identified by Aber and Rawlings (2011) is the shift in policy thinking toward approaches focused on human capital. This involves what they portray as a historic reconciliation of the imperatives of humanitarian aid and short-term assistance on the one hand, with the goals of long-term economic growth on the other. CCTs are held to achieve this by fusing cash assistance with future-oriented investments in the children of the poor (see Jenson 2010). It is recognized that "CCTs are highly ambitious," seeking as they do to "foster human capital accumulation among the young as a means to breaking the inter-generational cycle of poverty" (Aber and Rawlings 2011: 6), conceptualizing this as a multidimensional problem and endeavoring to mobilize positive synergies between education, nutrition, and health. With their distinctive emphasis on experimental practice, however, CCTs are credited with "pushing the boundaries of new thinking," as a programming technology positioned at "the threshold of the global policy debate" (Aber and Rawlings 2011: 7, 1). These boundaries are being pushed in such a way, however, as to *consolidate* new social-policy orthodoxies, certainly not to upend them.

CCTs, in this respect, can be seen as carriers of a new policy rationality, one that is continuously in the making in the style of an emergent form of deliber-

Table 1. Conceptions of social assistance, before and after CCTs

	Temporality	Philosophy	Tools	Barriers	Goals
Welfare	Assistance in times of need	Entitlement: social responsibility for the poor; "handouts"	Entitlement-based transfers	Dependency culture	Poverty alleviation; social redistribution
Postwelfare	Activation through targeted interventions	Reciprocity: partnership with the poor; "hand up"	Incentive-based transfers	Access to information, incentives	Exits from poverty, economic growth and human capital

Source: developed from Aber and Rawlings (2011)

ative technocracy. They not only encapsulate the "new thinking" on safety-net policy (see Table 1), which emphasizes social promotion over social protection, responsibilities over rights, and long-term investment over short-term amelioration, but they proactively substantiate an aspirational project that remains on the threshold of realization. This means that while the new generation of social-policy programs are globally diffused technologies, they are far from mature technologies. It is here, for all the uninterrupted soft sell of the best-practice industry, for all the debilitating barriers to entry and selection biases created by the "big science" evaluation regime, for all this paradigm-building momentum, that unscripted surprises continue to occur, new mutations appear in the wild, and alternative or vernacular models find their way into the limelight.

In its multiple roles as a funder, evaluator, and technical assistance provider, the World Bank has been directly engaged the purposeful pump-priming and rapid diffusion of this model of social protection, and it has been intimately involved in not only steering the course but managing the ecosystem of CCT experimentation. In supporting CCT experiments in approximately forty countries, including providing $5.4 billion since FY 2001 for the development and scaling up of thirty-nine CCT initiatives in twenty-two nations (Grosh 2011), the World Bank is positioned as the de facto principal global broker of CCT "best practice," even as (for understandable ideological reasons) this is typically represented in terms of an enabling, facilitating, or clearinghouse function. In this role as an especially proactive intermediator, the bank not only finances preferred lines of policy experimentation, it hosts international conferences; it bankrolls practitioner networks such as the South-to-South learning network, the "International CCT Community of Practice," and others for midlevel and senior program managers; and it has published countless programming briefs, technical reports, policy presentations, and blog posts advising governments on matters pertaining to CCT policy design, implementation, and evaluation.

Across these many channels, the World Bank's policy advice has tended to coagulate around three poles of CCT practice, which effectively define the pre-approved reform universe as well as the field of experimentation around CCTs: First (and foremost) the Mexican Oportunidades program, with its sophisticated targeting mechanisms, reliance on unambiguous conditionalities, and inbuilt evaluation infrastructure; second, the newer and relatively small-scale Chile Solidario program, which provides time-limited, highly targeted, and intensive interventions that are strictly contracted and closely managed by social workers; and third, Brazil's Bolsa Familia, which despite being the largest CCT program in the world credited for measurable reductions in both poverty and economic inequality, has a rather more questionable reputation—in orthodox circles—for having adopted a "softer" approach to conditionalities and targeting. World Bank researchers summarize these merits of these three CCTs as follows:

> What really makes Mexico's program iconic is the successive waves of data collected to evaluate its impact, the placement of these data in the public domain, and the hundreds of papers and thousands of references to them that this easy access has generated. . . . Brazil's CCT provides something of an interesting contrast to the Mexican case in various respects. [It] takes a softer, more gradual tack on conditions [and] puts a shade more emphasis on redistribution than on human capital formation. Also, unlike the Mexican program, the Brazilian programs did not explicitly incorporate impact evaluations in their design. . . . Chile Solidario . . . differs notably from classic CCT programs by customizing its conditions. Families initially work intensely with social workers to understand actions that could help them get out of extreme poverty, and then they commit to action plans that become the household-specific conditions of the benefit. . . . Chile Solidario is thus far a model unto itself, although other programs are moving to emulate it to a degree (Fiszbein et al. 2009: 36–9).

Not quite seen as a distinct model in and of itself, Bolsa Familia is typically positioned in the awkward space alongside Oportunidades and Chile Solidario, two "model programs" that stress strong conditionalities and social obligations, and that are most frequently presented as appropriate for emulation. In a sense, Bolsa Familia is too large to ignore, but the paucity of officially sanctioned evaluation evidence, the decentralized administration of the program, and what is seen as a "loose" approach to conditionalities combine to deny the program favored-model status in World Bank circles. The bank's definitive report on Bolsa Familia aptly travels under the unassuming title of *The Nuts and Bolts of Brazil's Bolsa Familia Program* (Lindert et al. 2007). As a leading figure on the international CCT evaluation scene later reflected, "*Nuts and bolts* was kind of self-effacing. 'We're just putting the thing together, and this is how it basically works.' There was no Model, *capital-M*, selling of it."[3] Crucially, what the Brazilian government chose to do with their "non-model" would depart from World Bank orthodoxy on the definitive terrain of conditionalities. In Brazil the first C of CCTs has a rather different meaning: a member of the World Bank team in Brasília explained it this way, "[here], the poor are poor because of a historical process of social exclusion, and we owe them a debt. That's fundamental in Brazilian thinking: they have citizens' rights [but] have not always had access to those rights, and we have to pay this debt back to the poor. . . . Their view is . . . if I have a child not attending school [but on the] program, are we going to take it [the allowance] away? Is my first response a penalty or a punishment? No, our response should be to go and investigate, to use it as a flag—use it as a flag for *more care*. For them, they would say that the C, as in CCT, is for care. [The idea is] not condition right away, it's not a contract right away."[4]

While it may not meet with the approval of World Bank economist-evaluators, Brazil's approach of combining soft conditionalities with social rights has resonated with program planners in sub-Saharan Africa, where large segments of the population live in abject poverty and where service delivery systems are, by and large, inadequate. Here, capacities for targeting and monitoring are likewise underdeveloped. Correspondingly, CCT programs do not stress conditionalities—partly out of choice, partly out of necessity—and there typically is no penalty for noncompliance (Garcia and Moore 2012). Across Africa's emerging CCT frontier, the centralized and tightly managed Oportunidades program has notably less traction. Instead, Brazil has proved to be a source of more prosaic and practical lessons, as well as a different kind of model for what might evolve into less conditional, rights-based CCTs. In this vein, Guy Standing (2008: 18) argues, "Even in Latin America, the desirability of the extensive conditionality imposed by [CCTs] has been called into question, which may prompt policymakers to conclude that a move towards less conditionality would be a more efficient and equitable way to go. The complexity of requiring potential beneficiaries to prove they are poor and vulnerable, and to demonstrate regular attendance at schools and clinics . . . is surely off-putting for people cowed by poverty and chronic insecurity." As a relatively late adopter of CCTs, Africa could potentially be a proving ground for alternative approaches, approaches that are not simply "suboptimal" in relation to the preferred models from Latin America, but which effectively redefine cash-transfer practice en route (see Ferguson, 2010).

Faced with extraordinarily high levels of poverty and social distress, a coalition of civil society organizations in Namibia sought to develop one such alternative model of social protection centered on *un*conditional cash transfers. Akin to citizen's income, Basic Income Grants (BIG) of 100 Namibian dollars ($11.90 U.S.) per month were disbursed to all residents of the settlement of Otjivero, where unemployment exceeds 70 percent and more than four in ten children are malnourished (Krahe 2009). While a randomized trial was ruled out as "ethically problematic," a nonrandomized evaluation of the two-year BIG pilot nevertheless revealed promising results: malnutrition plummeted, school attendance and health-clinic visits rose, and residents increasingly sought employment opportunities in outlying areas—outcomes that were achieved without the requirements imposed by conditionalities.[5] Yet the findings from this program have garnered little attention from the World Bank or other multilateral development agencies, and the Namibian program remains something of an anomaly, if not an ideological orphan, in international debates regarding the future of social-protection policy. The BIG stands as a case of largely unrequited model building, the relative isolation of which stems not from inferior performance but because it challenges the expert consensus in cash-transfer policy, which remains rooted in technocratic approaches to policy design predicated on means-testing, targeting, and, of course, conditionalities.

Countercultural experiments in unconditional cash transfers, such as the Namibian BIG, may indeed be exceptions that underscore the more general rule. But it would be premature to foreclose the possibility of mutation *beyond* the CCT consensus. In fact, the ILO has been taking up this cause in its evolving program on the "social-protection floor." This relatively progressive current in the multilateral policy debate diverges from the "liberal-residualist" approach of the World Bank, where targeting and conditionality remain axiomatic (if not dogmatic) principles, while at the same time transcending the accommodationalist approach to the "capabilities" and "social investment" paradigm favored by the OECD (cf. Jenson 2010; Mahon 2011). The Bachelet report on the social-protection floor diplomatically acknowledges the achievements of Oportunidades, Chile Solidario, and Bolsa Familia, but more assertively insists that the debate around conditionalities is "ongoing," while recognizing a "diversity of opinions and mixed evidence" on CCTs. It concludes that the conditionality "debate remains open," a position echoed on the progressive flank of OECD deliberations on social assistance (ILO 2011: 82). The more unvarnished position on the Global Social Protection floor website is that "*human rights are unconditional,* and as social security is a human right, it is therefore unacceptable to deny it through the enforcement of conditions."[6]

Thanks to these and other interventions, there may yet be surprising twists and turns in the global pathways of CCT experimentation. Despite the fact that only a fraction of the massive global "experiment" in cash-transfer programming has been devoted to testing the viability and effectiveness of progressive others to the dominant CCT model—such as unconditional transfers and basic-income initiatives—a perverse consequence of the single-minded focus on conditionality may have been to beg, by exclusion, questions around heterodox alternatives. Whatever the long-term fate of the ILO's social-protection initiative, this calls attention to the fact that policy development via model building remains a somewhat uncertain and inescapably political process. Heavily resourced attempts at technocratic (fore)closure will doubtless continue, and they will also continue to shape social-policy norms, but all such attempts at formatting, templating, and prescription are destined to remain incomplete and contradictory, no matter how asymmetrical the accompanying power relations. Model power may be formidable, but it is not boundless. What the World Bank calls the CCT "wave" may not yet have generated a substantial backwash, but there are unmistakable early indications of divergent eddies and countercurrents (see Table 2). For all of the evaluation scientism that has propelled the unprecedented global wave of CCT experiments, it has not been possible to maintain laboratory-like conditions of "closure" as these programs have entered the wild.

Conclusion. Beyond Conditionality?

Conditional cash transfers are a prime example of especially fast-traveling, if not hypermobile, policies. Realized through an international infrastructure of purposive experimentation and technocratic persuasion, buttressed by the favored evaluation technology of the randomized-control trial, and brokered to increasingly receptive nation-states, the status of CCTs as programs "that work" has been firmly secured in global debates on social policy. Sophisticated (and costly) experimental designs have facilitated the construction of a "postpolitical" veneer around CCTs, the bipartisan appeal of which can be traced to their intriguingly kaleidoscopic character: conservatives see in them a rejection of the something-for-nothing welfare ethos, while liberals place value on progress in

Table 2. Conditional cash transfers: in the laboratory and in the wild

	Model power	Unruly mutations
Ideational	Behavioral economics New paternalism	Social investment Basic income
Ideological	Late-neoliberal reformism Third-way pragmatism	Rights-based social assistance Social protection floor
Institutional	Technocratic propagation Paradigm-affirming experimentation	Countervailing practice Paradigm-disrupting cases

realizing social rights for marginalized populations. As a result, CCT models have come to define the innovative frontier in social policy across much of the global South and in parts of the global North (Peck and Theodore 2010), foreshortening policy-development phases and often preempting meaningful debate. These political valences, coupled with the formidable resources (in both dollars and expertise) of the multilateral organizations, mean that the CCT wave has had the benefit of a strong institutional and ideological tailwind, meeting relatively few serious obstacles in its rapid transnational diffusion. Needless to say, the policy would never have been likely to surge from just two or three to nearly fifty countries in the space of a little more than a decade had it been ideologically countercultural or seriously disruptive in political or macroeconomic terms. Built for speedy implementation and badged with expert approval, these models were *made* to travel.

Through the global diffusion of CCTs, the principle of behaviorally focused interventions, which at least at some level presumes that "corrective" action is both required and legitimate, has been consolidated as a postwelfare axiom across the political mainstream. In this context, fast-moving policy models also exert more subtle forms of normative influence by establishing parameters around "acceptable" policy options. In some cases, the propensity of best-practice models to arrive on the scene, almost fully formed, as policies that work (albeit somewhere else) can have the effect of forestalling, foreshortening, or completely circumventing processes of local deliberation, debate, and consensus-building around policy reform (Peck and Theodore, 2015). Indeed, even in those cases where imported policy models do not directly "format" local responses, they will often exert indirect effects by canalizing and prefiguring the terms of debate. Brazil may have been pursuing a *relatively* autonomous course as the architect and manager of its own regime of not-really-conditional cash transfers, but at the same time its approach is being increasingly "relativized," not least by the purveyors of authorized CCT expertise at the World Bank. Bolsa Familia duly becomes the least-loved corner of a triangular reform universe, with the "iconic" Oportunidades and the "compelling" Chile Solidario occupying the more favored corners (cf. Fiszbein et al. 2009). The effect of this triangulation strategy is not simply to lift the relatively modest Solidario program into a status of implied equivalence with the big-league players in Mexico and Brazil, it also tilts the field in favor of the two more strictly conditional schemes approved by the World Bank. In orthodox circles, there has been no squaring of this triangle through the elevation of Namibia's BIG or other *unconditional* cash transfer programs, despite their potential applicability elsewhere, although the ILO and others have more recently attempted to destabilize this premature consensus.

Despite the undeniable influence of the best-practice models backed by the multilateral development agencies and circulated through their distended networks of policy expertise, it would be incorrect to conclude that CCTs have been unilaterally remaking the social-policy world in their own image. There is certainly a tightly written and widely circulated script, but departures from the would-be frontal orthodoxy are routine, if not entirely predictable (Roy, this volume), and some threaten to rise to more-than-local significance. The CCT wave seems to be generating its own undertow, and the stubborn questions around unconditional cash assistance have refused to go away. These continue to animate a number of countercultural alternatives to the CCT, even as they remain largely sidelined within global policy debates. Meanwhile, unmet, real, and urgent needs demand alternatives that go beyond the newfound orthodoxy of targeted, temporary, and conditional social assistance, which has so clearly failed to reverse decades of immiseration. Sustaining the case for such alternatives will surely necessitate, however, quite different forms of model power.

NOTES

1. Accessed at http://www.oed.com.

2. See Heckhausen and Heckhausen (2008), Thaler and Sunstein (2008); cf. Ravallion (2009).

3. Evaluation manager, nonprofit research center, Washington, D.C., interviewed by Jamie Peck and Nik Theodore, May 2009.

4. Senior manager #1, World Bank Brasilia team, interviewed by Jamie Peck and Nik Theodore, May 2009.

5. Civil society representative, Windhoek, Namibia, interviewed by Nik Theodore, October 2009; senior manager, think tank, Windhoek, Namibia, interviewed by Nik Theodore, October 2009.

6. "Potential and Limitations of CCTs," at http://www.socialsecurityextension.org /gimi/gess/ShowTheme.do?tid=2845.

REFERENCES

Aber, Lawrence, and Laura B. Rawlings. 2011. "North-South Knowledge Sharing on Incentive-based Conditional Cash Transfer Programs." *Social Protection Discussion Paper* #1101. Washington, D.C.: World Bank.

Adato, Michelle, and John Hoddinott. 2010. *Conditional Cash Transfers in Latin America.* Baltimore: Johns Hopkins University Press.

Cohen, Jessica, and William Easterly, eds. 2009. *What Works in Development?* Washington, D.C.: Brookings Institution Press.

Dion, Michelle L. 2010. *Workers and Welfare.* Pittsburgh: University of Pittsburgh Press.

Dugger, Celia W. 2004. "Help Poor Be Pupils, not Wage Earners, Brazil Pays Parents." *New York Times*, January 3:A1.

Economist. 2010. "Give the Poor Money." *Economist*, July 31, 10.

Esping-Andersen, Gøsta. 1990. *The Three Worlds of Welfare Capitalism*. Princeton: Princeton University Press.

Ferguson, James. 2010. "The Uses of Neoliberalism." *Antipode* 41:1, 166–84.

Fiszbein, Ariel, and Norbert Schady, with Francisco H.G. Ferreira, Margaret Grosh, Niall Kelleher, Pedro Olinto, and Emmanuel Skoufias. 2009. *Conditional Cash Transfers*. Washington, D.C.: World Bank.

Garcia, Marito, and Charity M. T. Moore. 2012. *The Cash Dividend*. Washington, D.C.: World Bank.

Grosh, Margaret E. 2011. "CCTs: The Second Generation of Evaluations." Presentation at the workshop, CCTs: The Second Generation of Evaluations. World Bank. Washington, D.C., October 24–25.

Heckhausen, Jutta, and Heinz Heckhausen, eds. 2008. *Motivation and Action*. Cambridge: Cambridge University Press.

ILO (International Labour Office). 2011. *Social Protection Floor for a Fair and Inclusive Globalization*. Geneva: ILO.

Jenson, Jane. 2010. "Diffusing Ideas for After Neoliberalism: The Social Investment Perspective in Europe and Latin America." *Global Social Policy* 10:1, 59–84.

Krahe, Dialika. 2009. "A Basic Income Program in Otjivero." *Spiegel Online*, http://www.globalpolicy.org/component/content/article/211-development/48036-a-basic-income-program-in-otjivero.html.

Kukla, Rebecca. 2007. "Resituating the Principle of Equipoise: Justice and Access to Care in Non-Ideal Conditions." *Kennedy Institute of Ethics Journal* 17:3, 171–202.

Levy, Santiago. 2006. *Progress against Poverty*. Washington, D.C.: Brookings Institution Press.

Lindert, Kathy, Anja Linder, Jason Hobbs, and Bénédicte de la Brière. 2007. "The Nuts and Bolts of Brazil's Bolsa Família Program." Social Protection discussion paper 0709. World Bank. Washington, D.C.

Mahon, Rianne 2012. "Initial Reflections on the Social Protection Floor Initiative." *mimeo*. Waterloo, Ont.: Balsillie School of International Affairs.

Maluccio, John A., Michelle Adato, and Emmanuel Skoufias. 2010. "Combining Quantitative and Qualitative Research Methods for Evaluation of Conditional Cash Transfer Programs in Latin America." In *Conditional Cash Transfers in Latin America*, ed. Michelle Adato and John Hoddinott, 26–52. Baltimore: Johns Hopkins University Press.

Moreno-Dodson, Blanca, ed. 2005. *Reducing Poverty on a Global Scale*. Washington, D.C.: World Bank.

Mosley, Paul, Jane Harrigan, and John Toye. 1995. *Aid and Power*. New York: Routledge.

Naím, Moises. 2000. "Washington Consensus or Washington Confusion?" *Foreign Policy*, Spring, 87–103.

Peck, Jamie, and Nik Theodore. 2010. "Recombinant Workfare, Across the Americas: Transnationalizing 'Fast' Social Policy." *Geoforum* 41:2, 195–208.

Peck, Jamie, and Nik Theodore. 2015. *Fast Policy: Experimental Statecraft at the Thresholds of Neoliberalism.* Minneapolis: University of Minnesota Press.

Ravallion, Martin. 2009. "Should the Randomistas Rule?" *The Economists' Voice* 6:2, 1–5, http://www.bepress.com/ev.

Rodriguez, Evelyne. 2008. "Beating the Odds: How Progresa/Oportunidades Became Mexico's Major Poverty Alleviation Programme." In *Poverty Reduction that Works*, ed. Paul Steele, Neil Fernando, and Maneka Weddikkara, 287–302. London: Earthscan.

Romer, Paul. 2009. Comment by Paul Romer. In *What Works in Development?* ed. Jessica Cohen and William Easterly, 126–29. Washington, D.C.: Brookings Institution Press.

Roy, Ananya. 2010. *Poverty Capital: Microfinance and the Making of Development.* New York: Routledge.

Standing, Guy. 2008. "How Cash Transfers Promote the Case for Basic Income." *Basic Income Studies* 3:1, 1–29.

Steele, Paul, Neil Fernando, and Maneka Weddikkara, eds. 2008. *Poverty Reduction That Works.* London: Earthscan.

Stiglitz, Joseph E. 2002. *Globalization and its Discontents.* New York: W. W. Norton.

Sugiyama, Natasha Borges. 2011. "The Diffusion of Conditional Cash Transfer Programs in the Americas." *Global Social Policy* 11:2–3, 250–78.

Teichman, Judith. 2007. "Multilateral Lending Institutions and Transnational Policy Networks in Mexico and Chile." *Global Governance* 13:4, 557–73.

Teichman Judith. 2008. "Redistributive Conflict and Social Policy in Latin America." *World Development* 36:3, 446–60.

Teichman, Judith. 2009. "Competing Visions of Democracy and Development in the Era of Neoliberalism in Mexico and Chile." *International Political Science Review* 30:1, 67–87.

Thaler, Richard H., and Cass R. Sunstein. 2008. *Nudge.* New Haven: Yale University Press.

UNDP [United Nations Development Programme]. 2011. *Mexico: Scaling Up Progresa/Oportunidades.* New York: UNDP.

Wolfensohn, James. 2006. Foreword to *Progress against Poverty*, by Santiago Levy, vii–x. Washington, D.C.: Brookings Institution Press.

Data-Mining for Development?
Poverty, Payment, and Platform

BILL MAURER

As Ananya Roy argues in the introduction to this volume, the new territories of poverty are not merely new spaces or geographic locations. They are instead new political technologies. And they sit alongside, on top of, and interwoven with layers upon layers of the old. They are, with apologies to Foucault, problematizations that open up the assumptions and contingent connections between this or that claim, practice, or ethical stance. Poverty, generally understood as a condition, is more properly a political categorization and a set of techniques that institute that categorization, including often many of the techniques and claims that went before. This is not to imply, however, that territories of poverty are whole or encompassing without contradiction or messiness. As political technologies, they are contested within themselves, from within their own structuring logics or in terms of the conglomerations of people, capital, infrastructure, and space making them up. In the nineteenth century, Viviana Zelizer (1995) showed, social reformers advocated direct payments to the poor as a way to channel their consumption practices and thereby turn them into good citizens. Poor recipients of relief had other ideas of what to do with their welfare payments. We can see this as a contestation from below. I think the new territories of poverty are different insofar as the contestations come very much from within: for poverty professionals, territories of poverty are new kinds of problem-spaces that they actively construct and manipulate as they argue with one another and build often incompatible systems.

Compared to nineteenth-century social reform, late twentieth-century microfinance sought to institute a different kind of subjecthood, less a citizen than a businessperson whose entrepreneurial spirit would be unleashed by the provision of credit. Very much in line with a shift at the World Bank documented by Roy (2010), microcredit's proponents began to connect their effort to the wider financialization of the global economy as a means of further leveraging the assets of the world's poor—imagined to be a route to greater investment of the capital markets and thus presumably poverty alleviation. The sea change represented by C. K. Prahalad's (2009) *Fortune at the Bottom of the Pyramid* was not just its recapitulation of the poor as consumers as put forward by earlier social reformers. It was its claim that poor people's own knowledges and practices—collective, innovative, unexpected ways around and through the dilemmas of daily life in poverty in the midst of phenomenal and rapid global technological transformation—could be leveraged as assets to find new sources of value rather than hitching them to the old (Elyachar 2012).

The internal debates among those making the problem-space of poverty in the early twenty-first century have to do with both the absorption of the critique of microfinance and the focus on the poor as innovators (and the absorption of some of those innovative poor themselves into the professional poverty-alleviation workforce). Importantly, they take place in the context of widespread diffusion of communications technology and technology market actors. These actors are by definition always in competition with one another, yet they always must coordinate in order to realize the network effects their operations promise. The challenge to poverty scholarship is that if it could once focus either critically or appreciatively on the role of capital markets in the construction of (the category of) poverty, it now has to appreciate the weird complexity and internal problematizations of what we continue to call capitalist markets even after a global financial crisis and the animation of business models not based on accumulation or extraction or even profit in the traditional sense. This chapter is an effort to explain what I mean through a case study of the genesis and transformation of "mobile money."

Mobile phone–enabled money transfer, payment, and savings products—so-called mobile money services—have captivated industry and philanthropic attention since around 2007, when the Kenyan mobile network operator Safaricom launched M-Pesa. Now used by more than half of Kenya's population, and processing more transactions in Kenya than all of Western Union globally, M-Pesa is a money transfer service using the mobile network instead of the existing banking or payments infrastructure. Originally viewed as having the potential to "bank the unbanked" and provide an on-ramp to the "formal" financial sector, M-Pesa and other mobile money services are increasingly being imagined as payment platforms. That raises the question of what exactly a payment platform is, and how and why it can be imagined to have consequences for economic development and poverty alleviation. It also has ambiguous political, economic, and moral effects.

This chapter explores the practical consequences of the industry and philanthropic shift from mobile banking to mobile payment. In order to address the question of why some development practitioners are focusing on payment platforms for poverty alleviation, it proposes an analytical shift from poverty capital to poverty payment. It explains why payment, distinct from banking or other financial services, warrants closer scrutiny by critical development scholars and social scientists in general. It is based on my having followed and occasionally led mobile money professionals and policymakers into this realm of payments—the means of value transfer, sometimes understood to be a public good despite its privatization by credit card networks and, now, mobile network operators.

The payments industry is little studied or understood outside its own borders (see Evans and Schmalensee 2004; Maurer 2012c). In this chapter, I focus on the retail payments industry—the process of providing services that allow people, businesses, and governments to clear, settle, and process the movement of funds. "Payments" as an industry term (often pluralized) encompasses the purchase of goods at a physical or virtual point of sale; bill payment to a government agency or a corporation; payments made person to person, business to government, business to person, or government to person or business (for remittances, taxes or rents, salaries, or welfare or state subsidies or rebates, respectively). The payments industry is that collection of public and private entities that make sure value—generally in the form of funds denominated in state-issued currencies—gets from a sender to its intended recipient. The world of payments includes cash and checks, but increasingly is focused on electronic forms of value transfer, from credit card transactions to mobile phone–enabled services. When you hand over cash, the transmission of funds is straightforward. It is less so when any other payment mechanism besides cash is employed. Payment providers usually carry out this service for a fee. Payment is a basic operation on which exchanges of all sorts depend, but it is rarely focused on by people outside the infrastructures and processes that make it possible.

Payments are interesting because the payments industry business model does not square with market logic. The tolls and fees of private payment infrastructures pose challenges to competition law as well as to critical analyses of capitalism. Not set by the market mechanism in any conventional sense, these fees have vexed antitrust lawyers and consumer protection advocates, and have puzzled many a judge and legal scholar (see Levitin 2008; Porter 2008). They also raise the issue of the public interest in payment: most payment systems today are privately or shareholder owned, yet they are ever more essential to the forms and functions of value transfer, especially in a digitally connected world (Maurer 2012c). Traditionally, businesses and governments earned money from payments by levying fees on transactions when offering money transmission, clearance, and settlement services. Adding a lending function to a payment device provided a route to revenue from interest on funds extended (as well as, importantly, overcharge and late fees). This was the genius of the credit card. Even before the financial crisis that began in 2007–8, however, consumers were shifting their payment behavior away from credit cards and toward debit cards that drew directly from funds in bank accounts. In a world of debit, not credit, the motivation for offering payment is fee generation. Many new entrants into the payments business initially sought to capture a piece of that fee revenue.

Payments are also interesting because at this particular historical juncture the payments industry is itself undergoing a paradigm shift. Fees are receding; in some cases, they are being regulated away. Payment providers are experimenting with new ways to generate revenue—most notably, by seeking to profit from the promise of "big data." This represents a new business model: not based on interest or fees, but instead on accessing and leveraging vast troves of transactional data captured at the point of sale.

Where philanthropic and development attention to mobile money services like M-Pesa initially focused on their potential for "banking the unbanked" (Maurer 2012b) and could be seen as part of the phenomenon Roy terms poverty capital (Roy 2010), there is an emerging shift to poverty payment in places in the development world where mobile money services are being launched. By poverty payment, I refer to the idea that the design of digital platforms for the transfer of value, agnostic as to what value is being transited or what it is being used for, has positive spillover effects that ultimately benefit poor people. For philanthropic actors, poverty payment is mainly about reducing the costs of cash to the poor. For industry actors, poverty payment is increasingly oriented around the potential uses of transactional data to benefit the poor. It fits into an overarching belief that "big data" generally provides a "next frontier" in development (as Fengler 2012 puts it), that the increased connectivity and the overlaying and articulating of diverse databases may provide new solutions to old development problems. Attention focused first on the use of big data for tracking the spread of disease and social and economic conditions (Fengler 2012). By 2012, however, small startups and payments industry professionals were wondering whether transactional data could create new consumer markets in a sort of "bottom of the pyramid" approach to economic development (Prahalad 2009): knowing who was buying what, and how, could provide insight into new goods and services for the poor that would create business incentives to serve this new market niche.

As I have argued elsewhere, social science is ill equipped to understand payment (Maurer 2012c). One reason is that the social sciences, born in an age of capital, maintain capital as their reference point for economy. So, when we look at things like microfinance or development, we see reiterations of the original primitive accumulation via the enclosure of various commons in the name of the virtues of private property (as in de Soto and de Soto 2003), and we see attempts to liquefy the real assets of the poor—livestock and land (Shipton 2009), for example, but also expertise and relations (Elyachar 2005, 2010; Roitman 2005)—generally a first step toward their liquidation. We witness and criticize arguments about the virtues of debt, magically transformed into wealth (Peebles 2010), and we watch as people in specific institutional locations, from microfinance to global investment banks, seek to redefine the newly "freed" assets of the poor as "savings" to be leveraged in capital markets (Bruett 2007; Bystrom 2008). This all does little to help us understand payment, however, those infrastructures that enable value to move from one place to another, regardless of whether that value is involved in capital accumulation.

The following section briefly situates mobile money within the relatively short history of electronic payments at the point of sale (that is, at the till of a physical world shop). This historical digression is necessary in order more fully to explain the motivation of payments industry professionals in moving from a world of fees to one of data. Next, I will trace the history of the shift from mobile banking to mobile payments, along with a discussion of the realization in some circles around 2010–11 that providing electronic payment platforms could serve certain development agendas while at the same time, perhaps unwittingly, perhaps not, pose a challenge to the state's monopoly over the means of value transfer. Finally, I speculate on the political implications of seeing money as a private infrastructure versus a government utility, and the conundrum posed by big data to democracy and development more generally.

Payment at the Point of Sale

In 1973 IBM launched two electronic payment and inventory management systems: the 3650 Retail Store System and the 3660 Supermarket System. These were complete systems that included point-of-sale terminals with cash drawers, centralized data flow and storage, a magnetic label-maker for inventory control, a label-reader to be used at the point of sale, and a telephone modem to allow communication with warehouses and satellite stores. These systems represented a dramatic increase in the amount of data about inventory and payment available to retail businesses. If customers paid with cash, however—as was mostly the case when these machines were introduced—the data collected was limited essentially to cash in and inventory out, with ancillary data potentially to be collected on the performance of individual store employees assigned to specific terminals or stations.

The widespread acceptance of credit cards in retail stores added customer data to the ever-growing archive of retail transactional data. Even so, customer data was generally held only by the card companies, which could assemble records of customers' purchases. Without that data being cross-referenced with stores' inventories, however, a card company would acquire information about the amount and location of the purchase, but not the specific item bought. Stores carefully guard their purchase data, using it to offer coupons and rewards as part of loyalty marketing schemes (and at least once, to defend themselves in court against a consumer claim).[1] These schemes most often rely on the use of a store-branded payment card or a separate loyalty card presented at check out. In the United States, point-of-sale terminals at most major retail stores have one system for recording purchases for price scanning and inventory management, usually based on optical scanning technology and linked to a loyalty card (itself most often equipped with a bar code for optical scanning), and another for payment processing, usually based on magnetic stripe–enabled plastic cards. These two systems do not directly talk to each other (or, in the jargon of the industry, they do not interoperate). This is because the store is guarding its inventory and purchase data, which is linked to a specific customer only if the customer participates in a loyalty program, while the payment services are guarding their transaction data, recording only the purchase location and price.[2]

Imagine for a moment an everyday purchase of goods at a small shop. You make your selection and head to the till, money in hand. The clerk totals your purchases and tells you how much you owe. You tender cash and coin. The clerk provides change and a receipt, and off you go. The clerk may have a system for recording the goods purchased, for the purposes of inventory management. If the store uses any kind of mechanical or electronic cash register, it is likely that it can keep track of tax receipts and inventories. This information does not leave the store, however. And the clerk is left with your money but, most likely, no information about you at all, not even your name. Consider this a vast, unenclosed commons: in this scenario, very little "data" is produced—that is, very little information is objectified as such, demarcated from the flow of social and economic life, recorded, coded, stored, and then harnessed or sold for other purposes. This scenario, a retail point of sale with minimal "data capture," is the modal payment encounter around the world, in countless small shops and informal open-air markets, where goods and money change hands as if in a great bazaar. The bet of many new entrants and legacy players in the payments industry today (from Square and PayPal to Visa, American Express, Google, and Amazon) is that there is value to be gained by enclosing that commons of retail transactional data.

What does any of this have to do with poverty? As I argue below, some development actors' recognition of the shortcomings of microfinance as a poverty alleviation strategy, or desire to avoid its politics, led them to other "solutions," as some of my informants and research collaborators put it. Those solutions, in turn, were adapted and modified by their "targets," exemplifying the process

Prahalad (2009) hypothesized. Along the way, poverty payment emerged as a new problematic.

From Banking to Payments

The virtue of the focus on poverty capital is that one does not have to go too far to see it. Anthropologists, critical development scholars, and others have been documenting it for more than two decades. This does not mean that it is a seamless or single process, as Roy (2010) reminds us. It is "messy," "fragile," and "requires considerable and constant work"; it sits "uneasily alongside other poverty truths, such as those concerned with social protection or development infrastructure" (Roy 2010: 221). Roy finds in poverty capital not one dominant plan but multiple foldings and complicities, what Deleuze describes in another context as the incompossibilities that continually generate new borders between and lines across divergent worlds (Deleuze 1992: 81; see Maurer 2012a).

Some of those incompossibilities appear from "within" the beast, so to speak, when experts, academics, policymakers, and others—including the "targets" of development—articulate alternative visions and put them into practice. Much of the research for this chapter derives from the work I have conducted through the Institute for Money, Technology and Financial Inclusion, which I have directed since 2008. By funding and nurturing an extremely diverse group of specialists from the countries that development and philanthropic organizations have singled out for various financial inclusion interventions, the institute has created a vast repository of data and analysis that often lies in the way of some of the best-laid plans of the poverty alleviation apparatus. Replacing cleanliness with complexity, it agitates what Anke Schwittay (2011) has called the financial inclusion assemblage—arguing, for example, that savings could be denominated in goats or that technologies be developed to support, not subvert, the illiquidity preferences of many of the world's poor. Another aim has been to highlight the position of poor people not just as targets of finance but as monetary innovators in their own right, and, insofar as they are innovators in money itself, to highlight the political and theoretical consequences of the remaking of money through people's everyday practices with mobile technologies (Maurer 2012b).

Originally, much of the research at the institute had been on complicating certain stories or "hypotheses"[3] about savings: in particular, that the mobile phone could serve as a new "channel" for enhancing and mobilizing poor people's savings, harnessing the mobile network and capitalizing on the ubiquity of the mobile phone as an infrastructure for financial services rather than communication. The mobile phone—and new services like M-Pesa, originally imagined as a tool for microfinance loan repayment—could serve as a kind of "branchless banking." Where brick-and-mortar banks and electronic banking infrastructure are scarce or absent altogether, the mobile network and the basic communications channels of even the simplest mobile phones present a ready-to-hand information-processing and management system easily redirected from, say, voice and text to financial data.

A revisiting of the institute's output from 2008 to 2012,[4] my own field notes and interview notes with mobile money regulators and developers, the written products of experts from CGAP, the World Bank, the World Economic Forum, the Gates Foundation, and USAID indicates a slowly emerging understanding that mobile money represented something else besides a new channel for branchless banking. People started talking more and more about payment and found they had to give themselves a crash course in the existing payments industry in order even to begin examining their prior assumptions.

There are actually two shifts here: a first shift from microcredit to microsavings, and a second shift from microsavings to payment. The first shift is an effect of the absorption of the critique of microfinance levied by academics and others. The second is an effect of the operations of mobile money, and the increasing use of mobile money to serve payment functions by people in the countries where they have been deployed.

From the beginning, many observers believed that mobile money services would be used as de facto short-term piggy banks. People would load value into their account via an agent, handing over cash in exchange for electronic tokens of value (e-money, in the regulatory language), and instead of transferring it to another customer on the network—the modal use-case for mobile money—they let it sit there. This helped them avoid theft when traveling through the countryside. Today, some users of India's Eko mobile money service are using it to replace saving coins in clay pots (Nandhi 2012).

Directly related to this potential for mobile money itself to serve as a kind of savings account, mobile money intellectuals realized a fundamental contradiction in most countries' regulations around such services. Bank regulators from the start were understandably nervous about mobile network operators taking on quasi-banking functions. They worried about the potential for fraud and money laundering, since by running financial transactions over the mobile network there was no opportunity for monitoring by the established financial regulatory apparatus. But they were also worried about disintermediation of the banks themselves through the creation of a non-bank system for creating, storing, and transferring electronic value. The contradiction, however, was that although such services could function as small-value, short-term savings accounts (even if this was rarely realized in practice), the regulations did not permit either deposit insurance or interest. Loading funds into a non-bank entity but having no guarantee that the funds would be protected in the event of a bankruptcy, and saving money without the benefit of interest, the users of mobile money services were doing a kind of banking without its protections or benefits. Mobile-money intellectuals argued forcefully for the regulators to address these issues (see, e.g., Stephens 2012; Tarazi and Breloff 2010); regulators at times pushed back equally forcefully, but many adopted new rules. At the same time, mobile operators began to form partnerships with banks to provide basic financial services with the same protections and benefits of full-fledged banking (e.g., M-KESHO, a partnership between Safaricom and Equity Bank in Kenya).

Meanwhile, researchers started filling out with greater granularity and complexity users' behavior with M-Pesa and other mobile money services. When people used M-Pesa to send money to another person, researchers found, the recipient tended to "cash out" almost immediately—that is, upon receiving a text message notification that someone had sent them money, the recipient would immediately visit an M-Pesa agent and ask for cash, rather than letting the funds sit in their account or using them to make an over-the-air purchase of, say, a ringtone (Stuart and Cohen 2011). This was true even for the purchase of mobile phone airtime, bought from the same agent who disbursed the cash. Even when it was possible to pay directly for airtime using the electronic value held in the mobile network, people would still prefer to cash out, and then hand the cash over to the M-Pesa agent who provides both cash in/cash out services, and airtime sales. M-Pesa was not displacing the use of cash. Rather, it was functioning as a channel for *moving* money. Cash in/cash out was seen as the dominant use-case for mobile money. Some in the industry started wondering if there was a way to get people to keep their money in the system *forever* (in the words of one), not as a kind of savings but as a continually circulating pool of value endlessly looping through the mobile network. They wondered about this possibility not necessarily because of the presumed benefits to the poor of going cashless (benefits including protection from theft or loss, as well as the prevention of graft or extortion) but for the possibility of enhanced transaction-based fee income.

In Nairobi, meanwhile, a whole ecosystem of new services had sprung up around M-Pesa, with start-up businesses developing other products that used the mobile money channel as the primary or even sole means of moving money in order to achieve some other aim, like providing a health savings account product or agricultural insurance (Kendall, Maurer, and Machoka 2012). The payments industry frequently uses railroad metaphors to explain its infrastructures. For all intents and purposes, M-Pesa was functioning as a set of electronic payment "rails" for Kenya. It had become a new payment platform without anyone planning it as such.

Two authors nicely summed up the potential of mobile money as a new payments platform in 2010. At the time, both were at the Gates Foundation: "Where most financial inclusion models have employed either 'credit-led' or 'savings-led' approaches, the M-PESA experience suggests that there may be a third approach—focusing on building the payment 'rails' on which a broader set of financial services can ride" (Mas and Radcliffe 2010: 172). About a year later, USAID had announced its "Better Than Cash Movement," in which it cited the work of myself and my colleagues (Kendall, Maurer, and Machoka 2012) as demonstrating that mobile money had already come to serve as an electronic payment system more than a peer-to-peer money transfer or banking service:

> If you care about reducing poverty, then you must also care about reducing the reliance on physical cash. We begin a movement to do just that. USAID Administrator Rajiv Shah is announcing a broad set of reforms to use USAID's $22 billion financial footprint as a force for good—as a way to reduce the development industry's dependence on cash. This includes integrating new language into USAID contracts and grants to encourage the use of electronic and mobile payments and launching new programs in 10 countries designed to catalyze the scale of innovative payments platforms. (http://blog.usaid.gov/2012/02/we-must-do-better-than-cash/)

Then, having devoted itself primarily to savings since around 2008, the Financial Services for the Poor program at the Gates Foundation undertook a strategy refresh exercise in 2011, and in 2012 announced a new focus on payment, seeking to displace cash with digital payment platforms:

> After conducting a thorough analysis of the global financial inclusion landscape, we concluded that one of the main reasons why it is so costly to serve poor people with formal financial services is because most poor households conduct most or all of their economic and financial transactions in cash. We believe that the best way to reduce the cost of reaching poor people with financial services is to support efforts to shift the majority of their cash-based financial transactions into digital form through a mobile phone or other digital interface. Our new strategy aims to capitalize on the rapid evolution of mobile communications and digital payment systems to help catalyze this transition. (e-mail, March 28, 2012, copy in author's possession)

In the fall of 2012 and into early 2013, the newly formed Better Than Cash Alliance hosted a launch event in New York announcing a global effort to move people without access to electronic forms of value transfer into the digital money age. The event took place at the Ford Foundation headquarters in New York, and the alliance consisted of the Ford and Gates Foundations, the Omidyar Network, USAID, UNCDF, VISA, and Citi. Another event sponsored by Citi and

Imperial College was held in London in January 2013. The alliance has added new members since that time.

State and Market Moneys

The broader political-economic phenomenon co-occurring with the shift to cashlessness as a strategy for aiding the poor was the renewal of a profoundly antistate perspective on money. This was monetarism (Guyer 2007) combined with the belief that the state should get out of the business of money altogether. Since the 2008 financial crisis the Anglophone world has seen the drawing together of all manner of constituencies calling for the elimination of the state's monopoly of the means of exchange. These have ranged widely, from gold bugs, cryptocurrency advocates, and neo-Hayekian "denationalization of money" proponents, to legacy network partisans (meaning the card networks and the wire services), new payments industry startups like Dwolla and older ones like PayPal, journalists, authors (Wolman 2012; Boyle 2011), a few academics, local currency and Time Banking adherents (their numbers increasing during the recent recession), and at least one U.S. presidential candidate (Ron Paul) who ran unsuccessfully for his party's nomination in 2012.

Now, there is nothing necessarily anticash about antistate money proponents. One could imagine a private currency or currencies that take paper as one form. Yet the new constituencies of anti- or nonstate moneys are almost uniformly also antipaper, drawn by mobile and other information technologies to imagine private systems for the means of exchange that are almost exclusively digital.

Some states are in on the act, as well, even sometimes to the point of outsourcing the state's public function to provide a means of exchange. USAID's cashlessness initiative is in line with several sub-Saharan African central bankers' attempts to reduce reliance on physical cash in order to reduce fraud and theft as well as the costs of cash for the poor—costs related to transport, or loss due to climate (a significant concern where stashes of banknotes can rot or be eaten by vermin), not to mention cash's articulation to several "informal economy" money savings and transfer systems that often come with unclear or negligible protections and high transaction costs. The Central Bank of Nigeria, for example, began promoting a "cashless Lagos" project in 2012. This is in the context where interbank clearance and settlement can still involve bank employees with suitcases full of cash and receipts meeting in parking lots at the close of the business day. Again, lacking the basic electronic infrastructures necessary for the digitized financial transactions taken for granted in much of the global North, such projects make sense.

The broader emerging consensus on antistate money, however, includes skepticism toward any such state-led efforts. Canada, a leader in the provision of public infrastructure for payments,[5] recently issued a call to product designers, hackers, and app developers to come up with proposals for a digital currency to replace cash and coin. This Mint Chip project received fifty-seven entries. The reaction from the antistate money camp, however, is summed up nicely in the following article from a commentator in Forbes. Citing Bitcoin, the pseudo-anonymous (and anonymously created) cryptographic currency that received wide media attention in 2011 (Maurer, Nelms, and Swartz 2013), the author states: "My objection still lies with the fact that it is a non-free-market approach to the payments issue. Bitcoin has so far demonstrated its exchange value without being backed by anything that isn't backed by anything. Remove the standing armies and all money is essentially a mass illusion. Bitcoin just happens to be a voluntary, bottom-up mass illusion with scarcity, like gold" (Matonis 2012). The invocation of standing armies may be unexpected to some listeners. It is in fact a reference to the state and credit theorists of money (as opposed to commodity money theorists), who argue that the origins of money lie in the state's mandating of one method of payment for the purposes of raising revenue to support armies for territorial expansion.

The tax issue is not far from the minds of regulators charged with overseeing mobile money deployments. Mobile money offers the potential, after all, to track all exchanges—and therefore a way to ensure merchants and ordinary people are reporting taxable exchanges to the authorities.

There is more than tax on the mind of regulators, however. The shift from mobile banking to mobile payments also represents the rediscovery among regulators (not just academic observers like myself) that the means of payment—the technologies of value transfer, whether by government-issued paper notes or electronic infrastructures—serve an important public function. In many countries with mobile money, the race is on to build the rails for electronic value transfer. Companies from Visa to Citibank as well as global telecommunications network operators and traditional wire services like Western Union all see opportunities in creating for many countries in the global South what the card networks did in the North: an electronic payments network.

This is the first sense in which the shift to payments matters. It is a shift away from capital and from capital markets. Now, I do not mean to imply that these markets are withering away—far from it—or that, say, microfinance will not continue to bring profits to those leveraging it for capital gain and potentially further destitution for the already poor. However, something else is afoot here. And that something is a focus on generating revenue from the privatization of the means of value transfer.

Money, Data and Democracy

As I have been arguing for a number of years, payments are not like normal ex-changes, and capitalogocentric accounts (Gibson-Graham 2006) of them often miss the point of what they are and how they work. The value in payments comes not from value itself but tolls on its transfer. Tribute lives on in the modern-day fees levied on the passage of freight—in this case, financial data—going over the payment rails. Focusing on payment platforms rather than capital or credit thus throws a spotlight on those fees. This is important analytically because it also brings to the fore the centrality of noncapitalist relations within this thing we have been calling capitalism.

At the same time, my own analysis is anticipated by regulators and antitrust lawyers. They notice those fees, as well as the fact that they do not seem to follow the same rules of the game of other kinds of market-based processes. It is curious but not surprising that in most of the major antitrust cases levied against them, the card networks have chosen to settle out of court (see Maurer 2012c). The European Union recently promulgated regulations lowering the rate of interchange that the card networks can assess on transactions. One of the major accomplishments of the administration of U.S. President Barack Obama and the Democratic Senate during the president's first term was to do the same in the United States.

I would go so far as to argue that, with poverty capital, the state could adopt a laissez-faire approach: the capitalization of poor people's assets simply rep-resented another zone for financial speculation and accumulation, and not an affront to a state that was already captured or that had capitulated to financial interests. With poverty payment, in contrast, the state sees a threat to its tra-ditional authority to tax, expressed in terms of the concomitant threat to its ability to maintain a monopoly over the legitimate means of exchange. Thus, the regulators' concerns over interoperability, transaction fees, and the emer-gence of a (minority) position in the mobile money literature that the means of value transfer should not be privatized. In an important World Bank report on which I was asked to provide comment, Kevin Donovan sums up the position among some observers (like me) that "the provision of money by private com-panies over private infrastructure risks undermining an important function of the public sector, namely, that the means of value transfer are not 'owned' by anyone" (Donovan 2012:71).

Where a corporate-led mobile money effort promises to serve as a new set of payment rails, for example, central African regulators vociferously argue with donor agencies that "payments are a public good."[6] They are increasingly de-manding interoperability—that competing mobile money providers build their services such that a client of one can send money to a client of another, and that any customer on any network using any device should be able to access their funds without undue fees.

We arrive at the core of the problem of money, really: not only, as Keith Hart (1986) famously argued, is money ultimately a warrant of value underwritten by the state, or is money a commodity, or are these two sides of the same coin? But also, are money and the means of value transfer a *utility*?

The utility question is directly related to the data capture potential of electronic value transfer. If the new value proposition for mobile payments is based on leveraging transactional data, then who owns that data, who has access to it, and who can write and rewrite it? Rather than being based on leveraging the float in the system at any given time, or on levying tolls on transactions, the new business model capitalizes on the data being gathered when mobile or other electronic payments systems are used for purchases at the point of sale, realizing the potential of those old IBM 3660s.

By far the majority of economic transactions on the planet are undertaken with cash. Again, imagine this vast field of transactions as a commons—the common and collective property of the planet's human population, its "memory bank," as Hart has called it. "Once we accept that money is a way of keeping track of complex social networks that we each generate, it could take a wide variety of forms compatible with both personal agency and collective forms of association at every level from the local to the global. It is up to us to build them," Hart writes (2007). With electronic means of value transfer, transactions become sources of data; that data can be imagined as individual or collective property, and that data can be enclosed or mined, and, of course, monitored by governments.

I do not want to conclude on a dystopian note, however, where the privacy of even the world's poorest is evacuated as the billions of small transactions, this commons of transaction relations, is enclosed by private payment companies seeking a new business model when opportunities for fee income decline. This concedes too much to "big data," as well as to flatfooted conceptions of "privacy." My point is simply that the conversation and the technology are shifting: from concerns around liquefying (and maybe liquidating) poor people's assets via microfinance, to concerns that bind the world's poor with everyone else around questions of the nature and ownership and privacy of "personal data."

Is cash good, or bad, for the poor? Are transaction fees levied by corporate payment providers any better or worse? Does the privatization of payment diminish the public good, and does it even matter where people live in severe poverty? Poverty payment suggests that the contestation over these questions, and their messy connection to old debates and infrastructures for value transfer, opens new problematics, new territories of poverty that are themselves political technologies, requiring political not technical stances and solutions.

Making visible the transactional data in our everyday exchanges may, like making visible the rails and pipes of value transfer, have important public effects. In the face of antistate money proponents, therefore, I tend to imagine this public as a democratic polity, of the kind likely to make anarchist critics like David Graeber (2011) cringe. Not a state, then, but perhaps a new kind of archive. In an agenda-setting essay on critical questions for "big data," danah boyd and Kate Crawford provide a caution but also a prod to action. I close with their invocation of Derrida: "Effective democratization can always be measured by this essential criterion: the participation in and access to the archive, its constitution, and its interpretation" (Derrida 1996: 4, quoted in boyd and Crawford 2012:13).

Having already reopened money for interpretation and re-constitution, mobile money may provide just such access.

NOTES

The author would like to thank Ananya Roy and Emma Shaw Crane for the invitation to write and present the first version of this essay at the Territories of Poverty conference at the University of California, Berkeley. He is grateful for their hospitality and their critical feedback. He would also like to thank Taylor Nelms, Lana Swartz, Elizabeth Reddy, Nicholas Seaver, Robert Kett, Tom Boellstorff, Julia Elyachar and Scott Mainwaring for comments, criticisms and suggestions as this chapter was taking shape. Research has been supported by National Science Foundation, Law and Social Sciences Program (SES 0960423) and the Intel Science and Technology Center for Social Computing at the University of California, Irvine, of which the author was codirector. The author is the Director of the Institute for Money, Technology and Financial Inclusion, which is funded by the Bill and Melinda Gates Foundation. Any opinions, findings, and conclusions or recommendations expressed in this material are those of the author and do not necessarily reflect the views of the National Science Foundation, Intel Labs, or the Bill and Melinda Gates Foundation.

1. The case involved a supermarket's use of purchase data to challenge a customer's liability claim after a slip-and-fall incident inside the store. The supermarket used the fact that the customer was a regular liquor purchaser—as recorded in the supermarket's loyalty card records—to challenge his claim (and he lost; see Silverstein, 1999). This case in part led to the State of California's regulation of the loyalty card industry through the Supermarket Club Card Disclosure Act of 1999.

2. On the development of these competing standards, see Stearns, 2011.

3. This is an emic term among the development practitioners with whom I have worked on mobile money.

4. Much of this output is available on the Institute for Money, Technology and Financial Inclusion's website at http://www.imtfi.uci.edu.

5. Canada's Interac network links private debit and interbank networks much like Visa but has been denied for-profit status by the country's Competition Bureau. Thanks to Lana Swartz for this observation.

6. I did not directly overhear this assertion, but it was reported to me by an attendee of a closed-door conclave of banking regulators in an East African country in late 2010.

REFERENCES

boyd, danah, and Kate Crawford. 2011. "Six Provocations for Big Data." Paper presented at Oxford Internet Institute's "A Decade in Internet Time: Symposium on the Dynamics of the Internet and Society," September 2011. Available at SSRN: http://ssrn.com/abstract=1926431 or http://dx.doi.org/10.2139/ssrn.1926431.

Boyle, Mark. 2011. *The Moneyless Man: A Year of Freeconomic Living*. London: Oneworld Press.

Bruett, Tillman. 2007. "Cows, Kiva, and Prosper.com: How Disintermediation and the Internet are Changing Microfinance." *Community Development Investment Review* 3:2, 44–50.

Bystrom, Hans. 2008. "The Microfinance Collateralized Debt Obligation: A Modern Robin Hood?" *World Development* 36:11, 2109–26.

Deleuze, Gilles. 1992. *The Fold: Leibniz and the Baroque*. Minneapolis: University of Minnesota Press.

Derrida, Jacques. 1996. *Archive Fever: A Freudian Impression*. Trans. Eric Prenowitz. Chicago: University of Chicago Press.

de Soto, Hernando. 2003. *The Mystery of Capital: Why Capitalism Triumphs in the West and Fails Everywhere Else*. New York: Basic Books.

Donovan, Kevin. 2012. *Mobile Money and Financial Inclusion*. In *Information and Communication for Development 2012*, ed. Tim Kelly and Michael Minges, 61–73. Washington, D.C.: World Bank.

Elyachar, Julia. 2005. *Markets of Dispossession: NGOs, Economic Development, and the State in Cairo*. Durham: Duke University Press.

Elyachar, Julia. 2010. "Phatic Labor, Infrastructure, and the Question of Empowerment in Cairo." *American Ethnologist* 37:3, 452–64.

Elyachar, Julia. 2012. "Next Practices: Knowledge, Infrastructure, and Public Goods at the Bottom of the Pyramid." *Public Culture* 24:1, 109–29.

Evans, David, and Richard Schmalensee. 2004. *Paying with Plastic: The Digital Revolution in Buying and Borrowing*. 2nd ed. Cambridge, Mass.: MIT Press.

Fengler, Wolfgang. 2012. "Data—the Next Frontier of Development." World Bank blog, December 5, http://blogs.worldbank.org/africacan/data-the-next-frontier-of-development.

Gibson-Graham, J. K. 2006. *The End of Capitalism (As We Knew It): A Feminist Critique of Political Economy*. Minneapolis: University of Minnesota Press.

Graeber, David. 2011. *Debt: The First 5000 Years*. New York: Melville House.

Guyer, Jane I. 2007. "Prophecy and the Near Future." *American Ethnologist* 34:3, 409–21.

Hart, Keith. 1986. "Heads or Tails? Two Sides of the Coin." *Man* 21:4, 637–56.

Hart, Keith. 2007. "Money: Toward a Pragmatic Economic Anthropology." The Memory Bank blog, July 15, http://thememorybank.co.uk/2007/07/15/127/.

Kendall, Jake, Bill Maurer, and Phillip Machoka. 2012. "An Emerging Platform: From Money Transfer System to Mobile Money Ecosystem." *Innovations: Innovations: Technology, Governance, Globalization* 6:4, 49–64.

Levitin, Adam J. 2008. "A Critique of the American Bankers Association's Study on Credit Card Regulation." Georgetown Law and Economics Research Paper no. 1029191. Retrieved from http://papers.ssrn.com/sol3/papers.cfm?abstract_id=1029191.

Mas, Ignacio, and Daniel Radcliffe. 2010. "Mobile Payments Go Viral: M-PESA in Kenya." March 1 version. Reprinted in Capco Institute's *Journal of Financial Transformation*, no. 32, 169–82. World Bank, August 2011. Available at SSRN: http://ssrn.com/abstract=1593388.

Matonis, Jon. 2012. "MintChip Misses the Point of Digital Currency." Forbes.com blog, April 12, http://www.forbes.com/sites/jonmatonis/2012/04/12/mintchip-misses-the-point-of-digital-currency/.

Maurer, Bill. 2012a. "Credit Slips (But Should not Fall)." *Distinktion: Scandinavian Journal of Social Theory* 13:3, 283–94.

Maurer, Bill. 2012b. "Mobile Money: Communication, Consumption and Change in the Payments Space." *Journal of Development Studies*, June, 37–41.

Maurer, Bill. 2012c. "Payment: Forms and Functions of Value Transfer in Contemporary Society." *Cambridge Anthropology* 30:2, 15–35.

Maurer, Bill, T. Nelms and L. Swartz. 2013. "'When Perhaps the Real Problem is Money Itself!': The Practical Materiality of Bitcoin." *Social Semiotics* 23:2, 261–77.

Nandhi, Mani. 2012. *Impact of EKO's SimpliBank on the Saving Behaviour and Practices of Low Income Customers: The Indian Experience*. Delhi: Centre for Micro Finance (CMF), IFMR Research. http://www.centre-for-microfinance.org/wp content/uploads/attachments/csy/3164/Impact%20of%20EKO%20-%20Savings%20Behavior.pdf.

Peebles, Gustav. 2010. "The Anthropology of Credit and Debt." *Annual Review of Anthropology*, 39, 225–40.

Porter, Katherine. 2008. "The Debt Dilemma." *Michigan Law Review* 106, 1167–92.

Prahalad, Coimbatore Krishnarao. 2009. *The Fortune at the Bottom of the Pyramid: Eradicating Poverty through Profits*. Rev. ed. Upper Saddle River, N.J.: Wharton School Publishing.

Roitman, Janet. 2005. *Fiscal Disobedience: An Anthropology of Economic Regulation in Central Africa*. Princeton: Princeton University Press.

Roy, Ananya. 2010. *Poverty Capital: Microfinance and the Making of Development*. New York: Routledge.

Schwittay, Anke. 2011. "The Financial Inclusion Assemblage: Subjects, Technics, Rationalities." *Critique of Anthropology* 31:4, 381–401.

Shipton, Parker. 2009. *Mortgaging the Ancestors: Ideologies of Attachment in Africa*. New Haven: Yale University Press.

Silverstein, Stuart. 1999. "What Price Loyalty?" *Los Angeles Times*, February 7, http://articles.latimes.com/1999/feb/07/business/fi-5738.

Stearns, David L. 2011. *Electronic Value Exchange: Origins of the VISA Electronic Payment System*. London: Springer.

Stephens, Maria. 2012. "Promoting Responsible Financial Inclusion: A Risk-based Approach to Supporting Mobile Financial Services Expansion." *Banking and Finance Law Review* 27:2, 329–43.

Stuart, Guy, and Monique Cohen. 2011. *Cash In, Cash Out Kenya: The Role of M-PESA in the Lives of Low-Income People*. Washington, D.C.: Microfinance Opportunities.

Tarazi, Michael, and Paul Breloff. 2010. *Nonbank E-Money Issuers: Regulatory Approaches to Protecting Customer Funds*. Focus Note 63. Washington, D.C.: CGAP, July.

Wolman, David. 2012. *The End of Money: Counterfeiters, Preachers, Techies, Dreamers—and the Coming Cashless Society*. Cambridge, Mass.: DaCapo Press.

Zelizer, Viviana. 1995. *The Social Meaning of Money: Pin Money, Paycheck, Poor Relief, and Other Currencies*. New York: Basic Books.

REPRESENTATION

Fast Policy in a Mobile World

CHRISTINA GOSSMANN

In the early 1970s, as the Bretton Woods agreements ended, monetary markets underwent an enormous change: deregulation. This change created an entirely new set of financial products and relationships, and, as it turned out, it affected not only monetary markets but virtually every aspect of life. Over time, the abstraction of money spiraled to levels of mere fiction and finally resulted in the worst U.S. financial recession since the Great Depression. It seems that the world has lost control of its financial markets completely.

Whether coin, bill, or electronic currency, money was never more than a metaphor. The abstraction that accompanied the introduction of money has liberated people from age-old status distinctions, but it has also left them with nothing but money with which to evaluate their world. Increasingly detached from political control and material goods and labor, this "savage money" we now use is very different from what money once was: a universal yardstick quantifying objects, relations, services, and persons (Maurer 2006: 18). It is in this deregulated financial world that even assets of the "bottom billion," all the individuals living on less than $2 a day, become just another "zone for financial speculation and accumulation," as Bill Maurer describes it in this volume. Here is where what Ananya Roy (2010: 5) calls "poverty capital" or "bottom billion capitalism" is created and harnessed.

In his essay in this volume, Maurer argues that what we are witnessing today is a shift away from poverty capital toward "poverty payment." Maurer examines this shift based on the initial intent of financial inclusion whereby mobile phones, having reached an incredible level of penetration among the poorest, become a channel for enhancing and mobilizing poor people's savings.

A win-win situation? From the providers' side, mobile money allows for lower cost per transaction with reduced investment in physical infrastructure along with the possibility of offering additional services such as savings, credit, insurance and other products at a similarly low cost. Revenues are collected through fees associated with electronic monetary transactions. In the case of the Kenyan success story M-Pesa, most formal financial institutions have integrated their operations with mobile money, opening up a multitude of financial services. From the consumers' side, access to a financial platform such as M-Pesa allows for transfers, savings, and increasingly—according to Maurer—payments.

I was born in Russia, immigrated to Germany, where I spent most of my life, and came to the United States to study city planning as a graduate student at the University of California, Berkeley. I have progressively moved into the world of Visa, Citibank, Western Union, and Paypal, a world where digitized financial transactions have become so commonplace that I only use cash as a last resort for transactions: at the Laundromat, tipping at restaurants, and for the occasional morning coffee. But most of the world still relies on liquid cash for payments.

A *matatu* bus driver, having left his village to work in Nairobi, would save cash and occasionally travel home to bring money to his family. It could take him days, cost him money, and every now and again he might fall victim to robbers and lose all his money. Mobile money brought a solution to this dependency on liquid cash—and more. Now the *matatu* driver is able not only to make payments instantaneously using his mobile phone, he can also save on his M-Pesa account. But, possibly most significantly, when the *matatu* driver runs a red light and gets a ticket, he can pay that too through his phone.

This last transformation of mobile money—from microsaving to micro-payment—is taking place completely unplanned, writes Maurer in his essay here: it is an unintended, people-driven shift. As a consequence, mobile money regulators, developers, and experts from CGAP, the World Bank, the World Economic Forum, the Gates Foundation, and USAID are following the usage pattern laid out by customers. But as becomes clear in Maurer's discussion, while most everyone embraces mobile money, different actors do so for different reasons.

The world of international aid sees profound implications in enabling the poor to better protect their assets, invest in education and income-earning opportunities, and smooth economic shock curves in addition to creating entirely new product markets motivated by a boost in the participation of poor people. In Kenya more than five hundred organizations use M-Pesa to pay bills and conduct other transactions, including utilities and medical saving plans. In addition, the development of mobile money pathways builds an infrastructure that governments, donors, and charities can use to give money directly to the poor at low transaction cost. These payment platforms allow cheap, immediate deployment of (conditional) cash transfers, as discussed by Jamie Peck and Nik Theodore in their contribution to this volume. Industry is already making significant profits from the privatization of the means of value transfer and associated transaction-based fees. Safaricom, the Kenyan telecommunications company that launched M-Pesa in 2007, generates revenues of more than $1 billion per annum (Zuckerman 2010: 100).

The state, on the other hand and unlike in the case of poverty capital, has expressed interest in averting the privatization of poverty payment. Although M-Pesa value can be purchased at the local store along with other goods, cash is not an ordinary commodity after all. It is, insists the government, a state-issued instrument with specific properties and functions. The privatization of mobile banking would thus impede an important function of the public sector, concludes the state. What is telling of the larger transformation mobile banking has enacted is that the World Bank thinks so too.

If transferring money electronically should indeed become a public good, regulation and lower transaction costs will be necessary to avoid the enclosure of the culture of payments and enable the poorest to enter the financial market as well. Ironically, however, once regulatory practices are added to the equation, such as partnerships with commercial banks, classical financial inclusion barriers—such as specific identification requirements that mobile banking effectively avoids—are reintroduced.

The state is, as Maurer points out, also interested in the accumulation and potential dissemination of data. Personal transactional data, collected at the point of sale, provides opportunity for the state to track and tax all exchanges, impossible in the case of untraceable cash. The recording of any personal data, even if only available and used at the aggregate level, as so-called big data, will compel several questions: of whom? for whom? for what? In a time and place when every single electronic move we make—be it on Facebook, Google, or Twitter—leaves a trace on the World Wide Web, the protection of privacy is essential. As we fight to protect our virtual trail, companies pay millions to mine this commercial gold. Private information is regularly leaked to the public, through careless as well as illegal actions. While electronic financial transactions provide states and private actors with valuable information, it could also mean that we would expose those at the bottom of the pyramid to the risk (and paranoia) of the virtual space—identity theft, fraud, errors—that has come with the rise of the Internet. It is a risk many have learned to accept in a world of digitized transactions of all kinds, but does that mean that everyone should?

As great as the risks may be, the potential democratizing gains of big data are grand, as Maurer argues at the end of his paper here. Data collected from electronic value transfers make up what he calls an "individual or collective property," an archive of "big data" that, like a memory bank, should be shaped by and accessible to all. If total, free access to this data bank of financial transactions were possible, it could, like WikiLeaks, serve to democratize relevant, previously classified data—for anyone and free of charge.

The great enthusiasm with which the international development community has embraced it seems to indicate that mobile money may be just another extension of the world's love affair with the mobile phone. Unless, of course, it does indeed change the lives of the poor by opening up formerly inaccessible markets, be they financial, commodity, or information markets. Maurer's essay here seems to indicate the latter.

REFERENCES

Maurer, Bill. 2006. "The Anthropology of Money." *Annual Review of Anthropology* 35, 15–36.

Roy, Ananya. 2010. *Poverty Capital: Microfinance and the Making of Development*. New York: Routledge.

Zuckerman, Ethan. 2010. "Decentralizing the Mobile Phone: A Second ICT4D Revolution?" In "Special Edition 2010: Harvard Forum II Essays," special issue *Information Technology and International Development* 6, 99–103.

Section 2

The Ethics of Encounter

The chapters and essays presented in this section challenge the boundaries of traditional poverty research, instead taking up as objects of analysis middle-class interlocutors, bureaucracies of poverty, and practices of the self. We are interested in the spaces and moments of encounter in poverty action, and in the institutions and practices that create such encounters—from the millennial volunteer trip abroad to legal and juridical systems to philanthropic foundations. Such encounters are awkward and generate new subjectivities and questions. We pay particular attention to the affective economies of poverty work. Finally, this section invites readers to think about the temporalities of poverty—the ways in which poverty is situated relationally in time, often in the past, and how to imagine progress is also to conjure the future.

ESC

The Ethics of Encounter

Disaster Markets and the Poverty Factory

VINCANNE ADAMS

Disaster Markets

The waters . . . are receding but the damage is done.
—JOHN SCHWARTZ 2012

More than ever, large-scale flood and hurricane disasters are occurring at an unprecedented rate. Counting only the eighteen largest between 2001 and 2012 in the United States alone, these disasters accounted for roughly 3,600 officially reported deaths and over $281 billion in damages.[1] As climate change promises more disasters causing human and infrastructural devastation, it is worth exploring how disasters and our responses now form a growing sector of our economy, managed by both public- and private-sector interests.[2]

How we manage disasters tells us a great deal about how we manage poverty more generally and how well these strategies are working. Disaster-induced poverty generates public and private responses, authorizing a neoliberal form of "disaster capitalism" (Klein 2007) that persists long after disasters' initial impacts. Elsewhere I have explored how long-term recovery in post-Katrina New Orleans was also orchestrated by principles of market rule, tethering private for-profit interests not only to federally subcontracted relief but also to charity, volunteer, and "nonprofit" rebuilding (Adams 2013). As the safety net is increasingly privatized to profit and nonprofit entities, opportunities arise for what Roy (2012) calls an ethicalization of market rule (putting ideas about social responsibility into the logics of private profit). In this chapter, I build on the post-Katrina case to explore whether or not these new public and private assemblages work effectively to both ethicalize markets and relieve disaster-induced poverty or whether, alternatively, they create new opportunities for capitalization that perpetuate and extend poverty in new ways.[3]

Disasters, Responsibility, and Revolving Doors

Disasters are far from natural; they are nearly always intimately tied to growth industries of neoliberal capitalism, from the augmented crisis of environmental hazards associated with climate change to the social, infrastructural, and human-made environmental conditions that produce vulnerable people (Bolin 1982; Calhoun 2006, 2008; Erikson 1995; Freudenberg et al. 2009; Johnson 2011; Klinenberg 1999, 2002; Oliver-Smith 1996). In the case of floods and hurricanes in the United States, the growth industries surrounding the building of aqueducts and destruction of wetlands as natural protective barriers have played a huge role in the devastation caused by coastal hurricanes (Freudenberg et al. 2009). Federally subcontracted private corporations work through revolving-door relationships with government agencies like the Army Corps of Engineers and the merged offices of FEMA and Homeland Security, undermining effective federal support for civil infrastructure and contributing to the creation of risk zones. With profits in the mix, these agencies spend less and less of their federal funds on maintenance and repair of roads, bridges, aqueducts, levees, and floodplains, and more money on foreign oil and energy wars (Klein 2008; Calhoun 2006; Carde 2008). Added to this situation is the relative rise in low-income built environments (trailer parks, substandard housing) in high-risk areas that are particularly vulnerable to storm and flood destruction. Rising oceans and polar vortex effects affect communities built in what have now become vulnerable places. Here, preexisting patterns of poverty in relation to accessibility of evacuation, public notification for evacuations, medical care, and temporary housing also explain in large part how natural weather patterns become disasters, contributing to greater poverty (Klinenberg 1999). Finally, disasters usually authorize opportunities for the growth of disaster capitalism by mobilizing the neoliberal responses that allow for-profit industries to decide how and what type of recovery is warranted, bypassing many of the normal democratic and legislative processes that would enable careful deliberation, regulation, and legislative oversight of the industries called in to help (Laquer 1989; Calhoun 2004, 2008; Fassin and Vasquez 2005; Lakoff 2010; Roberts 2010).[4] Together these circumstances explain how market principles enable disasters to create, sustain, and entrench poverty.

What is less well understood is how capitalism also structures the long-term recovery of communities after a disaster. In the case of Hurricane Katrina, we know that allowing military subcontractors to provide the first line of relief led to inept responsiveness and human rights abuses during the immediate aftermath of storms and floods (Eggers 2009; Dyson 2005; Lipsitz 2006; Giroux 2006), but the floods were just the beginning of the disaster. A second-order disaster was ushered in by a multiyear recovery process that used similar mechanisms of market-driven private and for-profit companies to do the humanitarian work of delivering federally supported recovery assistance (Adams 2013). When these failed, recovery was left to charity and nonprofit grassroots volunteer organizations. As post-Katrina New Orleans suggests, however, even the charity sector that has grown to fill in the gaping holes in the safety net was affected by principles of market rule, shedding light on how well (or how poorly) pro-market strategies actually work for recovery.

In what follows, I argue that pro-market arrangements of charity work through an *affect economy* that mobilizes volunteer workers in and through sentiments of ethical responsibility. In step with neoliberal propositions, these arrangements offer new opportunities to shift our sensibility of how to make markets work in ethical (pro-poor) ways. At the same time, I also show how they can displace responsibility for recovery onto victims even while allowing profits to be made on the unpaid labor of volunteers. Relationships between disasters and capitalism may create a *poverty factory* that first allows profits to be made by businesses that, directly or indirectly, help create disasters, then allows profits to be made on disaster relief, and then finally, allows profits to be made on the unpaid and underpaid labor resources that actually do the work of recovery over the long run. All of these mechanisms, as I will show, run the risk of producing poverty even while ostensibly working toward its eradication.

Public Distributions of Disaster Risk/Private Allocations of Disaster Profit

How well do market-based strategies work to help people recover and avoid poverty after disasters? The abysmal performance in helping New Orleanians recover and rebuild their city offers an example of one of the most telling indictments of the privatization of federally funded humanitarian work ever seen.

The displacement of more than one million people from the Gulf region during and after Hurricanes Katrina and Rita and the flooding of Greater New Orleans in 2005 mobilized a set of responses that, over a roughly seven-year period, enabled only about 75 percent of displaced residents to return and rebuild.[5] Estimates are that some 140,000 residents were never able to return, but even those who did were subjected to a grueling, debilitating battle against the very programs deployed to help them, raising questions about why and how it could have taken this long, particularly given that an estimated $120.5 billion (roughly $45 billion of it from the federal government alone) was mobilized to help speed up the process.[6] People wondered: where did all the money really go?

Consider the options for help that were made available to returning residents. All of them were market-oriented infrastructures that enabled profits to be made on the business of humanitarian aid. Start with insurance companies: those who had insurance coverage for *hurricane damage* learned that they would not be eligible for payouts for damages that could be attributed to floods unless they also had *flood* insurance. Although homeowners argued that the hurricane *caused* the floods, and lobbied the U.S. Senate to require insurers to pay for flood damages, legislators refused to put this burden on insurance companies. This is despite the fact that the government initially supported the opposite claim in order to protect the Army Corps of Engineers from responsibility, saying floods *were due to the hurricane storm surge* rather than lack of repairs to levees. Most families were only able to collect minimal funds from insurance based on damages they could prove were from the hurricane but not floods.[7] Protecting the interests of insurance companies over those of homeowners ensured that most of the cost of recovery would be borne by homeowners themselves.

A second resource available to residents was the federally insured loan program, offered through the Small Business Administration (SBA), a program that was leveraged to help disaster victims during the Roosevelt Administration. To participate in this program, residents had to show some form of collateral, which for people who were "wiped out" meant being a good credit risk by simply having a job or equity in savings or property. The SBA loan program created opportunities for local banks to benefit with little risk by offering loans that were federally guaranteed. But for homeowners, this meant taking on additional debt beyond what they already carried on mortgages for homes they could no longer live in. In some cases, loan money was used to pay back taxes on properties that had been sitting in disrepair while homeowners struggled for year upon year to find a way to rebuild. This use of "poverty capital" is not unprecedented in the United States (Roy 2010), but the predatory character of it during the years after Hurricane Katrina was made visible in the large number of people who were dragged into poverty even while non-debt-creating federal resources should have been enough to prevent anyone from this fate.

Third, one of the lynchpin recovery programs was the Louisiana Recovery Authority's Road Home Program. This state program was designed to give federal funds to homeowners for the difference between what their insurance paid and the cost of rebuilding their home. Here too, the market was brought in; this program was subcontracted to a private, for-profit company called ICF International in a no-bid (noncompetitive) opportunity to run the program it designed. This company received over $10.3 billion in federal funds to help people, and despite the claim that they disbursed $8.95 billion in funds to 129,880 applicants, nearly half of the homeowners who applied for help from the Road Home Program did not get it. Meanwhile, ICF made profits on its contract from the very beginning. It initially went public with IPO stock offerings at $12 per share in 2006, a month before they were actually awarded the contract. A month later, when news of the Road Home contract was made public, their stock rose by 30 percent.

For homeowners trying to recover, the process of obtaining Road Home funds was long and complicated, sometimes taking up to four or even five years, and often resulting in settlements through arbitration that were far lower than what homeowners needed to rebuild.[8] The tactics used by ICF to audit legitimacy of claims and to offer payouts were surprisingly frustrating to residents, including homes being undervalued, claims of lost paperwork, refusals to accept affidavits in lieu of lost title papers, and inexplicable nonresponsiveness. Though the performance of this company was enough to prompt the formation of a citizen's action group (Citizens Road Home Action Team, or CHAT), ICF rewarded its executives with $2 million in bonuses, and they watched their stock grow to $33 per share in 2010 as their contract with Road Home came to an end and they obtained other new federal contracts. People were literally dying in their FEMA trailers waiting for funds while the company posted reports to shareholders about their strong fiscal performance.

One of the most visible signs that the relief and recovery arrangements encouraged the privatization of profits and public distribution of risk was the case of the FEMA trailers. In 2009, four years after the disaster, people still living in their trailers were offered the opportunity to buy their trailer for $25,000. The fact that Halliburton and Bechtel, among other federal subcontractors, had billed the government roughly $229,000 for each FEMA trailer they had made and shipped to New Orleans, in the initial months after the floods receded, gave these residents pause over the charge of $25,000. When it was learned these trailers contained dangerous levels of formaldehyde, the offer was withdrawn. Homeowners felt that had they each been given $229,000 at the outset, they could have both bought a trailer and rebuilt their homes quite quickly. The upward siphoning of federal funds toward for-profit corporations enabled these companies to make money on the business of "helping others" but produced remarkable inefficiencies when it came to helping New Orleanians recover.

The risks of capitalization for recovery were borne in large part by the residents and in virtually no part by the companies that were brought in to help. The production of poverty in and through these structural arrangements of disaster capitalism is evident in the fact that despite the large outpouring of government funds, the city did not eliminate its federally subsidized poverty. A few short years after Katrina, the city eliminated all but one of its public housing units and permanently displaced a large number of its poorest families (Adams, Van Hattum, and English 2009), but even six years later the city still had similarly high rates of families requesting federal support for housing assistance, only this time it was for middle-class elderly neighborhoods where people once owned their homes. With the abysmal failure of the publicly funded for-profit subcontractors called in to help with recovery, residents soon learned that the only real help would come from charities.

Responding to Need: The Charity Sector

William Foster, fifty-three years old, was living in his FEMA trailer on the front lawn of his single story brick home in Gentilly when we first met him. His story was typical of many returning residents. He'd been in his FEMA trailer nearly two years already. His single-story shotgun-style brick house that he could see sitting there, a mere twenty feet from the side window on his trailer, was still completely uninhabitable. It had been gutted and stripped to studs, and was somewhat moldy. Wiring in the walls was exposed, and there were a few remnants of bathroom fixtures, sinks, and countertops in rooms that had yet to be completely reamed out.

William was waiting to hear back from the Road Home program about his request for help. Insurance had only paid for damage to his roof, a paltry five thousand dollars. He figured he would need another eighty to a hundred thousand dollars to rebuild, and even though he was frustrated by the long wait, he was hopeful funding would come through from the state program and he'd be back in his house by the end of the year. Sitting in his little trailer, with piles of correspondence nearly covering his available counter space and the ledges behind the built-in dining seat, he started to talk about how hard it was to deal with all the losses. "It's crowded in here," he said. "Can you imagine having a family of four living in one of these?" I couldn't. The tiny toilet at one end wedged between a shower stall and a sink was hardly big enough for one person. The bed filled up the other end of the trailer, making it so there was virtually no real space to live in. Sitting at the table that filled up the midsection of the trailer, I felt sick to my stomach. "Two years now," he said. "I'm going on two years now in this trailer."

William was quick to tell us that the only people who really helped him after Katrina were the "church folks, the volunteers." Indeed, New Orleans witnessed the largest outpouring of grassroots, charity, nongovernmental, and faith-based volunteerism ever seen in the United States. Of the top ten charities that came to help rebuild the city, calculated by the size of their contributions, most of them were faith based (Sparks 2009; De Vita and Kramer 2008). Some charities started with minimal resources and a few hands: missionary evangelicals who set up ministries in their garages, or social justice–oriented church groups who formed rebuilding associations that went house to house and gutted, demolished, and hauled away debris. Other groups were already established charities: the Salvation Army, Feeding America, the American Red Cross, Catholic Charities, Habitat for Humanity. The Good News Camp, organized by the Disaster Pastor Network, Jerry Davis Ministries/Christian World Assemblies, appeared spontaneously in City Park in the weeks after the floods receded and, living in tents and using an open-air kitchen, eventually funneled some 17,000 volunteers from all over the world to homes, families, and neighborhoods that needed help.

William told us that a church group had come through sometime around February of 2007. It was a group of African American kids from a church in Florida. They were "big guys" he said. "They looked like a football team. I was so relieved. They just came in and started to empty it out." Wearing masks and gloves, "they just dug in," he said. "They ripped it all down to the studs, those guys. I couldn't believe it. I was so grateful to them." He got up and walked a few steps to his "bedroom," where he reached into the crack between the wall and his bed and pulled out a Bible. "I'm *not* really religious," he said, "but they left this Bible. You know, it reminds me of how much they did for me. I keep it right near my bed, in eyesight when I wake up in the morning. It gives me hope."

That churches and charities have played such an enormous role in disaster recovery programs of the past decades is not surprising. Although charity's role in creating social safety nets outside of government institutions in the United States is not new (Bartkowski and Regis 2003; Wuthnow 2004; Cnaan 2002), George Bush Sr.'s famous 1989 call for charity groups to rise up like a thousand points of light and fill in where the government could not (or would not) take care of the needy initiated a stream of government efforts that would make it possible for charities to become the first, and often only, resort for many Americans in need. The post–Bush Sr. era has offered altogether new commitments to growing the charity sector, forming a whole new chapter in the long history of government support for disaster relief, evading ethical conundrums that government aid might have aroused over concerns of moral hazard and the calibration of worthy vs. unworthy recipients of government help (Dauber 2008). By privatizing federal assistance programs through the charity world, the government washes its hands of moral hazard while growing this sector of the economy.

Today, new government programs help orchestrate and grow the charity sector, as well as the volunteers who fill their ranks. The Points of Light Foundation (later Points of Light Institute), for example, was formed in 1990 as a nonprofit agency with federal funding under Bush Sr. as an explicit effort to augment charity-based solutions to social welfare problems. The federal Corporation for National and Community Service, CNCS, designed in 1993 by Stephen Goldsmith (who also designed the Points of Light Campaign and Institute), is the government's solution to the neoliberal challenge of taking care of those in need without growing big government. CNCS recruits and places volunteers to do service work in the nation's neediest sectors (including education, health care, disaster relief, environment, and care for veterans). Now twenty years old, they advertise that, through organizations like theirs and others, one in four Americans now volunteer. CNCS is set up as a corporation so that it has more autonomy than other government agencies, operating as a public–private partnership. It is one of the main donors for the Points of Light Institute, but both organizations also raise money directly from the private sector through corporate and private wealth philanthropy.

It is important to note that the growth of the nongovernmental charity sector in disasters has not necessarily decreased the amount of federal resources that are spent. Calhoun noted that the charity sector in relation to disasters alone was a $10 billion a year industry (Calhoun 2006: 24), but in 2011 U.S. domestic federal disaster relief spending *alone* exceeded $32 billion.[9] Today, disaster recovery fuels an industry that is both public and private, nonprofit and for profit. Wolch (1990) warned that fueling such organizations through government funding and later through government regulatory processes would undermine the independence and autonomy of private volunteer charities. "As voluntary organizations become more central to the legitimacy of the welfare state," Wolch (1990: 189) writes, "their daily practices of planning and management, staffing and service delivery can be expected to come under increasing scrutiny." In fact, I would argue that the opposite has come true. Today, the state still relies on the charity sector to do safety-net work, but it does so in ways that endorse free-market legislative priorities rather than public-sector priorities and lessens government regulation at every step of the way.

The charity sector has grown since the 1990s in the United States at a rate that exceeds population growth. The number of 501(c)(3) organizations has more than quadrupled in the past thirty years, and social welfare organizations and nonprofits, including those devoted to disaster assistance work,[10] grew from roughly 1.1 million to 1.9 million.[11] The growth of the nonprofit sector in response to disasters has grown large enough today to spawn its own satellite industries. AIDMATRIX is an online relief and recovery agency network and distribution matrix support structure (getting donors connected to causes and making sure they can keep track of where there money or resources go). InterAction is an international NGO with similar goals, "respond[ing] to numerous natural disasters and complex emergencies around the globe, providing direct relief and support to affected populations."[12] The Center for Disaster Philanthropy is another such nonprofit organization, offering "the tools, expert analysis, and strategic one-on-one guidance to maximize the impact of dollars given for disaster preparedness, relief, and recovery."[13] One can even get a master's in fundraising for philanthropy these days. The University of Indiana, has "The Fund Raising School," which "helps thousands of fundraising professionals per year around the world achieve new levels of success."[14] Finally, the charity sector now has its own nonprofit NGOs (Charity and Guidestar, for instance), which are in the business of auditing the performance of charities.[15]

Charity organizations remain an important private-sector solution to the neoliberal state's problem of not wanting to give direct support for the public safety net, and will likely be so for a long time. We should keep in mind, though, that for all the good these organizations do, they are tax-exempt and they often rely on a largely volunteer labor pool.

Failed Recovery

On our second visit with William, he was still in his FEMA trailer. It was well into his third year post-Katrina. And he had not come much closer to his hoped-for return to living in his home. Compared with his optimism during our first visit, he was now visibly depressed. He missed the neighborhood, the people he may not have known intimately but was friendly with—the people who made him feel at home because they were familiar faces. Only a few were back. "We're banding together again," he said. "We help each other out. We keep an eye on the homes that are left." This had become more and more important because theft had become a huge problem. People would come back after a day at the Road Home offices and find that their old appliances had been taken, stolen by scavengers trading in metal and copper for cash. Worse, even new appliances they'd purchased to put back in their homes would be stolen, "right out from under their noses" while they slept in their trailers. It just felt like "a total collapse of society," he said. It was "as if everything had been taken away, even our sense of integrity."

He continued to tell us about his job. He previously worked as a city inspector, in the planning and permit department. He went back to work six months ago, and he thought having his job again would help him get his mind off the wait and the feeling of being "stuck." But it didn't. Going out to all these communities, and seeing how desperate people were only made him feel worse. He started to have doubts about whether he would ever be able to rebuild. So many people were struggling. His story was not unique. It was the norm.

While waiting, William became more and more depressed. He began to collect old wrought-iron grills, gates, and yard furniture that he found in emptied lots and un-gutted homes. He gathered them at first as a kind of service to his neighborhood. He figured if people returned, they'd be able to come retrieve their property. He stored them all in a backyard open-air garage behind his home. Over the many months, however, his intentions to help others return and recover started to shift. He started to realize that people were not coming back. For one reason or another, they gave up. It was as if a collective sense of possibility had been swamped, literally overturned, by the largesse of the devastation. He started to feel as if he were sinking from the weight of it. He now saw himself as a scavenger, not unlike those who had been collecting copper from old appliances. His collection of ironworks became an obsession—something that kept him focused—an activity that gave him a reason to get out of his trailer. It had also become a possible source of income. He envisioned being able to clean all this trash up and sell it to make money, and he needed money now, since he had been put on leave from his work as an inspector.

William's life had become a vivid example of postdiluvian survival and poverty. He kept trying to tell himself that things might get better, but gradually he realized these thoughts were a fiction he would tell himself to lift his mood. Eventually, that fiction too became a burden. He was drifting in and out of depression. When I asked to see him again in 2009, he first said yes but then called back a day before the meeting time to say that he'd have to cancel, saying simply, "Today isn't a good day." He said he just wasn't feeling up to it, and I detected a shaky tone in his voice, as if he were on the verge of tears. A few months later, when I was able to meet him again, he apologized for having canceled and confessed that he had not wanted to talk because he was embarrassed. He felt ashamed of the fact that he had not made any progress on his home, that he was still stuck in his trailer, plunged in poverty in a way he only imagined happened to others, but not him. He kept talking about how long he'd been stuck, and the thought that he was still stuck a year after we had seen him just overwhelmed him. He was shaky and tearful. It was too much for me too. Like in most of the interviews I did with returning residents, I also began to cry.

The Affect Economy and Its Surplus Values

In the wake of a disaster, emotions run high. Dramatic images circulate alongside startling statistics of lives lost and billions of dollars in damages.... We're moved to do something—anything—to help. Immediate needs must be met. Lives must be saved and vital functions restored.
—THE CENTER FOR DISASTER PHILANTHROPY (Mission Statement Used for Soliciting Donations)

Stories like that of William are important. They are important because they help orient us to the ways that affective experiences plunge through and pierce our comfortable narratives about how and why poverty exists, and about what might be done to address it. The sense of helplessness felt by William, and by so many others who live through the double disaster of not only storms and floods, but also delayed or stagnated recovery, is a key ingredient of the story of disaster-induced poverty. Affect directs us to share in the experiences of suffering and to imagine some connection to it. And this, in the end, is what drives a recovery process that relies on charity and volunteer labor, and it is what an economy that grows the charity sector relies on in order to work.

Disasters generate a type of affective surplus, an excess of emotion that begins with the victims of disaster and spills over into the communities that are roused to volunteer and help in the recovery process. Affect is built into the recovery industry as not just an experience but as a productive resource that, as we will see, enables money to be made on poverty. It circulates as a stimulus to productivity and as a surplus that can be transformed into fiscal profits for good causes. Some have described how "cause marketing" works in international development in ways that create an outpouring of fiscal support for humanitarian interventions and/or microfinance to pay for it (Roy 2010). Humanitarian relief often relies on representations of "suffering strangers" (Butt 2002; Maalki 1995; James 2010; Moodie 2013) and these representations traffic in affect in order to generate much needed aid. Similarly, in the United States, disaster zones arouse volunteer support by way of representational strategies that produce affect, and this affect is used in marketing the cause and arousing volunteer support: it may also play an important role in concealing the dynamics that enable unpaid labor to be another source of profit making.[16] How does this work?

People want to volunteer, in part, because it feels different than working for pay. Muehlebach (2011), writing about volunteer labor in contemporary Italy, notes that volunteer work enables people to rekindle a sense of belonging once found in older regimes of labor that have been abandoned or lost in a post-Fordist economy. In post-Katrina New Orleans, volunteers uniformly talked about similar feelings of emotional reward that came from providing help to people who needed it (Adams 2013). Through churches, these volunteers sometimes called themselves "kingdom laborers" and on the ground they talked about "putting the gospel to hands and feet." Outside of the churches, similar commitments to helping people were articulated around an ethic of American patriotism of building communities back "from the ground up," or of being "the foot soldiers" for recovery. The notion that volunteers helped people to "pull themselves up by their own bootstraps" was used in a collective sense—volunteers were "in it together" with the victims. The neoliberal arrangement that called upon charity to drive the economy and to engender a sense of collective self-responsibility is noteworthy, lending credence to the notion that charity was "ethicalizing market rule."

Far beyond New Orleans, the ranks of volunteers in America are vast. People with charitable intentions sign on as volunteers or as "voluntourists," often absorbing the entire cost of travel, lodging, and food in the places where they work. Called to action by the affective pull of service, these volunteers sometimes even pay to do volunteer work. Just because the labor is free, however, does not mean that money is not circulating in the charity sector. In fact, it is partially the way in which affect can be transformed into free labor that enables charities to not only survive (and do good work) but also that makes this sector of the economy so attractive to neoliberal policymaking.

The Charity Business

What kind of economic sector is charity, after all? Beyond the many small NGO nonprofits that have risen up like a thousand points of light to rebuild the safety net, there are also large corporate and nongovernmental organizations involved in this sector. Indeed, neoliberal arrangements don't necessarily eliminate government so much as drive decision-making and resource allocation to the market on the way to helping people. Thus, it is important to note that affect here is leveraged all the way from the level of the state, through organizations like the Corporation for National and Community Service and the Points of Light Institute. One of the newest players in this sector is HandsOn Network, a nonprofit volunteer organization deploying hundreds of thousands of volunteers and placing them in organizations like AmeriCorps, Teach for America, HealthCorps, and Vista, as well as in hundreds of small nonprofit grassroots organizations that operate on the ground in postdisaster settings across the country. In 2014 HandsOn Network boasted mobilizing more than 2.6 million volunteers, which they valued at "$576 million in human capital toward our nation's critical problems."[17] In 2010 HandsOn merged with the Points of Light Institute and created the largest volunteer network in the history of the United States.

Like its predecessors, HandsOn Network operates in an interstitial space that is both public and private—funded with public money and protected by public legislation but also able to operate with the autonomy of a private-sector company. It is not publicly traded (yet), but as a nongovernmental nonprofit organization, it is able to leverage federal allocations to raise additional money through large corporate philanthropy from donors like Fidelity Investments, American Express, Target, and the University of Phoenix, among others, and these donor companies play an important role in the networks' sense of purpose (while taking tax deductions for their philanthropic giving).

In reality, as the private sector is asked to take on more and more responsibility for relief and recovery work (as evidenced by the public–private structure of federally supported organizations and by the amount of corporate wealth that is used to sustain them), there has been a steady encroachment of market-driven values in the charity sector. That is, the charity volunteer industry has increasingly come to look and feel a lot like the for-profit corporate world. Charity Navigator describes this well:

Many of these charities are complex organizations, with multi-million dollar budgets, hundreds of employees, and thousands of constituents. Most charity executives could inevitably make much more running similarly sized for-profit firms. Charities provide vital, life-saving tasks such as providing food, collecting and distributing blood, and providing medical care. In order to attract the kinds of executives that can provide the leadership these organizations need, charities must offer a competitive salary. (Heck 2007)

A good example is this advertisement from 2012 for executive leadership at the Points of Light Institute:

Points of Light is looking for a strategic and innovative individual to develop relationships and financial support from a portfolio of external facing corporate prospects to revenue goals and develop Points of Light's Programs division. This individual will be required to prospect for and secure new business as well as grow existing accounts with a defined multi-million revenue goal. Additionally, the Vice President must be able to effectively work across teams to ensure the execution of corporate partnership goals and success. This is a leadership position based in Atlanta that is integral to the development team's ability to support signature programs at Points of Light that will propel the organization's capacity to ignite a new spirit of service and civic engagement across the world.[18]

Today, the job of doing big-business charity entails much of the same skill set one would find on Wall Street, where fundraising entails far more than hanging out one's tin cup and asking for money for a worthy cause. It now entails managing investment portfolios and looking for business opportunities that will grow to meet revenue goals that will generate enough to not only run the business but also create new corporate investment opportunities for growth. This is not a criticism. This is a reality of the world of nonprofits today.

Under neoliberal policies that favor the business model for not just the commercial sector but for all social sectors, nonprofits are forced to compete with the for-profit sector. As Bishop and Green (2010) have illustrated, this means they often end up having to do things just like the for-profit sector to stay in business. Take this interview with a leader in the world of market philanthropy for the health sector. When asked, "How has philanthropy changed?" he said:

Over the last couple of decades, an enormous amount of wealth has been created in the private sector. Many of the people who have benefited the most have sought to give back to society by forming foundations and other organizations that drive social change. Their arrival in that landscape has really transformed philanthropy.

They are playing differently from the way that many of the traditional philanthropists have played. They are more willing to engage the private sector to be part of the solution. They take a business-style approach to problem solving. Their vision of themselves as social entrepreneurs has changed the way philanthropy is carried out.[19]

The optimists see this as a win-win scenario in which money (and strategic planning) are finally pouring into the coffers and offices of those who do social good. But such arrangements might have a down side as well. The problem of compensation is just the beginning of the challenges for a charity sector that relies on the private, for-profit world. In leveraging public funds to raise private donations, these organizations subject themselves to new kinds of demands. Taking large sponsorship from the corporate world and even partnering with large for-profit corporations can mean adopting performance measures that are more suited to the corporate sector and the markets they serve than they are to the public sector. Jones (2007) describes this as a process in which corporate sponsorship starts to transform into a kind of corporate governance managed all the way down through its accounting, investing, and management practices. Jenkins (2011) refers to the way that corporate philanthropy influences nonprofit and humanitarian work as a form of "muscle philanthropy."

John Arena (2012) describes the downside of allowing nonprofit NGOs to decide how to protect the interests of the poor when they are under the pressure of for-profit interests. Even before Hurricane Katrina, but particularly in its aftermath, nonprofit organizations became coopted as part of the neoliberal industrial complex and, in the end, advanced the interests of developers over those of low-income publics who needed subsidies for housing. Privatization, he notes, killed the radical call for public-sector rules and regulations that were ultimately needed to protect the interests of the poor.

In perhaps the most ironic twist in this story, for-profit federal subcontractors now see opportunities to invest in the world of charity in order to sustain their access to federal safety-net funding. ICF International decided to get involved in the nonprofit volunteer business when, in 2009, it merged with a company called Macro that specialized in services in the social sector, including victim services and disaster relief. As part of their new growth strategy, ICF noted its desire to partner with grassroots faith-based groups: "Currently, ICF is working with a wide range of faith-based and neighborhood partnerships throughout the country, providing expert training and technical assistance in an effort to help these programs improve their programming, build their capacity, and enhance their ability to promote self-sufficiency for individuals, families, and communities" (Good, Orell, and Hercik 2009; ICF Macro n.d.).[20]

If evidence from ICFs work in post-Katrina New Orleans suggests that there are numerous obstacles that get in the way of turning for-profit work into effective humanitarian relief, then we should probably ask what their commitments to the charity sector will do. Since charities are already effective at the grassroots level, it is hard to imagine how companies like ICF International will make this work. In many ways, it looks suspiciously rather like this will simply amount to a form of double-dipping at the trough of disaster capitalism.

The shift in the way capital flows in and out of the public and private sectors to fuel and support a postdisaster public safety net is one in which the outcomes *feel* promising. There are, in fact, clear positives to these new arrangements, not least of which is that nonprofits are often able to respond in much more pluralistic ways to people in need. Moreover, there are differences in the degree to which market forces are able to penetrate these charities, with churches being better able to resist pressure from both the market and corporate donor demands than other nonprofit groups. Still, the growth of the disaster relief NGO charity sector constitutes a shift in the public and private distributions of humanitarian and social services work, and its outcomes are still yet to be fully understood. There is a largely undertheorized set of differences between for-profit philanthropy and nonprofit work even though they are now being merged (Brakman Reiser 2008).

One thing for sure is that these industries rely on a lot of unpaid and underpaid labor, and this labor is productive in ways that exceed the immediate emotional, social, and physical benefits to recipients and volunteers. Volunteers generate a surplus, calibrated in social capital and emotional rewards but also in fiscal profits. Affect does a sort of double work here: it arouses the call to labor, and it conceals the ways that profits flow into and upward in this industry, taking resources away from the people who need it most who are trying to rebuild or dig out of their new poverty. To the extent that charities must now be attentive to growing their business investments, paying retention bonuses, and seeking new revenue sources, the question might be raised of what is *not* getting done for the poor with that money.

The Virtuous Circle and the Un- and Underpaid Labor It Relies On

Again, putting profit into the mix of humanitarian relief and social services is seen by some to be a virtuous circle in which everyone potentially wins, including executives as well as those who volunteer and those who receive the help of volunteers. After watching the effects of volunteer charity in New Orleans, it would be hard to disagree with this view. At the same time, the New Orleans case also foregrounded some of what Roy (following Derrida) identifies in her introduction to this volume as the aporias emerging in our attempts to address poverty. Here too is an irresolvable incompleteness of translation, in this case between market rule and humanitarianism. As helping the poor (or those made poor by disaster) becomes an ethical option (rather than a government guarantee), and as more and more for-profit companies are asked to invest in these social causes by way of charity (often lending not only funds but business advice), it is important to pay attention to not only how money is made and how charity businesses are sustained but also how the labor of charity gets done, who pays for it, and who profits from it.

There are, of course, differences between disaster recovery volunteers and the low-paid volunteers who work for AmeriCorps, Teach for America, Ameri-Saves, VISTA, and the like, who are often pre-professional interns. Still these "volunteers" are connected through organizations like HandsOn Network, and they play similar roles in relation to the public safety net in that they both solve a problem for the economy: how to take care of those in need while shrinking government spending *and* allowing the charity sector to grow in the same way that for-profit companies grow. Thus, in places like New Orleans, volunteer labor might be read in relation to the other activities of profiteering that were deployed in the disaster by companies that were subcontracted to help people rebuild but in large part failed to do so. And, as large companies like ICF get in the mix of charity, competing with or working together with organizations like HandsOn Network and the CNCS, one might ask: how much should they be paid and how much should they be allowed to profit, in view of the fact that much of the actual work is being done by unpaid volunteers? If companies like HandsOn are calibrating the monetary value of their work ($700 million in man hours), who is shouldering the burden of this invisible capital other than the volunteers themselves, and what work does this invisible capital do to sustain corporate-style profits at the top? Here, as the case of post-Katrina New Orleans suggests, publics are often being asked to pay twice for the safety net: first through taxation that pays for companies like ICF to deliver federal aid, and then through their work as volunteers.

Even the use of volunteers in pre-professional internship tracks at organizations like HandsOn Network are part of a new assemblage that expands the role of unpaid or underpaid labor in the economy. Volunteering in low-paid internships removes a paid salary opportunity from the landscape and displaces older and more highly paid workers (which is especially true in public education). Small nonprofits in New Orleans complained about the temporary character of this workforce, which meant valuable time had to be spent retraining new volunteers annually, which took time away from project work and effectively eliminated long-term expertise. Enormous displacement of skilled craftsmen by temporary volunteers in New Orleans completely reshaped the landscape of labor in the post-Katrina era.

These new unpaid and underpaid labor regimes are changing the dynamics of wealth and poverty across the board in America. A different kind of moral hazard arises in the use of labor that is unpaid and in the ways human suffering is used to generate surplus wealth for others. This is particularly true when we consider that most of the poverty in America today is among the "working" poor. A HealthCorps intern who shadowed me for a day confessed to me that she was only being paid around nine thousand dollars for her year of full-time work at a northern California health clinic, and, to my surprise as well as hers, she was told by her supervisor on her first day of work to take paid time off to go stand in line to register for food stamps.

Considering that the minimum wage is 21.4 percent less today than it was in 1979,[21] that 15.1 percent of people living in the United States live in poverty,[22] that the number of Americans living below the official poverty line in 2011 was 46.2 million people,[23] and that poverty persists today because of too many low-wage jobs and single-income households,[24] the logic of creating ever larger cadres of unpaid or underpaid workers is somewhat inscrutable. Again, we should remember that this sector *is* making profits for some people.

The slow drift in the world of humanitarian relief work from public and charity sectors to private for-profit sectors (or some entangled blurring of the two) results in a growth industry in which stock trades and investment capital will surely figure as prominently in the measures of success as do outcomes for the public in need. The seamless drift toward market-driven models of charity starts with the recasting of the world of philanthropy as an industry that should use its business smarts to run the charity sector. It may end, however, with the formation of ever-new kinds of poverty.

The Poverty Factory

Optimists might talk about the privatization of safety-net philanthropy as creating opportunities to ethicalize market rule, to get the private sector more involved in doing good work by being socially responsible. In fact, privatizing safety-net responsibilities has made it possible for decision-making about whether or not to help the poor to become a question of ethical choice (should I volunteer or not?) rather than a requirement of citizenship (through taxation and redistribution). We might ask, Have the new regimes of charity affected market rule in ways that make it more ethical in pro-poor ways, or is market rule affecting charity and subjecting it to the needs of profit and accountability that have little to do with aid and much to do with executive bonuses?

The story told here about the pitfalls of thinking that poverty is a problem that can be solved in and through the for-profit private sector is a cautionary one. Ananya Roy (2012) has interrogated the arrangements that allow global poverty to become a source of market profit-making, reminding us that rhetorics that justify predatory microfinance aid are often deployed in and through charity. It is time, perhaps, to recognize that these same dynamics are at work in the global core as well (albeit through arrangements) and post-Katrina New Orleans offers a good case in point. Certainly for the case of disaster-induced poverty, there are important questions that could be raised about not simply whether or not this arrangement works but also about what else it does besides, or sometimes instead of, the work of helping people who are recovering. As concerns over profit indices start to seep into the nonprofit world in ways that are nefarious and persistent, we need to ask more about what accounting and auditing practices work and for whose benefit they are working. My interest is not necessarily in undermining this infrastructure, but rather in taking stock of our current predicament in order to understand how we might rethink the contours of our investments of time, affect, and labor, both paid and unpaid.

NOTES

1. Jamal Knight and Rick Piltz, "Federal Disaster Assistance Budgeting: Are We Weather Ready?" posted on August 5, 2011, by *Climate Science Watch*, http://www .climatesciencewatch.org/2011/08/05/federal-disaster-assistance-budgeting-are-we -weather-ready/.

2. As of the writing of this paper, this is roughly the same amount of welfare spending on housing, family and children and unemployment subsidies for one year ($281 billion); see "U.S. Welfare Spending," usgovernmentspending.com, http://www.usgovernment spending.com/us_welfare_spending_40.html. See also Bruce R. Lindsay, William L. Painter, and Francis X. McCarthy, "An Examination of Federal Disaster Relief under the Budget Control Act," Congressional Research Service 7-5700 www.crs.gov R42352, February 10, 2012, http://www.hsdl.org/?view&did=701332. Their calculation of the total federal expenditures on disaster relief/recovery for hurricanes and storms since only 2003 is roughly $62 billion.

3. I acknowledge the support of the National Institutes of Health (NIA) grant #5R01AG28621 on which the research on New Orleans post Katrina was based. I also thank Louise McCune, Edwina Newsom and Taslim van Hattum, along with other research assistants and colleagues who helped with data collection, transcription, and archival research.

4. This is allowed under the Stafford Act, Lindsay, Painter, and McCarthy, "An Examination of Federal Disaster Relief." See also Singer (2010) on the new partnerships between humanitarian intervention and private military contractors.

5. This is based on the 2011 indicators. For full report, see Allison Plyer, "What Census 2010 Reveals about Population and Housing in New Orleans and the Metro Area," Greater New Orleans Community Data Center, released March 17, 2011, https://gnocdc .s3.amazonaws.com/reports/GNOCDC_Census2010PopulationAndHousing.pdf.

6. Here too, exact numbers are hard to get. See this report, which combines relief and rebuilding expenditures and includes Katrina as well as hurricane Rita, which followed shortly after: Rick Weil, (Department of Sociology at Louisiana State University), LSU Post-Katrina Studies of Community Resilience, http://www.lsu.edu/fweil/lsukatrinasurvey/FourNeighborhoodsSlides.pdf. I also call attention to John Arena's (2012) analysis of how the process of displacing the poor from New Orleans began long before Hurricane Katrina.

7. In the end, the average insurance payout was roughly $15,000 per household.

8. For specifics on amounts awarded, see Adams 2013.

9. Jamal Knight and Rick Piltz, "Federal Disaster Assistance Budgeting: Are We Weather ready?" *Climate Science Watch*, August 5, 2011, http://www.climatesciencewatch.org/2011/08/05/federal-disaster-assistance-budgeting-are-we-weather-ready/.

10. See Sandy Deja, "The Way We Were," www501c3book.com, 2011, http://501c3book.org/uploads/The_Way_We_Were.pdf.

11. See Chronicle of Higher Philanthropy http://philanthropy.com/article/Charting-the-Tax-Exempt-World/127014/.

12. "Humanitarian Practice," InterAction, http://www.interaction.org/work/humanitarian-practice.

13. See their website at http://disasterphilanthropy.org/.

14. The Fund Raising School at the University of Indiana, http://www.philanthropy.iupui.edu/TheFundRaisingSchool/.

15. The IRS seems to have a studied ambivalence about auditing these organizations.

16. Roberts (2010) notes that it was, in part, this affective component of disaster relief that enabled FEMA to become one of the federal government's most powerful and well-funded agencies.

17. The numbers change regularly. In 2012, the posted numbers were more like 30 million volunteers and $700 million worth of service. See HandsOn Network website, http://www.handsonnetwork.org/ (accessed July 20, 2012 and November 20, 2014).

18. Job Opportunities, Points of Light, July 20, 2012, http://www.pointsoflight.org/jobs.

19. The BCG (Boston Consulting Group) Expert Interview with Colin Boyle, http://www.bcg.com/about_bcg/social_impact/Philanthropy/ExpertInterview.aspx?interviewId=tcm:12-26170&personId=tcm:12-10877&pt=UGFydG5lciAmIE1hbmFnaW5nIERpcmVjdG9y&practiceArea=Philanthropy (accessed August 21, 2012).

20. For more on the merger, see "ICF International Completes Acquisition of Macro International Inc.," ICF International archives, April 1, 2009, http://www.icfi.com/news/archives/2009/icf-completes-acquisition-of-macro-international-inc.

21. See Jack Rasmus, "Wages in America: The Rich Get Richer and the Rest Get Less," Kyklos Productions Presents: Articles, 2004, http://www.kyklosproductions.com/articles/wages.html.

22. "Poverty in the United States," Wikipedia, http://en.wikipedia.org/wiki/Poverty_in_the_United_States.

23. Sabrina Tavernise, "Soaring Poverty Casts Spotlight on 'Lost Decade,'" *New York Times*, September 13, 2011, http://www.nytimes.com/2011/09/14/us/14census.html?pagewanted=all.

24. Peter Edelman, "Poverty in America: Why Can't We End It?" *New York Times*, July 28, 2012.

REFERENCES

Adams, Vincanne. 2013. *Markets of Sorrow, Labors of Faith: New Orleans in the Wake of Katrina*. Durham: Duke University Press.

Adams, Vincanne, Taslim Van Hattum, Diana English. 2009. "Chronic Disaster Syndrome: Displacement, Disaster Capitalism, and the Eviction of the Poor from New Orleans." *American Ethnologist* 36:4 615–36.

Arena, John. 2012. *Driven from New Orleans: How Nonprofits Betray Public Housing and Promote Privatization*. Minneapolis: University of Minnesota Press.

Bartkowski, John P., and Helen A. Regis. 2003. *Charitable Choices: Religion, Race and Poverty in the Post-Welfare Era*. New York: New York University Press.

Bishop, Matthew, and Michael Green. 2010. *Philanthrocapitalism: How Giving Can Save the World*. London: Crown Books.

Bolin, Robert. 1982. *Long-Term Family Recovery from Disaster*. Boulder: University of Colorado, Institute for Behavioral Science.

Brakman Reiser, Dana. 2008. "For-Profit Philanthropy." ExpressO, http://works.bepress.com/dana_brakman_reiser/14.

Butt, Leslie. 2002. "The Suffering Stranger: Medical Anthropology and International Morality." *Medical Anthropology* 21:1, 1–24.

Calhoun, Craig. 2004. "A World of Emergencies: Fear Intervention and the Limits of Cosmopolitan Order." CRSA/RCSA 41:4, 373–95.

Calhoun, Craig. 2006. "The Privatization of Risk." *Public Culture* 18:2, 257–63.

Calhoun, Craig. 2008. "The Imperative to Reduce Suffering: Charity, Progress, and Emergencies in the Field of Humanitarian Action." In *Humanitarianism in Question: Power, Politics and Ethics*, ed. Thomas G. Weiss and Michael Barnett, 73–97. Ithaca: Cornell University Press.

Carde, Leslie, dir. 2008. *America Betrayed*. First Run Features Distributors.

Cnaan, Ram A. 2002. *The Invisible Caring Hand: American Congregations and the Provision of Welfare*. New York: New York University Press.

Dauber, Michelle L. 2005. "The Sympathetic State." *Law and History Review* 23, 2.

De Vita, Carol J., and Fredrica D. Kramer. 2008. "The Role of Faith-Based and Community Organizations in Providing Relief and Recovery Services after Hurricanes Katrina and Rita." ASPE: Office of the Assistant Secretary for Planning and Evaluation. U.S. Department of Health and Human Services (DHHS), http://www.urban.org/publications/1001244.html.

Dyson, Michael Eric. 2005. *Come Hell or High Water: Hurricane Katrina and the Color of Disaster*. New York: Basic Civitas Books.

Eggers, Dave. 2009. *Zeitoun*. San Francisco: McSweeney's Books.

Erikson, Kai T. 1995. *A New Species of Trouble: The Human Experience of Modern Disasters*. New York: Simon and Schuster.

Fassin, Didier, and Paula Vasquez. 2005. "Humanitarian Exception as the Rule: The Political Theology of the 1999 Tragedia in Venezuela." *American Ethnologist* 32:3, 389–405.

Freudenburg, William R., Robert Gramling, Shirley Laska, and Kai T. Erikson. 2009. *Catastrophe in the Making: The Engineering of Katrina and the Disasters of Tomorrow*. Washington, D.C.: Island Press.

Giroux, Henry. 2006. *Stormy Weather: Katrina and the Politics of Disposability*. London: Paradigm Publishers.

Good, Josh, Brent Orell, and Jeanette M. Hercik. 2009. "Faith-Based and Neighborhood Partnerships—Learning from the Past, Building on the Promise." ICF International Presidential Transition 2009. http://thehill.com/images/stories/whitepapers /pdf/ICFI_FaithBasedWhitePaper.pdf.

Heck, Andrew. 2007. "Five Charity Myths Dispelled." Charity Navigator, July 1, http:// www.charitynavigator.org/index.cfm?bay=content.view&cpid=617.

ICF Macro. n.d. Faith-based and Community Initiatives. www.macrointernational.com /projects/faithbased/default.aspx.

James, Erica. 2010. *Democratic Insecurities: Violence, Trauma and Intervention in Haiti*. Berkeley: University of California Press.

Jenkins, Garry W. 2011. "Who's Afraid of Philanthrocapitalism?" *Case Western Reserve Law Review* 61:3, 1–69.

Johnson, Cedric. 2011. "Introduction: The Neoliberal Deluge." In *The Neoliberal Deluge: Hurricane Katrina, Late Capitalism, and the Remaking of New Orleans*, ed. Cedric Johnson, xvii–l. Minneapolis: University of Minnesota Press.

Jones, Bryn. 2007. "Citizens, Partners or Patrons? Corporate Power and Patronage Capitalism." *Journal of Civil Society* 3:2, 159–77.

Klein, Naomi. 2007. *The Shock Doctrine: The Rise of Disaster Capitalism*. New York: Henry Holt and Company.

Klinenberg, Eric. 1999. "Denaturalizing Disaster: A Social Autopsy of the 1995 Chicago Heat Wave." *Theory and Society* 28, 239–95.

Klinenberg, Eric. 2002. *Heat Wave: A Social Autopsy of Disaster in Chicago*. Chicago: University of Chicago Press.

Lakoff, Andrew, ed. 2010. *Disaster and the Politics of Intervention*. New York: Columbia University Press.

Laqueur, Thomas. 1989. "Bodies, Details, and Humanitarian Narrative." In *The New Cultural History*, ed. Lynn Hunt, 176–204. Berkeley: University of California Press.

Lipsitz, George. 2006. "Learning from New Orleans: The Social Warrant of Hostile Privatism and Competitive Consumer Citizenship." *Cultural Anthropology* 21:3, 451–68.

Maalki, Liisa. 1995. *Purity and Exile: Violence, Memory and Native Cosmology among Hutu Refugees in Tanzania*. Chicago: University of Chicago Press.

Moodie, Megan. 2013. "Microfinance and the Gender of Risk: The Case of Kiva.org" *Signs* 38:2, 279–302.

Muehlebach, Andrea. 2011 "On Affective Labor in Post-Fordist Italy." *Cultural Anthropology* 26:1, 59–82.

Oliver-Smith, Anthony. 1996. "Anthropological Research on Hazards and Disasters." *Annual Review of Anthropology* 25, 303–28.

Roberts, Patrick W. 2010. "Private Choices, Public Harms: The Evolution of natural Disaster Organizations in the United States." In *Disasters and the Politics of Intervention*, ed. Andrew Lakoff, 42–69. New York: Columbia University Press.

Roy, Ananya. 2010. *Poverty Capital: Microfinance and the Making of Development.* New Brunswick: Routledge.

Roy, Ananya. 2012. "Subjects of Risk: Technologies of Gender in the Making of Millennial Poverty." *Public Culture* 24:1, 131–55.

Schwarz, John. 2012. "Cost of Minnesota Flood Estimated at $100 Million." *New York Times*, June 22.

Singer, Peter W. 2010. "Strange Brew: Private Military Contractors and Humanitarianism." In *Disasters and the Politics of Intervention*, ed. Andrew Lakoff, 70–99. New York: Columbia University Press.

Sparks, Randy J. "'An Anchor to the People': Hurricane Katrina, Religious Life, and Recovery in New Orleans." *Journal of Southern Religion* After the Storm: A Special Issue on Hurricane Katrina, http://jsr.fsu.edu/Katrina/Sparks.pdf accessed Dec 3, 2009.

Wolch, Jennifer R. 1990. *The Shadow State: Government and Voluntary Sector in Transition.* New York: Foundation Center.

Wuthnow, Robert. 2004. *Saving America? Faith-Based Services and the Future of Civil Society.* Princeton: Princeton University Press.

REPRESENTATION

The Privatization of Everything?

REBECCA PETERS

During a period of field work in Cochabamba, Bolivia, in June 2012, I witnessed the ways that socioeconomic status determined who had access to safe water and who did not. The reassertion of public control of water in Cochabamba after a privatization contract that made water both inaccessible and unaffordable is a frequently cited example of poor peoples' movements overcoming transnational capitalist impulses. Despite the rejection of undemocratic models for water provision, contemporary advocates of privatization regard state institutions as vehicles for enabling the handoff of public services to the private sphere as part of a market-based approach to international development. This manifestation of capitalist expansion is characterized by unfettered deregulation, undeterred by objections regarding the brutalities produced by structural adjustment policies on marginalized people harmed by patterns of exploitation and the removal of social protections such as affordable water pricing.

Adams's discussion in this book of disaster capitalism sharpens my own academic focus on access to and control of water resources. Although her analytical field is distinct from my own, the application of her insights provides me with critical theoretical tools to use in reflecting on the complex intersections of poverty, power, and water. As a hopeful millennial scholar skeptical of the beneficence of the free market, I find that the simultaneously pro-poor and pro-market approach to water provision as a method for alleviating poverty contributes to novel contradictions and opportunities to grasp the evolving logic behind international development strategies. Improved water provision as a means of reducing poverty was enshrined in the Millennium Development Goal target 7(c), aimed at cutting in half by 2015 the proportion of the global population that lacks sustainable access to safe drinking water and basic sanitation. Interventions in the water sector to reduce poverty have created a generative space for a multiplicity of actors—non-governmental organizations, charities, and private companies—while unduly attenuating the responsibility of states to provide affordable, accessible, and safe water to the public. The modern water barons providing services for profit do not belong to a single archetype, but instead represent a variety of private sellers and buyers, ranging from multinational corporate behemoths to quasi-governmental organizations.

While market control of water resources is perhaps more overt in the global South, similar forms of water grabs have perniciously insinuated themselves into the daily management and consumption practices of the global North. Adams examines the lack of water management in the case of the devastating flooding and unrelenting hurricanes deluging the coasts of the United States, along with the industries that benefit from the destruction of wetlands as natural barriers from storms. The transfer of postdisaster responsibility to private companies to ensure public safety represents the abandonment of a primary function of government. The responses to catastrophic disasters involving nonstate actors with neoliberal agendas, as discussed in Adams, are reminiscent of the way the everyday disaster that is poverty encourages private actors to fill the void left by an unresponsive state, entrusting "the poor" in the global North and South alike to the good will of charities and corporations rather than addressing institutionalized inequality. In this way, the regulation and management of water and the poor through disaster capitalism addressed in American poverty scholarship aligns with themes of private involvement in water provision in global poverty scholarship.

This socialization of risk and privatization of profit in the water sector that I see in my work mirrors the way that exposure to postdisaster capitalization risks were borne by residents along the Gulf Coast and not by private companies as discussed by Adams in this volume. In the global North, markets for private providers are manufactured by instigating distrust in the quality of public drinking water sources (Natural Resources Defense Council 2013). The undermining of federal support for civil infrastructure creates territories of risk as agencies spend less on maintaining and repairing pipes, aqueducts, levees, and dams (cf. Adams, this volume). This is particularly discernable in rural communities, where the regulation of water supplies is conspicuously absent and many families rely on unmonitored sources of drinking water. In California, the Salinas Valley is home to Latino farming communities that are disproportionately impacted by odorless, colorless, and tasteless arsenic and nitrate contamination that has a significant impact on health. After a private company was found guilty of manipulating quality results to avoid responsibility for treating the water, nonprofits in the region have taken up the burden of mitigating the impact of private companies using fertilizers that leach into the groundwater and cause debilitating public health hazards (*United States v. Alisal Corporation* 2005).

The privatization of water and corresponding public disinvestment contributes to distinctive geographies of poverty and its management, and creates novel territories of wealth for those benefiting from the commoditization of water resources. The rise of disaster capitalism entails the authorization of "for-profit industries to decide how and what type of recovery is warranted," frequently circumventing "democratic and legislative processes" (Adams, this volume). In Adams's description of the no-bid contracts issued for the rebuilding of areas devastated by Hurricane Katrina, I see similarities to the way multinational corporations are awarded non-competitive awards for the private enclosure of public water resources as a means to control access to water in the global North and South alike. This is evident in the unregulated and uninhibited $400-billion-a-year bottled-water industry which turns what has been established as a basic human right by the United Nations into a market opportunity (Kreiser 2006).

As I reflect on the ways Adams emboldens my interdisciplinary academic understanding of the water sector, I am reminded that any meaningful change in approaches to water management and provision must simultaneously confront both poverty and inequality through policy and direct action. Diverse acts of resistance to institutionalized market mechanisms in the water sector reflect Polanyi's (1944) idea of a double movement reacting to the profound havoc unleashed by markets through the commoditization of natural resources. However, such dissent is not solely a saga of "poor peoples'" movements; the repudiation by social movements in the global North of water privatization suggests that movements against profit-motivated interventions in the water sector may indeed be a global phenomenon. When the privatization of publically held resources is understood to be a symptom of a weak civil society unable to protect itself from the lures of the free market, then it is possible to reform, reconceptualize, and reimagine understandings of the problem of poverty as something actively produced, regulated, and managed. Adams's theoretical work reacquaints me with the importance of not turning political processes into technical solutions, which is often the path of least resistance in the water sector when the default remedy for subpar water provision is turning to private providers with little accountability or regulation.

REFERENCES

Kreiser, John. 2006. "Investors Have a Big Thirst for Water." CBS News, August 16, http://www.cbsnews.com/news/investors-have-a-big-thirst-for-water/.

Natural Resources Defense Council. 2013. "Exploding Sales: Marketing a Perception of Purity." *Bottled Water: Pure Drink or Pure Hype?* July 15.

Polanyi, Karl. 1944. *The Great Transformation: The Political and Economic Origins of Our Time.* Boston: Beacon Press.

United States v. Alisal Corporation. 2005. *Find Law.* United States Court of Appeals, Ninth Circuit, October 13.

Our Past, Your Future: Evangelical Missionaries and the Script of Prosperity

JU HUI JUDY HAN

Encountering the past as foreign

The past is a foreign country: they do things differently there.

—L. P. HARTLEY, *The Go-Between* (1953: 9)

The rather famous opening line of L. P. Hartley's novel, *The Go-Between* (1953), usually appears in discussions of past-in-the-present (see Lowenthal 1975; Traub 2008). The idea that "the past is a foreign country" depicts the past as unfamiliar and distant, defined in terms of estrangement from the present time and space. The past appears so far receded into the remote distance that it feels as unfamiliar as a foreign country. In the second half of the famous line is an observation of the way of life in this foreign country: "*they* do things differently *there*" in the past. Both the subject of their lives and the content of their practical activities— the doing of "they do things"—as well as their location *there* are all approached in terms of difference and departure from the territory of the present. The past and its occupants are as distant as a foreign country, marked by their difference from here and now.

There are certainly other ways of tying the future to the memory of the past, and there is an enormous body of writings on the subjects of history, memory, and futurity (see Rosaldo 1989; Munn 1992; Yoneyama 1999; Muñoz 2009). A protagonist in William Faulkner's (1950: 92) novel *Requiem for a Nun* speaks this often-quoted line: "The past is never dead. It's not even past." Then-Senator Barack Obama (2008) was embellishing this Faulkner quote in his 2008 speech on race relations when he said, "The past isn't dead and buried. In fact, it isn't even past," referring to the project of "being bound to, but struggling to overcome the past" of racial injustice and slavery (Horton 2008). Similar sentiments of a persistent and ever-present past haunting the present serve as a key theme in such works as Frederick Cooper's (2002) *Africa since 1940: The Past of the*

Present, Allan Pred's (2004) *Past Is Not Dead*, and Derek Gregory's (2004) *The Colonial Present*. In many of these works, the idea is not that we are perpetually bound to an unjust past, but that this past must be conjured and recognized in order for the past to be overcome. The future depends on it.

Futurity is thus a key constitutive element of territories of poverty. The affective capacity of past poverty and the ethics of aspirational work involved in overcoming poverty have captivated my attention throughout my long-term ethnographic research of Korean/American (shorthand for South Korean and Korean American) evangelical Christian spaces. I was struck early on by how powerfully time-and-space narratives compelled people to embrace far-reaching worldviews and far-fetched aspirations, and how these narratives pulsed through people's memories, lives, and imaginations on and off the mission field. Especially on short-term overseas mission trips, far from home in a foreign country and usually traveling without family, Korean/American evangelical Christians rehearsed stories and staged scenes from South Korean history, portraying poverty as an undesirable condition of a painful past, vanquished thereafter through Christianity. The missionaries held themselves up as model protagonists in a triumphant script to overcome poverty and to progress into prosperity (Han 2009, 2011). This essay discusses the perceived remoteness and foreignness of poverty, as articulated through the missionary performance and experience of hardship and compassion. Mission encounters with poverty past and present, I argue, lend credence to the evangelical message of becoming Christian and becoming prosperous, becoming saved and becoming capable of saving others. The script of prosperity in this sense moves from poverty to capacity through the register of experience and empathy.

Staging a Short-Term Mission Trip

> If the Americans hadn't brought us the Gospel and saved us, we would be
> living like this!
> —an elderly Korean woman missionary in Uganda

> You don't understand until you see it with your own eyes. To see how they
> ["Africans"] live, and to remember that we used to live like them, that's what
> I learned on the short-term mission.
> —Housewife in her late 40s, about her trip to Tanzania the previous year.
> Seoul, 2006.

Thirty minutes outside Kampala, Uganda, a missionary-run primary school building was transformed into a temporary hostel and base camp for a group of

150 short-term Korean/American missionaries from South Korea and the United States. Classroom floors were strewn with thick blue foam pads and sleeping bags, pop-up mosquito nets and suitcases, with socks and underwear drying on makeshift clotheslines. For over a week, the short-term missionaries slept on red dirt-covered floors, ate simple meals on plastic plates, and coped with unpredictable access to the toilet and running water. Most of them were remarkably unconcerned by the humble accommodations and inadequate amenities. They had plenty of experiences with similar challenges on school trips and church camps in Korea; this was simply a group travel experience longer in duration and a trip farther in distance from home.

I participated in the monthlong mission trip to East Africa in 2006 to examine how transnational missionary networks mobilized both beliefs and believers, and how global religious imaginaries played out on the ground in the mission field. The trip was organized by Global Mission Frontier (GMF), a transnational Korean/American missionary organization with offices in Seoul and California, and the official itinerary involved South Korean and Korean American evangelical Christian missionaries who spent an estimated total of $1.5 million in travel and operating expenses for the summer program devoted to "bringing together Korea and Africa under the wings of God."[1] There were subgroups; some were sent to visit children's group homes to perform Bible-story puppet shows and hold face-painting events, and some traveled to refugee camps and remote villages to distribute vitamins and shoes. Every summer, GMF also produced large-scale outdoor prayer rallies in soccer stadiums, and organized several educational seminars and workshops for pastors and local government officials. But between the official events, and throughout the schedule, the days were also full of time spent off the stage and off the clock; in addition to rehearsals and prayers, there was plenty of unstructured social time for the missionaries to get to know each other, and share stories (see Han 2010a).

Four classrooms at the school-turned-hostel were assigned according to gender and age: one room each for older men over the age of forty, younger men, older women over the age of forty, and younger women. Age and gender, however, were not the only social categories organizing the mission field. Missing from the school grounds were the teenage and early-twentysomething Korean Americans who arrived separately in Uganda as part of a semiprofessional performance troupe. They were a traditional Korean dance and drumming group from the United States, and since most of them did not speak Korean well— many of them having been born in the United States or being transnational adoptees—they did not socialize closely with the Korean-speaking missionaries from South Korea. As it turned out, Korean Americans in this performance troupe stayed elsewhere on their own. The staff person in charge of local logistics explained to me that the Korean Americans could not be housed at the base camp at the primary school like the other Korean participants because they required special attention. They were deemed unfit essentially because they were too American in disposition and sense of entitlement, unaccustomed to the modest and regimented group living arrangements. This decision was apparently a lesson gleaned from past experience. I was told that Korean Americans in previous years had been disgruntled about sleeping on the floor day after day, and their complaints had eventually become a distraction to other mission participants and the people they were there to serve. So this year, most Korean American missionaries were placed at a nearby guesthouse where rooms were air conditioned and floors laminated. There were beds and chairs. Instead of washing and brushing their teeth with water collected in plastic tubs the night before, they could take warm showers every morning. The guesthouse where the Korean Americans slept, however, was not the pinnacle of the accommodations hierarchy. Also part of the mission trip was a VIP delegation of high-ranking politicians from South Korea, traveling with their wives, teenage children, and personal assistants, and staying at a four-star hotel in downtown Kampala. Such was the local spatial arrangement of a world mission project; gender and age differentiation, and social status hierarchies structured the lived geography of itineraries.

It is worth noting here that, regardless of how arduous a mission trip may be, all short-term travel itineraries have a predefined beginning and an end. Voluntary suffering has a finite duration, and it is precisely this temporal and spatial finitude that makes the difficulties bearable. In turn, the very structure of intentional and temporary privation effectively underscores the passage of time as a key feature of endurance and survival. Put differently, one must first suffer before being delivered from that suffering. Economic development and Christian deliverance require poverty and misery as necessary points of departure.

Overseas mission itineraries like this are designed for the participants to embody an ethical orientation of charity and to act on a commitment to witness the world's suffering. In order to accomplish this, mission participants voluntarily experience misery, however temporarily that may be, rehearsing and performing the affective script of compassion and empathy. They are tasked with seeing firsthand others' suffering elsewhere, and in the process try to build an emotional and ethical kinship with others. Melani McAlister (2008: 873) has described similar evangelical engagements as a distinctly American ethical-political construct she calls "enchanted internationalism," one that "combines an imperialist-style imaginary with something else—a sense of genuine religious community and even global solidarity, however attenuated." Her discussion of ideas such as the imaginary, community, and solidarity builds on an understanding of religion not simply as a site of belief, but as a form of practice (McAlister 2008: 874), turning our attention to not only theological doctrines and religious beliefs, but also to evangelical Christian *practices*. Accordingly, I approach evangelical missions not simply as vehicles for disseminating faith but as a set of practices that negotiate how and toward whom to direct the affective registers of care and compassion. The missionary script of empathy I describe here is akin to what Geraldine Pratt has described as "the seduction of feeling good about feeling bad" (Pratt and the Philippine Women Centre of BC 2012: 80).[2] By feeling bad about the poverty and poor living conditions in the developing world, Korean/American missionaries gain an opportunity to feel good about their own capacity for compassion. As in development, evangelical missions are often a seductively empowering process, one in which participants gain a sense of purpose as contributing agents of social and spiritual change. The discrepancy between temporary mission experience and permanent living conditions—a difference in mobility and territory of suffering—does render some mission participants feeling ineffectual and ultimately powerless in transforming structural conditions and creating lasting change. But for many others, even a fleeting engagement with "doing good" yields long-term personal rewards—at least for the missionaries themselves.

The Script of Progress

The Korean/American missionary script of prosperity unambiguously connects progress through development. One quiet afternoon during the mission trip, I struck up a conversation with a South Korean teenager who was practicing dance moves for an upcoming skit. I recall he was playing the role of a teenager high on drugs and was working on the movement of faltering and stumbling. His encounter with a Jesus figure later in the skit was to save him, at which point he would start walking confidently and with poise. When I asked if he found anything to be particularly difficult or challenging on the trip, this teenager shrugged and said, "To me, Africa doesn't feel that different from Korea. It feels just like Korea in the sixties." I must have chuckled audibly. He was much too young to reminisce about the 1960s; he was likely not born until the 1990s. What did he then mean by "just like the sixties"? His explanation was simple and earnest: "The older people keep telling me this is what Korea used to be like, so I figure it used to look like this." In interpreting the foreign present through the register of Korean history, he was experiencing the present as a simulacrum of the past, seeing Uganda's present and Korea's past as equivalent and mutually constitutive. This young man was not alone in contemplating Korea's past during the mission trip. In fact, the South Korean and U.S.-born Korean American missionaries were so inundated with historical comparisons on the mission trip that one Korean American youth at one point quipped with irritation, "I've learned more about Korea in Africa than Africa." To challenge the "older people's" narrative would involve an inquiry into Korea's past, for which the youth lacked the critical knowledge and the experiential authority. To challenge the "idiom of equivalence" would require a deeper knowledge of the present location, which all short-term mission participants lacked.[3]

The "older people" the young man referred to are the women and men of the "Development Generation," who typically narrate their evangelical missionary calling through dramatic and compelling personal tales of poverty and suffering, endurance and survival, and deliverance and redemption. This is the war generation born either in the last days of Japanese colonial rule or the decade soon after, a generation that came of age during the Korean War and the accompanying destruction and chaos.[4] The war has left indelible marks on nearly everyone's biography, in forms of family separation and untimely death, lost fortune and devastating displacement. For many in the Development Generation, the profound sense of grief and trauma in their lifetime is paralleled only by a sense of gratitude and indebtedness—they cannot believe they have survived. They consider themselves to have been rescued from the past, thanks to the grace of God. This generation of workers had constituted the labor force mobilized for rapid industrialization and nation building throughout the sixties and the seventies, and they have lived through a succession of repressive military-authoritarian regimes, waves of growing democracy, and expanding political liberties. The Development Generation's biographical timeline essentially runs parallel to Korea's economic development and modernization. The national euphoria of hosting the 1988 Seoul Olympics was like a congratulatory pat on the back for the Development Generation, and South Korea's initiation into the OECD in 1996 set another important milestone, announcing to the world that South Korea had arrived as a member of the league of the world's richest nations.

Only the Development Generation can claim to have experienced the full range of bitter hardship and sweet success, and only the Development Generation can claim to have not only *aspired* to but also *achieved* progress through their own blood, sweat, and prayers. The territory of their generational biography is defined affectively in terms of loss, resilience, and triumph. Their survival itself is seen as an achievement and a sign of deliverance. This is the generation that today constitutes the top rank among elders, pastors, theologians, mission strategists, and evangelical politicians leading and coordinating the project of world missions. They are the Christian status quo. Granted, all collective biographies—of generations, racial(ized) communities, sexual minorities, and so forth—risk drawing overly rigid boundaries and overstating their internal coherence in favor of clear periodization and tidy schematics. But the intent here is not an ontological one. A generation is defined not only by a shared range of birth dates but also a lifetime of historical experiences, discourses, and understandings. Discussions of generations need not espouse facile claims of uniformity or consensus. In fact, it is the contradictory complex of meanings and narratives within a generational time-space that could be useful in generalizing historical subject formation, transition, and transformation. Keeping in mind that generational identity and rhetoric remain fluid and multiple, I find it epistemologically useful to map the contours of a distinct aspirational ethos of the evangelical Development Generation. There is both a geography and a shared faith in development. Aspiring to get better and to become better—this ethos of progressive improvement helped drive the explosive "church planting" and "church growth" phenomenon in recent decades. To build, to expand, to spread—these aspirations have launched not only the careers of celebrity megachurch pastors but also mobilized countless volunteers into reproductive labor, supporting pastor husbands, providing childcare, cooking and cleaning in church kitchens and on the backstage of every world mission field. Gender implications are no doubt enormous in this voluntary political economy; the heavily male-dominated political structure of Protestantism in Korea, and especially the project of world missions, rely heavily on women's labor, and a gendered embrace of care, service, and unpaid labor.

An elderly woman burst out in tears during a conversation in Uganda. It was her first time traveling outside of Korea, and I saw her wipe away tears on numerous occasions during the trip. She said, "If the Americans hadn't brought the Gospel to Korea and saved us, we would still be living like this!" She was referring to the work of American Protestant missionaries who arrived in Korea during the early nineteenth century with Western medicine and ideas of enlightenment, but she was also talking about American soldiers who arrived during the Korean War and the American troops stationed in Korea to this day. Her uncritical gratitude toward the United States as a benevolent rescuer and provider shaped her own aspirations. She wanted to rescue and save others as she herself had been saved. This is a distinctly—though probably not uniquely—evangelical disposition: to convert the deeply felt register of appreciation and gratitude into a desire to express and share that joy with others. The fact that this dynamic of "paying forward" depends on the geopolitical structure of U.S. military and economic aid to South Korea very much shapes the evangelical geopolitics of South Korea's missionary enterprises. While scholars have increasingly focused on the importance of the "unchurched" and private, inward looking forms of faith in the United States, what I find significant among Korean/American evangelical Christians is an embrace of historically contingent sociality.

"We would still be living like this!"—by "this," the elderly woman was point-ing to what she regarded as a landscape of poverty and undeveloped potential. In spite of what was largely regarded by the Korean missionaries as an envious abundance of natural resources—in contrast to resource-poor Korea—Uganda seemed to be trapped in a uncultivated time-space that she associated with Ko-rea's past. To the missionaries, what Uganda needed was precisely what Korea once needed: a will to develop, a helping hand, and an acceptance of the Gospel. Recurrent power outages and water stoppages prompted bittersweet recollec-tions of a time when such inconveniences used to be a daily occurrence in Seoul, as well. Unpaved streets and foul-smelling outhouses reminded Korean mission-aries of a childhood and home that no longer was. Elderly women reminisced about when they used to draw water from a communal well and balanced the heavy pails on their heads on the long walk home. Men kicking around a soccer ball talked about how they used to play with poorly inflated soccer balls when they were young, and how they discovered later that they could not play nearly as well with properly inflated ones. For the Development Generation, their mission encounter experience in Uganda seemed to corroborate their personal journey and historical purpose: to make Africa better by remembering how *they* got better. They were on a mission trip to "help Africa" to become better through development, modernization, education, wage labor, and above all else, by cul-tivating a model of Christian leadership that prioritizes Godly governance as good governance. It is perhaps not surprising, then, that none of the Korean/American missionaries seemed even slightly perturbed about the fact that Ugan-dan President Yoweri Museveni has been in power since 1986. The evangelical Korean script for state-led modernization already contained several chapters of dictatorship, euphemistically referred to as "strong leadership," an effective governance structure for the promotion of discipline and hard work.

The affective script of seeing hardship, remembering misery, and offering relief operated across multiple lines of national affinity and racial difference. Korean-born and Korean American missionaries certainly considered them-selves to be equal to the white American missionaries in duty and status. They also thought Koreans could empathize better with people in developing coun-tries and connect with them in a more intimate and visceral way because, the way they saw it, Koreans themselves also had firsthand experiences with coloni-zation, poverty, and development. But there were still lines not ever meant to be blurred. An unmarried woman missionary in her late forties laughed out loud when I asked if she could imagine finding a potential spouse at the mission post. Though she herself was the foreigner in this context, she said that she would never "date a foreigner." Romance or marriage between a Korean missionary and a non-ethnic Korean person on the mission field would be highly discouraged if not explicitly forbidden, she said, and besides, she thought the whole prospect ridiculous. Short-term dalliances on mission trips would most certainly be frowned upon, and even on long-term, sometimes lifelong mission posts, Korean missionaries are expected to lead a somewhat ascetic unmarried life or a "properly" heterosexual life, but only with ethnically Korean spouses who could help with the missionary work. There are some exceptions out there, such as a man I met who had married his Filipina wife while he lived as a missionary in the Philippines, but for the most part, sharing the Gospel and inviting the world into one's close circles and intimate spaces of faith do not require relaxing the ethnic boundaries around sex and marriage, at least in theory.

On the first morning of a weeklong economic development seminar in Uganda, the electricity went out three times during the first fifteen or twenty minutes. When the power finally came back on and the LCD projector could be used, the missionaries played a short video for a room full of civil servants and local politicians. This was an organizational promotion video introducing GMF's history and spiritual mission, narrated as a dramatic tale of Korea's deliverance from poverty to prosperity. The video began with scenes of barefoot children and pregnant women from black-and-white documentary films and jumped from colonial-era Korea to the arrival of American and European missionaries who, according to popular Christian narrative, devoted their lives to uplifting the poor presumed-to-be-ignorant Korean masses. With rousing background music and triumphant narration, the video declared that Korea had achieved success and was now in a position to reach out to the rest of the world. Evangelical missionaries are working tirelessly throughout the world, the narrator in the video excitedly proclaimed, building schools and teaching the poor, organizing and leading prayers wherever they are most needed, and spreading faith and work ethic.

The video, narrated authoritatively from a purportedly singular and unified perspective of Korean Christians, fell on the ears of confused and disinterested audience. The need for interpretation between Korean, Swahili, and English made communication difficult and extremely time consuming, and the tone of the video narrative left the audience uneasy. Were the Ugandan and Tanzanian participants supposed to applaud with the Koreans at the end of the video? Were they expected to feel encouraged by Korea's success or envious of Korea's good fortune? Questions from several participants revealed that what they sought in the economic development seminar were specific and technical forms of development knowledge: what specific water-treatment and soil-testing technology were the missionaries going to teach about? Which specific governmental bureaucratic units were involved in launching rural reform policies in Korea, and what was the path of least resistance? How did farmers negotiate the pros and cons of using chemical fertilizers on their crops? How are Koreans different from the Chinese? How is South Korea different from North Korea?

GMF missionaries were certainly not the first or only group of foreign missionaries and so-called development experts to roll through town. Christianity, development, and foreign aid all have a long sordid history throughout Africa. Most if not all seminar participants in Uganda and Tanzania already identified themselves as Christian and regular churchgoers, and they were recruited through their churches to attend the missionary-led seminars. They were not in need of conversion. Many in fact told me they regularly attended similar seminars and focus groups organized by donors from afar, and one woman admitted to me during a lunch that she came only for the stipend and free meal. She regularly attended these seminars, she said, but had no real interest in economic development or Korean Christianity. She was a marginally employed municipal employee bored at work, and thought the seminar would be mildly entertaining and she would earn some pocket money. In a way, she was also performing to the script of mission encounter, one between benevolent strangers and grateful natives. For six hours every day for an entire week, the missionaries taught an economic development seminar by narrating Korean history, reenacting scenes from Korean development programs, and leading Bible study on work and prosperity. On the final day of the seminar, a pastor from the nearby church came by to thank the missionaries and the participants. Surrounded by smiles and hellos, the pastor held an envelope given to him by the Korean missionaries and handed out cash stipends to each participant.

Missionary Actors as Agents of Change

GMF had begun as the brainchild of one man, Pastor Kim, a modestly successful Silicon Valley entrepreneur and publisher of a local Korean-language Christian weekly newspaper. In 1994 he went to Rwanda to report on the genocide for a journalistic assignment, and he was so devastated by the violence and destruction he witnessed that he made a career- and life-changing decision upon his return—he founded GMF and began working full time on world missions. By 2001 he had been ordained as a Presbyterian minister and was running GMF as its full-time director. By the time I met Pastor Kim in 2006, GMF was a registered nonprofit organization with several paid staff and volunteers, dedicated to identifying and proselytizing to "unreached people groups" especially in East Africa. A stern man in his early fifties, Pastor Kim personally oversaw most aspects of the programs. He frequently gave guest sermons at Korean American churches and raised money for his projects, and he traveled between Africa, California, and South Korea several times a year. His salary and travel expenses, as well as the entire operation of GMF, were supported by donations from individuals and sponsoring churches in the United States and South Korea, as well as the few small business ventures affiliated with GMF. His teenage Korean American children often accompanied Pastor Kim to Africa, as they did in 2006 when I participated in the mission trip. While Pastor Kim led delegations of Christian politicians from Korea in meetings with Ugandan and Tanzanian government officials, his son and daughter participated in proselytizing activities on the mission field, and his wife worked at her full-time job as a nurse back in California.

Short-term missions like the GMF program are derided by critics as the "amateurization of missions" or "drive-by missions," but they remain a key part of evangelical programs and mission strategies today (see Hancock 2013). Short-term missions bring a concentrated infusion of attention and funding and complement ongoing long-term GMF projects such as the year-round operation of mission centers, medical clinics, primary schools, and small factories. Short-term visitors can bring new energy and enthusiasm and help alleviate the feelings of isolation and loneliness that can beset missionaries in the field. However, when I spoke with several long-term missionaries unaffiliated with GMF, they expressed mixed feelings about the influx of volunteers and donations. They worried about how short-term missions exhausted fragile local networks and exploited relations that had taken time and care to cultivate over a long period of time. They were also troubled by how poorly trained the short-term volunteers often were in terms of language competency, historical knowledge, and ethics of aid work. While most appreciated the enthusiastic flurry of activities every summer—the peak season for short-term missions—the long-term, career missionaries also wished for more attention to the less spectacular programs in the more immediate present. Instead of a minivan full of balloons and face-painting supplies, for example, the long-term missionaries wished for a regular supply of writing paper and sketchbooks. One seasoned missionary working with a different Christian NGO was appalled that GMF missionaries were handing out shoes to random children on the street—did they know if another short-term mission team had visited the previous week? Was that particular neighborhood considered most in need? Did they know if those shoes will actually be worn by the children, or sold to support the household? Do they know that gifts like shoes and other material objects often foment jealousy and tension among children, damaging social relations in the community? Do the short-term missionaries have any idea of the longer-term consequences of their actions? One former missionary back in Korea even offered this terse advice: "What can Korean missionaries do to improve their short-term missions? They can *stop*."[5]

Evangelical mission encounters effectively articulate personal and historical memories with scripts of compassion and empathy. They invoke historical commonality and developmental solidarity and obscure geopolitical and geoeconomic inequalities and uneven power relations. By framing the encounter with the developing world as a nostalgic encounter with a past overcome, Korean-led evangelical Christian missions corroborate the self-serving narrative of advancement, and renew the missionaries' own faith in progress. By repeatedly narrating national poverty as a condition they have left behind, the missionaries were also cultivating hope in future prosperity, when in reality the future is far from certain or bright. In fact, most of the South Korean missionaries in their twenties and thirties faced bleak prospects for full-time and stable employment, and they talked often during the mission trip about scarce job opportunities and limited career options.

Whereas the Development Generation saw and experienced the mission trip in ways that corroborated their progress thus far, Korea's postdevelopment generation tended to express a greater inclination toward mission as a structure of self-discovery and self-discipline with poverty and hardship as the backdrop. One night in Tanzania, when twenty or so missionaries rooming together in a large rented house gathered for informal worship and prayer, conversations gradually led to talk about what had brought everyone on the mission trip. It was a cross-generational and mixed-age meeting with both staff and volunteers, men and women from South Korea and the United States, but everyone spoke in Korean. The Development Generation tended to paint their motivations in broad and remarkably standardized strokes. Their stories typically began with overcoming some sort of financial or personal hardship, leading to a born-again experience, and concluding with renewed devotion and a commitment to service as an expression of gratitude. Especially the well-off missionaries in the group tended to embrace charity as a way to review the balance sheet of their own lives, to account for providence and grace, and to show gratitude by being generous toward others. As a recently retired tax accountant from southern California put it, she had received plenty of blessings from God, and it was time to share her dividends with the rest of the world.

Not many of the postdevelopment generation came from prosperous backgrounds, however. I will share three vignettes here. Suah, in her early twenties and wearing a black Sex Pistols T-shirt at the time, came from a city in the southern region in South Korea. She told the group that she had spent the last few years hanging out with the wrong people. "Theater crowd, you know how they are," she said wryly, to which there was a collective "Ah!" and disapproving shake of the head. There was a lot of drinking and other immoral behavior, Suah confessed, and she described herself as having been a lost lamb who did not want to be found. A couple of years ago, her parents faced a sudden catastrophic financial loss, forcing her middle-class family to adapt to a significantly more modest quality of life. They had to move far out of the city, in part to find cheaper housing and in part to avoid the debt collectors. It was humiliating turn of events, Suah said, and it was devastating to see her parents suffer such loss. And for all this, Suah blamed herself. She blamed her lack of faith and misbehavior for her parents' misfortunes. She believed that God was punishing her guiltless, hardworking parents for the sins of their ungrateful daughter. When Suah came across a description of GMF's Africa mission program on the Internet, she said it immediately made sense to her: she was meant to go to Africa. She maxed out her credit cards, borrowed money from friends and family, and received help from her church to join the mission trip. The mission was about penitence for Suah, a step in atonement and self-rehabilitation. "I have nothing here in Africa," she emphasized, "no money, no job, and no pride." She wanted to "lower herself to nothing" so that she could start a new life when she returned to Korea. She saw Africa as a place of life laid bare, a blank slate, and this was a common narrative for many of the younger missionaries who planned to return to Korea to start a new chapter in life. This trope, as many have pointed out, not only represents Africa as the "supreme receptacle" of the West's obsession with "absence," "non-being," and "nothingness," but also as a frontier where fortunes can be made (see McClintock 1995; Mbembe 2001). Such representation is certainly not a uniquely Western projection; South Koreans fully deployed this colonial perspective, frequently describing Africa as "the dark continent" and "the ends of the earth."

Another young Korean woman in her early twenties, Mina, had spent the last two years caring full time for her terminally ill father. When he was diagnosed with late-stage cancer, she had been preparing to leave for Vienna, Austria, to study classical musical composition on a prestigious full scholarship. Instead, she had to put her studies on indefinite hold and help her mother make ends meet and care for her father. Mina's life was now filled with hospital visits and administering pain-management medications, and her father's recovery remained unlikely. One day, her mother suggested that Mina take a break from the constant cloud of dread and sadness at home, and go somewhere far away to take her mind off things. The mission trip was hardly a vacation, but it was a welcome break, Mina said. The trip was about a temporary reprieve from her own pain. Soft-spoken and earnest, Mina said that she saw far more pain and misery on the mission field than she had ever imagined back in Korea. Witnessing firsthand how much suffering there was in Africa, she said that she felt stronger about returning home to face the inevitable—her father's death. "After Africa," she said, "I can handle anything." Like Suah, Mina saw "Africa" as a spatiotemporal break, a place for a fresh restart.

Lastly, there was Jimin, a vivacious social worker with aspirations to become a long-term missionary. She was one of the very few who took the time to learn a few Kiswahili phrases and songs before the mission trip. Positive in disposition and remarkably hard-working, she volunteered for tasks that no one else wanted to do, went out of her way to make conversations with people she did not know, and was brilliant with children—energetic, funny, and patient. It turned out that Jimin had a deeply personal reason for why she joined the mission trip. She was an orphan; she had lost both of her parents in a car accident when she was only two years old, and, not having any family members who could take her in, Jimin grew up in an orphanage outside of Seoul. Though she was repeatedly made available for adoption, she never was. She explained that growing up in an orphanage and trying to be chosen for adoption had trained her well—she has always had to be bright and likable, as this was a matter of survival. She had persevered with well-practiced positivity as her friends were taken away for adoption one by one. But one of Jimin's fondest memories growing up was of white American visitors who came to the orphanage. A small group of Christian volunteers including some soldiers from a nearby American military base visited the children regularly with gifts and affection, and Jimin recalled vividly how their visits excited the children, who eagerly awaited them. The crinkling sound of certain candy wrappers, she said, still makes her smile because she remembers how happy she used to be to receive those American treats. She eventually became a social worker and a residential staff at the same orphanage where she grew up, and though she found the work gratifying, she felt ready for change. After all, Jimin was in her early thirties, and had never lived anywhere but the orphanage. When her pastor at church suggested the GMF summer mission trip, she jumped at the chance to work with orphans in Africa because, she said, she knew firsthand how visitors from afar—like the American soldiers she fondly remembered—can bring the gifts of joy and happiness. She could not wait to be on the *giving* end of aid and compassion. "African orphans" for her was not just an abstraction in charity; she herself was an orphan, and as she said, she would always be an orphan. She was convinced she had a special calling.

The Present Past and Alternative Futures

Missions by definition are spatiotemporal projects of purpose-driven mobility, and they produce an uneven geography of aspirations. It is by now a common contention that missionaries played a key role within the workings of colonial domination. Proselytizing missions have equipped colonial projects with an enabling moral pretext, carried out colonial agendas as de facto agents of empire, and pacified the colonized populations with teachings that stressed submission and acquiescence (see Comaroff and Comaroff 1986, 1991; Stoler 2002, 2006).

Beyond benevolence, foreign missions in Korea were also a "moral equivalent for imperialism" (Hutchison 1987: 91), and the three pillars of American Protestant missionaries—the "spirit of white supremacy, religious triumphalism, and cultural imperialism" (Oak 2002: 3)—sought to eradicate Korean traditions, religions, and customs as antithetical to modernity.

Today, with tolerance of difference being promoted as a political virtue, even diehard fundamentalist evangelicals begrudgingly admit that the so-called romance of missions is over. These changes are of course not limited to evangelical missions. In contemporary travel narratives, an emphasis on adventure and danger has arguably faded with awareness of uneven power relations and calls for cultural sensitivity, though by no means have they vanished. Popular depictions of alien cultures and unfamiliar places—presented for instance on long-running American reality TV programs like Survivor and The Amazing Race, as well as countless travel programs and National Geographic television shows—continue to depict foreign places as exotic playgrounds full of bewildering practices even as the participants sometimes acknowledge the still-present past of colonialism, war, and poverty. Narratives of humanitarian volunteerism and internationalism dominate today's mission programs and travel itineraries alike. Emphasized instead of conquest and adventure are service, compassion, and empathy. In missionary literature, overtly racialized expressions like "heathen regions" have been replaced by pseudoscientific terms like "unreached ethnolinguistic people groups" and the flagrantly imperialist depictions of "civilizing missions" are reinterpreted as "cross-cultural endeavors." In fact, mission training curricula draw significantly from cultural anthropology for "in-depth knowledge of cultural differences" that promote "cross-cultural understanding."[6] As I discuss elsewhere, the evangelical reliance on cultural anthropology, statistics, demography, and cartography together constitute a "missionary geoscience" (Han 2010b). For example, a popular notion among missiologists and mission strategists is that proselytizing missions should no longer depend on the success of cross-cultural missions because the cross-cultural model is no longer considered suitable for the postcolonial present. Instead, missionaries are urged to support and cultivate "cultural neighbors" who are better suited for evangelizing those "near" them—geographically, ethnically, and linguistically (see Johnstone, Mandryk, and Johnstone 2001; Barrett and Johnson 2001). But beyond these new catchphrases and rephrased sentiments, the narratives of encountering difference still produce a familiar geography of preexisting racial and cultural difference and a missionary pursuit of rescue and salvation as a way of life.

Korean/American evangelical missionaries—as emissaries of faith both in development and in Christianity—reinscribe an uneven geography of privilege and generosity in which the world is divided between saved and unsaved, mission-sending and mission-receiving. As a formerly aid-receiving nation that has become an aid-sending donor nation, South Korea claims a special stature for overcoming poverty and achieving progress (see Kim 2011a, 2011b). For this, Korean/American missionaries insist they are differently qualified to be the "good guys" in mission. There are parallels in exceptionalism, such as with Canada's national narrative of being the "good guys" in the international arena in contrast to the imperialist United States (see Heron 2007). For Korean evangelical missionaries, though, the national narrative emphasis is on having *overcome* poverty, and having *become* one of the "good guys." In preaching and proselytizing a distinctly Korean model of developmentalism and millennial capitalism, the missionaries not only produce geographical imaginaries and ethics of charity, but also an affective script of prosperity that emphasizes the possibility of this becoming. As I have discussed in this article, this script certainly prefigures achievement of wealth and prosperity as the end result, but poverty, misery, and struggle are key and necessary ingredients for that outcome. In other words, overcoming poverty and overcoming the past are constitutive acts within the scripts of prosperity.

At stake is not simply the place of Korean missionaries in the world or the changing landscape of global Christianity. With the complex geographies of international development and the ethical and political tensions between charitable service and social justice, the work of Korean missionaries and their participation as nonstate actors in poverty alleviation in the developing world pose new questions and challenges in understanding territories of poverty and prosperity. It is important to remember that the Korean/American missionaries from Seoul and California experienced their monthlong trip to Uganda and Tanzania as a kind of an offering in itself, sharing what they themselves have recently gained. This is not to discount in any way the colonial continuities in missionary intent and practice, and I certainly do not dismiss the significance of neocolonial Korean missionary projects in places like Iraq and Afghanistan. Nonetheless, what I see as critically important in Korean/American evangelical missionary practices is the insistence that they possess a greater capacity for empathy and compassion for the developing world precisely because Korea was also once poor. But rather than acknowledging the persistence of poverty and the intensifying economic polarization in contemporary Korea, the missionary script of prosperity relegates poverty to the first opening acts in their chronological narrative. The bright spotlight is on the protagonists in this optimistic developmental narrative, and they expect the audience to eagerly follow the script toward a future of prosperity. But this is mostly a story they tell themselves, and it is one of many stories possible. If the missionaries had only recognized that poverty is not past or already overcome but very much still present and persistent in Korea, they might have encountered the foreign country differently—not as a territory of their past but a sobering reflection of their present. To recognize the present and imagine alternative futures, the missionary script of prosperity must be reinscribed.

NOTES

1. GMF and all names used in this article are pseudonyms. This paper is based in part on research supported by the Academy of Korean Studies Grant funded by the Korean Government (MEST) (AKS-2011–AAA-2104)

2. Also see Book Review Symposium—"Geraldine Pratt's 'Families Apart: Migrant Mothers and the Conflicts of Labor and Love,'" Antipode Foundation, blog post, May 7, 2013, http://antipodefoundation.org/2013/05/07/families-apart/.

3. "Idiom of equivalence" is a phrase used by Sylvia Nam, personal communication, June 5, 2013. Also see Nam 2012.

4. I am grateful to Janice Kim at York University for helping me think through the continuities between the "Development Generation" and the "War Generation." Personal communication to author, June 6, 2013.

5. Interview with a former missionary, Seoul, July 20, 2007.

6. In Korea, the anthropologist-theologian Paul G. Hiebert has been particularly influential in this regard, and four of his books have been translated into Korean and are distributed by a leading missionary research agency. Hiebert was a well-known theologian who taught mission and anthropology at Trinity Evangelical Divinity School, Kansas State University, and Fuller Theological Seminary, where he had ample opportunity to work with and train Korean and Korean American seminary students. See Hiebert 1996, 1997, 2006, 2010.

REFERENCES

Barrett, David, and Todd Johnson. 2001. *World Christian Trends, AD 30–AD 2200: Interpreting the Annual Christian Megacensus*. Pasadena, Calif.: William Carey Library.

Comaroff, Jean, and John Comaroff. 1986. "Christianity and Colonialism in South Africa." *American Ethnologist* 13, 1–22.

Comaroff, Jean, and John Comaroff. 1991. *Of Revelation and Revolution*. Chicago: University of Chicago Press.

Cooper, Frederick. 2002. *Africa since 1940: The Past of the Present*. Cambridge: Cambridge University Press.

Faulkner, William. 1950. *Requiem for a Nun*. New York: Random House.

Gregory, Derek. 2004. *The Colonial Present: Afghanistan, Palestine, and Iraq*. Malden, Mass.: Blackwell.

Han, Ju Hui Judy. 2009. "Contemporary Korean/American Evangelical Missions:

Politics of Space, Gender, and Difference." PhD diss., University of California, Berkeley.

Han, Ju Hui Judy. 2010a. "Neither Friends nor Foes: Thoughts on Ethnographic Distance." *Geoforum* 41:1, 11–14.

Han, Ju Hui Judy. 2010b. "Reaching the Unreached in the 10/40 Window: The Missionary Geoscience of Race, Difference and Distance." In *Mapping the End Times: American Evangelical Geopolitics and Apocalyptic Visions*, ed. Jason Dittmer and Tristan Sturm, 183–207. Hampshire: Ashgate Publishing.

Han, Ju Hui Judy. 2011. "'If You Don't Work, You Don't Eat': Evangelizing Development in Africa." In *New Millennium South Korea: Neoliberal Capitalism and Transnational Movements*, ed. Jesook Song, 142–58. London: Routledge.

Hancock, Mary E. 2013. "New Mission Paradigms and the Encounter with Islam: Fusing Voluntarism, Tourism and Evangelism in Short-Term Missions in the USA." *Culture and Religion*, February, 1–19.

Hartley, L. P. 1953. *The Go-Between*. London: H. Hamilton.

Heron, Barbara. 2007. *Desire for Development: Whiteness, Gender, and the Helping Imperative*. Waterloo: Wilfrid Laurier University Press.

Hiebert, Paul G. 1996. *Sŏn'gyowa Munhwa Illyuhak* (Anthropological Insights for Missionaries). Trans. D. H. Kim. Seoul: Joy Mission Publishers.

Hiebert, Paul G. 1997. *Illyuhakjŏk Chŏpkŭnŭl T'onghan Sŏnkyo Hyŏnjangŏi Munhwa Ihae* (Anthropological Reflections on Missiological Issues). Trans. Y. D. Kim. Seoul: Joy Mission Publishers.

Hiebert, Paul G. 2006. *Inshinronjŏk Chŏnhwanŭi Sŏn'gyohakjŏk Ŭiŭi*. Seoul: Korea Research Institute for Missions.

Hiebert, Paul G. 2010. *21-segi sŏn'gyo wa segyegwan ŭi pyŏnhwa* (Transforming worldviews: an anthropological understanding of how people change). Trans. P. N. Hong. Soul T'ukpyolsi: Pok innun Saram.

Horton, Scott. 2008. "The Past Is Not Past. Or Is It?" *Harper's Magazine*, March 24, http://harpers.org/blog/2008/03/the-past-is-not-past-or-is-it/.

Hutchison, William R. 1987. *Errand to the World: American Protestant Thought and Foreign Missions*. Chicago: University of Chicago Press.

Johnstone, Patrick, Jason Mandryk, and Robyn Johnstone. 2001. *Operation World: When We Pray, God Works*. 21st-Century ed. Cumbria: Paternoster Lifestyle.

Kim, Soyeun. 2011a. "Bridging Troubled Worlds? An Analysis of the Ethical Case for South Korean Aid." Journal of International Development 23: 802–22. doi:10.1002/jid.1811.

Kim, Soyeun. 2011b. "To Be or Not to Be (emerged), 'DAC-ability' Is the Question: Lessons from Japan and Korea." Paper presented at the joint conference of the European Association of Development and the Development Studies Association, University of York, September 19–22.

Lowenthal, David. 1975. "Past Time, Present Place: Landscape and Memory." *Geographical Review* 65:1, 1–36.

Mbembe, Achille. 2001. *On the Postcolony*. Berkeley: University of California Press.

McAlister, Melani. 2008. "What Is Your Heart For?: Affect and Internationalism in the Evangelical Public Sphere." *American Literary History* 20:4, 870–95.

McClintock, Anne. 1995. *Imperial Leather: Race, Gender, and Sexuality in the Colonial Contest*. New York: Routledge.

Munn, Nancy D. 1992. "The Cultural Anthropology of Time: A Critical Essay." *Annual Review of Anthropology* 21, 93–123.

Muñoz, Jose Esteban. 2009. *Cruising Utopia the Then and There of Queer Futurity*. New York: New York University Press.

Nam, Sylvia. 2012. "Speculative Urbanism: The Remaking of Phnom Penh". PhD diss., University of California, Berkeley.

Oak, Sung-Deuk. 2002. "The Indigenization of Christianity in Korea: North American Missionaries' Attitudes towards Korean Religions, 1884–1910." PhD diss., Boston University School of Theology.

Obama, Barack. 2008. "Barack Obama's Speech on Race." *New York Times*, March 18, http://www.nytimes.com/2008/03/18/us/politics/18text-obama.html.

Pred, Allan. 2004. *The Past Is Not Dead: Facts, Fictions, and Enduring Racial Stereotypes*. Minneapolis: University of Minnesota Press.

Pratt, Geraldine, and Philippine Women Centre of BC. 2012. *Families Apart: Migrant Mothers and the Conflicts of Labor and Love*. Minneapolis: University of Minnesota Press.

Rosaldo, Renato. 1989. "Imperialist Nostalgia." *Representations* 26, 107–22.

Stoler, Ann Laura. 2002. *Carnal Knowledge and Imperial Power: Race and the Intimate in Colonial Rule*. Berkeley: University of California Press.

Stoler, Ann Laura. 2006. *Haunted by Empire: Geographies of Intimacy in North American History*. Durham: Duke University Press.

Traub, Valerie. "The Past Is a Foreign Country? The Times and Spaces of Islamicate Sexuality Studies." In *Islamicate Sexualities: Translations across Temporal Geographies of Desire*, ed. Kathryn Babayan and Afsaneh Iajmabadi, 1–40. Cambridge, Mass.: Harvard University Center for Middle Eastern Studies.

Yoneyama, Lisa. 1999. *Hiroshima Traces: Time, Space, and the Dialectics of Memory*. Berkeley: University of California Press.

REPRESENTATION

Moving Beyond the Geography of Privilege

ANH-THI LE

As I was growing up, my parents constantly impressed on me the importance of serving the most vulnerable populations—the poor, the elderly, the homeless, the disabled. I spent the majority of my youth volunteering with food banks and other community projects as a member of the Girl Scouts of America, Air Force Junior Reserve Officer Training Corps, and student government. In many ways, these principles of service and volunteerism are rooted in my parents' struggles as refugees during the Vietnam War and the political, financial, and communal support that they received when they first arrived in the United States. As a first-generation Vietnamese American from the global North, my commitment to social justice and poverty action is in many ways shaped by my family's history.

When I came to UC Berkeley, I took courses on wealth inequality and poverty-related issues and found a community of likeminded peers who were as passionate about social justice as I was. Many of us spent our summers working with community development organizations in the United States and abroad. Before my final undergraduate year at UC Berkeley, I volunteered with a U.S.-based fair-trade women's empowerment organization in India. I was one of forty students in my academic program involved in an international service learning experience that summer. The organization I worked with was committed to alleviating poverty by providing market access and capacity-building opportunities for artisans around the world. By living and immersing myself in the community where I worked, I was given a rare opportunity to constantly learn, reflect, and build on my understanding of the development space that I was engaging in.

Over a three-month period, I was tasked with building on-the-ground partnerships with community leaders and collecting qualitative data from in-depth interviews, life histories, and testimonials from artisans. I had studied the social, economic, and political history of India, so I was excited to work directly with a partner organization on the ground. However, when I arrived in India and began conducting monitoring and evaluation surveys, I found myself acutely aware of my identity as a young, educated volunteer from the United States, and I worried about how the women I surveyed and worked with perceived me. The surveys not only highlighted the poverty of the women but also highlighted the stark economic and political differences between my life and theirs. As a volunteer from the global North interviewing an artisan from the global South, our relationship reflected a geography of privilege in which there is a division "between the saved and unsaved, mission-sending and mission receiving, and between aid-sending donor nations and aid-receiving nations in the developing world" (Han, in this volume). Gathering personal information about the artisans I worked with seemed to produce the notion that I had the technical expertise that would alleviate the obstacles they faced.

On the one hand, I was able to overcome feelings of insecurity about wealth and cultural differences once we began working collaboratively on handicraft projects and spent time together outside of our regular work hours. I came to see these women as partners, friends, and extended family—not just as poor people. On the other hand, nothing could change the fact that our relationship was defined by my role as a volunteer, and theirs as beneficiaries.

While I was able to support the organization through a host of monitoring and evaluation surveys and partnerships with new buyers in the United States, I questioned how I, as a young, American woman could play a role in addressing issues of the global South. I carried these sentiments back to UC Berkeley, where I found my peers in similar predicaments. We questioned our identities and privilege as short-term volunteers from the global North working to help those living in the global South. But how effective could we be as workers in a place where we did not speak the local language, and where our specific skill sets might bear only a passing resemblance to what is actually needed? If we go somewhere else to help people, what assumptions are we making about those we are trying to help? How can we really address issues of inequality if we are geographically distant from the social and political challenges that shape the everyday lives of the poor?

It was after deep reflection we found that though we were all volunteers from the global North, our identities and intentions varied greatly. This variation allowed us to conceptualize our encounters with poverty individually and move beyond the global North–global South framework. For me, traveling and working in India supplemented my academic and professional development, as I was interested in learning about the role of international NGOs in addressing women's issues in India. For some, it was about gaining professional experience, contributing expertise, or adding a service experience to their resume. And for others, it was much more nuanced and about empowering their own local communities or reengaging and giving back to their parents' home country. Our diverse motivations and engagements with poverty reflect our studies, service background, and personal identities in a way that may not be represented by a global North–global South divide.

This geography of privilege delineates the characteristics and histories of the global North and the global South, the developed from the developing and effectively, the volunteers and the poor. Volunteerism produces the geography of privilege, as the relationship often represents a transfer of services from the global North to the South, reinforcing paternalistic power imbalances as interactions are about giving and receiving across wealth, class, and geographic boundaries. As the reflections of my peers show, our motivations and encounters with poverty present another way to look at engagements with poverty that studies individual sources of affect and moves beyond the hierarchical global North–global South relationship.

I am reminded of Han's discussion in this volume of how cross-national and intergenerational volunteers from South Korea shared their own imaginations of development, producing a geography of privilege rooted in a global South–global South interaction that is not strictly defined by the global North–global South divide. While I am geographically from the global North, my histories and experiences are rooted in generations of struggle that go well beyond my personal identity as an American. Thus, my encounters with poverty are shaped by my identity as a child of Vietnamese refugees in a way that is not and should not be defined by a stark global North–global South binary.

I acknowledge the inherent cultural, social, and economic differences between myself and those I worked with in India. However, the notion that the relationship is distinctly and geographically defined by the global North and the global South leaves out other histories. Reframing the global North and the global South framework of development in a way that moves beyond the geography of privilege allows us to understand and orient how our identities shape our encounters with poverty, that is, in a relationship not only defined by our geographic differences but also grounded in our personal and individual identities and histories.

The Duration of Inequality:
Limits, Liability, and the Historical
Specificity of Poverty

ALYOSHA GOLDSTEIN

The "persistence of poverty" is a constitutive dilemma for the idea of historical progress. Despite proclamations to the contrary, this is not because poverty is a foundational problem to be solved as such, but rather because the idea of progress demands the counterpoint of destitution in a variety of ways, especially as it is articulated with economic development, capitalist accumulation, and the promise of prosperity. However, for poverty to be plausible as a contradiction or residual circumstance within the advance of progress, it is a problem that requires moments of apparent incremental resolution and institutional mechanisms that enact periodization and confer closure. Progress depends upon that which it ostensibly overcomes. Law has been among the most prominent of such mechanisms for the ways in which it passes judgment—assessing past wrongs and establishing precedent for the future—and how it institutes epochal shifts toward the presumably immanent realization of the greater good of justice. In this sense, *history* appears as the ultimate judgment, as in to be "on the right side of history" and the divine "last judgment" (Koselleck 2002: 218–47). This essay focuses on the particular series of legal settlements funded by the Claims Resolution Act (CRA) as a means of considering how and why poverty is made history—rendered progressively past, resolved, and reconciled—in the context of the contemporary United States. What follows is an inquiry into the tension between demands for the redress of historical injustice and the genealogies of dispossession that are ongoing but that exceed the conventional terms of the "persistence of poverty."

Upon signing the CRA into law in December 2010, President Barack Obama declared that the legislation was not "simply a matter of making amends. It's about reaffirming our values on which this nation was founded—principles of fairness and equality and opportunity. It's about helping families who suffered through no fault of their own get back on their feet. It's about restoring a sense of trust between the American people and the government that plays such an important role in their lives" ("Remarks by the President" 2010). Indeed, this legislation assembled and funded a series of historic class-action lawsuit settlements that were milestones for civil rights and Native American claims litigation in the United States. The CRA appropriated $3.4 billion for the settlement reached in *Cobell v. Salazar*, a case against the Interior and Treasury Departments for their mismanagement of American Indian trust accounts created by the 1887 General Allotment Act. The legislation also included *In re Black Farmers Discrimination Litigation*, a suit against the U.S. Department of Agriculture that was the single largest civil rights settlement in U.S. history. Additionally, the CRA funded a series of prodigious Indian water rights cases, as well as extending the Temporary Assistance to Needy Families (TANF) program. If the duration of dispossession and impoverishment addressed by the Claims Resolution Act surpassed and suppressed the lifetimes of many of those affected, the settlements and the legislation as a whole promised to bring closure to the longstanding wrongs perpetrated by the federal agencies involved.

This essay focuses specifically on the temporal provisions through which the Claims Resolution Act purports to either resolve or render provisional the forms of inequity collected under its auspices (for further discussion of the CRA, see Goldstein 2014a). I argue that the CRA's juridical bundling of cases brings into proximity discrepant histories and geographies of expropriation and poverty so as to situate these within an overarching teleology of progress and improvement in the face of contemporary economic and social volatility. This proximity ultimately suggests historical and present-day entanglements that unsettle the proposed terms of juridical closure. This prospective closure reduces racialized logics of dehumanization, property, and dispossession to aberrant acts of discrimination, mismanaged accounting, and temporary need.

For the purposes of this essay, I limit my analysis of the legislation to the *Cobell* and *In re Black Farmers* settlements and the provisions for extending TANF block grants. The first part of the essay provides an overview of the two settlements and the stakes of bringing closure to the issues raised by each of the two class-action lawsuits. As Ananya Roy emphasizes with regard to the "aporias of poverty" in the introduction to this volume, I am interested here in what Jacques Derrida calls "the time of the problematic closure," which "assigns a domain, a territory, or a field to an inquiry, a research, or a knowledge" (Derrida 1993: 44, 40).[1] The next section of the essay looks at the legislative assemblage of the Claims Resolution Act and situates the CRA and the two settlements in the dynamics of the present. My focus in this section is on how and why the perspective of the present renders the disparate histories of impoverishment legible in particular ways. The essay's third part examines the temporalization of inequality evident in the stipulations for time limits, sanctions, and marriage promotion in the Temporary Assistance to Needy Families block grants included in the CRA. I argue that the time-limited and conjugal terms through which these social policy provisions insist that poverty and need can only be temporary express a corollary to the historical foreclosures enacted by *Cobell* and *In re Black Farmers*. Furthermore, these measures aim to bestow incremental forms of privatized resolution through expressions of personal responsibility that ultimately enable the intensification of expropriation and disposability evident in the ongoing forms of immiseration that exceed the settlements pledged by the CRA. The essay itself concludes with an analysis of the evocations of reconciliation and resolution in relation to the CRA settlements as methods of deferral and displacement. I suggest that such deferral and displacement convey the ongoing reconfiguration of genealogies of dispossession that are at once mutually constitutive and distinct. As such, they refuse the attribution of poverty as a transhistorical counterpoint to progress. Poverty is not a single axiomatic condition that persists throughout time and changes only in degrees of intensity. Poverty is not a universal condition of deficiency and misery against which the supposedly fitful advance of progress can be measured.

Yet, as a gesture toward such progress, the resolution sanctioned by the CRA presumes that those who are aggrieved aspire to inclusion and strives to shore up the prevailing social and economic order. In this essay, I aim to trouble this presumption of inclusion as the self-evident logic of resolution and as in certain respects commanding the collective trajectory of desire to have and to be in particular ways because those ways hold the promise ultimately of life and survival. If poverty is understood as designating economic and social relations of antagonism—rather than simply a lack of money or resources—how might living under particular historical conditions of dispossession perform what Elizabeth Povinelli (2011: 125) describes as "the entwinement of endurance and exhaustion" in ways that serve as the source of others' well-being and material accumulation?

Settlement and Conclusion

Remarkable for the sheer magnitude of their historical scope and monetary compensation, *Cobell* and *In re Black Farmers* each entail challenges to egregious practices of expropriation, displacement, and outright theft perpetrated with the United States as accomplice against peoples already incessantly exposed to poverty, racialized subordination, and early death. Inasmuch as the circumstances under contention in *Cobell* are those of U.S. settler colonial administration and *In re Black Farmers* are arguably a consequence of the afterlife of chattel slavery, the historical conceits of property and value in the United

States are implicated in the stakes of the settlements. Rather than indicating poverty as an outcome of anomalous acts, these cases specify dispossession as a social and economic relation that endures while also substantively changing over time. More than simply taking and displacing, dispossession here presupposes and conforms possession itself.

In North America the entangled histories of colonialism, slavery, and racism serve as present conditions of possibility. As Jodi Byrd (2011: 122–23) contends, "That the continued colonization of American Indian nations, peoples, and lands provides the United States the economic and material resources needed to cast its imperialist gaze globally is a fact that is simultaneously obvious within—and yet continually obscured by—what is essentially a settler colony's national construction of itself as an ever more perfect multicultural, multiracial democracy." Audra Simpson (2011: 209) likewise forcefully insists: "It is in these complicated relationships to the past, to territory, and to governance that Indigeneity . . . fundamentally interrupts what is received, what is ordered, what is supposed to be settled." To attend to colonialism, and to slavery and its afterlives, is to acknowledge that continental conquest and the diverse forms of unincorporation, inclusion, and attenuated sovereignty perpetrated by the United States remain unsettling and ongoing. Saidiya Hartman (2002: 758) thus asks: "How might we understand mourning, when the event has yet to end? When the injuries not only perdure, but are inflicted anew? Can one mourn what has yet ceased happening?" Hence, for Hartman (2002: 759) "the time of slavery" as "the relation between the past and the present, the horizon of loss, the extant legacy of slavery, the antinomies of redemption . . . and irreparability . . . negates the common-sense intuition of time as continuity or progression, then and now coexist; we are coeval with the dead." The historical reciprocities of territorial dispossession and forms of racialized coerced labor remain directly tied to the economic logic of property and value, even as their particular valences change over time. Indeed, despite bestowing conclusion, such legislation as the Claims Resolution Act testifies to this endurance. Neither a historical deviation nor a passing moment in the nation's development, U.S. colonialism is a perpetually incomplete project that strives to resolve and to preserve its logic of possession and finality by disavowing the sustained defiance that it encounters and violent dislocation that it demands (Goldstein 2014b). The racial logic of slavery likewise fundamentally persists as a calculus of valuation and expendability. Rather than diminishing in consequence, these collisions and confrontations remain unabated in the colonial present.[2]

The *Cobell v. Salazar* class action lawsuit was filed in 1996 on behalf of approximately five hundred thousand individual Indian owners of the trust lands that were a result of the 1887 General Allotment Act (also known as the Dawes

Severalty Act). Allotment followed a century of escalating seizure of tribal lands, the removal and circumscription of tribal nations to reservations, and intensifying war and extralegal violence against indigenous peoples in North America. Reformist advocates for allotment such as the Indian Rights Association argued that privately held land titles and cultivating liberal individualism were necessary to defend Indians against further land theft and annihilation. The act sought to dismantle collectively held tribal lands into individually owned and alienable property and to sell off land considered in surplus of the individual allotments. Native landholding fell sharply from 138 million acres in 1887 to 52 million acres in 1934, when allotment policy officially ended.[3] The legislation also imposed competency criteria to assess the degree of federal oversight required on behalf of the individual Indians who held fee-simple title to the newly apportioned parcels. In the many cases where such oversight was deemed necessary, the Department of the Interior (DOI) continues to hold the parcels in trust and to negotiate leases with private companies and non-Indian proprietors for the extraction of oil, timber, coal, and other minerals, as well as to broker grazing and agricultural agreements. Fees for the leases are paid to the Individual Indian Money (IIM) Trust Fund accounts administered by the U.S. Treasury Department and the DOI's Bureau of Indian Affairs, which in turn are supposed to disburse regular payments to the individual account holders. The *Cobell* suit charged the United States government with gross neglect of its fiduciary obligations for the Interior and Treasury Departments' flagrant mismanagement of the IIM accounts since their creation in 1887. Indeed, the plaintiffs estimated $137.2 billion in unpaid trust funds between 1887 and 2000 by cross-referencing the historical records of the companies that leased trust lands from the Bureau of Indian Affairs and adding interest.[4]

The *Cobell* lawsuit generated more than thirty-six hundred filings, eighty published opinions, and eleven appellate decisions between 1996 and 2009. Although reports on the federal government's negligent administration of the leases and accounts go back at least as far as 1915, momentum for what became the *Cobell* suit reached a turning point between the 1970s and early 1990s (U.S. Joint Commission 1915). In 1975 the allottees of Quinault Tribe sued the federal government to recover damages resulting from the mismanagement of timber resources on the Quinault Reservation, which eventually led to the 1983 Supreme Court ruling in their favor in *United States v. Mitchell* (Nagel 1983). A public scandal ensued when a BIA accountant leaked internal audits of the agency as evidence of its egregious and endemic fiscal misconduct (Henry 1994). The scandal prompted a 1992 Congressional Oversight Hearing report and the subsequent Indian Trust Fund Management Reform Act of 1994, although no substantial changes in the Interior Department's operations were in place by the time the

Cobell suit was filed two years later. When brought to court, *Cobell* demanded two measures. First, it sought a full accounting of the money owed to IIM beneficiaries. Second, it called for a substantial reform of the Interior Department's administration of the Indian trust funds (Files 2004). As Richard Monette, Angelique EagleWoman, Kimberly Craven, and other critics of the 2009 settlement have pointed out, the settlement ignored both of these demands and instead substituted a monetary award to the class-action plaintiffs. Significantly less than the initial plaintiff estimate, the suit was settled for a total of $3.4 billion.

In 1998, early in the litigation, the Reagan-appointed Federal District Court judge Royce Lamberth ruled that in managing IIM accounts, federal agencies would be held to the same account management standards as any other trustee, such as a bank, rather than to the less-strict statutory governmental standards. The following year, and then again in 2002, Judge Lamberth held the Secretary of the Interior, Assistant Secretary of the Interior, and Treasury Secretary in contempt for withholding evidence and failing to cooperate with the inquiry. In 2002 the *New York Times* reported that "the physical records have fallen into disrepair, been lost, or, in some cases, been purposefully destroyed," and indeed the Department of Treasury acknowledged that it had destroyed 162 boxes of relevant documents while the case was pending ("Contempt at Interior" 2002). In 2005 Lamberth wrote that "our 'modern' Interior department has time and again demonstrated that it is a dinosaur—the morally and culturally oblivious hand-me-down of a disgracefully racist and imperialist government that should have been buried a century ago, the last pathetic outpost of the indifference and anglocentrism we thought we had left behind" ("Memorandum and Order," 07/12/05, reprinted in Stein 2005). The following year, at the request of the Justice Department, a federal appeals panel removed Lamberth from the case because he "lacked objectivity," declaring that "our ruling today presents an opportunity for a fresh start" (Files 2006: A18).

Notably, the temporal terms of Lamberth's condemnation—that the racism and imperialist disposition of the Interior Department was out of step with today's more enlightened norms, that it was behind the times, as it were—charged that, rather than Indian claimants, it was the federal government that was "out of time"—"the last pathetic outpost of the indifference and anglocentrism." Yet even the moral outrage expressed by Lamberth is in the final instance nonetheless an affirmation of U.S. historical progress, a narrative itself predicated on situating Native Americans as "out of time" and awaiting inclusion. Thus, he contends that "it reminds us that even today our great democratic enterprise remains unfinished" ("Memorandum and Order," 07/12/05, reprinted in Stein 2005). However, the court's support for a "full and accurate accounting" to IIM beneficiaries ended with Lamberth's dismissal. His replacement, Judge James Robertson, ruled in

January 2008 that the Interior Department's accounting for the funds was un-
feasible "as a conclusion of law," because the department could not "achieve an
accounting that passes muster as a trust accounting" (quoted in Kim 2010: 6)
due to inadequate appropriations by Congress. The U.S. Court of Appeals for
the District of Columbia likewise supported "an administrative balancing of
cost, time, and accuracy." The appeals court concluded that "the unique nature
of this trust requires the district court to exercise equitable powers in resolving
the paradox between classical accounting and limited government resources,"
and recommended "low-cost statistical methods of estimating benefits across
class sub-groups" (U.S. Court of Appeals for the District of Columbia Circuit
2009: 4) rather than a full accounting. In other words, rather than calculating
the amounts owed based on the records themselves, a statistical sampling based
on the discretion of the Interior Department would be used to estimate average
totals.

And it was under these circumstances that lead plaintiff Elouise Cobell remarked at the case's settlement in December 2009: "We are compelled to settle
by the sobering realization that our class grows smaller each day as our elders
die and are forever prevented from receiving just compensation" (quoted in
Savage 2009: A1).[5] Speaking in an interview on CNN in November 2010, John
Boyd, founder and president of the National Black Farmers Association and
a principal force behind the African American farmers' discrimination suits
against the Department of Agriculture, similarly emphasized the need to vin-
dicate and bring "justice to black farmers who had been waiting so very very
long . . . [so long that] many black farmers have died at the plow while waiting
for justice."[6] Gary R. Grant, president of the Black Farmers and Agriculturists
Association, was among those present at the Claims Resolution Act presidential
signing ceremony the following month. Grant was decidedly less sanguine than
others commenting on the event, observing, "Seemingly forgotten in the process
are those Black farmers who are in the Administrative Process or have outstanding court claims, like my parents, not to mention those who filed Civil Rights
claims during the 'Bush years' who are now threatened with loss of their claims
because of the Statutes of Limitations being used against them since the Bush
Administration did pretty much as the Reagan Administration by stripping the
office of Civil Rights and not following up on filed claims" (quoted in McBride
2010, 1A). Grant noted that the settlement, as with so many of the federal government's USDA discrimination inquiries before, conveyed no penalties for the
agency or those of its representatives who were directly culpable for the racist
practices identified in the suit. Furthermore, many of the African American
farmers who actually do get compensation from the discrimination settlements
will pay the money toward costs related to their previous bankruptcy. Neither

did the settlement resolve the consequences of their past debts nor did it substantially provide for future possibilities to resume farming. What the settlement did—through a standardized and finite distribution of payments—was insist that federally institutionalized racial inequality was past, finished, and resolved in the progressive realization of justice presumably immanent to law.

Although hostile to black farmers since its inception, during the economic crisis of the 1930s the Department of Agriculture's newly created loan programs directly contributed to diminishing the hard-won gains of African Americans since Emancipation. Despite the failures of the Freedmen's Bureau and the 1866 Southern Homestead Act to redistribute property to emancipated African Americans, 20 percent of black agriculturalists managed to purchase at least some arable land by 1880. Although by comparison 60 percent of all southern white farmers owned their land at this time, which on average was valued at twice as much as their black counterparts, African American farmers continued to increase their property holdings in spite of concerted white hostility and violence (Daniel 1972; Biegert 1998; Clark 2012). By 1910 African Americans held title to approximately 16 million acres of farmland, and by 1920 there were 925,000 black-owned farms in the United States (Browne 1973).

New Deal legislation established the USDA as the "lender of last resort" and created local county committees to administer loans to qualifying farmers. These local boards, acting subsequently under the auspices of the USDA's Farmers Home Administration and then the Farm Service Administration, were responsible for making supervised long-term loans to farmers who were unable to find other financing. The county committees had considerable influence on agricultural development and individual farm capacity. The committees not only served as self-interested gatekeepers to financing and capricious fiscal overseers, they also set limits on the maximum amount of acreage upon which farmers could raise their crops. In the South, until as late as the mid-1960s, these committees were comprised entirely of white farmers who used their fiscal and planning authority to systematically dispossess and eliminate black farmers in the South. Loans were especially crucial during this period and after the Second World War, because of the cost of new agricultural technologies required for modernized production—which also had the effect of decreasing the labor required to farm—and the increasing competition from corporate argibusiness. Small farmers, as a group, tend to be looked upon as uncreditworthy by both public and private lenders (Conkin 2008; Fite 1984; Havard 2001; Hurt 2003; Schulman 1994). The 1946 Farmers' Home Administration Act—which is the source of the USDA's current loan programs—and the 1961 Consolidated Farmers' Home Administration Act—which sought to address the increasing need for credit as a result of agricultural mechanization—continued to expand and refine the

USDA's function as a fiscal safety net, yet once again largely bypassed farmers of color (Grim 1995, 1996). Small-scale farming declined significantly over the course of the twentieth century as a result of the industrialization and corporatization of agribusiness, but there was a considerable disparity between the 98 percent decrease of black farmers as compared to 66 percent among whites. Increased reliance on financing and less access to credit than their white counterparts left black farmers with little recourse. By 1997, the year the first *Pigford* class-action lawsuit was filed, African American farmers owned and operated only 18,451 farms, a bleak number compared with the 925,000 farms during peak black ownership in 1920 (Daniel 2013). Increased reliance on financing and less access to credit than their white counterparts, left black farmers with little recourse.

The discrimination suits brought by black farmers demonstrated the federal government's direct role in the decline of African American farm ownership. USDA impropriety had been identified by numerous government investigations. In the wake of the Civil Rights Act of 1964 the U.S. Commission on Civil Rights initiated an inquiry into the discriminatory practices of the Department of Agriculture, sometimes referred to as "the last plantation." The commission's 1965 report found that despite the agency's significant contributions to "raising the economic, educational, and social levels of thousands of farm and rural families," African American farmers were "a glaring exception to this picture of progress" (U.S. Commission on Civil Rights 1965: 8). The commission also reported that USDA assistance to black farmers was "consistently different from that furnished to whites." Black farmers routinely had their property seized, while white farmers were allowed to restructure loans or purchase needed equipment. In 1982 the U.S. Commission on Civil Rights published the results of another inquiry into the USDA that demonstrated that since the 1965 report, the agency had—apart from establishing a division for reviewing civil rights violations—made little or no progress in eliminating discriminatory actions against African American farmers (U.S. Commission on Civil Rights 1982). The Reagan administration's response was to close the USDA's Office of Civil Rights Enforcement and Adjudication in 1983. In 1997 a Civil Rights Action Team (CRAT) report observed that the USDA was commonly perceived as playing a key role in forcing nonwhite and independent farmers off their land through discriminatory loan practices (Civil Rights Action Team 1997).

The CRAT study had been prompted by events that began in December 1996, when a group of African American farmers protested outside the White House, calling for President Bill Clinton to ensure fair treatment for them in the federal government's agricultural lending programs. The farmers also filed suit in court against then Secretary of Agriculture Dan Glickman demanding an end to farm foreclosures and restitution for bankruptcy that was a result of discrimination.

The class action lawsuit *Pigford v. Glickman* was settled in 1999 for discrimination between 1983 and 1997—the period since the confluence of the Reagan administration's decision to close the USDA's Office of Civil Rights Enforcement and Adjudication and the devastating farm financial crisis of the 1980s (Grant, Wood, and Wright 2012; Daniel 2013).

In his opinion for the original consent decree for *Pigford I*, filed in April 1999, U.S. District Court Judge Paul L. Friedman observed that the Department of Agriculture was created on May 15, 1862, "as Congress was debating the issue of providing land for freed former slaves" ("Civil Actions" 2007: 666). What Friedman regarded as "a fair resolution of the claims brought in this case and a good first step toward assuring that the kind of discrimination that has been visited on African American farmers since Reconstruction will not continue into the next century," had acquired the full force of historical conclusion by the signing of the Claims Resolution Act ("Civil Actions" 2007: 667). The deadline for submitting a claim as a class member was September 2000, but as of November 2010, only 69 percent of the eligible class members had final adjudications approved. Many voiced concern over the structure of the settlement agreement, the large number of applicants who filed late, and reported deficiencies in representation by class counsel. A provision in the 2008 farm bill permitted any claimant who had submitted a late-filing request under *Pigford* and who had not previously obtained a determination on the merits of his or her claim to petition in federal court to obtain such a determination. A maximum of $100 million in mandatory spending was made available for payment of these claims, and the multiple claims that were subsequently filed were consolidated into a single case, *In re Black Farmers Discrimination Litigation* (commonly referred to as *Pigford II*).

In February 2010 Attorney General Eric Holder and Secretary of Agriculture Tom Vilsack announced a $1.25 billion settlement of these *Pigford II* claims. With the funding appropriated by the Claims Resolution Act, South Carolina congressman James Clyburn declared that "we removed this stain on our country's history. What happened to our nation's African American farmers and Native Americans was wrong, and we have made it right" (quoted in Southall 2010). In his formal statement on the CRA, Vilsack (2010) remarked that the legislation would "finally allow USDA to turn the page on past discrimination against black farmers. . . . The process has been long and often difficult, but we can't wait any longer to close this sad chapter in USDA's history." That the legislation would "finally allow" Vilsack and the USDA to "close this sad chapter" of course implies a peculiar inversion whereby the USDA—rather than the African American farmers who initiated the lawsuit—was "waiting for justice" and hoping for the juridical possibility of ending its long-standing institutionalized practices of racial discrimination.

Both adjudication and settlement serve as a means of indemnifying defendants against future claims. Yet settlement means that plaintiff and defendant have agreed to forgo full litigation through trial in favor of a mode of alternative dispute resolution (ADR) that does not entail the admission of wrongdoing on the part of the defendant. Critics of settlement, such as Owen Fiss, contrast adjudication as public deliberation to settlement as private negotiation and argue for the social good of adjudication (Fiss 1984; Erichson 2009). According to Judith Resnik (2008: 796), the "worldwide movement toward ADR is propelled by political and social forces trumpeting deregulation and privatization and is staffed by lawyers and other professionals seeking and shaping new markets."

As the number of cases going to trial continues to decline—partially due to the enormous and often preemptive cost of litigation—settlement has become an increasingly common element of ADR. Most relevant in the context of the Claims Resolution Act are the ways in which the form of settlement itself signals outstanding conflicts and the current market dynamics of privatization (A. Cohen 2009, 2011; Issacharoff and Nagareda 2008).

Poverty and the Present Tense

Cobell and In re Black Farmers reached settlement, but both required Congressional authorization and hence legislation to fund the settlements. The first deadline for congressional authorization for Cobell was set for February 28, 2010. This was extended by two months just before the Obama administration announced the settlement of In re Black Farmers contingent on congressional authorization by deadline of March 31. Throughout the year, authorization for both settlements was separately debated and the deadline extended. Efforts to appropriate funding for each settlement independently turned to their strategic placement within other legislative proposals. An act to provide emergency relief to earthquake victims in Chile and Haiti eventually became the Claims Resolution Act, first with a proposed amendment "making emergency supplemental appropriations for disaster relief and summer jobs . . . and for other purposes," including Cobell and In re Black Farmers, and next with the removal of the emergency assistance to Chile and Haiti. In the interim, there were attempts to include both settlements (along with the TANF block grant extension) in May as part of a bill titled the American Jobs and Closing Tax Loopholes Act and in July within an act authorizing supplemental war funding. In its final form, the Claims Resolution Act used fines collected under the Continued Dumping and Subsidy Offset Act, a protectionist trade law that the World Trade Organization had forced the United States to repeal in 2005, to fund the settlements. The diverse elements that ultimately made up the CRA were thus negotiated and threaded together across a tumultuous geopolitical landscape that included emergency disaster relief abroad, a jobs bill prompted by massive unemployment in the wake of the 2006–8 financial crisis, expanded military spending to underwrite the proliferation of U.S. global warfare, and protectionist trade legislation as a counterpoint to free-market international policy. Each discrete settlement, even if arbitrarily combined in the CRA, relied on the broader assemblage in which it was placed to successfully navigate the maneuvers of legislative expediency.

The CRA requires an analysis of the historical conjunctures within which these legislative negotiations were undertaken and the class-action lawsuits settled, as well as an accounting of the multiple intertwined pasts that at once fill, exceed, and are made reconcilable by this juridical framing. Methodologically, this entails foregrounding what Walter Benjamin has described as the dialectical "relation of what-has-been to the now." Benjamin (1999: 462, 463) argues that "each 'now' is the now of particular recognizability" that attains or accedes "to legibility only at a particular time." With the CRA, this legibility emerges precisely through juridical terms that claim to conclude multiple pasts, which now appear to have lost their hold in the present tense through which they are visible. To discern this particular recognizability is thus to decipher elements of the specific dialectical constellation of now while also conceding the distinctions and incommensurabilities that inhere in what-has-been. During the current moment, with accelerated financialization and market speculation deferring the present to an anticipated future time of augmented value for some and dispossession for many, efforts to foreclose and conclude the past in particular ways acquire a deliberate urgency. It is within this interval that those who are expended and devalued by such speculative regimes struggle to make what Neferti Tadiar (2013: 23) so evocatively calls "remaindered life-times" under "conditions of their own superfluity or disposability."

In the logic of limiting liability that animates the structure of settler colonialism and the mechanisms of "neoliberal multiculturalism" (Melamed 2011), recognition and accommodation provide a means of justifying and invigorating colonial sovereignty and racial capitalism (Coulthard 2014). The calculated distribution of limits and liabilities is, among other things, a temporal strategy. The Claims Resolution Act participates in the making of what Kevin Bruyneel (2007: 171) calls "colonial time"—a temporal location that situates "tribal sovereignty as a political expression that is out of (another) time, and therefore a threat to contemporary American political life and political space." Indeed, the binding force of law and juridical reason has been among the most prevalent forms of rendering indigenous peoples as out of time. But this is certainly not a dynamic limited to the domain of law. Elizabeth Povinelli's conception of "social tense" as a technique for governing social difference is particularly useful in this respect. She argues that "late liberal governance makes use of an array of social tenses to legitimate its powers over life and death" with the social divisions of tense helping to "shape how social belonging, abandonment, and endurance are enunciated and experienced within late liberalism" (Povinelli 2011: 51, 11). The ways in which social difference is attributed temporal difference "are at hand when accounts of ongoing structural social harm are explained from a neoliberal or late liberal perspective." Moreover, as is especially pronounced in the Claims Resolution Act, the social divisions of tense "continually deflect moral sense and practical reason from the durative present to an absolute difference between presence and absence or the critical difference between the future anterior and the past perfect" (Povinelli 2011: 13).

This partitioning of tense was amply on display as Congress deliberated on the CRA. Debated in the wake of the midterm elections of 2010, congressional statements on the question of appropriating funds for settlements clearly registered both the persistent fiscal insecurities of the economic crisis and the recent Republican electoral victories. The legislation's Democratic supporters framed their arguments in terms of debt and the moral imperatives of fiscal responsibility. Congresswoman Sheila Jackson Lee (D-Tex.) contended: "America is a place of equality. . . . [L]egitimate issues addressing native lands have now been resolved. This is not a handout. This legislation is paid for" (*Congressional Record*, November 30, 2010: H7656). Representative Ed Perlmutter (D-Colo.) insisted: "America needs to pay its debts and not allow this kind of discrimination to go forward. . . . This country pays its bills" (H7654, H7657). Nick Rahall (D-W.V.) likewise declared "I am proud to say that we have been able to resolve these longstanding litigation matters without adding to the Federal deficit" (H7686). Reiterating the racially inflected paternalistic language of "handouts" and "responsibility," Democrats emphasized the correlation between legitimacy and solvency as a national imperative.

It was in this context that Congressman Doc Hastings (R-Wash.) nonetheless reprimanded the Democrats sponsoring the bill, claiming that "the message from the voters in November's election was unmistakable: It's very clear the American people do care about Congress acting in a transparent, open, and fiscally responsible manner." Hastings contended, "at a time of record deficit spending and record Federal debt, it is the duty of Congress to ask questions to ensure that these settlements are in the best interest of the taxpayers" (*Congressional Record*, November 30, 2010: H7686). Not surprisingly, neither the taxpayer nor the interest he invoked coincides with the Native American or African American claimants. Moreover, Representative Steve King (R-Iowa) dismissively characterized the *Pigford II* settlement in particular as "modern-day reparations" and, along with Congresswoman Michele Bachmann (R-Minn.), argued that its claims process was rife with fraud. King bemoaned "spending money that we don't have for causes that don't have the support of the American people." Suggesting that between 75 and 90 percent of the Pigford applicants were fraudulent, he declared: "We can't be paying modern-day slavery reparations thinking we compensate what took place in the past. We have the future to worry about" (*Congressional Record*, December 1, 2010, H7845, H7850). Regrettable as aspects of this past may have been, according to King, racial opportunists now threatened the vitality of the United States with duplicitous claims that neither served nor had the endorsement of the "American people." Congresswoman Virginia Foxx (R-N.C.) maintained that "the growing deficits under the Democrats' leadership will ultimately lead to a lower standard of living and less opportunity for future generations of Americans. As spending by the Federal Government grows to unsustainable levels, the U.S. will sacrifice its sovereignty by becoming dependent on debt borrowed from foreign countries" (*Congressional Record*, November 30, 2010, H7656). Thus, the specter of dependency, debt, and national economic decline not only underwrites the neofeudalization of society, but also fast-tracks the upward redistribution of wealth and the prospects for perpetual war in order to maintain U.S. geopolitical power. Yet the racial and affective claims evident here also require further parsing the domains of proper and improper dependency through a reassertion of the operative division between public and private, and in this sense, the terms through which Temporary Assistance to Needy Families was extended in the CRA were indispensable.

Limits and Liabilities

Title 8(b) of the Claims Resolution Act extended Temporary Assistance to Needy Families and its initiatives for "healthy-marriage promotion" and "pathways to responsible fatherhood" for a year. Notably brief in duration, the TANF extension provided time-limited assistance for dire circumstances it determines can only be temporary. Although perhaps strikingly out of place amid the settlements with which it was grouped in the CRA, such temporary assistance affirms and repeats—over and over again—bringing deprivation to closure and resolution. However bureaucratically fictive this closure and resolution proves to be, it emphatically conjures a postwelfare alibi for the CRA settlements' emphasis on limiting liability and securing the present from past claims. As such, proponents of so-called welfare reform point to steady decline in TANF recipients as proof of the program's success in ending poverty, which they often equate with "dependency" on government assistance. From this perspective, a reduction in TANF caseloads is evidence of social progress that can be best encouraged only by the grudging temporary extension of the program. If time limits and discouraging eligibility requirements hasten this attrition, then marriage and heteronormativity ostensibly offer the privatized stability and support no longer available as public welfare.

The Personal Responsibility and Work Opportunity Reconciliation Act (PRWORA) of 1996 ended "welfare as we know it" by replacing Aid to Dependent Families with Children with the newly created TANF block grants (Marchevsky and Theoharis 2006; Katz 2008; Morgen, Acker, and Weigt 2010; Gustafson 2011; Soss, Fording, and Schram 2011). The temporalization of destitution inscribed in TANF functions as a compulsory directive. The law prohibits states from using federal TANF funds to assist most families for more than a lifetime total of sixty months (although some states have used their discretionary authority to work around this cutoff point) (Lindhorst and Mancoske 2006).[7] In addition to work requirements and sanctions for noncompliance, one of the most controversial features of the PRWORA was the imposition of time-limited eligibility. The PRWORA not only imposed strict limits on the parsimonious benefits provided to recipients, but it set funding for TANF itself to expire in 2002. A series of short-term measures for the temporary extension of the "temporary assistance" allocated by TANF preserved the program between its designated expiration in 2002 and its reauthorization by Congress for another five years as part of the Deficit Reduction Act of 2005. The Claims Resolution Act extended TANF for five years once again in 2010. The provisionality and legislative precarity of the program mirror the deliberate impermanence of the support provided. If *Cobell* and *Pigford* promise historical closure and the resolution of past inequality, the TANF extension insists that, apart from the truly incorrigible, poverty exists as an interim moment en route to future prosperity for, in President Obama's words, "families who suffered through no fault of their own" ("Remarks by the President" 2010). By contrast, time will properly dispose of those who by implication suffered by their own fault—those who do not adequately perform the role of willful subject and economic agent—or, perhaps worst of all, refuse to conform to the acceptable conjugal demarcation of the family.

Obama's prominent role in the call for "responsible fathers" and his administration's Fatherhood, Marriage, and Families Innovation Fund was preceded by more than twenty years of a growing concurrence between liberals and conservatives that heteronormative marriage and the nuclear family were essential for the stability and future economic well-being of children (Heath 2012). In Dan Quayle's infamous 1992 campaign speech castigating the fictional television character Murphy Brown for denigrating family values he declared: "A welfare check is not a husband, the state is not a father. It is from parents that children learn how to behave in society ... marriage is probably the best anti-poverty program of all" (quoted in Heath 2013: 568). A year later, in an *Atlantic Monthly* article titled "Dan Quayle Was Right," Barbara Dafoe Whitehead (1993) wrote:

"welfare dependency . . . takes two forms: first, single mothers particularly un-wed mothers, stay on welfare longer than other welfare recipients. . . . Second, welfare dependency tends to be passed on from one generation to the next." Contending that public welfare was eroding the foundation of private life, she asserted: "The family is responsible for teaching lessons of independence, self-restraint, responsibility, and right conduct, which are essential to a free, demo-cratic society." Thus, according to Whitehead, the two degenerate temporalities were mutually constitutive. An extended reliance on public welfare and the in-tergenerational effects of "broken" homes perpetuating dependency threatened freedom and democracy. During the mid-1990s a number of organizations were established to promote marriage and fatherhood as key to public policy, includ-ing the National Fatherhood Initiative, Promise Keepers, the National Marriage Project, Marriage Savers, the Institute for American Values, and the Coalition for Marriage, Family, and Couples Education. Arguably, there has been some movement to expand the heteronormative imperative to include homonorma-tive marriage as well, especially after the Supreme Court overturned the Defense of Marriage Act in 2013.

Directly tied to the terms of compliance and sanctions, the focus on mar-riage and fatherhood in TANF likewise serves to privatize poverty and enforce heteropatriarchy by punishing single motherhood and nonconjugal familial arrangements (Monnat 2010; Bentele and Nicoli 2012; Mannix and Freedman 2013; Weaver 2014). As delineated in PRWORA, TANF was designed to "end the dependence of needy parents on government benefits by promoting job prepara-tion, work, and marriage"; "prevent and reduce the incidence of out-of-wedlock pregnancies"; and "encourage the formation and maintenance of two-parent families" (PRWORA 1996). Marriage promotion—and hence the penalization of nonconjugal families or unwed mothers—has become increasingly central to TANF policy. Father initiatives as part of TANF were first proposed with the Fathers Count Act in 1998. In 2002 the Bush administration announced that one of its highest priorities in "welfare reform" was "healthy" marriage. That same year, the House and the Senate Finance Committee passed two bills that included marriage provisions. The reauthorization of TANF as part of the Deficit Reduction Act of 2005 included Title IV-A Healthy Marriage and Responsible Fatherhood grants programs—made competitively available to "states, territo-ries, Indian tribes and tribal organizations, and public and non-profit groups (including religious organizations" (Deficit Reduction Act 2006). Funding for such initiatives has since been a continuous feature of TANF.

These funding initiatives work in tandem with a broader discourse on the role of "the family" in the persistence of poverty. In July 2013, in anticipation of the fiftieth anniversary of the Economic Opportunity Act and the War on Poverty, the House Budget Committee chaired by Paul Ryan (R-Wis.) convened a series of hearings. In his opening remarks, Ryan insisted: "If you work hard and play by the rules, you can get ahead. That is something that we all believe in and that we all care about. This is the central promise of this country. We want to protect that idea, and we want to preserve it for the next generation" (*War on Poverty* 2013: 1). Not surprisingly, given the partisan character of the committee, the subsequent report on the hearings stated that "Federal programs are not only failing to address the problem [of poverty]. They are also in some significant respects making it worse" (House Budget Committee 2014: 9). Although the authors note "many reasons why poverty persists to such a wide extent today," they nonetheless conclude: "Perhaps the single most important determinant of poverty is family structure. . . . The Moynihan Report identified the breakdown of the family as a key cause of poverty within the black community. More recent research on Americans of all backgrounds has backed up Moynihan's argument" (House Budget Committee 2014: 4, 5). Indeed there has been a notable revival of the Moynihan Report and other versions of the "culture of poverty" thesis, which argue that single-mother households—as crucibles of deviant black matriarchy and the emasculation of African American males— propagate intergenerational racial pathology.[8] Journalistic accounts have similarly (re)embraced this argument. A 2012 *New York Times Magazine* cover story called "Obama vs. Poverty" maintained that although poor people in the United States are materially better off than they were fifty years ago, what has become most pronounced is what the author calls a "social gap" between poor people and the so-called middle class, a social gap made and perpetuated, according to the article, by "family dynamics and their effects on child development" (Tough 2012, 345; also P. Cohen 2010; Lowrey 2014). Thus, marriage is the happy ending that not only promises to bring closure to inherited social dysfunction but also the means through which to direct the provision of care from the state to the institutions of private life. In this sense, the heteronormative two-parent family ostensibly allows for appropriate provisional forms of dependency in the private sphere while ultimately cultivating independence.

But the supposed vindication of Moynihan as a means of asserting the primacy of marriage is important in another way as well. What makes Moynihan's argument so interesting is that—contrary to much of the criticism aimed at his report in the 1960s—he in fact emphasized the historical trauma of structural racism and its consequences for the present. Yet he did so in such a way that situated the reproduction of these consequences in the supposed breakdown of African American families rather than the ongoing realities of white racism and racial capitalism. The "tangle of pathology" phrase most associated with his report indexes this transposition from the public legacies of slavery to the supposed private psychic dysfunction of single-mother households. The TANF extension provides an analogous transposition as a component of the Claims Resolution Act. On the one hand, it further privatizes the terms through which "trust" in government is to be secured and racism disavowed. It offers normative personal responsibility to suggest that the force of individual will alone can fore-close the violence of historical dispossession. On the other, it promises repeat-edly to end poverty in the present tense—one time-limited case at a time—and in so doing to ease anxiety about the crisis that is capitalism. This repetition is at once the persistence of insecurity and the postponement of futurity.

Borrowed Time

In May 2011 a Gallup poll found that only 44 percent of Americans surveyed believed that young people will be better off economically as adults than their parents, the lowest percentage since the polling agency began asking this ques-tion in 1983 (Mendes 2011; Pew 2012). If such a poll easily lends itself to narratives of the loss of an ostensibly unproblematic and undifferentiated "golden age" of U.S. affluence and upward mobility following the Second World War, it likewise presumes a teleology of progress and improvement wherein poverty is a con-dition that always already implies its own overcoming, a provisional stage en route to prosperity. On November 24, 2012, the *Cobell* settlement appeal period expired and, with the U.S. Supreme Court having dismissed the two appeals petitions submitted for its consideration, two days later President Barack Obama announced "the final approval of the Cobell settlement agreement, clearing the way for reconciliation between the trust beneficiaries and the federal govern-ment" (Capriccioso 2012; "Statement of the President" 2012).

It hardly seems a coincidence that the systemic historical dispossession of Native peoples and African American farmers should take on new significance during an era of mass eviction and foreclosure, and that, when the national fic-tion of intergenerational mobility and ever-increasing accumulation appears so scandalously unattainable for most everyone, new appeals to "restoring a sense of trust" are made in relation to American Indians whose historic assimilation and disappearance has been the very condition upon which progress has been predicated. Indeed, the federal government is bound by very specific and indeed legally mandated terms of trust to American Indians based on past treaty obli-gations and fiduciary duty. As such, national integrity and sovereign authority here appear anxiously entwined with the resolution of indebtedness and fiscal insecurity in the aftermath of the 2008 economic crisis.

Financialization provided capitalist institutions and governments with a means to defer and seemingly depoliticize—at least until 2008—the effects of economic decline since the 1960s (Dardot and Laval 2013; Duménil and Lévy 2011; Krippner 2011; Peck 2010). The restructuring and deregulation of global capital markets and exponential expansion of credit and debt during this period nevertheless continued to attribute debt as credit-worthiness for some and pejoratively as dependency for others in highly uneven and racially overdetermined ways. Under conditions of the crisis this time, at the very moment when the neoliberal fantasy of market-based salvation has imploded and the Keynesian model of regulatory remediation appears equally untenable, the foundational violence, territorial seizure, and social obliteration on which settler colonial expansion has been based once again potentially comes into view. This unseemly presence in the present—a present that is ostensibly the progressive outcome of ever-advancing improvement and enlightenment—belies and disrupts the liberal conceits of equality, opportunity, and colorblindness, perhaps opening new spaces for sovereign claims and even transforming the substance of jurisprudence itself.

In the introduction to their volume on the politics of state apology and reconciliation of historical injustice that have become ubiquitous during the last twenty years, Elazar Barkan and Alexander Karn underscore what they consider to be the common value of the "negotiated history" they attribute to such collective deliberation and possible resolution. According to Barkan and Karn (2006: 8), "Through a process of open dialogue, victims and perpetrators can exchange perspectives, combine their memories, and recover their lost dignity. As they allow themselves to become enmeshed in each other's stories, historical adversaries uncover new possibilities for self-definition and fresh avenues for cooperation" (also see Gibney et al. 2008; Kauanui 2014). While acknowledging criticism of apology and reconciliation, Barkan and Karn nonetheless argue that such resolution ultimately contributes to greater societal well-being. Yet, apology and reconciliation, as they have been articulated in liberal jurisprudence and the conventions of international law, pose an ethical encounter that presumes closure and commensurability in the deliberative exchange between equivalent if not equal parties. Past injustices are ostensibly reconciled to a single shared narrative of mutual recognition by plaintiff and defendant, who as such agree to move forward together having resolved present-day conflicts originating from previous offenses and inequities. Without entirely dismissing the potential forms of redress that state apology and reconciliation might provide, it is nevertheless worth asking what the normative force of these juridical mechanisms presumes and toward what end. How might such resolution variously strive toward restoration, reparation, and settlement—each of which conveys distinct trajectories of encounter and relation?

A different, yet directly relevant, mode of reconciliation is evident in the

Personal Responsibility and Work Opportunity Reconciliation Act that established TANF. Reconciliation here refers to the budget reconciliation process, a procedure first initiated by the Congressional Budget Act of 1974 that has increasingly been used by lawmakers as a strategy for securing a majority vote on legislation (Keith 2010). In the context of the PRWORA there is reason to consider how and why thinking about moral and fiscal reconciliation together, as well as their place in law and policy, might matter for understanding contemporary inequalities. Brenna Bhandar (2007: 94) argues that "The much vaunted social and political objective of reconciliation, prevalent in colonial settler societies which attempt to grapple with the injustices that accrued during the course of violent settlement, demands a settled, unified notion of what transpired, which in turn compresses history into a seamless, progressive narrative of nation formation" (also see Schaap 2005). Acknowledgment and accommodation in this context serve as a means of justifying and invigorating settler sovereignty and racial capitalism. In jurisprudence and legislation, as Bhandar (2007: 95, 99) argues, "the injustices of the colonial past and its history of racist discriminatory laws" are acknowledged "only in order to close off and contain this past. The past is remembered only so that it may be forgotten in the push toward maintaining the foundation of the existing economic and social order." To be reconciled is thus to make one account consistent with another, while anticipating or allowing for transactions begun but not yet completed.

In the summer of 2014 *Cobell* and *In re Black Farmers* claimants were still awaiting their settlement payments, and TANF was set to expire once again and slated for debate on reauthorization. This perpetual delay and recursive impermanence are among the techniques of social tense that unevenly partition the durations of inequality. The prevailing social and economic order is predicated in this way on distinguishing past and present while holding the future in abeyance. Returning to Derrida's (1993) theorization of aporias mentioned earlier, it is important that *Aporias* is largely concerned with the temporal modalities of death, thought partially in relation to Heidegger and waiting as not advancing but anticipating. The "persistence of poverty" as a constitutive dilemma for the idea of historical progress similarly extends this manner of anticipation and deferral. In everyday experience, as Javier Auyero (2012: 9, 156) argues, the bureaucratic and institutional manner of being habituated to waiting teaches those who are destitute that they "have to remain temporarily neglected, unattended to, or postponed," and, in effect, this waiting in perpetuity binds the poor to the state. The logic of reconciliation and settlement likewise insists on patience and waiting so as to disavow irreparability and to safeguard the forms of compensatory closure pledged by the Claims Resolution Act. Yet, at the same time, waiting is not merely to be passively resolved, but is rather evidence of the profound and ongoing forms of dispossession that make compensation equivalent to the very possibility of survival.

NOTES

1. Discussing "the relation to death *as such*," Derrida (1993: 44) is concerned here with the "already" in Heidegger's use of "the classical idea of order, an order of priority, precedence, and presupposition (*vorliegen, voraussetzen*), which is also an order of foundation: there is the *founding* basis of foundation and the *founded* structure that presupposes it."

2. By "colonial present" I mean the spectrum of forces that currently animate and derive from the fraught historical accumulation and shifting disposition of colonial processes, relations, and practices. As with Derek Gregory's (2004) notion of the colonial present, I am interested in how "the capacities that inhere within the colonial past are routinely reaffirmed in the colonial present." My conception of the colonial present, in contrast to Gregory's focus on imperial formation, emphasizes how forms of colonial administration, property form, and jurisprudence continue to impinge on and be contested or negotiated by indigenous peoples today. I aim to highlight these contemporary conditions, as well as how they shape political, economic, and social formations more broadly and variously manifest the continuities between past and present. Ann Laura Stoler (2010, xviii) likewise usefully insists, "Understanding what constitutes the colonial present calls into question both the selective geographic and analytic space within which postcolonial studies has concentrated and what it has assumed characterizes a colonial situation."

3. Indicative of the pace of dispossession once the Allotment Act was implemented, tribal landholding was reduced by 20 million acres between the beginning of 1890 and mid-1891 alone (Otis 1973: 84–85).

4. Annual lease and asset transactions remain immense. For instance, as reported by the Office of the Special Trustee for American Indians in 2014, "The Indian trust includes 55 million surface acres and 57 million acres of subsurface minerals estates held in trust by the United States for American Indians and Indian tribes. Over 11 million acres belong to individual Indians and nearly 44 million acres are held in trust for Indian tribes. On these lands, Interior manages over 119,000 leases for such things as mineral development, oil and gas extraction, and grazing. It also manages approximately $4.6 billion in trust funds. For fiscal year 2013, income from financial assets and from leases, settlements and judgments, use permits, and land sales, totaling approximately $791 million, was collected for about 393,000 open IIM accounts. Approximately $642 million was collected in FY2013 for about 3,000 tribal accounts (for over 250 tribes)" (Office of the Special Trustee for American Indians 2014: 1).

5. Cobell herself died of cancer less than two years later (Hevesi 2011: A25). Not surprisingly, Cobell's remarks shifted in emphasis over the course of the litigation. Testifying before Congress in July 2005, she contended: "We are in the 10th year of this litigation and more than 1 century of mismanagement of individual Indian trusts has already passed. Justice has been delayed for individual trust beneficiaries. Every individual trust beneficiary I have spoken with has told me that they want a fair resolution even if it takes

longer. They do not want to be sacrificed at the altar of a political expediency as they have so many times before" ("Statement of Elouise P. Cobell" 2005: 93).

6. This temporal framing was characteristic of much of the rhetoric in favor of the settlement. Following the successful passage of the legislation in the Senate, for instance, an NAACP (n.d.) press release invoked similar consequences of such "long overdue" justice: "There is an urgency to pass this appropriation to settle the class action lawsuits of African-American farmers and Native Americans. Many of the farmers who would qualify for monies under the settlement have waited as long as 10 years to be compensated; some have already died or lost their farms. After years of discriminatory treatment by USDA credit and program agencies, these farm families have already waited almost a decade for compensation for these well-established claims. It is time to allow these farmers to focus on the future, and move forward unencumbered by the racial discrimination of the past."

7. Time limits work in tandem with the overall punitive discourse of "welfare reform." Thus, for instance, Gary D. Alexander, Secretary of Public Welfare in Pennsylvania, testified before Congress: "unfortunately, I think in our other programs like food stamps and Medicaid, there is scant—there is a scant work requirement or no work requirement at all. I think what we have learned from TANF from 1996 is that there was a focus on self-reliance, personal responsibility, the focus on work, it was time-limited, and that there was a focus on bringing families together in a healthy marriage. And I think that if we are going to proceed in the future and end dependency, we are going to have to work harder at encompassing all of our programs across the welfare spectrum and bring all of these together" (U.S. House of Representatives 2011: 86).

8. Michael B. Katz (2013, 220–30) provides an excellent account of the recent reclamation of Moynihan (also see Mayeri 2013).

REFERENCES

Auyero, Javier. 2012. *Patients of the State: The Politics of Waiting in Argentina*. Durham: Duke University Press.

Barkan, Elazar, and Alexander Karn. 2006. "Group Apology as an Ethical Imperative." In *Taking Wrongs Seriously: Apologies and Reconciliation*, 1–32. Stanford: Stanford University Press.

Benjamin, Walter. 1999. *The Arcades Project*. Trans. Howard Eiland and Kevin McLaughlin. Cambridge: Harvard University Press. (Orig. written 1927–40.)

Bentele, Keith Gunnar, and Lisa Thiebaud Nicoli. 2012. "Ending Access as We Know It: State Welfare Benefit Coverage in the TANF Era." *Social Service Review* 86:2, 223–68.

Bhandar, Brenna. 2007. "'Spatialising History' and Opening Time: Resisting the Reproduction of the Proper Subject." In *Law and the Politics of Reconciliation*, ed. Scott Veitch, 93–110. London: Ashgate.

Biegert, M. Langley. 1998. "Legacy of Resistance: Uncovering the History of Collective Action by Black Agricultural Workers in Central East Arkansas from the 1860s to the 1930s." *Journal of Social History* 32:1, 73–99.

Browne, Robert S. 1973. *Only Six Million Acres: The Decline of Black Owned Land in the Rural South*. New York: Black Economic Research Center, June.

Bruyneel, Kevin. 2007. *The Third Space of Sovereignty: The Postcolonial Politics of U.S.-Indigenous Relations*. Minneapolis: University of Minnesota Press.

Byrd, Jodi A. 2011. *Transit of Empire: Indigenous Critiques of Colonialism*. Minneapolis: University of Minnesota Press.

Capriccioso, Rob. 2012. "Indians Pull Appeal to Cobell Settlement." *Indian Country Today*, November 8, http://indiancountrytodaymedianetwork.com/article/indians-pull-appeal-to-cobell-settlement-government-says-payments-by-years-end-144690.

"Civil Actions, Nos. 97–1978, 98–1693 [1999]: Opinion." 2007. In *Redress for Historical Injustices in the United States: On Reparations for Slavery, Jim Crow, and Their Legacies*, ed. Michael T. Martin and Marilyn Yaquinto, 665–67. Durham: Duke University Press.

Civil Rights Action Team. 1997. *Civil Rights at the United States Department of Agriculture*. Washington, D.C.: USDA.

Clark, Christopher. 2012. "The Agrarian Context of American Capitalist Development." In *Capitalism Takes Command: The Social Transformation of Nineteenth-Century America*, ed. Michael Zakim and Gary J. Kornblith, 13–37. Chicago: University of Chicago Press.

Cohen, Amy J. 2009. "Revisiting 'Against Settlement': Some Reflections on Dispute Resolution and Public Values." *Fordham Law Review* 78:3, 1143–70.

Cohen, Amy J. 2011. "The Family, the Market, and ADR." *Journal of Dispute Resolution* 2011:1, http://scholarship.law.missouri.edu/jdr/vol2011/iss1/6.

Cohen, Patricia. 2010. "'Culture of Poverty' Makes a Comeback." *New York Times*, October 17.

Conkin, Paul K. 2008. *A Revolution Down on the Farm: The Transformation of American Agriculture since 1929*. Lexington: University of Kentucky Press.

"Contempt at Interior." 2002. *New York Times*. September 19, A34.

Coulthard, Glen S. 2014. *Red Skin, White Masks: Rejecting the Colonial Politics of Recognition*. Minneapolis: University of Minnesota Press.

Daniel, Pete. 1972. *The Shadow of Slavery: Peonage in the South, 1901–1969*. Urbana: University of Illinois Press.

Daniel, Pete. 2013. *Dispossession: Discrimination against African American Famers in the Age of Civil Rights*. Chapel Hill: University of North Carolina Press.

Dardot, Pierre, and Christian Laval. 2013. *The New Way of the World: On Neoliberal Society*. Trans. Gregory Elliott. New York: Verso.

Deficit Reduction Act of 2005. 2006. Public Law 109-171. 42 USC § 1305. February 8.

Derrida, Jacques. 1993. *Aporias*. Trans. by Thomas Dutoit. Stanford: Stanford University Press.

Duménil, Gérard, and Dominique Lévy. 2011. *The Crisis of Neoliberalism*. Cambridge, Mass.: Harvard University Press.

Erichson, Howard M. 2009. Special forum on *"Against Settlement*: Twenty Five Years Later." *Fordham Law Review* 78:3.

Files, John. 2004. "One Banker's Fight for a Half-Million Indians." *New York Times*, April 20, A-15.

Files, John. 2006. "Appeals Panel Removes Judge Presiding Over Indian Lawsuit." *New York Times*, July 12, A18.

Fiss, Owen M. 1984. "Against Settlement." *Yale Law Journal* 93:6, 1073–90.

Fite, Gilbert C. 1984. *Cotton Fields No More: Southern Agriculture, 1865–1980.* Lexington: University of Kentucky Press.

Gibney, Mark, Rhoda E. Howard-Hassmann, Jean-Marc Coicaud, and Niklaus Steiner, eds. 2008. *The Age of Apology: Facing Up to the Past.* Philadelphia: University of Pennsylvania Press.

Goldstein, Alyosha. 2014a. "Finance and Foreclosure in the Colonial Present." *Radical History Review* 118, 42–63.

Goldstein, Alyosha. 2014b. "Toward a Genealogy of the U.S. Colonial Present." In *Formations of United States Colonialism*, ed. Alyosha Goldstein, 1–30. Durham: Duke University Press.

Grant, Gary R., Spencer D. Wood, and Willie J. Wright. 2012. "Black Farmers United: The Struggle against Power and Principalities." *Journal of Pan African Studies* 5:1, 3–22.

Gregory, Derek. 2004. *The Colonial Present: Afghanistan, Palestine, and Iraq.* Malden, Mass.: Blackwell.

Grim, Valerie. 1995. "The Politics of Inclusion: Black Farmers and the Quest for Agribusiness Participation, 1945–1990s." *Agricultural History* 69:2, 257–71.

Grim, Valerie. 1996. "Black Participation in the Farmers Home Administration and Agricultural Stabilization and Conservation Service, 1964–1990." *Agricultural History* 70:2, 321–36.

Gustafson, Kaaryn S. 2011. *Cheating Welfare: Public Assistance and the Criminalization of Poverty.* New York: New York University Press.

Hartman, Saidiya. 2002. "The Time of Slavery." *South Atlantic Quarterly* 101:4, 757–77.

Havard, Cassandra Jones. 2001. "African-American Farmers and Fair Lending: Racializing Rural Economic Space." *Stanford Law and Policy Review* 12:2, 333–60.

Heath, Melanie. 2012. *One Marriage under God: The Campaign to Promote Marriage in America.* New York: New York University Press.

Heath, Melanie. 2013. "Sexual Misgivings: Producing Un/Marked Knowledge in Neoliberal Marriage Promotion Policies." *Sociological Quarterly* 54:4, 561–83.

Henry, David L. 1994. *Stealing from Indians: Inside the Bureau of Indian Affairs—an Exposé of Corruption, Massive Fraud and Justice Denied.* Billings, Mont.: Thunder Mountain Press.

Hevesi, Dennis. 2011. "Elouise Cobell, 65; Sued for Indian Funds [Obituary]." *New York Times*, October 18, A25.

House Budget Committee Majority Staff. 2014. *The War on Poverty: 50 Years Later—A House Budget Committee Report.* March 3.

Hurt, R. Douglas, ed. 2003. *African American Life in the Rural South, 1900–1950.* Columbia: University of Missouri Press.

Issacharoff, Samuel, and Richard A. Nagareda. 2008. "Class Settlements Under Attack." *University of Pennsylvania Law Review* 156:6, 1649–722.

Katz, Michael B. 2008. *The Price of Citizenship: Redefining the American Welfare State*. Rev. ed. Philadelphia: University of Pennsylvania Press.

Katz, Michael B. 2013. *The Undeserving Poor: America's Enduring Confrontation with Poverty*. 2nd ed. New York: Oxford University Press.

Kauanui, J. Kēhaulani. 2014. "A Sorry State: Hawaiian Land and Legal Fictions in the Court of the Conqueror." In *Formations of United States Colonialism*, ed. Alyosha Goldstein, 110–34. Durham: Duke University Press.

Keith, Robert. 2010. *The Budget Reconciliation Process: The Senate's "Byrd Rule."* Washington, D.C.: Congressional Research Service, July 2.

Kim, Yule. 2010. *The Indian Trust Fund Litigation: An Overview of* Cobell v. Salazar. Washington, D.C.: Congressional Research Service. April 9.

Koselleck, Reinhart. 2002. *The Practice of Conceptual History: Timing History, Spacing Concepts*. Stanford: Stanford University Press.

Krippner, Greta R. 2011. *Capitalizing on Crisis: The Political Origins of the Rise of Finance*. Cambridge, Mass.: Harvard University Press.

Lindhorst, Taryn, and Ronald J. Mancoske. 2006. "The Social and Economic Impact of Sanctions and Time Limits on Recipients of Temporary Assistance to Needy Families." *Journal of Sociology and Social Welfare* 33:1, 93–114.

Lowrey, Annie. 2014. "50 Years Later, War on Poverty Is a Mixed Bag." *New York Times*, January 5, A1.

Mannix, Mary R., and Henry A. Freedman, 2013. "TANF and Racial Justice." *Clearinghouse Review: Journal of Poverty Law and Policy*, September–October, 221–29.

Marchevsky, Alejandra, and Jeanne Theoharis. 2006. *Not Working: Latina Immigrants, Low-Wage Jobs, and the Failure of Welfare Reform*. New York: New York University Press.

Mayeri, Serena. 2013. "Historicizing the 'End of Men': The Politics of Reaction(s)." *Boston University Law Review* 93:3, 729–44.

McBride, Earnest. 2010. "Black and Indian Farmers Gain from Largest Civil Rights Settlement in History." *Jackson Advocate*, December 16, 1A.

Melamed, Jodi. 2011. *Represent and Destroy: Rationalizing Violence in the New Racial Capitalism*. Minneapolis: University of Minnesota Press.

Mendes, Elizabeth. 2011. "In U.S., Optimism about Future for Youth Reaches All-Time Low." May 2, http://www.gallup.com/poll/147350/optism-future-youth-reaches -time.low.aspx.

Monnat, Shannon M. 2010. "The Color of Welfare Sanctioning: Exploring the Individual and Contextual Roles of Race on TANF Case Closures and Benefit Reductions." *Sociological Quarterly* 51:4, 678–707.

Morgen, Sandra, Joan Acker, and Jill Weigt. 2010. *Stretched Thin: Poor Families, Welfare Work, and Welfare Reform*. Ithaca: Cornell University Press.

NAACP. n.d. "Senate Passes Funding for Pigford II Black Farmer Racial Discrimination

Law Suit." http://www.naacp.org/action-alerts/entry/us-senate-passes-funding-for
-pigford-ii-black-farmer-racial-discrimination.

Nagel, Patricia McKeown. 1983. "The Reemergence of the Trust Relationship after
United States v. Mitchell." *Land and Water Law Review* 18:2, 491–512.

Office of the Special Trustee for American Indians. 2014. *Fiscal Year 2013: Annual Report to Congress*. Washington, D.C.: Department of the Interior, March 10.

Otis, D. S. 1973. *The Dawes Act and the Allotment of Indian Lands*. Norman: University
of Oklahoma Press. (Orig. pub. 1934.)

Peck, Jamie. 2010. *Constructions of Neoliberalism*. New York: Oxford University Press.

PRWORA (Personal Responsibility and Work Opportunity Reconciliation Act of 1996).
1996. Public Law 104-193. 42 USC § 601. August 22.

Pew Social and Demographic Trends. 2012. *Fewer, Poorer, Gloomier: The Lost Decade of
the Middle Class*. Washington, D.C.: Pew Research Center, August 22.

Povinelli, Elizabeth A. 2011. *Economies of Abandonment: Social Belonging and Endurance in Late Liberalism*. Durham: Duke University Press.

"Remarks by the President at Bill Signing for the Claims Resolution Act." 2010. White
House, December 8, http://www.whitehouse.gov/the-press-office/2010/12/08
/remarks-president-bill-signing-claims-resolution-act.

Resnik, Judith. 2008. "Courts: In and Out of Sight, Site, and Cite." *Villanova Law
Review* 53:5, 771–810.

Savage, Charlie. 2009. "U.S. Will Settle Indian Lawsuit For $3.4 Billion." *New York
Times*, December 9, A1.

Schaap, Andrew. 2005. *Political Reconciliation*. New York: Routledge.

Schulman, Bruce J. 1994. *From Cotton Belt to Sunbelt: Federal Policy, Economic Development, and the Transformation of the South 1938–1980*. Durham: Duke University Press.

Simpson, Audra. 2011. "Settlement's Secret." *Cultural Anthropology* 26:2, 205–17.

Soss, Joe, Richard C. Fording, and Sanford F. Schram. 2011. *Disciplining the Poor: Neoliberal Paternalism and the Persistent Power of Race*. Chicago: University of Chicago
Press.

Southall, Ashley. 2010. "Black Farmers Settlement Approved." *New York Times*—The
Caucus: The Politics and Government Blog of the Times. November 30, http://the
caucus.blogs.nytimes.com/2010/11/30/black-farmers-settlement-approved/.

"Statement of Elouise P. Cobell, Blackfeet Reservation Development Fund." 2005.
Indian Trust Reform Act: Hearings before the Committee on Indian Affairs. United
States Senate, 109th Congress, 1st session, July 26. Washington, D.C.: U.S. Govern-
ment Printing Office.

"Statement of the President on the Final Approval of the Cobell Settlement." 2012.
White House. November 26. http://www.whitehouse.gov/the-press-office/2012
/11/26/statement-president-final-approval-cobell-settlement.

Stein, Jonathan. 2005. "Contempt from Court: The Blistering Eloquence of Judge
Royce C. Lamberth." *Mother Jones*, September 1. http://www.motherjones.com
/politics/2005/09/contempt-court-blistering-eloquence-judge-royce-c-lamberth.

Stoler, Ann Laura. 2010. *Carnal Knowledge and Imperial Power: Race and the Intimate in Colonial Rule.* Berkeley: University of California Press.

Tadiar, Neferti X. M. 2013. "Life-Times of Disposability within Global Neoliberalism." *Social Text* 31:2, 19–48.

Tough, Paul. 2012. "Obama vs. Poverty." *New York Times Magazine*, August 19.

U.S. Commission on Civil Rights. 1965. *Equal Opportunity in Farm Programs: An Appraisal of Services Rendered by Agencies of the United States Department of Agriculture.* Washington, D.C.: Government Printing Office.

U.S. Commission on Civil Rights. 1982. *The Decline of Black Farming in America: A Report.* Washington, D.C.: The Commission.

U.S. Court of Appeals for the District of Columbia Circuit. 2009. *Cobell v. Salazar.* No. 08-5500. July 24.

U.S. House of Representatives. 2011. *Improving Work and Other Welfare Goals: Hearing before the Subcommittee on Human Welfare of the Committee on Ways and Means.* 112th Congress, 1st Session, September 8. Washington, D.C.: Government Printing Office.

U.S. Joint Commission to Investigate Indian Affairs, Bureau of Municipal Research. 1915. *Business and Accounting Methods, Indian Bureau: Report to the Joint Commission of the Congress of the United States, Sixty-third Congress, Third session, to Investigate Indian affairs, Relative to Business and Accounting Methods Employed in the Administration of the Office of Indian Affairs.* Washington, D.C.: Government Printing Office.

Vilsack, Tom. 2010. "Turning the Page on Discrimination at USDA." November 30. http://blogs.usda.gov/2010/11/30/.

The War on Poverty: A Progress Report—Hearing before the Committee on the Budget. 2013. House of Representatives, 113th Congress, 1st session, July 31. Washington, D.C.: Government Printing Office.

Weaver, R. Kent. 2014. "Compliance Regimes and Barriers to Behavioral Change." *Governance* 27:2, 243–65.

Whitehead, Barbara Dafoe. 1993. "Dan Quayle Was Right." *Atlantic Monthly*, April, http://www.theatlantic.com/magazine/archive/1993/04/dan-quayle-was-right/307015/.

Funding the Other California:
An Anatomy of Consensus and Consent

ERICA KOHL-ARENAS

> Consensus politics can mean, from the general sense, policies undertaken
> on the basis of an existing body of agreed opinions. It can also mean, and in
> practice has more often meant, a policy of avoiding or evading differences
> or divisions of opinion in an attempt to "secure the centre" or "occupy the
> middle ground."
>
> —RAYMOND WILLIAMS, *Keywords*

Introduction

The conception of successful political negotiation as a process of building consensus through the identification of common interests has reached near-hegemonic status. In the fields of environmental sustainability and community development, for example, the antagonistic organizing style of the 1960s and 1970s is often critiqued as dated and ineffectual, while projects that are claimed to serve common interests or "build bridges" among diverse stakeholders are embraced as unquestionably "good" (Peterson, Peterson, and Peterson 2005; Graham 2012). President Barack Obama brought the idea of consensus-based politics to new heights, commonly avoiding racial politics and stating that there are very few issues that we cannot find a solution for that most people would be happy with.[1] His efforts to build consensus around health-care reform, the financial crisis, and the wars in the East are all examples of the often unexplored belief that consensus is the most viable political strategy of our politically, socially, and economically polarized time. Even new activist movements whose discourse draws attention to entrenched inequality and the corruption of elite-serving economic systems, such as the United States' Occupy Wall Street and Spain's Indignados, attempt to bring large masses of people together in a common crusade for economic justice through specifically consensus-driven processes.

One realm where the notion of consensus politics has become predominant is the field of development and poverty alleviation. In this chapter I explore the specific consensus-based politics engaged through philanthropic investments in addressing migrant poverty across California's Central Valley. While there have been relatively few critical studies of large-scale antipoverty initiatives launched by private foundations in the United States, critical global development scholars have described the depoliticizing approach to development as an Anti-Politics Machine. Monographs such as James Ferguson's *The Anti-Politics Machine* and Tania Murray Li's *The Will to Improve* define the field of global development by processes of depoliticization through the rule of stakeholder politics, bureaucratic power, professionalization, and the misrepresentation of local and regional political economies through development discourse and technical programs. At the heart of these critiques is the claim that the "development apparatus" hides the violence wrought by global capital behind popular discourses of technological progress and participatory democracy. Cloaked in conceptual frameworks that misrepresent local realities, these initiatives inevitably fail to solve the problems they set out to address.

Since the Millennium Development Goals' (2000) commitment to eradicating extreme poverty, the "antipolitics" approach to development has expanded its reach. A growing number of global philanthropists (e.g., Bill Clinton, Warren Buffet, and Bill Gates), social entrepreneurs, and pro-development scholars propose to end poverty through "double bottom-line development" by integrating the poor into a singularly defined "civil society" and global economy (Moyo 2010; Prahalad 2004; Bishop and Green 2008; Clinton 2007). One particular thread, and some argue a relatively new direction, of this approach to poverty alleviation is the call to action for the poor to "help themselves" in programs that aspire to interrupt the cycle of entrenched poverty and simultaneously build economies and local infrastructure (Roy 2010). Critical development scholars describe this trend as "revolutionary" and "hegemonic," representing a new neoliberal rationality of "self-responsibilization" that structures the lives of the poor around solving their own problems while obscuring the structural relationships that maintain poverty in the global South (Ilcan and Phillips 2010; Karim 2008; Roy 2010). From the antipolitics machine to self-responsibilization schemes to the double bottom-line approach of global philanthrocapitalists and social entrepreneurs, the project of development becomes one of consensus building. Often relying on agreed upon development knowledge and technocratic and behavioral solutions to structural political and economic problems, large-scale poverty alleviation initiatives propose ways in which diverse and sometimes greatly divergent stakeholders can work together to create a greater good, reifying an, "existing body of agreed opinions . . . (while) avoiding or evading differences or divisions of opinion in an attempt to 'secure the centre' or 'occupy the middle ground'" (Williams 1985: 77).

Yet is this antipolitics or consensus-building approach to poverty alleviation new, particularly global, or even neoliberal? My study of philanthropic investments in addressing migrant poverty across California's Central Valley, from the historic Farm Worker Movement to the present, shows that this approach is not new and has origins that stretch beyond the neoliberal era and the global South. Extending the historical and geographic reach of critical development studies, this paper highlights the encounter between California farmworker organizers and their public and private funders through programs framed within consensus-based discourses and institutional relationships in California's Central Valley. Focusing on two cases, at two very different historical conjunctures, I show how the process of building consensus among greatly unequal partners is a central element of generating consent. Whether during the social movement era of the 1960s or the entrepreneurial double bottom-line development projects of today, philanthropic initiatives have promoted projects that ask the poor to "participate" in programs to contribute to a greater common good for agricultural communities while evading the root causes of migrant poverty and inequality.

With the work of Nancy Fraser (1997) and Chantal Mouffe (2006) as a point of departure, I argue that the idealized notion of a fully accessible and equitable deliberative arena where diverse stakeholders build common ground often disguises differences, conflicts, and the political stakes of the less powerful—ultimately generating consent. Embracing the liberal ideal of an open and accessible public deliberative arena, large-scale philanthropic initiatives often ignore questions of differential access, marginalization within participatory processes, and the alternate spaces and ways that migrant workers organize and support one another (Habermas 1989: 30). They also exclude questions that threaten the interests of those in power. In other words, as stated by Nancy Fraser (1997: 76) rephrasing Italian cultural theorist Antonio Gramsci, "The official bourgeois public sphere is . . . the prime institutional site for the construction of the consent that defines the new, hegemonic mode of domination." By asking migrant farmworkers, the poorest Californians, to participate in consensus-building projects *as equals* alongside the wealthiest agriculture producers in the world "secures the center" where both parties care about the health of agricultural communities, but evades questions about the massive inequality produced by industrial agriculture.

Through a historical and an ethnographic case study I show how the discursive evasions constructed by philanthropic investors, the practical political negotiations involved in building common ground among unequal partners, and the strategic articulations constructed to support or confront the dominant framework compose a broader theory of consensus and consent. In keeping with the intentional pairing of ethnographic and historical approaches within *Territories of Poverty* this paper "defamiliarizes" the recognizable story of the

California Farm Worker Movement by pairing it with a ethnographic case study of a recent $50 million farmworker organizing initiative. As legacy farmworker movement institutions continue to address enduring migrant poverty the ethnographic case challenges the silences and assumptions of the well-chronicled social movement of the past.

Case #1: From Farm Worker Movement to "Hustling Arm of the Union"

Sometimes called "the other California," in reference to Michael Harrington's 1962 exposé on poverty in the United States (*The Other America*), the Central Valley stretches 450 miles down the state's interior from the Sacramento Valley in the north to Bakersfield in the south. In stark contrast, it is at once the most productive agricultural region in the world and home to the poorest Americans.[2] In the public imagination of California, when pictured the Valley is usually represented by its agricultural riches, featuring vibrant wine vineyards and an overflowing cornucopia of farm produce.[3] What remains unseen is the enduring migrant poverty, hidden beyond the main highways and thoroughfares, created and maintained through century-old farming practices reliant on the recruitment of increasingly undocumented low-wage seasonal migrant labor. Since before the California Gold Rush racialized immigration, land ownership and labor policies and practices frustrated immigrant and migrant efforts to own land, marry, educate children, and participate in political life. These practices and patterns fostered the present circumstance of hidden poverty in the midst of great agricultural wealth—a form of territorial governance that David Harvey calls "organized abandonment" (Harvey 1989: 303). Produced and maintained by ongoing processes of appropriation and dislocation—including seasonal low-wage migrant employment, excessive land and water usage, and competition and financialization in global agricultural markets—farmworker communities are among what Ruth Wilson Gilmore (2008: 32) describes as advanced capitalism's *forgotten places*, "exhausted by the daily violence of environmental degradation, racism, underemployment, overwork, shrinking social wages, and the disappearance of whole ways of life" (see also Bradshaw 1993: 218–56).

Yet migrant poverty in California's Central Valley is not new, and people who struggle financially in this region are not silent, destitute, hopeless, or without agency. Periodic outrage at and organizing against California's industrial agricultural system has cast national attention on the region, from John Steinbeck's *Grapes of Wrath* (1939) and Carey McWilliams's *Factories in the Fields* (1939), to Dorothea Lange's Works Progress Administration photographs of Dust Bowl migrants, to Edward R. Murrow's nationally televised 1960 exposé *Harvest of Shame*, to multiple waves of agricultural labor organizing during the twentieth century. As these historic moments and more recent studies have brought to light, much of the region's poverty is maintained through a fragmented, multiple-farm industry organized around what Philip Martin (2003) calls the "three *c*'s" of farm labor. The first *c* stands for *concentration*: since the turn of the twentieth century, the vast majority of farmworkers have been employed on the largest farms that rely on labor-intensive seasonal work from which a majority of field workers are without wages for significant portions of the farm cycle. The second *c* stands for *contractors*: farm labor is managed by contractors who negotiate, and profit from, the difference between what the farmer will pay to have a job done and what the workers are paid. Farmers benefit from this arrangement because it streamlines the hiring process and also makes it difficult for worker advocates to directly negotiate and enforce wage standards, farm labor health, safety, and fair treatment regulations. To this day, it is easier for large growers to pay fines for labor and environmental abuses than to follow the regulations established by the struggles of the Farm Worker Movement and its allies.

The third *c* of California farm labor stands for *conflict*, a history of protest that continues but that has been unable to significantly change an industry whose profit relies on constant flows of poor migrant workers. In the course of the twentieth century, this previously alluvial valley basin was made and remade by sometimes violent struggles over minerals, water, farmable land, and multiple socioeconomic, cultural, and political stakes—including the Farm Worker Movement at its height during the 1960s and 1970s.[4] Through an innovative combination of place-based community organizing, self-help Mexican mutual aid associations, community service unions, culturally inspired leadership, and international boycotts, Cesar Chavez and the Farm Worker Movement showed how people in a forgotten place can build pride, form powerful worker-led institutions, and connect local struggles beyond regional landscapes—breaking patterns of territorial governance by large-scale agriculture in favor of self-determination through a multifaceted social movement.[5] These intersecting relationships of land, labor, capital, and social movements across the Valley and over time can be understood as "fields of power" (Roy 2003), or, as Doreen Massey (2204: 265) describes them, "power-geometries," a complex web of social relations "full of power and symbolism . . . of domination and subordination, of solidarity, and cooperation." The Farm Worker Movement emerged from a particular "power geometry" of crisis and opportunity. With the various civil rights movements of the early 1960s raging across the country, a growing population of settled Mexican migrant field workers, and the eventual end of the United States–Mexico bracero contract, which made it nearly impossible to organize farm labor (due to the ease of replacing striking labor with bracero migrant workers), the stage was set for Cesar Chavez and Dolores Huerta's grassroots organizing campaign across California's Central Valley (Taylor, Martin, and Fix 1997).

Part of the great success of the farmworker movement during the 1960s was its ability to dramatize the stark differences in life experience, in privilege, and in power between the farmworker (*la campesina/el campesino*) and the grower (*el mayordomo*) to farm-working families based on their own lived experiences. Through their stark and simplified plays of campesino vs. mayordomo, friend vs. enemy, good vs. evil, El Teatro Campesino, a roving theater troupe that toured the picket lines, the nation, and the globe showed workers that every identity is relational and that the conditions and the very existence and suffering of the campesino was determined by its opposition to the wealthy grower, his "constitutive outside" (Butler 1990). Wielding new understandings of power and change, these images were spread through Radio Campesina and the pages of the movement's paper, *El Malcreado* ("the mischievous," or those who speak back to their parents, named after the paper of the Mexican Revolution). Despite the complexity and diversity within the farmworker population, these relational representations of conflict between "us" and "them" served as strategic articulations (Hall 1980) of farmworker power that prompted anger, action, and a sense of collective struggle—the seeds of a movement. Through diverse representations and actions, a generation of farmworkers, college student volunteers, legal aid workers, Catholic priests, and movement leaders learned from critical praxis, that, as articulated by Paolo Freire (1985: 122), "Washing one's hands of the conflict between the powerful and the powerless means to side with the powerful, not to be neutral."

In contrast to the critical praxis that fueled the early movement, private foundations were initially interested in supporting the farmworker struggle for its potentially unifying claims of addressing migrant poverty through the promotion of dignity in work, cultural pride, and especially the unique place-based community union service model. The idea of a community union to address migrant poverty through reciprocal relationships of peer service, self-help, and leadership training was popularly embraced by funders, which set it apart from traditional union organizing, which is seldom supported by private foundations, and attracted as much as three hundred thousand dollars a year in foundation grants at the height of the movement—a significant amount in the 1960s.[6] However, just as foundations were attracted to the "community union" philosophy, they refused to fund the strikes, boycotts, and labor organizing strategies included in the broader vision of Chavez.

The first appeal to a foundation to support the UFW came in a 1966 letter to the Field Foundation from Office of Economic Opportunity programmer and national community development leader Edgar Cahn. Cahn drafted legislation for Johnson's War on Poverty and was particularly influential in encouraging the participation of the poor in multi-stakeholder Community Action Programs (CAPs) designed to build local consensus around how to best address questions of poverty and urban abandonment. In a December 10, 1966, memo to the Field Foundation's Leslie Dunbar, Cahn listed the characteristics of what a farmworker community union model could become with support from Field. Within the context of the then innovative Community Development Corporations (CDCs), Cahn described the potential of the community union model as limited to a defined geographical area, governed by a diverse array of local residents, comprised of a mix of trade union functions with community service and programming, utilizing strong streams of governmental and private funding, and governed by outside citizen review committees to evaluate and monitor the union activity. In this letter, Cahn proposed that if funded by Field, the community union could, like the CDCs of the inner city and the rural South (a product of Ford Foundation intervention to inner city conflict), "attempt to stabilize the fluid labor market picture of the migrant workers by adaptation of the 'community corporation' concept that Milt Kotler, Robert Kennedy and others have been exploring."[7] In other words, through the eyes of funders and planners the community union model would not mainly serve to organize workers but would rather introduce regional multi-stakeholder consensus processes of the emerging War on Poverty to a movement that was at the time experiencing strikes, boycotts, and increasing violence on the picket lines.

While Dunbar responded positively to Cahn's proposition and made several grants to the movement, he became cautious of continued funding to the UFW when he found out that the community union did indeed organize workers and was associated with a major union, the AFL-CIO. In a firm letter to Chavez, Dunbar warns that funding work in "the economic sphere" conflicts with the mission of all general purpose foundations and that Field would only continue funding if Chavez could frame his work in a way that benefited all stakeholders in agricultural communities beyond the economic grievances of workers,

> The farmworker's movement seems something very special and fine to a great many of us . . . to me, its great character is its faith in the people and its resolve to see them all live in dignity; and its commitment to non-violence and peace. Those of us who feel this way . . . want to be able to assist without at the same time giving our support to any other economic organization, such as the AFL-CIO or any other national union. . . . I think you would see why if you asked yourself how many other unions, AFL-CIO or otherwise, get foundation support. Few if any. (Leslie Dunbar, letter to Cesar Chavez, October 20, 1969, Field Foundation Archives, box 2T143 National Farmworker Service Center folder)

After months of heated correspondence between Chavez and Dunbar about what a community union should and should not do, with Chavez arguing for labor organizing and workers' rights and Dunbar arguing for an approach in keeping with the model proposed by Cahn, funding to the union was halted, and Chavez was convinced to transform his community union vision into an apolitical nonprofit 501(c)(3) organization, the National Farm Worker Service Center (NFWSC), which Field, and eventually other foundations including the Ford and Rockefeller Foundations, could funnel funds through. Soon after its incorporation, minutes of an NFWSC board meeting reveal that Chavez started to call the new nonprofit the "Hustling Arm of the Union," referencing its distance from the actual organizing and its ability to attract large tax-deductible grants (Meeting Minutes of National Farm Worker Service Center, 1969, Field Foundation Archives, box 2T143, National Farmworkers Service Center folder). Ultimately, in the face of intense conflict both within the movement leadership and with external competitors such as the Teamsters Union and opponents such as large grower associations and conservative politicians, Chavez eventually retreated from union organizing to the foundation-funded "Hustling" service center that would help farmworkers build mainstream institutional relationships and the skills and capacities necessary to fully participate in and theoretically improve agricultural communities, but not to strike or organize. Ultimately, through negotiations with funders, additional newly incorporated "movement institutions" required a separation of the social service approach of the movement from the focus on confronting the economic structures that maintain farmworker poverty and powerlessness—disarticulating the social from the economic, and the movement from the union. In the end, the approach that the foundation and the movement leadership could both agree upon limited what the movement could achieve.

Instead of concluding that service center work itself, as opposed to union organizing, represents the triumph of hegemonic counterrevolutionary forces in philanthropy (a common trend in critical philanthropy studies), I argue that through specific evasions in the "economic sphere" and through the political process of building consensus with funders, the service model was strategically rearticulated as both funders and Chavez witnessed growing conflict in the movement (Roelofs 2003; Rodriguez 2007). For example, in contrast to Rebecca Dolhinow's (2005: 558–80) recent study of the relationship between nonprofit organizations, activists, and residents in migrant colonies in New Mexico, which concludes that the neoliberal agenda is embodied in the implementation of "service" provision models that evade questions of structural inequality, I argue that the service model is not bad in and of itself but has rather been transformed through consensus processes. For Chavez, community *service* was originally a long-term strategy for radical economic independence, pride, and movement building based on collective ownership, mutual aid, and self-love (Levy 2007). Various movement leaders shared the ideology of service to self and to community as a means of radical self-sufficiency, defense against racist institutions, and the building of a new network of mutual aid support systems outside of mainstream society (interview with Farm Worker movement leader, October 2009; Garcia 2012; Bardacke 2011). Archival correspondence between Chavez and the Field Foundation revealed that philanthropic investors saw the movement's service center orientation attractive in its multi-stakeholder consensus-building potential, and through the founding of nonprofit institutions privileged this aspect of the work while evading and excluding questions of unionization, strikes, and the conflictual praxis that originally inspired broad-based participation in the movement. Through negotiations with movement leaders and the eventual founding of the nonprofit National Farm Worker Service Center, several foundations came to support the social service *tradition* while "disarticulating" the radical aspects of the approach from the framework and "re-articulating" it within the apolitical nonprofit model. Not unitary or controlling by definition, a radical idea is reinscribed on hegemonic terms through the process of negotiating with powerful stakeholders such as foundation program officers. In keeping with a Gramscian theory of consent, we can understand the role of "tradition, (as) a process of disarticulation and rearticulation of elements characteristic of hegemonic practices" (Mouffe 2006: 18). Ultimately, through building consensus among unequal partners, a radical idea held the seeds to its undoing.

Case #2: Farm Worker Community Building Initiative and the "New Win-Win Paradigm"

Despite the struggles and victories of the Farm Worker Movement, migrant poverty endures. Throughout the 1980s and 1990s, the rapid expansion of low-wage, immigrant-intensive production systems and the active recruitment of undocumented workers from poor regions in Mexico—with increasingly fewer services and rights in the United States—exacerbated an already impoverished farmworker population (Martin 2003; Holmes 2013). The environmental and labor regulations won in the 1970s are often unenforced, and growers find it more economical to operate above the law and pay fines when caught. The window that opened in 1964—the concrete conjuncture of Chavez's unified vision of a community union, the ending of the bracero program, the rising civil rights activism, the settling of once-migrant families, the support from political, media, and philanthropic institutions—just as quickly closed. With the practical defeats in the fields, internal leadership crisis, increasing undocumented immigration, the conservative political turn marked by the election of George Deukmejian to the California governor's office in 1983, the restructuring of the agricultural economy, and the availability of public and private funding to build nonprofit institutions and now extreme drought and related financial pressures for workers and growers alike, the terrain was immeasurably changed.

In the most recent moment, explicitly consensus-oriented approaches to addressing agricultural poverty are promoted in the context of the union–grower alliance around immigration reform (inspired by the "AGJOBS" legislative proposal—designed through an unprecedented compromise between farmworker advocates and major agricultural employers to address labor supply concerns as related to the current immigration crisis).[8] Despite worsening conditions for migrant field workers, many advocates believe that in the current climate of global financial crisis and competition, and the increasingly threatened status of undocumented workers, consensus-based partnerships with growers is the only thinkable strategy for improving the lives of farmworkers. For the first time in history, farmworker advocates' rhetoric (at least) is about saving California agriculture from the dangers of global competition and the need to ensure a sustainable workforce through new guest worker programs. This is a far cry from Cesar Chavez's (1984) dramatic call to "*overthrow* a farm labor system in this nation that treats farmworkers as if they were not important human beings." As part of the new worker-industry alliance, historic movement nonprofit organizations are working with growers to improve production strategies and increase industrial efficiency, thereby increasing profit and competitiveness of farmers while also increasing the output (and theoretically the wages) and sustainability of workers. I found through my ethnographic field work that growers and farmworker advocates alike argue that in the context of the rapid globalization of agriculture, where the cost of doing business is more expensive (e.g., land, water, equipment, labor, and regulation costs) in California than in the global South, the human worker is the only malleable input to increase competitiveness. Instead of "fighting" for workers' rights and enforcing existing regulations, former farmworker advocates are looking for ways to save California agriculture by building consensus or double bottom-line partnerships with growers. Theoretically there is a "win-win" in this approach, increasing farm profit and worker wages at once.

Between 2007 and 2009 I conducted ethnographic research on an explicitly consensus-based $50 million foundation initiative in farmworker communities in the San Joaquin Valley, the Western Foundation's Farm Worker Community Building Initiative (FWCBI).[9] The vision of this initiative was to create win-win strategic partnerships among workers, growers, and public and nonprofit service providers to collaboratively envision and ultimately implement strategies to address regional poverty and improve conditions in Central Valley agricultural communities. Through complex, multilayer partnership and committee structures (engaging local community organizing and service provider institutions), it was hoped that consensus-based planning would reveal how workers, growers, and diverse Valley residents might benefit from decentering the historic antagonisms of workers' rights vs. growers' abuses by charting a new shared vision. One of the frequently quoted mottos of the initiative was, "Let's diffuse the poles, and create a new center." Through extensive interviews and observation of this initiative, I observed how consensus-based institutional governing structures and professional program frameworks prohibited organizations from addressing the long-standing unfair labor practices that have kept farmworkers living in unhealthful and unjust conditions. In this case the particularly "asset-based" approach to community development,[10] the overwhelming concern with collaborative processes and structures, and the need for "all stakeholder" concerns to be heard (even though not all were present) seriously confined and frustrated grassroots organizations already challenged by the pessimistic political climate and decades of institutional competition and restrictions.

Within the Western Foundation's FWCBI several specific consensus-based processes diffused antagonism and proposed new ways of working with Valley growers and stakeholders. The first was through the process of research and the diluting role of the appointed task force in translating research into policy recommendations—including recommendations that seem to hold farmworkers responsible for their own health and well-being and exclude questions that hold growers accountable. The second technique was the "asset-based" community development model. The asset-based model engaged farmworker organizers in meetings, training sessions, and processes to document their own strengths and resources, a frame that disallowed the problem-centered model that most partnering FWCBI community organizers were trained in. The third was the specifically win-win collaborative model to both improve business and the conditions of workers at once.

To make a very long and perhaps convoluted story short, because the FWCBI avoided issues that farmworker advocates were concerned with, and because the asset-mapping approach did not appeal to action-based organizers, and because partners (farmworker and growers) of such divergent power could not find ways to come to the table together,[11] the project failed. With only paid professionals and no workers and/or growers consistently participating in the initiative, and with program coordinators advised to "stick to mapping assets" and not address any concrete issue until workers and growers were present, the project could not move forward. In the midst of this standstill, and with a threat from the foundation board that the project had better show measurable outcomes if funding was to be continued, the lead program officer required the partnership to take on antipesticide organizing. However, this last-ditch attempt to rally partners did not work, both because it contradicted the original consensus-driven model and because of the foundation's lack of knowledge about antipesticide strategy and fear of confrontation with growers.

A fatal critique of the foundation's last-minute attempt to take on a pesticide drift alert system came not from growers but from FWCBI partners with experience working on this issue. A staff person with a pesticide action partner to the FWCBI rejected the program officer's call to pesticide organizing as mismatched with the consensus-based ideology of the initiative:

> For anything to really happen we are going to need to make some demands, protest, but of course that doesn't fit with the consensus model. "We are not there yet" is what they'd say. The Tulare Country Board of Supervisors is made up of all Republican, conservative growers. So collectively taking on pesticides in Tulare Country is laughable when we can't even get growers or supervisors to participate. We are just so far apart from those in power. We need to shake things up but the foundation won't let us push on anything. (interview with FWCBI partner, 2008)

Unable to garner support from partners, and unwilling to take on growers or county officials, the program officer slowly retreated from pesticide organizing. In the end, the failure of the pesticide action attempt reveals how the general approach of the initiative was deeply flawed, poorly planned, and against the grain of the culture of the community organizing partners the foundation recruited. At a larger level it also reveals how, in the context of industrialized agriculture and its deeply embedded political support system, consensus among diverse and unequal groups is nearly impossible and sometimes undesirable. According to the consensus model, truly addressing the life, work, and health problems experienced by workers would raise too many issues that immediately scare off growers. Yet the irony in this situation is that in a time marked by fear of worker deportation, economic desperation, hopelessness, and competition, the consensus model is least helpful but does makes most sense. In an unimaginative (and increasingly policed, with increasing surveillance by the federal Secure Communities deportation program) environment where everyone is fearful of confronting growers, the consensus-based process keeps people engaged, yet it further entrenches a way of thinking that sees working on behalf of industry as the best way to help improve the lives of workers. The FWCBI was closed in 2009 due to a lack of "measurable outcomes," and defunded partnering organizations sought out new resources from a similarly consensus-driven foundation initiative in Bakersfield.

Conclusion

One might easily conclude that the current consensus-oriented win-win moment has top-down imperialist neoliberal origins. However, in keeping with my claim that consent is generated through the politics of translating historically divergent ideas into nonthreatening approaches acceptable to diverse stakeholders, my archival research revealed that the origins of the FWCBI's win-win approach are found not in the neoliberal moment but rather in the management ideas and vision of Cesar Chavez. Different from a story of straightforward neoliberal rule, the win-win model represents a strategic rearticulation of Chavez's long-term strategy to transform farm labor into a strong, stable, and well-respected profession inspired by his relationship with business management gurus such as Peter Drucker and Patrick Below.[12]

In the early 1990s the UFW was struggling to keep contracts due to increased competition with the Teamsters and dramatic staff and leadership fall-outs that occurred from 1979 through the 1980s, and due to a general failure to organize members and gain contracts.[13] Initially introduced to the union by Cesar Chavez, management consultant Patrick Below helped to develop a new project at a rose farm called Bear Creek Roses. Drawing on management theory, this project proposed that instead of organizing workers to strike, it might make more sense over the long haul to work with industry to "create a mission of mutual prosperity and respect, and innovative thinking for improving the company."[14] According to longtime UFW organizer David Villarino,

> This was genius thinking because we don't usually work with growers in this kind of context of mutual prosperity. It was also genius because we created a 1.5 million dollar profit after implementing a 30% production increase for the two types of roses they produce. The workers were better educated and more trained and in the end the worker crews were making decisions and did not even need a foreman anymore. This helped to raise wages and earnings for the piecemeal work and doubled vacation time. The normal lost days in December that year decreased by 1,000 percent. This was a huge paradigm shift because the company was using the farmworkers' knowledge, utilizing it to the benefit of the enterprise. And the company committed to sharing the gains and maintaining employment for workers not the job. For us this was a revolutionary lesson for the Union. (Villarino 2008)

In the end the Bear Creek project broke down because "it was ultimately their [growers'] vision and us helping them reach it. Eventually the manager took credit for all of it and distrust amongst workers ended it all" (Villarino 2008). However, the idea of win-win planning and organizing for "mutual prosperity" became central to the new approach of the UFW. In 2000, nearly a decade after the Bear Creek experience, the UFW engaged all of its various institutions (the union and eight nonprofit "movement office" organizations) and leaders in a strategic planning process. The meetings served as a wake-up call, and it was agreed that, "everyone has failed farmworkers. The growers have not changed, educational institutions are failing farmworker children, training and workforce development efforts have done nothing for farmworkers . . . and the union failed with 98% of the industry with no contracts" (FIELD planning document, 2000, shared with the author by David Villarino). At this meeting it was agreed that everyone would focus less on contracts and direct organizing and instead look at poverty, the whole life of the farmworker, and how to make farmwork a livable career. One of the ways it was proposed that this new direction would be implemented was to use the Bear Creek model through the union-associated nonprofit, Farm Worker Institution for Education and Leadership Development (FIELD). When I interviewed the founding program officer of the FWCBI, he cited FIELD's "New Win-Win Paradigm" as his main inspiration. Yet he also mentioned wanting to reinspire the radical movement for farmworker rights that Chavez and Huerta ignited almost half a decade before. Yet in practice those aspects of Chavez's vision remained in the history books.

The projects that emerged out of the win-win framework do propose incentives for industry to become more environmentally friendly, and some propose ways to increase worker productivity and thus wages. Some even advocate for immigration reform, alongside agricultural industry allies. In order to build consensus with growers, none take on issues of regulation or holding industry accountable for persistent financial, safety, sexual, and environmental abuses in the fields, or of failure to implement legislation passed under the leadership of the California Farm Worker Movement. Obviously, none of these initiatives address worker ownership, cooperatives, or banning the corrupt labor contractor system and below–minimum wage undocumented immigrant workforce that makes agricultural wealth possible. While inconceivable now, models of collective worker ownership, land reform, and business accountability were imaginable only a few decades ago. While "saving jobs" or "saving industry" take center stage, what is left out of the public agenda? What is not conceivable to accomplish or even attempt to change through the process of consensus-based collaboration? What kind of changes do consensus-based politics allow, and more importantly, what does it exclude, hide, or make unthinkable?

As proposed in the introduction of this chapter, I argue that building consensus among unequal partners is central to the process of generating consent. Consensus itself is not "bad" or "good" but is rather the terrain of negotiation upon which agendas are set and ideas become hegemonic. It is also the site in which these very ideas are contested. Through specific exclusions, negotiated political processes and professional frameworks, and strategic articulations of dominant and counter frameworks, hegemony is always at work translating and redefining the interests and aspirations of its opposition. I show how the "antipolitics machine" of development and philanthropy often does not solve the problems it sets out to address. Instead, it translates the struggles, identities, and interests of migrant field workers into programs and collaborative structures most palatable to those in power. Counter to recent studies that claim that philanthropy controls through a more straightforward process of neoliberal governance or cultural imperialism, the cases featured in this paper show how "a class is hegemonic not so much to the extent that it is able to impose a uniform conception of the world on the rest of society, but to the extent that it can articulate different visions of the world in such a way that their political antagonism is neutralized" (LaClau 1977, 161).

Of course, central to the two cases featured in this paper are the inherent political limits of mainstream philanthropy. From the founding of the early American philanthropies such as the Rockefeller, Carnegie, and Ford Foundations to the multiple general-purpose foundations making grants to nonprofit organizations today, philanthropic giving has clearly defined limits (Arnove 1980; Coon 1990; Covington 1997; Dowie 2001; INCITE! 2007; Jenkins 1998; Roelofs 2003). Created and maintained through wealth generated from the surplus of capitalist production, foundations interested in poverty alleviation will generally not fund labor organizing or labor rights. Foundations interested in environmental degradation generally don't fund global corporate accountability. Foundations interested in immigrants prefer to fund citizenship education but not immigrant rights. In other words, foundation priorities reveal the grand paradox of funding working-class organizing through the surplus of capital. The surplus of capital is generally understood as the profit generated from unpaid or underpaid labor. In the globalized world of the twentieth and twenty-first centuries, unpaid or underpaid labor is one of the main causes of deepening inequality and embedded poverty. This is as true for global agriculture as any industry (Goodman and Watts 1997). In the face of global competition, even certified organic farms replicate labor practices set by the very industrialized agriculture sector that they set out to change (Guthman 2004). Can the surplus of capitalist exploitation be used to aid those upon whose backs this surplus is generated? Can these surplus dollars contribute to seriously addressing entrenched poverty if systemic questions of labor, migration, and human rights organizing are not addressed? The social movement leaders, organizational staff, and foundation program officers and consultants featured in this chapter struggle with these questions as they negotiate encounters between philanthropic institutions and the grassroots organizations they believe in and support.

NOTES

1. For a recent analysis of Obama's middle ground politics, see Frederick Harris, "Still Waiting for Our First Black President," *Washington Post*, June 1, 2012, http://www .washingtonpost.com/opinions/still-waiting-for-our-first-black-president/2012/06/01 /gJQARsT16U_story.html?socialreader_check=0&denied=1.

2. "California is the nation's most productive agricultural state, and is home to a $35 billion agricultural industry. Of the ten most productive agricultural counties in the United States, nine are in California, and the San Joaquin Valley is the single richest agricultural region in the world. California produces more than 400 commodities. It is the nation's sole producer of a dozen crops, including almonds, artichokes, olives, raisins, and walnuts, and is the leading producer of five dozen more. The state employs 27 percent of the nation's farm workers, and produces nearly half domestically grown fruits, nuts, and vegetables. Almost 22 percent of the nation's milk and cream is produced in California, and the state is by far the nation's largest producer of dairy products" (U.S. Environmental Protection Agency 2013).

3. Isao Fujimoto's description of the "front" and "back" of California documents the public representations of Central Valley towns and provides a framework for studying the "invisible" poverty amid great wealth that defines the region. See the working paper series, CALIFORNIA CASES II, Central Valley Partnership for Civic Participation (Isao Fujimoto, Human and Community Development, UC Davis).

4. For a complete labor history of the material and ideological struggles over the California landscape, including the role of migrant workers, see Don Mitchel, *The Lie of the Land* (Minneapolis: University of Minnesota Press, 1996).

5. For a complete labor history of the material and ideological struggles over the California landscape, including the role of migrant workers, see Mitchel, *The Lie of the Land*. Also see Richard Walker, *The Conquest of Bread: 150 Years of Agribusiness in California* (New York: The New Press, 2004), and recent Farm Worker Movement histories: Bardacke 2011; Marshall Ganz, "Five Smooth Stones: Strategic Capacity in the Unionization of California Agriculture" (PhD diss., Harvard University, 2008); Garcia 2012.

6. Funding and institutional data for this chapter was gathered from interviews with movement leaders and archival research at the United Farm Workers archives at the Walter P. Reuther Library at Wayne State University (Foundations Folder, individual foundation folders) and the Field Foundation archives at the Center for American History at the University of Texas, Austin (UFW, Farm Labor, Cesar Chavez, and Roger Baldwin Folders). See specific archival citations where directly referenced.

7. Cahn is referring to Marion Wright Edelman, legal advocate for the Child Development Group of Mississippi who would later help found the Children's Defense Fund. Cahn is wishing for a similarly catalytic legal advocate for Cesar Chavez's growing movement. See Edgar Cahn, letter to Leslie Dunbar, December 10, 1966, Field Foundation Archives, Center for American History, University of Texas, Austin, box 2T143, National Farmworker Service Center folder.

8. AGJOBS is the Agricultural Job Opportunities, Benefits and Security Act, which was

designed through an unprecedented compromise between farm worker advocates (primarily United Farm Workers) and major agricultural employers to address labor supply concerns as related to the current immigration crisis. If passed AGJOBS would ensure a legal, stable labor supply and would create pathways to legalization. It also contains a proposal to create a new "guest worker" program.

9. All foundation, initiative, and individual names are disguised according to the Human Subjects Protocols for this project. All subsequent individual and organizational names in this chapter are disguised to protect the identity of informants.

10. The asset-based community development approach was popularized by John McKnight and John Kretzmen, and in the rural context by Cornelia Flor Butler. The general model proposed that a problem-centered approach to community development mires communities in debate and antagonistic blame, while ignoring the strengths and assets already existent but not necessarily connected and mobilized within a community. The FWCBI was specifically inspired by M. Emery, S. Fey, and C. B. Flora, "Using Community Capitals to Build Assets for Positive Community Change," *CD Practice* 13 (2006); M. Emery and C. B. Flora, "Spiraling-Up: Mapping Community Transformation with Community Capitals Framework," *Community Development* 37 (2006): 19–35; Cornelia Butler Flora, "Rural Community Economic Development Case Review," Claude Worthington Benedum Foundation (2003–2004); Cornelia Butler Flora "Developing Indicators to Refine and Test a Theory of Equitable Change for Rural Communities of Interest and of Place" National Rural Funders Collaborative (2003–2004); Robert Putnam, *Bowling Alone: The Collapse and Revival of American Community* (New York: Simon and Schuster, 2000).

11. In most cases, growers did not respond to the call to participate in a project about farmworkers, migrant poverty, or community improvement. Farmworkers themselves were underrepresented because the FWCBI coordinators did not find them "ready" to participate as equals alongside the other stakeholders, such as city officials and nonprofit organizational directors.

12. Cesar Chavez's meeting with Peter Drucker in 1981 is marked by movement leaders as a significant moment in his shift away from union organizing and toward institutional management and planning. In this meeting Drucker also suggested that "immigrants" and not "farmworkers" are the central constituents to the UFW, and if embraced as such would move the union toward greater power and success in the agriculture industry (1981 Meeting with Peter Drucker debrief transcript, United Farm Workers of America Archives, Walter P. Reuther Library, Wayne State University, Detroit, box 52 UFW Information and Research Department Files folder). It is not clear whether Drucker's advice had anything to do with the UFW's decision to focus their attentions on immigration reform through the AGJOBS legislation, as Chavez did not move in this direction during his lifetime.

13. Discussions of internal leadership problems and multiple staff resignations can be found in multiple files labeled "The Purge" in the United Farm Workers of America archives at Wayne State University. While beyond the scope of this chapter, it is relevant to mark this time of crisis as one where Cesar Chavez had become paranoid about lead-

ership loyalty and generally feared of internal surveillance. These fears resulted in Chavez and an inner circle of UFW leaders "purging" volunteers and staff in question from the movement, for more information, see Bardacke (2011) and Garcia (2012).

14. According to an article in the October 2000 issue of *Rural Migration News* (vol. 6, no. 4: http://migration.ucdavis.edu/rmn/more.php?id=470_0_3_0), "The UFW says that its agreement with Bear Creek (Jackson & Perkins Rose) Production Company in Wasco, California is an example of how the 'new UFW' is willing and able to cooperate with farm employers to enhance employer profitability while increasing wages and benefits for workers. . . . The UFW won an election to represent Bear Creek workers December 16, 1994, and signed a three-year contract on March 17, 1995 that increased wages and benefits 22 percent over the life of the contract. . . . The UFW-Bear Creek relationship got off to a rocky start, with 136 grievances filed in the contract's first 18 months. In July 1996, Bear Creek contacted the UFW about the troublesome relationship, and a two-day session was held in September 1996 to resolve outstanding grievances; it resulted in a pledge to work together as the UFW-Bear Creek partnership. Under the partnership, supervisors and union representatives were retrained to enable them to resolve disputes before they escalated into grievances. Bear Creek workers were asked to make productivity increasing suggestions without fear of layoffs. As a result, the quality of the bare-root roses produced at Bear Creek increased markedly, from 40 percent premium in 1996 to 54 percent premium in 1999. . . . According to the UFW, average hourly earnings rose from $7.62 in 1997 to $8.02 in 1999, the number of foremen was reduced, and the number of workers' compensation claims reduced by half."

REFERENCES

Arnove, Robert. 1980. *Philanthropy and Cultural Imperialism*. Boston: G. K. Hall.

Bardacke, Frank. 2011. *Trampling Out the Vintage: Cesar Chavez and the Two Souls of the United Farm Workers*. London: Verso.

Bishop, Mathe, and Michael Green. 2008. *Philanthrocapitalism: How the Rich Can Save the World*. New York: Bloomsbury Press.

Bradshaw, Ted K. 1993. "In the Shadow of Urban Growth: Bifurcation in Rural California Communities." In *Forgotten Places: Uneven Development in Rural America*, ed. Thomas A. Lyson and William W. Falk, 218–56. Lawrence: University Press of Kansas.

Butler, Judith. 1990. *Gender Trouble: Feminism and the Subversion of Identity*. New York: Routledge.

Chavez, Cesar. 1984. Public address by Cesar Chavez, President, United Farm Workers of America. AFL-CIO, November 9, San Francisco.

Clinton, Bill. 2007. *Giving: How Each of Us Can Change the World*. New York: Knopf.

Coon, Horace. 1990. *Money to Burn*. New Brunswick, N.J.: Transaction. (Orig. pub. 1938.)

Covington, Sally. 1997. *Moving a Public Policy Agenda: The Strategic Philanthropy of*

Conservative Foundations. Washington, D.C.: National Committee for Responsive Philanthropy.

Dolhinow, Rebecca. 2005. "Caught in the Middle: The State, NGOs, and the Limits to Grassroots Organizing along the U.S.–Mexico Border." *Antipode* 37:3, 558–80.

Dowie, Mark. 2001. *American Foundations, An Investigative History*. Cambridge Mass.: The MIT Press.

Ferguson, James. 1994. *The Anti-Politics Machine: "Development," Depoliticization, and Bureaucratic Power in Lesotho*. Minneapolis: University of Minnesota Press.

Fraser, Nancy. 1997. *Justice Interruptus: Critical Reflections on the "Postsocialist" Condition*. New York: Routledge.

Freire, Paolo, with Donald Macedo and Henry Giroux. 1985. *The Politics of Education: Culture, Power, and Liberation*. New York: Continuum.

Garcia, Matt. 2012. *From the Jaws of Victory: The Triumph and Tragedy of Cesar Chavez and the Farm Worker Movement*. Berkeley: University of California Press.

Gilmore, Ruth Wilson. 2008. "Forgotten Places and the Seeds of Grassroots Planning." In *Engaging Contradictions: Theory, Politics, and Methods of Activist Scholarship*, ed. Charles R. Hale, 31-61. Berkeley: University of California Press.

Goodman, David, and Michael Watts. 1997. *Globalizing Food: Agrarian Questions and Global Restructuring*. London: Routledge.

Graham, Leigh. 2012. "Advancing the Human Right to Housing in Post-Katrina New Orleans: Discursive Opportunity Structures in Housing and Community Development." *Housing Policy Debate* 22:1, 5–27.

Guthman, Julie. 2004. *Agrarian Dreams: The Paradox of Organic Farming in California*. Berkeley: University of California Press.

Habermas, Jürgen. 1989. *The Structural Transformation of the Public Sphere: An Inquiry into a Category of Bourgeois Society*. Trans. Thomas Burger. Cambridge, Mass.: MIT Press.

Hall, Stuart. 1980. "Race, Articulation and Societies Structured in Dominance." In *Sociological Theories: Race and Colonialism*, 305–45. Paris: UNESCO. Repr., Oxford: Blackwell, 2001.

Harrington, Michael. 1962. *The Other America: Poverty in the United States*. New York: Macmillan.

Harvey, David. 1989. *The Limits to Capital*. Chicago: University of Chicago Press.

Holmes, Seth. 2013. *Fresh Fruit, Broken Bodies: Migrant Farmworkers in the United States*. Berkeley: University of California Press.

Ilcan, Suzan, and Lynne Phillips. 2010. "Developmentalities and Calculative Practices: The Millennium Development Goals." *Antipode* 42:4, 844–74.

INCITE! 2007. *The Revolution Will Not Be Funded: Beyond the Non-Profit Industrial Complex*. New York: INCITE! and South End Press Collective.

Jenkins, J. Craig. 1998. "Channeling Social Protest: Foundation Patronage of Contemporary Social Movements." In *Private Action and the Public Good*, ed. Walter W. Powell and Elisabeth S. Clemens, 206–16. New Haven: Yale University Press.

Karim, Lamia. 2008. "Demystifying Micro-Credit: The Grameen Bank, NGOs, and Neoliberalism in Bangladesh." *Cultural Dynamics* 20:1, 5–29.

LaClau, Ernesto. 1977. *Politics and Ideology in Marxist Theory: Capitalism, Fascism, Populism*. London: NLB.

Levy, Jacques. 2007. *Cesar Chavez: Autobiography of La Causa*. Minneapolis: University of Minnesota Press.

Li, Tania. 2007. *The Will to Improve: Governmentality, Development, and the Practice of Politics*. Durham: Duke University Press.

Martin, Philip. 1997. "Promises Unfulfilled: Unions, Immigration, and the Farm Workers." PhD diss., Cornell University.

Massey, Doreen, 2004. *Space, Place, and Gender*. Minneapolis: University of Minnesota Press.

Mouffe, Chantal. 2006. *The Return of the Political*. Brooklyn: Verso.

Moyo, Dambisa. 2010. *Dead Aid: Why Aid Is Not Working and How There Is a Better Way for Africa*. New York: Farrar, Straus and Giroux.

Peterson, M. N., M. J. Peterson, and T. R. Peterson. 2005. "Conservation and the Myth of Consensus." *Conservation Biology* 19, 762–67.

Prahalad, C. K. 2004. *The Fortune at the Bottom of the Pyramid: Eradicating Poverty Through Profit*. Upper Saddle River, N.J.: Wharton School Publishing.

Rodriguez, Dylan. 2007. "The Political Logic of the Non-Profit Industrial Complex." In *The Revolution Will Not Be Funded: Beyond the Non-Profit Industrial Complex*, ed. INCITE! Women of Color against Violence, 21–40. Cambridge, Mass.: South End Press.

Roelofs, Joan. 2003. *Foundations and Public Policy: The Mask of Pluralism*. Albany: State University of New York Press.

Roy, Ananya. 2003. *City Requiem, Calcutta: Gender and the Politics of Poverty*. Minneapolis: University of Minnesota Press.

Roy, Ananya. 2010. *Poverty Capital: Microfinance and the Making of Development*. New York: Routledge.

Taylor, J. Edward, Philip L. Martin, and Michael Fix. 1997. *Poverty amid Prosperity: Immigration and the Changing Face of Rural California*. Washington, D.C.: The Urban Institute.

U.S. Environmental Protection Agency. 2013. "State Agricultural Profiles: California." http://www.epa.gov/region9/ag/ag-state.html.

Villarino, David. 2008. Interview with author.

Williams, Raymond. 1985. *Keywords: A Vocabulary of Culture and Society*. Oxford: Oxford University Press.

Section 3

Geographies of Penality and Risk

From the ghettos of the North Atlantic to the cities of the global South—and at the militarized borders that confound such neat analytic categories—the question of poverty is also and always a question of surplus populations. Poverty programs may seek to integrate the poor and transform poor neighborhoods, but they are also calculative strategies for managing risky bodies and stigmatized places. In arguing for an analytical shift from spaces of poverty to territories of poverty, we are particularly attentive to how practices of security normalize and reproduce the ways in which poverty is spatialized and bordered. We are also interested in the question of praxis in territories and spaces of poverty: collective imagination that reinvents public institutions and rearranges geographies of knowledge production and expertise.

ESC

Class, Ethnicity, and State in the Making of Marginality: Revisiting Territories of Urban Relegation

LOÏC WACQUANT

To relegate (from the late Middle English, *relegaten*, meaning to send away, to banish) is to assign an individual, population, or category to an obscure or inferior position, condition, or location. In the postindustrial city, relegation takes the form of real or imaginary consignment to distinctive sociospatial formations variously and vaguely referred to as inner cities, ghettos, enclaves, no-go areas, problem districts, or simply rough neighborhoods. How are we to characterize and differentiate these spaces, what determines their trajectory (birth, growth, decay, and death), whence comes the intense symbolic taint attached to them at century's edge, and what constellations of class, ethnicity, and state do they both materialize and signify? These are the questions I pursue in my book *Urban Outcasts* through a methodical comparison of the trajectories of the black American ghetto and the European working-class peripheries in the era of neoliberal ascendancy (Wacquant 2008b).[1] In this chapter, I revisit this cross-continental sociology of "advanced marginality" to tease out its lessons for our understanding of the tangled nexus of symbolic, social, and physical space in the polarizing metropolis.

To speak of *urban relegation*—rather than "territories of poverty" or "low-income community," for instance—is to insist that the proper object of inquiry is not the place itself and its residents but the multilevel structural processes whereby persons are selected, thrust, and maintained in marginal locations, as well as the social webs and cultural forms they subsequently develop therein. Relegation is a *collective activity*, not an individual state; a *relation* (of economic, social, and symbolic power) between collectives, not a gradational attribute of persons. It reminds us that, to avoid falling into the false realism of the ordinary and scholarly common sense of the moment, the sociology of marginality must fasten not on vulnerable "groups" (which often exist merely on paper, if that) but on the *institutional mechanisms* that produce, reproduce, and transform

247

the network of positions to which its supposed members are dispatched and attached. And it urges us to remain agnostic as to the particular social and spatial configuration assumed by the resulting district of dispossession.[2]

Urban Outcasts is the summation of a decade of theoretical and empirical research tracking the causes, forms, and consequences of urban "polarization from below" in the United States and Western Europe after the close of the Fordist-Keynesian era, leading to a diagnosis of the predicament of the *postindustrial precariat* coalescing in the neighborhoods of relegation of advanced society. The book brings the core tenets of Bourdieu's sociology to bear on a wide array of field, survey, and historical data on inner Chicago and outer Paris to contrast the sudden implosion of the black American ghetto after the riots of the 1960s with the slow decomposition of the working-class districts of the French urban periphery in the age of deindustrialization. It puts forth three main theses and sketches an analytic framework for renewing the comparative study of urban marginality that I spotlight to help us elucidate the relations of poverty, territory, and power in the postindustrial city.

From Ghetto to Hyperghetto, or the Political Roots of Black Marginality

Urban Outcasts opens by parsing the reconfiguration of race, class, and space in the American metropolis because the foreboding figure of the dark ghetto has become epicentral to the social and scientific imaginary of urban transformation at century's turn.[3] On American shores, the abrupt and unforeseen involution of the "inner city"—a geographic euphemism obfuscating the reality of the ghetto as an instrument of ethnoracial entrapment imposed uniquely on blacks—was the target of a fresh plank of policy worry and scholarly controversy. Across Western Europe, vague images of "the ghetto" as a pathological space of segregation, dereliction, and deviance imported from America (with rekindled intensity after the Los Angeles riots of spring 1992) suffused as well as obscured journalistic, political, and intellectual debates on immigration and inequality in the dualizing city.

The first thesis, accordingly, charts the *historic transition from ghetto to hyperghetto* in the United States and stresses the pivotal role of state structure and policy in the (re)production of racialized marginality. Revoking the trope of "disorganization" inherited from the Chicago school of the 1930s and rejecting the tale of the "underclass" (in its structural, behavioral, and neo-ecological variants) that had come to dominate research on race and poverty by the 1980s, *Urban Outcasts* shows that the black American ghetto collapsed after the peaking of the civil rights movement to spawn a novel organizational constellation: the hyperghetto. To be more precise, the "Black Metropolis," lodged at the heart of the white city but cloistered from it, that both ensnared and enjoined African American urbanites in a reserved perimeter and a web of shared institutions built by and for blacks between 1915 and 1965 (Drake and Cayton 1993), collapsed to give way to a dual sociospatial formation. This decentered formation, stretching across the city, is composed of the *hyperghetto* proper (HyGh), that is, the vestiges of the historic ghetto now encasing the precarized fractions of the black working class in a barren territory of dread and dissolution devoid of economic function and doubly segregated by race and class, on the one hand, and of the burgeoning *black middle-class districts* (BMCD) that grew mostly via public employment in satellite areas left vacant by the mass exodus of whites to the suburbs, on the other. Whereas space unified African Americans into a compact if stratified community from World War I to the revolts of the 1960s, now it fractures them along class lines patrolled by state agencies of social control increasingly staffed by middle-class blacks charged with overseeing their unruly lower-class brethren (Pattillo 2000, 2007). The encapsulating dualism of the Fordist half-century inscribed in symbolic, social, and physical space, summed up by the equation White:Black :: City:Ghetto has thus been superseded by a more complex and tension-ridden structure White:Black :: City::BMCD:HyGh according to a fractal logic according to which the residents of the hyperghetto find themselves doubly dominated and marginalized.

Breaking with the stateless cast of mainstream U.S. sociology of race and poverty, *Urban Outcasts* then finds that hyperghettoization is economically underdetermined and politically overdetermined. The most distinctive cause of the extraordinary social intensity and spatial concentration of black dispossession in the hyperghetto is not the "disappearance of work" (as argued by Wilson 1996) or the stubborn persistence of "hypersegregation" (as proposed by Massey and Denton 1993), although these two forces are evidently at play. It is government policies of urban abandonment pursued across the gamut of employment, welfare, education, housing, and health at multiple scales—federal, state, and local—and the correlative breakdown of public institutions in the urban core that has accompanied the downfall of the communal ghetto. This means that the conundrum of class and race (as denegated ethnicity) in the American metropolis cannot be resolved without bringing into our analytic purview the shape and operation of the state, construed as a stratification and classification agency that decisively shapes the life options and strategies of the urban poor.

The "Convergence Thesis" Specified and Refuted

The second part—and central thesis—of *Urban Outcasts* takes the reader across the Atlantic to disentangle the same spatial nexus of class, ethnicity, and state in postindustrial Europe. Puncturing the panic discourse of "ghettoization" that has swept across the continent over the past two decades, it demonstrates that zones of urban deprivation in France and neighboring countries are not ghettos *à l'américaine*. Despite surface similarities in social morphology (population makeup, age mix, family composition, relative unemployment, and poverty levels) and representations (the sense of indignity, confinement, and blemish felt by their residents) due to their common position at the bottom of the material and symbolic hierarchy of places that make up the metropolis, the remnants of the black American ghetto and European working-class peripheries are separated by enduring differences of structure, function, and scale as well as by the divergent political treatments they receive. To sum them up: repulsion into the black ghetto is determined by *ethnicity* (E), inflected by *class* (C) with the emergence of the hyperghetto in the 1970s, and intensified by the *state* (S) throughout the century, according to the algebraic formula $[(E > C) \times S]$. By contrast, relegation in the urban periphery of Western Europe is driven by class position, inflected by ethnonational membership, and mitigated by state structures and policies, as summed up by the formula $[(C > E) \div S]$. It is not spawning "immigrant cities within the city," endowed with their own extended division of labor and duplicative institutions, based on ethnic compulsion applied uniformly across class levels. It is not, in other words, converging with the black American ghetto of mid-twentieth century characterized by its joint function of social ostracization and economic exploitation of a dishonored population.

To lump variegated spaces of dispossession in the city under the label of "ghetto" bespeaks, and in turn perpetuates, three mistakes that the book dispels. The first consists in invoking the term as a mere rhetorical device intended to shock public conscience by activating the lay imaginary of urban badlands. But a ghetto is not a "bad neighborhood," a zone of social disintegration defined (singly or in combination) by segregation, deprivation, dilapidated housing, failing institutions, and the prevalence of vice and violence. It is a *spatial implement of ethnoracial closure and control* resulting from the reciprocal assignation of a stigmatized category to a reserved territory that paradoxically offers the tainted population a structural harbor that fosters self-organization and collective protection against brute domination (Wacquant 2008a, 2011). The second mistake consists in conflating the communal ghetto with the hyperghetto: impoverishment, economic informalization, institutional desertification, and the depacification of everyday life are not features of the ghetto but, on the contrary, symptoms of its disrepair and dismemberment. The third error misreads the evolution of traditional working-class territories in the European city. In their phase of postindustrial decline, these defamed districts have grown more heterogeneous ethnically while postcolonial migrants have become more dispersed even as nodes of high density have emerged to fixate media attention and political worry (Pan Ké Shon and Wacquant 2012); their boundaries are porous and routinely crossed by residents who climb up the class structure; the number and variety of organizations in them have dwindled, and they have failed to generate a collective identity for their inhabitants—notwithstanding the fantastical fear, coursing through Europe, that Islam would supply a shared language to unify urban outcasts of foreign origins and fuel a process of "inverted assimilation" (Liogier 2012). In each of these five dimensions, neighborhoods of relegation in the European metropolis are consistently moving away from the pattern of the ghetto as device for sociospatial enclosure: they are, if one insists on retaining that spatial idiom, *anti-ghettos.*

To assert that lower-class districts harboring high densities of bleak public housing, vulnerable households, and postcolonial migrants are not ghettos is not to deny the role of ethnic identity—or assignation—in the patterning of inequality in contemporary Europe. *Urban Outcasts* is forthright in stressing the "banalization of venomous expressions of xenophobic enmity" and the "cruel reality of durable exclusion from and abiding discrimination on the labor market" based on national origins; it fully acknowledges that "ethnicity has become a more salient marker in French social life" (Wacquant 2008b: 195–96) as in much of the continent. But *cognitive salience is not social causation.* The sharp appreciation of the ethnic currency in the political and journalistic fields does not mean that its weight has grown *pari passu* as a determinant of position and trajectory in the social and urban structure, nor that it now routinely skews ordinary interactions and everyday experience.[4] Moreover, ethnic rifts, when they do surge and stamp social relations, do not assume everywhere the same material form.

To maintain that ghettoization is *not* at work in the pauperized and stigmatized districts of the European city is simply to recognize that the modalities of ethnoracial classification and stratification, including their inscription in space, differ on the two sides of the Atlantic, in keeping with long-standing differences in state, citizenship, and urbanism between Western Europe and the United States. In the urban periphery of the Old World, resurging or emerging divisions based on symbolic markers activated by migration do not produce "ethnic communities" in the Weberian sense of segmented collectivies, ecologically separate and culturally unified, liable to act as such on the political stage (Banton 2007), as the inflexible hypodescent-based cleavage called race has for African Americans—and only for them in the sweep of history in the country. Ethnicity is defined by shifting and woolly criteria that operate inconsistently across institutional domains and levels of the class structure, such that it does not produce a coordinated alignment of boundaries in symbolic, social, and physical space liable to foster a dynamic of ghettoization.[5]

The "Emergence Thesis" Formulated and Validated

Refuting the thesis of transatlantic convergence on the pattern of the black American ghetto leads to articulating the thesis of the *emergence of a new regime of urban marginality*, distinct from that which prevailed during the century of industrial growth and consolidation running roughly from 1880 to 1980. The third part of *Urban Outcasts* develops an ideal-typical characterization of this ascending form of "advanced marginality"—thus called because it is not residual, cyclical, or transitional, but rooted in the deep structure of financialized capitalism—that has supplanted both the dark ghetto in the United States and traditional workers' territories in Western Europe. A cross-sectional cut reveals six synchronic features (chapter 8) while a longitudinal perspective ferrets out four propitiating dynamics (chapter 9), including the polarization of the occupational structure and the reengineering of the state to foster commodification. Here I want to spotlight two of those features, the one material and the other symbolic, to emphasize the novelty of advanced marginality.

The paramount material attribute of the emerging regime of marginality in the city is that it is *fed by the fragmentation of wage labor*, that is, the diffusion of unstable, part-time, short-term, low-pay, and dead-end employment at the bottom of the occupational structure—a master trend that has accelerated and solidified across advanced nations over the past two decades (Cingolani 2011; Kalleberg 2011; Pelizzari 2009). Whereas the life course and household strategies of the working class for much of the twentieth century were anchored in steady industrial employment set by the formula 40–50–60 (40 hours a week for 50 weeks of the year until age 60, in rough international averages), today the unskilled fractions of the deregulated service proletariat face a simultaneous dearth of jobs and plethora of work tenures that splinter and destabilize them. Their temporal horizon is shortened as their social horizon is occluded by the twin obstacles of endemic unemployment and rampant precarity, translating into the conjoint festering of hardship and proliferation of the "working poor" (Shiple 2004, Clerc 2004; Andress and Lohmann 2008).

This double economic penalty is particularly prevalent in lower-class neighborhoods gutted out by deindustrialization. One illustration: in France between 1992 and 2007, the number of wage earners in insecure jobs (short-term contracts, temporary slots, government-sponsored posts, and traineeships) increased from 1.7 to 2.8 million to reach 12.4 percent of the active workforce against the backdrop of a national unemployment rate oscillating between 7 and 10 percent; for those ages fifteen to twenty-four that proportion jumped from 17 to 49 percent (Maurin and Savidan 2008). But in the 571 officially designated "sensitive urban zones" (ZUS) targeted by France's urban policy, the combined share of unemployed and precariously employed youths zoomed from 40 percent in 1990 to above 60 percent after 2000. Far from protecting from poverty as it expands, fragmented wage labor is a vector of *objective* social insecurity among the postindustrial proletariat as well as *subjective* social insecurity among the inferior strata of the middle class—whose members fear social downfall and are proving unable to transmit their status to their children due to intensified school competition and the loosening of the links between credentials, employment, and income. On this count, *Urban Outcasts* is an invitation to *relink class structure and urban structure* from the ground up and a warning that an exclusive focus on the spatial dimension of poverty (as fostered, for instance, by studies of "neighborhood effects")[6] partakes of the obfuscation of the new social question of the early twenty-first century: namely, the spread and normalization of social insecurity at the bottom of the class ladder and its ramifying impact on the life strategies and territories of the urban precariat.

But the inexorable propagation of "McJobs"—*petits boulots* in France, *Billig-Jobs* in Germany, *lavoretti* in Italy, *biscate* in Portugal, and so on—is not the only force impinging on the precariat. A second, properly symbolic vector acts to entrench the social instability and redouble the cultural liminality of its constituents: *territorial stigmatization*. Mating Bourdieu's theory of symbolic power with Goffman's analysis of the management of spoiled identities (Bourdieu 1990; Goffman 1964), I forged this notion to capture how the blemish of place affixed on zones of urban decline at century's turn affects the sense of self and the conduct of their residents, the actions of private concerns and public bureaucracies, and the policies of the state toward dispossessed populations and districts in advanced society. First, I document that territorial taint is indeed a distinctive, novel, and generalized phenomenon, correlative of the dissolution of the black American ghetto and of the European working-class periphery of the Fordist-Keynesian period, that has become superimposed on the stigmata traditionally associated with poverty, lowly ethnic origins, and visible deviance. Since the publication of *Urban Outcasts*, proliferating studies have documented the rise, tenacity, and ramifying reverberations of spatial stigma in cities spread across three continents (Wacquant, Slater, and Pereira 2013).

Next, I show that the denigration of place wields causal effects in the dynamics of marginality via cognitive mechanisms operating at multiple levels. Inside districts of relegation, it incites residents to engage in coping strategies of mutual distancing, lateral denigration, retreat into the private sphere, and neighborhood flight that converge to foster diffidence and disidentification, distend local social ties, and thus curtail their capacity for proximate social control and collective action. Around them, spatial disgrace warps the perception and behavior of operators in the civic arena and the economy (as when firms discriminate based on location for investment and residential address for hiring),[7] as well as the delivery of core public services such as welfare, health, and policing (law enforcement officers feel warranted to treat inhabitants of lowly districts in a discourteous and brutal manner). In the higher reaches of social space, territorial stigma colors the output of specialists in cultural production such as journalists and academics; and it contaminates the views of state elites, and through them the gamut of public policies that determine marginality upstream and distribute its burdens downstream. To label a depressed cluster of public housing a *cité-ghetto* fated by its very makeup to devolve into an urban purgatory closes off alternative diagnoses and facilitates the implementation of policies of removal, dispersal, or punitive containment.

Lastly, I propose that territorial stigmatization actively contributes to *class dissolution* in the lower regions of social and physical space. The sulfurous representations that surround and suffuse declining districts of dispossession in the dual metropolis reinforce the objective fragmentation of the postindustrial proletariat stemming from the combined press of employment precarity, the shift from categorical welfare to contractual workfare, and the universalization of secondary schooling as a path to access even unskilled jobs. Spatial stigma robs residents of the ability to claim a place and fashion an idiom of their own; it saddles them with a noxious identity, imposed from the outside, which adds to their symbolic pulverization and electoral devalorization in a political field recentered around the educated middle class. So much to say that the precariat is *not* a "new dangerous class," as proposed by Guy Standing (2011), but a miscarried collective that can never come into its own precisely because it is deprived not just of the means of stable living but also of the means of producing its own representation. Lacking a shared language and social compass, riven by fissiparity, its members do not flock to support far-rightist parties so much as disperse and drop out of the voting game altogether as from other forms of civic participation.

A Bourdieusian Framework for the Comparative Sociology of Urban Inequality

Urban Outcasts sketches a historical model of the ascending regime of poverty in the city at century's turn. It forges notions—ghetto, hyperghetto, anti-ghetto, territorial stigmatization, advanced marginality, precariat—geared to developing a comparative sociology of relegation capable of eschewing the uncontrolled projection across borders of the singular experience of a single national society tacitly elevated to the rank of analytic benchmark. It does so by applying to urban questions five principles undergirding Pierre Bourdieu's approach to the construction of the sociological object (Bourdieu and Wacquant 1992). These principles are worth spotlighting by way of closing since this is a facet of the book that has been overlooked even by its more sympathetic critics.

The first principle derives directly from "historical epistemology," the philosophy of science developed by Gaston Bachelard and Georges Canguilhem, and adapted by Bourdieu for social inquiry: clearly demarcate folk from analytic notions, retrace the travails of existing concepts in order to cast your own, and engage the latter in the endless task of rational rectification through empirical confrontation (Bourdieu, Chamboredon, and Passeron 1991). Such is the impulse behind the elaboration of an institutionalist conception of the ghetto as a Janus-like contraption for ethnoracial enclosure, commenced in *Urban Outcasts* and completed in its sequel, *The Two Faces of the Ghetto*, which further differentiates the ghetto from the ethnic cluster and the derelict district; compares it with its functional analogues of the reservation, the camp, and the prison; and stresses the paradoxical profits of ghettoization as a modality of structural integration for the subordinate population (Wacquant 2015). Second comes the relational or topological mode of reasoning, deployed here to disentangle the mutual connections and conversions between symbolic space (the grid of mental categories that orient agents in their cognitive and conative construction of the world), social space (the distribution of socially effective resources or capitals), and physical space (the built environment resulting from rival efforts to appropriate material and ideal goods in and through space).

The third principle expresses Bourdieu's radically historicist and agonistic vision of action, structure, and knowledge: capture urban forms as the products, terrains, and stakes of struggles waged over multiple temporalities, ranging from the *longue durée* of secular constellations to the midlevel tempos of policy cycles to the short-term phenomenological horizon of persons at ground level. In this perspective, America's Black Belt and France's Red Belt, like districts of relegation in other societies, emerge as historical animals with a birth, maturity, and death determined by the balance of forces vying over the meshing of class, honor, and space in the city. Similarly, the hyperghetto of the U.S. metropolis and the anti-ghettos of Western Europe are not eternal entities springing from some systemic logic but time-stamped configurations whose conditions of genesis, development, and eventual decay are sustained or undermined by distinct configurations of state and citizenship. The fourth tenet recommends the use of ethnography as an instrument of rupture and theoretical construction, rather than simple means for producing an experience-near picture of ordinary cultural categories and social relations. It implies a fusion of theory and method in empirical research that overturns the conventional division of intellectual labor in urban inquiry marked by the routine divorce of microscopic observation and macroscopic conceptualization.[8]

Last but not least, we must heed the constitutive power of symbolic structures and track their double effects, on the objective webs of positions that make up institutions, on the one side, and on the incarnate systems of dispositions that compose the habitus of agents, on the other. As illustrated by territorial stigmatization, this principle is especially apposite for the analysis of the fate of deprived and disparaged populations, such as today's urban precariat, that have no control over their representation and whose very being is therefore molded by the categorization—in the literal sense of *public accusation*—of outsiders, chief among them professionals in authoritative discourse such as politicians, journalists, and social scientists. So much to say that the sociologist of marginality must punctiliously abide by the imperative of epistemic reflexivity and exert constant vigilance over the myriad operations whereby she produces her object, lest she get drawn into the classification struggles over districts of urban perdition that she has for a mission to objectivize.

These five principles propel the comparative dissection of the triadic nexus of class (trans)formation, graduations of honor, and state policy in the nether regions of metropolitan space across the Atlantic presented in this book. They can also fruitfully guide a triple extension of the sociology of urban relegation in the era of social insecurity across continents, theoretical borders, and institutions. Geographically, they can steer the adaptation of the schema of advanced marginality via sociohistorical transposition and conceptual amendment to encompass other countries of the capitalist core as well as rising nations of the Second World where disparities in the metropolis are both booming and shape shifting rapidly (Atkinson, Roberts, and Savage 2012; Murray 2011; Perlman 2010; Wu and Webster 2010). Theoretically, taking Bourdieu's distinctive concepts and propositions into city trenches offers a formidable springboard to both challenge and energize urban sociology *in globo*. It does not just add a new set of powerful and flexible notions (habitus, capital, social space, field, doxa, symbolic power) to the panoply of established perspectives: it points to the possibility of reconceptualizing the urban as the domain of accumulation, differentiation, and contestation of manifold forms of capital, which effectively makes the city a central ground and prize of historical struggles.

On the institutional front, the consolidation of a new regime of urban marginality begs for a focused analysis of the policy moves whereby governments purport to curb, contain, or reduce the very poverty that they have paradoxically spawned through economic "deregulation" (as re-regulation in favor of firms), welfare retraction and revamping, and urban retrenchment. It calls, in other words, for *linking changing forms of urban marginality with emerging modalities of state-crafting*. I do this in my book *Punishing the Poor*, which enrolls Bourdieu's concept of bureaucratic field to diagram the invention of a punitive mode of regulation of poverty knitting restrictive "workfare" and expansive "prisonfare" into a single organizational and cultural mesh flung over the problem territories and categories of the dualizing metropolis (Wacquant 2009b, 2009c, 2012). The wards of urban dereliction wherein the precarized and stigmatized fractions of the postindustrial working class concentrate turn out to be the prime targets and testing ground on which the neoliberal Leviathan is being manufactured and run in. Their study is therefore of pressing interest, not just to scholars of the metropolis, but also to theorists of state power and to citizens mobilized to advance social justice in the twenty-first century city.

NOTES

1. For a recapitulation of the biographical, analytic, and civic underpinnings of this project, see Wacquant 2009a, especially 106–10.

2. In particular, we cannot presume that the resulting social entity is a "community" (implying at minimum a shared surround and identity, horizontal social bonds, and common interests), even a community of fate, given the diversity of social trajectories that lead into and out of such areas. We also should not presuppose that income level or material deprivation is the preeminent principle of vision and division, as persons with low incomes in any society are remarkably heterogeneous (artists and the elderly, service workers and graduate students, native homeless and paperless migrants, etc.) and form at best a statistical category. For a historical recapitulation of the loaded meanings and persistent ambiguities of the notion of "community" in U.S. history, see Bender 1978.

3. The mutual contamination and common intermingling of scholarly and ordinary visions of urban life is stressed by Hall 1988 and Low 1996.

4. Collapsing these three levels conflates collective conscience with social morphology, elite discourse, and everyday action, and it mechanically leads to overestimating both the novelty and the potency of ethnicity as determinant of life chances, as does Amselle 2011.

5. For a model study breaking down ethnicity across social forms and scales, see Brubaker et al. 2008; a germane argument from an analytic angle is Wimmer 2013.

6. The built-in blindness of such research to macrostructural economic and political forces is stressed by Tom Slater 2013.

7. In April 2011 the High Council for Fighting Discrimination and for Equality (HALDE) recommended to the French government that residential location be added to the eighteen criteria on the basis of which national labor law sanctions discrimination, in recognition of the prevalence of "address discrimination."

8. The peculiar genre of research unthinkingly labeled "urban ethnography" in the English-speaking academy is blissfully atheoretical, as if one could carry out embedded observation of anything without an orienting analytic model, while grand theories of urban transformation show little concern for how structural forces imprint (or not) patterns of action and meaning in everyday life. One of the aims of *Urban Outcasts* is to bridge that chasm and to draw out the manifold empirical and conceptual benefits arising

from continual communication between field observation, institutional comparison, and macroscopic theory.

REFERENCES

Amselle, Jean Loup. 2011. *L'Ethnicisation de la France*. Fécamp: Nouvelles Éditions Lignes.

Andress, Han Jürgen, and Henning Lohmann, eds. 2008. *The Working Poor in Europe: Employment, Poverty, and Globalization*. Cheltenham: Elgar Publishing.

Atkinson, Will, Steven Roberts, and Michael Savage, eds. 2012. *Class Inequality in Austerity Britain: Power, Difference and Suffering*. Basingstoke: Palgrave Macmillan.

Banton, Michael. 2007. "Max Weber on 'Ethnic Communities': A Critique." *Nations and Nationalism* 13:1, 19–35.

Bender, Thomas. 1978. *Community and Social Change in America*. New Brunswick: Rutgers University Press.

Bourdieu, Pierre. 1990. *Language and Symbolic Power*. Cambridge: Polity Press, 1990.

Bourdieu, Pierre, Jean Claude Chamboredon, and Jean Claude Passeron. 1991. *The Craft of Sociology: Epistemological Preliminaries*. New York: Walter de Gruyter. (Orig. pub. 1968.)

Bourdieu, Pierre, and Loïc Wacquant. 1992. *An Invitation to Reflexive Sociology*. Chicago: University of Chicago Press.

Brubaker, Rogers, Margit Feischmidt, Jon Fox, and Liana Grancea, 2008. *Nationalist Politics and Everyday Ethnicity in a Transylvanian Town*. Princeton: Princeton University Press.

Cingolani, Patrick. 2011. *La Précarité*. Paris: PUF.

Clerc, Denis. 2004. *La France des travailleurs pauvres*. Paris: Grasset.

Drake, St. Clair, and Horace Cayton. 1993. *Black Metropolis: A Study of Negro Life in a Northern City*. Chicago: University of Chicago Press. (Orig. pub. 1945).

Goffman, Erving. 1964. *Stigma: Notes on the Management of Spoiled Identity*. Englewood Cliffs, N.J.: Prentice-Hall.

Hall, Peter. 1988. *Cities of Tomorrow: An Intellectual History of Urban Planning and Design in the Twentieth Century*. Oxford: Basil Blackwell.

Kalleberg, Arne. 2011. *Good Jobs, Bad Jobs: The Rise of Polarized and Precarious Employment Systems in the United States, 1970s-2000s*. New York: Russell Sage Foundation.

Liogier, Raphaël. 2012. *Le Mythe de l'islamisation. Essai sur une obsession collective*. Paris: Seuil.

Low, Setha. 1996. "The Anthropology of Cities: Imagining and Theorizing the City." *Annual Reviews in Anthropology* 25: 383–409.

Massey, Douglas, and Nancy Denton. 1993. *American Apartheid: Segregation and the Making of the Underclass*. Cambridge, Mass.: Harvard University Press.

Maurin, Louis, and Patrick Savidan. 2008. *L'État des inégalités en France 2009. Données et analyses*. Paris: Belin.

Murray, Martin J. 2011. *City of Extremes: The Spatial Politics of Johannesburg*. Durham: Duke University Press Books.

Pan Ké Shon, Jean Louis, and Loïc Wacquant. 2012. "Le grand hiatus: tableau raisonné de la ségrégation ethnique en Europe." Paper presented at the Journée INED on "La ségrégation socio-ethnique: dynamiques et conséquences," Institut national d'études démographiques, Paris.

Pattillo, Mary. 2000. *Black Picket Fences: Privilege and Peril among the Black Middle Class*. Chicago: University of Chicago Press.

Pattillo, Mary. 2007. *Black on the Block: The Politics of Race and Class in the City*. Chicago: University of Chicago Press.

Pelizzari, Alessandro. 2009. *Dynamiken der Prekarisierung: Atypische Erwerbsverhältnisse und milieuspezifische Unsicherheitsbewältigung*. Konstanz: UVK Verlag.

Perlman, Janet. 2010. *Favela: Four Decades of Living on the Edge in Rio de Janeiro*. New York: Oxford University Press.

Shiple, David. 2004. *The Working Poor: Invisible in America*. New York: Knopf, 2004.

Slater, Tom. 2013. "Your Life Chances Affect Where You Live: A Critique of the 'Cottage Industry' of Neighbourhood Effects Research." *International Journal of Urban and Regional Research* 37:2, 367–87.

Standing, Guy. 2011. *The Precariat: The New Dangerous Class*. London: Bloomsbury, 2011.

Wacquant, Loïc. 2008a. "Ghettos and Anti-Ghettos: An Anatomy of the New Urban Poverty." *Thesis Eleven* 94, 113–18.

Wacquant, Loïc. 2008b. *Urban Outcasts: A Comparative Sociology of Advanced Marginality*. Cambridge: Polity Press.

Wacquant, Loïc. 2009a. "The Body, the Ghetto and the Penal State." *Qualitative Sociology* 32:1, 101–29.

Wacquant, Loïc. 2009b. *Prisons of Poverty*. Minneapolis: University of Minnesota Press.

Wacquant, Loïc. 2009c. *Punishing the Poor: The Neoliberal Government of Social Insecurity*. Durham: Duke University Press.

Wacquant, Loïc. 2011. "A Janus-Faced Institution of Ethnoracial Closure: A Sociological Specification of the Ghetto." In *The Ghetto: Contemporary Global Issues and Controversies*, ed. Ray Hutchison and Bruce Haynes, 1–31. Boulder, Colo.: Westview Press.

Wacquant, Loïc. 2012. "Crafting the Neoliberal State: Workfare, Prisonfare and Social Insecurity." *Sociological Forum* 25:2, 197–220.

Wacquant, Loïc. 2015. *The Two Faces of the Ghetto*. New York: Oxford University Press.

Wacquant, Loïc, Tom Slater, and Virgílio Borges Pereira. 2013 "Territorial Stigmatization in Action." *Environment & Planning A* 46, 1270–80.

Wilson, William Julius. 1996. *When Work Disappears: The World of the New Urban Poor*. New York: Knopf.

Wimmer, Andreas. 2013. *Ethnic Boundary Making: Institutions, Power, Networks*. New York: Oxford University Press.

Wu, Fulong, and Christopher Webster, eds. 2010. *Marginalization in Urban China: Comparative Perspectives*. New York: Palgrave Macmillan.

REPRESENTATION

Poverty Action in Neighborhoods of Relegation

STEPHANIE ULLRICH

As a student, scholar, and activist, I have participated in poverty action in solidarity with the people of the Gulf Coast after Hurricane Katrina. During volunteer student trips to the greater New Orleans region, I have advocated for legal protections for homeowners, worked with youth on increasing their job preparedness, and have trained community members in organizing skills they can use to combat marginality and exclusion. This service work has taught me that poverty action in what are called neighborhoods of relegation—territories that have been consigned to an inferior position in society—is determined by how these neighborhoods are conceptualized and bounded. I ask: How can critical understandings of neighborhoods of relegation help shape the creative and collective imaginations of poverty actors, organizers, activists, and scholars?

Most of my service work in the city has been in the Lower Ninth Ward, one of the wards hardest hit by Hurricane Katrina. Prior to the hurricane, this was a neighborhood with one of the highest rates of African American homeownership in the United States. With fourteen thousand residents, it had five schools, parks, medical facilities and businesses. Today, nearly a decade after the storm, this community is a wasteland of alternating empty lots and demolished housing units resembling a neighborhood drowned out. Less than 20 percent of its former residents have returned, only one school is operational, and there are no grocery stores or banks. Decaying homes still display search-and-rescue crews' spray painted "X" markings, tallying death counts and destruction in the flooding and its aftermath. Is there hope for poverty action in such neighborhoods of relegation?

We must consider why this community has not been rebuilt the same way that others in New Orleans have. Vincanne Adams's work explains how the city remained in disarray even after relief efforts were dispersed, accelerating the growth industries of neoliberal capitalism (Adams 2013). To mitigate the extension of poverty in new ways after disasters, should we ask, following Teddy Cruz, how can we use our collective imagination to redesign institutions? Cruz calls our moment in time a cultural crisis, a crisis of institutions unable to re-think their own protocols. Has the Lower Ninth Ward fallen victim to the city's inability to reimagine growth after the hurricane? Alternatively, we can use Loïc Wacquant's conceptualization of neoliberal state regulation and containment to explain why growth in the Lower Ninth Ward has stagnated. Wacquant argues that poverty is managed within the realm of political control whereby neighbor-hoods of relegation become the primary targets of punitive containment, a gov-ernmental technique for managing problem territories. Indeed, the destruction of New Orleans by the hurricane and the subsequent recovery process demon-strated the relative power of a variety of actors—governmental, nonprofit, and private sector—to rearrange and contain neighborhoods. Disaster relief poured into the city through streams of donations, volunteers, temporary governmental infrastructure, and new private sector investment. The spatially unequal flow of these resources further exacerbated preexisting social, physical, and economic vulnerabilities (Adams 2013), effectively regulating and bounding space in the city based on race and class.

Practices of bounding of conceptualized and lived space are a main mecha-nism for the production of neighborhoods of relegation. The Orleans Parish is delineated into wards, a system which represents a geographical-historical map of marginalization. Even before the hurricane, the Lower Ninth Ward was con-ceptually and territorially bounded by stigma as a low-income and high-crime black neighborhood. Wacquant engages this idea of bounding when he defines two processes that occur in neighborhoods of relegation: territorial stigmatiza-tion and the symbolic dissolution of the populations living in these territories of poverty. Hurricane Katrina exacerbated these perceived and lived socioeco-nomic divisions in New Orleans; national media outlets broadcast images of people "looting" stores for food and goods, maintaining the negative portrayal of low-income residents as unrestrained and depraved. What mainstream media outlets haven't highlighted is that the most dramatic and extensive hurricane damage was in the poorest, most stigmatized areas of the city and the recovery process in these areas has been the slowest.

The city's levee system is an extension of the physical and social boundaries of the city; it delineates privilege and supports systems of inequality. Ground at higher sea levels of the city has natural levees often in the form of parks and public spaces, while ground at lower sea levels like the Lower Ninth Ward has vertical cement-wall levees. On August 29, 2005, the levees that lined the Indus-trial Canal of the Lower Ninth Ward could no longer hold the storm surge and floodwater began to pour over the concrete, toppling the walls designed to keep the water out and submerging the entire Lower Ninth Ward. Around the city, the water destroyed homes and infrastructure, leaving over twelve hundred dead in its wake (Smith 2006). Three years later, the Army Corps of Engineers rebuilt the levees in the Lower Ninth Ward to their original form—fourteen-foot gray concrete walls—carefully consigning this neighborhood back to the fringes of the city, and either keeping the water out, or keeping the people in.

In sites of relegation, poverty management occupies many spaces, from short-term evangelical Christian missions in Sub-Saharan African villages (Han, this volume) to postdisaster rehousing projects in New Orleans. After the hurricane, rehousing support varied by neighborhood, and Federal Emergency Management Agency (FEMA) disaster housing trailers became semipermanent dwellings. Vincanne Adams notes that since the storm, the number of housing units has decreased in the parishes most damaged by floods—parishes that are generally lower income—and increased in outlying parishes (Adams, this volume). Government rehousing efforts also came through federal funds in the Road Home program, which offered people cash grants to rebuild or sell their severely damaged houses. Yet black homeowners in the Lower Ninth Ward struggled through years of bureaucratic poverty-management and discriminatory distribution of funds under this scheme. It is an injustice to call Hurricane Katrina evidence of a vengeful Mother Nature; instead, the storm highlighted the vengeful power of institutionalized exclusion and the swift redistribution of housing resources, capacity, and ownership (Smith 2006).

A tension between Wacquant's and Cruz's analyses is whether marginal neighborhoods are sites for production of the neoliberal state or sites of cultural production and innovation for urban development. In the case of New Orleans, do these neighborhoods demonstrate the power of the punitive state or the cultural production of resistance among the most marginalized? Perhaps the two conceptualizations are not so separate, and instead these neighborhoods of relegation are produced through ever-changing dual processes of external intervention and internal poverty action. To examine how these neighborhoods in New Orleans are sites of both control and of cultural production, we must ask *where* is the city being rebuilt and *which* poverty actors are rebuilding the city and for *whom*. These are inherently political inquiries that problematize poverty and expose regimes of power, social regulation, and government action or inaction. In the Lower Ninth Ward this action/inaction dichotomy manifests spatially in how the government cares for itself (i.e., the full restoration of Jackson Barracks—headquarters of the Louisiana National Guard—within three years of the storm), versus how it cares (or doesn't care) for its citizens, demonstrated through vacant public land and condemned housing that still remains in the Lower Ninth Ward nine years after the hurricane.

However, collective imagination for poverty action in neighborhoods of relegation combats marginality and exclusion. New forms of innovation and inclusive urbanization are constantly emerging. One example is the Lower Ninth Ward Village nongovernmental organization colloquially termed "the Village" in the neighborhood, which transformed a dilapidated airplane hangar–like warehouse into a community center to build self-sustaining capacity for the ward's residents after the hurricane. The Village has reclaimed this public space for healing, recovery, and resilience. It facilitates job training for local youth, hosts town hall meetings and debates, supports entrepreneurial initiatives in sustainable food systems in the ward, and has housed volunteers (like me and fifty thousand others from institutions nationally). Founded and run by Lower Ninth Ward resident Ward "Mack" McClendon and his team, this organization is co-creating a vision for rebuilding the Lower Ninth Ward with new rationalities of poverty alleviation. Poverty action from within neighborhoods of relegation redistributes power, illuminating the importance of harnessing innovation and problematizing poverty management.

Reflecting on containment, practices of bounding, and poverty action in neighborhoods of relegation shifts territories of poverty and relinks civic engagement to social justice. The Lower Ninth Ward in New Orleans has been managed as a problem area, yet it is still harvesting citizen innovation, rearticulating and dismantling the boundaries around the neighborhood. Expanding conceptualizations of neighborhoods of relegation like this one moves us beyond analysis of structural containment in marginalized territories to one that captures the collective imaginations of new generations, sustaining equitable processes of poverty action and deterritorializing poverty. Many voices like mine and those of my fellow activists and poverty scholars can move toward a new reality, where urban centers and postdisaster zones are spaces for home-grown and proactive—versus reactionary—innovation for poverty solutions.

REFERENCES

Adams, Vincanne. 2013. *Markets of Sorrow, Labors of Faith*. Durham: Duke University Press.
Smith, Neil. 2006. "There's No Such Thing as a Natural Disaster." Understanding Katrina: Perspectives from the Social Sciences. New York: Social Science Research Council. http://understandingkatrina.ssrc.org/Smith/.

From Poor Peripheries to Sectarian
Frontiers: Planning, Development,
and the Spatial Production of
Sectarianism in Beirut

HIBA BOU AKAR

"An urban planner is like a fashion designer," Mr. I, one of the main urban planners involved in the planning and zoning of Sahra Choueifat,[1] a formal yet poor
periphery southeast of Beirut, told me:

> I now design a master plan like a fashion designer designs a dress—you see, there
> is no difference, not at all. In fashion: you ask me for a dress, I design it and tailor it
> for you. After you take it home, you can take off the ribbon, remove the ruffles, and
> shorten the sleeves. It is none of my business anymore. Same for urban planners
> like me in Lebanon: I do my job and give "them" a master plan. If after that, they
> want to remove a road, add floors, transform a zone, destroy the entire conceptual
> design, it is none of my business.[2]

While I was still processing the political implications of the parallels between
designing a dress and producing a zoning plan for Beirut's marginalized peripheries, I met with another well-established urban planner, Mr. H., who was also
involved in planning a number of Beirut's southern peripheries. In response to
my question on how he approaches zoning plans and building regulations, he
said:

> Urban planning should be like jewelry design; as a planner you need to combine
> art and science in order to produce finely calibrated master plans.
>
> You are a planner, right? Can you believe how they are changing the street
> alignments? Take the example of Sahra Choueifat: Have you ever seen a street
> in the U.S. where the buildings are not aligned? This is unacceptable planning![3]

Large-scale planning and construction projects have come to define the "formal"
planning scene of postwar Beirut. The highest profile of these is Beirut's Central
District, which has been undergoing reconstruction by the real estate company

Solidere (Sawalha 1998). Elyssar and Linord, two unrealized grand planning projects for Beirut's southern and northern coastal suburbs respectively, have also been discussed at length (Rowe and Sarkis 1998; Harb 2001). More recently, Project Waad, Hezbollah's large-scale effort to reconstruct Beirut's southern suburbs (which were largely destroyed during Israel's July 2006 war on Lebanon) has been the subject of several studies (Ghandour and Fawaz 2008; Harb 2008; Fawaz 2009; Al-Harithy 2010). In addition, scholars have foregrounded the relevance of Beirut's informal settlements to understand the production of space in the city (Hamadeh 1987; Charafeddine 1991; Harb 2001; Fawaz 2004; Clerc 2008). Of these, Fawaz's (2004) study of Hayy el-Selloum (an informal settlement just north of Sahra Choueifat) provides key insights about the entanglement of formal practices in the production of informality in Beirut. However, unlike Beirut's Central District or its informal peripheries, which have been the subject of numerous urban studies, the periphery in question, Sahra Choueifat, is a marginal, understudied, and overlooked area. Inhabited by mostly poor (many were previously displaced by war) families, it suddenly found itself in May 2008 to be on a deadly frontier of a renewed sectarian conflict that gripped Beirut.[4]

Before I explain Mr. I's and Mr. H's outlooks toward planning the peripheries that they laid out in their interviews with me, I will first discuss the spatial production of peripheral Sahra Choueifat as a frontier. Second, I will examine the theoretical and political implications of peripheries as frontiers. In the third section, I will introduce how the spatial and temporal logics of what I call the war yet to come regulate Beirut's peripheries, shaping their poverty and urban growth, and violence and marginality. I will then focus on the role of urban planning in the production of these geographies. Finally, I will address the shift from development to planning in the approach toward governing Beirut's peripheries, discuss the role of experts like Mr. I and Mr. H in this shift, and consider its political implications on everyday life in Beirut's peripheries-as-frontiers.

This essay is based on an ethnography and archival investigation of spatial practices. I sought to understand the multitude of practices, policies, and discourses that produced Sahra Choueifat as a contest frontier in 2008. I conducted archival and ethnographic work over two time periods: before the May 2008 events (2004–5), and after (2009–10). These timeframes were critical to understanding how the transformation of a periphery into a frontier changed and became rearticulated over time.[5] Examining the transformation of a peripheral area from a "territory of poverty" into a polarized and contested frontier is a complex exercise in a deeply divided city like Beirut, where one is always categorized as "with" or "against" this or that group. The research necessitated crossing emergent dividing lines again and again — both physical ones produced by the May 2008 battles and consequent social, political, and psychological ones.

In addition, despite lengthy engagement with my research sites (more than ten years), I had to continuously negotiate my access to information over time as new political alliances between religious-political organizations emerged and others dissolved.

My interlocutors in Choueifat and Sahra Choueifat included residents, municipal officials, developers, planners, landowners, real estate brokers, officials from the religious-political organizations, journalists, intellectuals, and former militiamen. Since practices of zoning and urban planning in Sahra Choueifat take place on multiple bureaucratic levels, from the municipality to the national level, I conducted observations and interviews with planners and heads of planning units in different public agencies and private companies. My historical research on political events, planning, development, contestation, and wars draws on newspaper and media archives, the American University of Beirut libraries' archives, and records, maps, and reports stored in public administration offices (municipalities, ministries, councils, etc.).[6] Together, these different research methods resulted in a situated understanding of the changing geography of Sahra Choueifat as produced and contested over time, through master plans, territorial struggles, and everyday discourses of fear, tolerance, coexistence, and conflict.

Sahra Choueifat: A Periphery as a Frontier

Sahra Choueifat is in the vicinity of the Beirut International Airport, located between areas ascribed to different religious-sectarian groups. One would only pass through the area if one works or lives there. Despite the fact that middle-income people inhabit Sahra Choueifat alongside poorer families, Sahra Choueifat is often described as a zone of poverty. This popular view of Sahra Choueifat is in part shaped by the presence of Hayy el-Selloum, one of Beirut's largest informal settlements, next door.[7]

During the civil war (1975–90), the area remained agricultural, heavily guarded by its Druze landowners against Shiite expansion from the neighboring Al-Dahiya, Hezbollah's stronghold in the southern suburbs of Beirut.[8] At that time, Hayy el-Selloum was already a dense informal settlement, part of Al-Dahiya, and a stronghold for Shiite militias that were fighting at times against the Druze militia.[9] By the end of the war, seeing it as an "empty land," Hezbollah and its affiliated developers worked through the land and housing markets to provide housing in this area especially for the poor war-displaced populations that had been squatting in Beirut for more than fifteen years, and who were mostly Hezbollah supporters. In 1993 large-scale low-income housing complexes started mushrooming in the area.[10] During Israel's 2006 war on Lebanon, seen as part of Al-Dahiya, Sahra Choueifat was bombed, which inserted it as a node in the regional Arab–Israeli conflict. On the local level, while the low-income Shiite residents saw it as a new affordable and formal residential area on the fringes of the city, the Druze residents saw its transformation into a "Shiite neighborhood" as an invasion of their "territory."

This contestation turned deadly during the civil strife events of May 2008. The now Shiite Sahra Choueifat and its neighboring Druze Choueifat witnessed the most severe battles fought between two main religious-political organizations, the Shiite Hezbollah and the Druze Progressive Socialist Party (PSP). Dozens were killed. Since then, a parade of Lebanese Army tanks reinforces the newly formed frontier lines. These dividing lines have been further reinforced through contested planning exercises over different imagined futures of development and war.

The PSP and Hezbollah have different purposes and histories of militarization and social service. There is a vast difference in their size and scales of operation. Hezbollah is a much more complex and powerful entity. Yet, in a country where the balance of power between sectarian groups cannot be jeopardized, both entities continue to play significant political roles. The PSP was established as a secular political party in 1949 and was responsible for a Druze militia during the civil war. Despite its disarmament at the end of the war, the PSP has remained an influential political actor in Lebanon. Hezbollah emerged in 1982 primarily to resist the Israeli occupation of southern Lebanon. Hezbollah continues to hold a large armory and operate one of the region's largest service-provision networks. It is also a major regional actor and power broker. Depending on one's perspective, Hezbollah can be considered a nongovernmental organization, a Lebanese political party, a resistance movement, or an armed organization central to the "War on Terror." Such categories, however, selectively emphasize or blur Hezbollah's various activities in the areas of politics, military organization, resistance to occupation, and service provision—all of which characterize its diverse activities.

The local and institutional power dynamics between the two actors in Sahra Choueifat are quite complex, but for the sake of this essay, it is sufficient to say that for the most part, Hezbollah and its allies are in control of the housing and real estate markets, and the PSP had, up until the last municipal elections in June 2010, control over the municipality. Also, due to the complex voting laws in Lebanon, the municipal board does not have a Shiite representative.

I will discuss in greater detail this shift in Sahra Choueifat's geography in times of peace from a periphery to a frontier, but before I do that I will briefly discuss the logics of these two spatial categories, peripheries and frontiers, vis-à-vis issues of marginality, poverty, violence, and hope. I will then consider the political implications of the overlapping geographies of these two seemingly mutually exclusive categories.

Peripheries as Frontiers

Peripheral areas like Sahra Choueifat found themselves in 2008 to be the frontiers of the new round of sectarian conflict that rocked Beirut. Before then, in 2006, Sahra Choueifat, marked as part of Al-Dahiya, was targeted in the Israeli war on Lebanon. Until then, the area had been seen as marginal, associated with agricultural supply, the informality of Hayy el-Selloum, rural migrant workers, and industries (PepsiCo is one).[11] Nowadays, the area is seen as a frontier of urban growth, violence, fear, and environmental degradation. However, what this study shows is that the contestation over the development of Sahra Choueifat had been unfolding for decades before then: through paramilitary interventions during the civil war, and through real estate and housing markets as well as urban planning and zoning policies since the end of the war. Marginal yet contested, Sahra Choueifat is shaped simultaneously by the spatial logics of peripheries and frontiers. It is the juxtaposition of these two logics that has so far shaped the possibilities for housing for Beirut's poor and middle-income families in Sahra Choueifat. The area has provided the opportunity for low-cost formal housing on the outskirts of Beirut. At the same time, this association has also defined a politics of closure, segregation, borderlines, and a "tactics of anticipation" for possible violent futures (Pradeep 1998).

Peripheries and frontiers have played a significant role in the understanding of uneven geographies. As operational categories of spatial understanding and theorization, their different uses point to different sets of socioeconomic, geographic, and political processes. The temporalities of their becoming are also distinct. As a result, theoretically, the two categories remain mutually exclusive. Yet, the case of Sahra Choueifat points to the fact that the spatial and temporal logics of peripheries and frontiers can overlap in contested geographies. How then can we understand the socioeconomic, spatial, and political logics that govern such territories?

Peripheries are usually spaces of marginalization, neglect, economic disadvantage, and an incomplete urban citizenship that is yet to come. The periphery has been a powerful concept whether in discussions of peripheries in the global South or in general as an aspect of urban theory (Tsing 1993; Yiftachel 2000; Caldeira 2000; Roy 2009; Watson, 2009; Miraftab 2009). Commonly, peripheries constitute the urban outskirts (Simone 2010). As such, they have been key to discussions of urban informality (Roy and AlSayyad 2004; Holston 2009). They may also be sites for the relocation of "unwanted" populations standing in the way of a city's "development" (Ghannam 2002). Peripheries are constituted by specific sets of social, economic, and political conditions that usually contribute to the exclusion of peripheries but can also lead to the destabilization of the center (Dikec 2007; Simone 2010). Because of their exclusion, peripheries can often be imbued with hope, a "volatility that is permitted to go nowhere and a completion always yet to come" (Simone 2007: 464). In the peripheries, Holston (2009: 245) shows the move to stake claims to urban citizenship. He has written that "struggles . . . for the basic resources of daily life and shelter have also generated new movements of insurgent citizenship based on their claims to have a right to the city and a right to rights."

Frontiers, on the other hand, are spaces of exploration and excitement, encroachment and conquest, danger and violence. They are another powerful concept in anthropological and urban research. They are quite often discussed as dystopic spaces where regimes of power and capital are in the process of reconfiguring space in their own image. Frontiers are often thought of as spaces of capital accumulation and/or racial or ethnic domination. Smith (1996) examined how inner city neighborhoods in American cities became urban frontiers where poor people are driven from their neighborhoods by forces of gentrification. In Israel, frontier settlements have allowed the expansion of control by a dominant group into adjacent areas, assisting "both in the construction of national-Jewish identity, and in capturing physical space on which this identity could be territorially constructed" (Yiftachel 2006: 108). The elasticity of such a frontier, according to Weizman (2007: 173), allows it to "continually remold itself to absorb and accommodate opposition," diverting the debate around its existence to issues of inclusion and exclusion. Frontiers also shape the geographies of the "War on Terror," where distance has been mapped into difference. Gregory (2004) shows how, by transforming borders into frontiers, spaces in Baghdad or Kabul are constructed as "imaginative geographies," whose destruction is necessary for the safety of "the West." Frontiers are also spaces of uncertainty. In Gupta and Ferguson's (1992: 18) account, borderlands as frontiers are a "place of incommensurable contradictions" and "an interstitial zone of displacement and deterritorialization that shapes the identity of the hybridized subject." Frontiers could also be "liminal zones of struggle, between different groups for power and influence—each seeking to expand their influence by shaping these zones on their own terms. In this view, the frontier is a fuzzy geographic space where outcomes are uncertain" (Leitner, Peck, and Sheppard 2007: 311). Within such framings, frontiers are dystopic spaces of capital and resource accumulation, war and violence, often characterized by class, racial, religious, or ethnic domination battles over contested futures.

Within this dichotomy of peripheries as left-out, hopeful spaces and frontiers as emerging, dystopic spaces, how can we then understand the transformation of marginal peripheries into violent frontiers, or more accurately the overlapping geographies of peripheries and frontiers that shape areas like Sahra Choueifat?

What are the spatial logics that govern these territories of poverty as simultaneously marginal and neglected yet on the forefront of local sectarian and regional geopolitical wars? And what is the significance of such overlapping logics?

Not many studies have interrogated the theoretical implications of the overlap of these seemingly distant logics of spatial categorization. In his essay "On Cityness," Simone (2010: 39) states that "the periphery is many things." According to Simone (2010: 40), "the periphery can exist as a frontier in that it has a border with another city, nation, rural area, or periphery." As an area of overlap, the periphery is thus a hybrid space "where different ways of doing things, of thinking about and living urban life, can come together" (Simone 2010: 40–41). It is a space "that absorbs tensions inherent in the intersection of substantially different ways of doing things" (Simone 2010: 41). In this approach, the periphery-as-frontier is a hopeful space imbued with possibilities of improving one's life.

In this essay, on the other hand, I argue that geography and politics of peripheries as frontiers in contested cities like Beirut are shaped simultaneously by feverish urban growth and abject neglect, profit and poverty, violence and indifference. These processes are configured through an anticipated future of conflict, informed by pasts and presents of wars and violence. In Beirut, where the specters of war always lurk, I call these the governing logics of the war yet to come.[12]

For the War Yet to Come: Governing the Peripheries

My analytic of the war yet to come does not treat war and peace as distinct categories. It approaches war not as a temporal aberration in the flow of events, with a beginning and an end. Rather the war yet to come focuses on how wars and their anticipation have become governing modalities of Beirut's peripheries, regulating their urban growth and poverty, marginality and violence. It is hence a regulating logic that articulates political, spatial, and economic orders within a temporal framework through which spaces of poverty, marginality, otherness, and violence are configured and contested over and over again.

The war yet to come does not produce poor localities per se. Instead, as the case of Sahra Choueifat shows, its spatial and temporal logics produce patchworks of lavishness and poverty, sectarian violence and development growth, mixed neighborhoods and segregated ones. The borderlines of these geographies are continuously shifting, momentarily solidifying through violence, only to be contested and reconfigured again. The war yet to come further regulates these territories through its foreclosure of urban politics and the possibility of action for social change outside the sectarian political order.

In the war yet to come, there is no state monopoly over sovereignty, war, and their geographies. Critical to these geographies are nontraditional actors, like religious-political organizations, that challenge established state-market, private-public, and government-insurgency binaries. These actors play a significant role in the exercise of ordering the present through their expected role in the futures of violence and local and regional wars yet to come. At a time in which such actors are increasingly engaged in the production of cities, it is important to investigate their role in producing urban space and the ensuing dynamics of urban politics, its ruptures and possibilities, contestations and transgression. This is particularly true with regard to cities divided along religious and ethnic lines, where the spatiality of constructed differences may affect decisions of inclusion and exclusion, peace and war.

The case of Sahra Choueifat shows that these geographies of the war yet to come are shaped by the articulation of at least four main processes: urbanization, neoliberalization, paramilitarization, and the reproduction of a spatial order of sectarian difference. I will briefly discuss the ways in which these four interrelated processes have shaped Beirut's peripheries as frontiers.

A congested and expensive city, Beirut has been experiencing a massive urbanization toward its peripheries to accommodate the city's expansion and provide housing for those who after the end of the war could not afford to live in the city anymore for many reasons, including gentrification, squatting, war displacement, and changes in the rent-control law. As bulldozers ploughed through the hills and the fields surrounding Beirut, some of these mushrooming peripheries developed without much contestation. However, the peripheries that have become contested frontiers are those that have been witnessing an influx of populations of a different sectarian group than the one that had inhabited the area at the end of the war. Sahra Choueifat is one.

The widely debated neoliberal policies that postwar Lebanon governments adopted played a critical role in this urbanization. The end of the war in Lebanon coincided with the shift in the global political and economic orders toward neoliberalism, structural adjustment, privatization of welfare, and so forth, and also with the dissolution of the Soviet Union and the demise of the communist project. The postwar Lebanese government followed that global economic and political neoliberalization rationale by promoting privatization policies especially in the approach toward the reconstruction of Beirut and in dealing with the problem of the war-displaced populations. In that vein, socioeconomic development was left to the de facto rulers on the ground, former civil war militias that had transformed into powerful religious-political organizations that constitute the Lebanese government. Space constraints do not allow for a full discussion about this here. However, two key issues are important to highlight:

one, the Lebanese government's policies toward the poor and those displaced by war left many to the market to sort our their housing needs (Bou Akar 2005). For example, the postwar Lebanese government opted to evict war-displaced families who were squatting in abandoned houses during the war, by providing them with small monetary compensation packages to move elsewhere. The government did not supplement these cash handouts with any meaningful housing policies that could help these families find affordable housing in the city. In fact, the aim of the cash compensation packages was to move families who had lived in Beirut for more than twenty years back to their villages in south and east Lebanon. However, to many of these families, Beirut was home. It is where they had established their livelihoods. Returning to their villages of origin was not a real option. They had to find housing in the city or its outskirts. Through such policies of indifference, the government relegated the livelihood needs of these families to the market. Certainly, the task proved most challenging for the poorer families. Second, the role that the religious-political organizations have played in operating the housing and real estate markets as well as shaping the urban planning practices and infrastructure provision have had critical spatial implications on shaping Beirut's peripheries as frontiers. These actors, which were part of the process of overseeing the compensation enumeration and partaking in the distribution of the packages, provided channels that many lower income families came to rely on when looking for affordable housing, as the case of Sahra Choueifat illustrates. Many scholars have argued that such a rollback of the Lebanese state as part of its neoliberal policies allowed for religious-political organizations to take over that space left vacant by the government (Fawaz 2009). In Lebanon, most of these actors were former civil war militias who have become the major political constituents of the Lebanese government since the end of the civil war. In Sahra Choueifat, the two main actors are Hezbollah and the PSP. Common discussions around such actors, especially Hezbollah, describe them as operating "a state within a state." However, such descriptions tend to gloss over the fact that these actors also constitute the state. This study instead takes seriously how since the 1990s these religious-political organizations form and operate as part of the Lebanese state while also operating outside it. These organizations are not discrete entities but are constellations of public and private actors, who for example implemented the compensation policy and oversaw it at the same time (and received a cut in both capacities). Individuals within these networks may range from street-level bureaucrats, to heads of municipalities, ministers and parliamentarians, draftsmen in planning agencies, housing developers, real estate brokers, religious charity workers, micro-loan officers, and workers in an asphalt company. As I show elsewhere (Bou Akar 2012a), their geographic interventions cannot be easily categorized; they are shaped by the continuities and discontinuities of these actors' spatial and neoliberal practices with practices of religious affiliation, sectarian constructions, service provision, resistance ideologies, and militarization.

In addition, these actors together form the Lebanese army and maintain the state's sovereignty. Yet, individually, they operate their own paramilitary groups that continuously challenge the state's sovereignty in varying degrees as they operate within the overlapping geographies of Lebanese sectarian wars, the Arab-Israeli conflict, transnational geographies of Islamic "resistance[s]," and those of the global "War on Terror."[13]

As they anticipate engaging with different contestations or wars on local and regional levels, the religious-political organizations' paramilitary strategies shape the mundane geographies of Beirut's contested peripheries, turning them into sectarian frontiers through the twin logic of militarization and profitable real estate and housing transactions. In weaving their militarization logics into the built environment, these actors use the vast knowledge acquired during their involvement in the civil war's battles that mostly unfolded in residential areas and on street corners. They are also informed by the more recent rounds of violence that accompanied major political events in the country, including the assassination of Prime Minister Rafik Hariri and the withdrawal of the Syrian armed forces in 2005, the July 2006 Israeli war on Lebanon, and the May 2008 sectarian violence, to name a few. Previously ad hoc, during times of peace these military spatial logics are now intrinsic and built-in in the everyday geographies of the wars yet to come.

The practice of urban planning is at the nexus of the four aforementioned processes: urbanization, neoliberalism, paramilitarization, and the sociospatial production of sectarian difference. Planning tools, practices, and outcomes have become the primary terrain of contestation in Beirut's times of peace. Plans and their implementation are continuously being drawn and redrawn, contested and reconciled, with severe implications on the everyday lived spaces of the city. The discussion on the zoning of Sahra Choueifat in the following section illustrates how the practice of urban planning in Beirut involves innovative techniques to continuously balance a spatiality of political difference in order to keep a war at bay while simultaneously allowing for urban growth and development profit.

These geographies of the war yet to come render the possibility of social change outside the sectarian political order unimaginable or unattainable. Through its policies and practices, the Lebanese government (an assembly of religious-political organizations) has led people, especially vulnerable populations, to depend on these same religious-political organizations to access affordable housing, infrastructure, security, jobs, and so forth—not solely through charity but most importantly through their "channeled markets" (Bou

Akar 2012a). As inhabitants of these peripheries-as-frontiers become reliant on religious-political organizations for a decent living and a sense of security, it becomes increasingly difficult for residents to challenge the sectarian sociopolitical order perpetuated by these actors. This order is further reinforced through sporadic rounds of fighting, discourses of fear, and circulation of rumors about the religious Other living across the road. These practices shape the geographies of the war yet to come, which in turn further reinforce this sociopolitical order of sectarian difference. As violence continues to rage on local and regional levels under the banner of sectarianism, these borderlines are further solidified making it increasingly difficult for people to challenge the governing modalities of the wars yet to come—that keep their neighborhoods mired in poverty, without infrastructure, and environmentally unsafe—outside the political order of sectarian difference.

The Planned Geographies of the War Yet to Come: The Urbanization of Sahra Choueifat

A brief discussion of the contestations over the urban development of Sahra Choueifat will illustrate the role of planning in producing and reproducing the geographies of the war yet to come.

As mentioned earlier, while Sahra Choueifat's urban development has been taking place through the land and housing markets, the contestations over its expansion are taking place mostly through zoning, planning, and building law battles. For example, since 1996 the zoning ordinance for Sahra Choueifat has been modified at least eight times back and forth between residential and industrial zones. While Hezbollah has been pushing to zone the area as residential, the PSP municipality wants it to be an industrial one. In the last iteration of the master plan in 2008, the PSP municipality celebrated its triumph of being able to pass a new zoning law that will decrease the height and density of future buildings in the now residential Sahra Choueifat. It also enforced the use of expensive stone cladding instead of the tin sheets and the cheap concrete blocks that were previously allowed, and it limited buildings to two apartments per floor. These regulations aimed at increasing the price per square meter, and thus, the same size apartment could cost up to twice as much, curbing the expansion of Sahra Choueifat by significantly decreasing affordability of its housing. It hence aimed to eliminate future possibilities of housing more low-income families in the area. They were also able to zone Choueifat's hilltops as villa areas—that is, upscale single-family houses—which means one would need large piece of land to build a small house with expensive finishing materials as per the zoning code. And the portion of the highway that goes through Sahra Choueifat, what residents were hoping would one day bring them closer to the city and its jobs, had yet to be completed.

In urban planning terms, this all sounds normal: density, height, and proposed infrastructure aim, among other things, to redistribute resources, facilitate industrial production, and protect ecologies. However, in Sahra Choueifat these practices are also the tools that the religious-political organizations are using to order the present in anticipation of future wars. Here, "industrial zone" is a synonym for Druze territory, and "residential zone" is a synonym for Shiite territory, as one planner put it. Hezbollah has been pushing to zone the area as residential to help in housing more of its low-income supporters. By designating it as industrial, PSP is trying to avoid a further urbanization of the area, which would mean "more poor 'Shiite'—and hence more Hezbollah ideologically committed supporters—in the area," as one municipal employee told me.

However, zoning designations are not easy to change in Lebanon. In order to do so, a proposed master plan must be endorsed by the Directorate General of Urbanism and studied by the prime minister's advisory board on planning and development and the Council of Ministers. If approved, the legal change is then issued as a government decree signed by the president of the Lebanese Republic, the prime minster of the Lebanese government, and the concerned ministers, which always includes the Minister of Public Works and Transportation. The decree is published in the official gazette and becomes immediately binding. Considering this cumbersome process, the high stakes in the contest over Sahra Choueifat is reflected in the fact that the different religious-political organizations have managed to make large-scale legal changes to its zoning eight times in twelve years, resulting in a patchwork of competing residential, industrial, and agricultural developments.

Paramilitary urban strategies are also key to understanding these peripheral geographies. As explained earlier, both Hezbollah and PSP function as paramilitaries. What emerged during my fieldwork is how the creation of weapon tunnels, the domination of hilltops, and the ability to distribute militias in space is key to their geographies. Therefore, attempting to turn the hilltops into a "beautiful villa area" is an attempt by the PSP to ensure that Hezbollah could not afford to create a low-income dense settlement from which the PSP areas could be attacked in the event of future wars.

Between the industrial and the residential, this low-income periphery is now a patchwork of apartment buildings, in the vicinity of industries, next to one of the most active urban agricultural areas around Beirut. Every winter the area witnesses an environmental disaster when waste water mixed with rain water— carrying with it industrial waste and soil—fills up the streets, causing new phases of displacement among the small segment of families who can leave, and leaving behind those who cannot afford to go—basically leading to displacement along class lines.

The governing logic of war yet to come, hence, is in many ways the antithesis of Simone's city yet come. For Simone (2004: 9) the "city is the conjunction of seemingly endless possibilities of remaking," where precarious structures, provisional locations, potholed roads "even in their supposedly depleted conditions, all are openings onto somewhere." However, the case of Sahra Choueifat briefly discussed above shows that in cities in conflict, like Beirut, the mundane geographies of peripheries-as-frontiers may be both hopeful and dystopic. Low-income war-displaced families have been able to secure low-cost housing in Sahra Choueifat, as they were priced out from skyrocketing housing prices of Beirut. This has allowed many of them to keep their jobs in the city and commute to peripheral areas like Sahra Choueifat. Nonetheless, the new spaces are also zones of conflict and contestation where fears of future local and regional wars shape everyday life. These are geographies that provide the possibility for some sort of "right to the city" (Mitchell 2003). But they are also spaces where the futures of violent engagements and displacements are drawn and redrawn every day. With this logic, Beirut's southern peripheries-turned-frontiers are simultaneously centers and nodes in the transnational geographies and circulations of the Arab-Israeli conflict, the militarization of Islamic organizations, and also those of the global "War on Terror."

As concurrent frontiers of both—urban growth and sectarian conflict—these peripheries also emphasize how, in the geographies of the war yet to come, the practice of urban planning with its tools, processes, and outcomes have become the primary terrain of contestation.

From Development to Planning: Rethinking Beirut's Territories of Poverty

What I would like to highlight here is that the war yet to come as a spatial logic that shapes Beirut peripheries at this moment signals a shift in the experts' approach toward the peripheries as territories of poverty.

Since the establishment of the Lebanese nation-state in 1943 and throughout the civil war, the expert discourses on the built environment focused on how the uneven development of the peripheries, due to their poverty, informality, unruliness, had become the primary source of instability, witnessing recurrent labor unions' uprisings. In the 1950s and 1960s, Lebanon was not far from the global sweep of communist sentiments that manifested themselves in class struggles, student uprisings, and civil rights movements around the world. Poor areas were assumed to be the breeding grounds for the foot soldiers that championed these revolutionary sentiments, which were threatening to disrupt the world's hegemonic capitalist and religious orders. These revolutionary manifestations were causing anxiety among global powers, especially the United States, Western European countries, and the Catholic Church. In Lebanon this anxiety was sharpened by the rise in support for secularist Pan-Arabism, which reached its peak when Syria and Egypt united (1958–61) under the charismatic leadership of Gamal Abdel Nasser, who assumed the presidency of Egypt in 1956.[14] Pan-Arabism positioned the region as a socialist field with an Arab identity. The poorer segments of the Arab populations saw in Pan-Arabism their hope for a better future.

Poverty alleviation and economic development were seen as ways to stop communist aspirations from taking hold in the alleyways of the informal and poor peripheries of cities in developing countries. As a result, the poor and their spaces globally became an obsession of international aid and development institutions. Hence, in cities around the globe, slums were cleared and experimentations with public housing were underway, followed by widespread "sites and services" projects that aimed to facilitate access for the poor to formal and hygienic housing within a clear spatial order.

The push toward spatializing development was crystallized by the shift in the apparatus of international development. This apparatus became more salient in 1960 when the United Nations started playing a crucial role in "building international consensus on action for development" (see the UN website at http://www .un.org/en/development/other/overview.shtml). Beginning in 1960, the General Assembly helped set priorities and goals through a series of ten-year International Development Strategies. "Development is not growth, Development is growth plus change," the United Nations (1962) declared in its 1962 conference in Beirut, as part of its global initiative at the time to include social development alongside economic development, and that social change was seen as possible through "change in the built environment." Putting these ideas together, the United Nations was promoting at the time development through change in the built environment, which one could argue may have crystallized the spatial turn in development studies.

It was at that time that Beirut became the convention hub in the Middle East for experts and relevant institutions to discuss development and poverty alleviation.[15] In 1968, for example, representatives of the Catholic Church, joined by United Nations personnel, convened in Beirut to discuss world development.[16] The conveners discussed development strategies that aimed to alleviate poverty and eradicate disparities among nations and within each nation (Munby, Vatican Commission on Peace and Freedom, and World Council of Churches 1969). Several documents on planning and development from that time, especially documents developed by the Catholic Church, mentioned the slum clearance of

Qarantina, an informal settlement and a refugee camp on the north entrance to Beirut (Verdeil 2008).[17] The slum clearance and eradication approach to informal settlements continued in conversations on development and planning in the 1960s. In 1964 Michel Ecochard delivered his now famous master plan for Beirut and its suburbs.[18] Ecochard's plan articulated the problematic of the periphery as target of spatial planning. His planning scheme was basically aimed at ordering the peripheries by facilitating their gradual urbanization, proposing low land-exploitation factors and low building heights. Many aspects of that scheme remained ink on paper. Having been issued as a government decree, however, the Ecochard master plan still haunts the everyday spaces of the peripheries, including those of Sahra Choueifat. Almost fifty years later, many land plots are still held hostage to Ecochard's planning schemes that are never to come.[19]

The spatiality of the sectarian problematic and how it intersected with these proposed development and planning schemes were silenced. Despite the fact that the sectarian problem was being discussed in several forums, in discussions of the built environment it was masked by the concept of the "unruly" periphery. Modernization and the formation of the modern state provided the larger umbrella of the debates, discussions, and plans of action that focused on poverty and class difference rather than on other axes of difference like sectarianism.

What is interesting to note is that even after the civil war took shape in its known format—that is along sectarian lines in 1975—the experts of the built environment in Lebanon continued with the same diagnosis of the urban problematic. The economic crisis of uneven development between the peripheries and the hinterland was assumed to be the underlying cause of the war (that turned sectarian) (Traboulsi 2007).[20] Even in 1983, eight years after the onset of civil war, one can quote Samir Khalaf (1983: 18), the most prominent Lebanese urban sociologist, saying in a workshop on reconstructing Beirut that "virtually all the urban problems of Beirut stem from one fundamental source: unguided, uncontrolled, and unplanned urban growth."

To recap, these trouble areas were hence located as "targets of development" to stem causes of instability, especially at the height of a global moment of anxiety around the rise in communist and pan-Arab socialist aspirations. Consequently, they became sites of urban planning interventions with proposals aimed at poverty alleviation, housing provision, industrial jobs, and tenure security. For the most part, these plans remained blueprints.

Through this brief engagement with the planning aspirations that were prevalent in 1950s and 1960s, this essay argues that the logic of the war yet to come indicates a major shift in this previous governing logic toward the peripheries and its populations. As the case of Sahra Choueifat illustrates: the planning of the war yet to come is the result of layers upon layers of contested planning exercises over different imagined futures. That's why Sahra Choueifat's 1996 master plan that was meant to be the blueprint for its development for the next thirty years was changed at least eight times in twelve years. And the promised highway is never to come. Its ghost lanes not only haunt Sahra Choueifat's everyday spaces, but also the dreams of residents who are still hopeful that that highway would bring the city to them.

Therefore, rather than understanding Beirut's peripheries as an unmapped and unplanned geography (Roy 2002; Elyachar 2005), or in terms of possibilities yet to come (Simone 2004; Holston 2009), the geographies of Beirut's peripheries-as-frontiers are in fact "intricately planned" according to imagined present and futures of simultaneous urban growth and conflict on the local, regional, and transnational levels.

The Technicians of the War Yet to Come

It is within this context that one ought to locate Mr. I's and Mr. H's descriptions of their approaches to planning, whether designing fashion or jewelry, in a contested periphery like Sahra Choueifat. They are symptomatic of the spatial logics of the war yet to come and the role that planners take within it: as technicians of this regulating spatial logic. However, Mr. I and Mr. H are not anomalies among their planning peers. They are in fact two of the more respected planning experts in the city.

During my more than twenty interviews with planners working in Beirut about their approaches to planning, most of the discussions were focused on the logic of traffic and vehicular arteries, how a "proper" city should look, and of course lots of talk about Solidere, Elyssar, Linord, and Hezbollah's reconstruction project Waad. Only a handful of my interviewees were interested in discussing, for example, the newly approved National Physical Master Plan. I learned a lot about urban-planning practices during these interviews that I am grateful for. For the most part, my interviewees were respected urbanists with many years of experience in Lebanon.

Nonetheless, what was striking to me during these conversations was that only a handful of my interviewees mentioned poverty alleviation, informality, precarious living conditions, lack of jobs, middle-class inability to access housing in the city, or unequal distribution of resources between the city and its peripheries, even when asked about areas like Sahra Choueifat. Discussions that involved talking about equal or unequal distribution were related to the government's unequal investment in physical planning projects across regions. Many argued that investment in public planning projects has been happening along sectarian lines, benefiting areas that are inhabited by certain political-religious organizations while ignoring other areas.[21] Even in public forums (media, workshops, etc.), the talk about socioeconomic development was barely present.[22]

However, when I interrogated these planning discourses further, a different picture emerged about the practice of urban planning in Beirut. A number of planners, especially Mr. I and Mr. H, provided a more nuanced genealogy of their planning practices that have shaped their positions and approaches to planning in Lebanon. Mr. I, a planner in a private company who was affiliated with planning Sahra Choueifat for more than a decade, described to me the threats, abuses, and humiliations that he had to endure during the process. After a while, I realized that Mr. I is in fact a planning idealist who has found himself in an unfortunate situation, apparently common in the Lebanese planning practice. A graduate of a prestigious university in North America, he believes in the power of planning to "beautify, develop, and improve" living conditions. However, he painfully recounted the many times when politically backed landowners, militiamen, and land developers intercepted his arrival to his office, threatened his planning team in the field, and banged on his drawing table, all for the purposes of demanding he makes changes to his zoning and planning proposals of Sahra Choueifat. In the end, Mr. I was "instructed" to just draw the lines as he was "told" to do so by the religious-political organizations' representatives or their affiliates. During one of our discussions, Mr. I pulled out a pile of papers from a dusty corner. These papers showed his initial planning scheme for Sahra Choueifat. His vision included a cutting-edge industrial zone, a low-income residential neighborhood that supplies the labor for the industries, and a green buffer and recreational zone between the two areas. What ended up on his drawing board and on the ground are overlapping zones of industrial and residential areas with the dangerous environmental and political repercussions briefly aforementioned.

Mr. I's engagement with planning Sahra Choueifat provides the context of his current approach to planning of these peripheries as "fashion design," and that any changes by the "clients"—in this case the clients are in reality the warring religious-political organizations—to his planning project are "none of his business." Mr. I has been transformed into a technician of the regulating logic of the war yet to come. He told me that he still practices his planning ideals, however, in picturesque mountain villages away from Beirut's contested frontiers.

Mr. H encountered similarly aggressive experiences when he attempted to put forward alternative planning visions. Mr. H has vast knowledge and outstanding expertise in the field of planning. We had a great conversation, for example, on social justice and the ideal city. But when I asked him about Beirut's peripheries, his discussion scaled down to focus on the failure of street alignments in areas like Sahra Choueifat, areas that had just witnessed a small-scale civil war.

Post-poverty Beirut?

Based on these interviews with urban planners in the city, I concluded that it seems that postwar Beirut has witnessed a complete shift in approaches to planning: from planning as a tool of social and economic development to planning as an end in itself. Planning has been emptied of its development discourse, a discourse that was resilient even during the most difficult years of war.

This shift in the approach to planning from the quests and questions of social and economic development centered on issues of poverty and illegality, to an exercise in spatializing sectarian difference changed the discourse around Beirut's southern peripheries from that of "informal and poor peripheries" to "Shiite neighborhoods," the new frontiers of sectarian conflict. This reformulation of the political consciousness vis-à-vis the periphery, its economy, marginality, and inhabitants has had major repercussions on poverty, segregation, violence, and environmental degradation, as illustrated by the case of Sahra Choueifat. It is important to point out here, however, that Shiites inhabited the southern peripheries long before the onset of the civil war. However, as discussed earlier, in the 1950s and 1960s it was rare that any of the academic volumes published on planning and development in Beirut discussed the peripheries in sectarian terms. Rather, the discussion embodied a modernization approach to social and human development that was common back then. Certainly, these modernization discourses were not devoid of an underlying discriminatory logic against a certain sect, but that prejudice was targeted more against the "backward" rural to urban migrants and less against "the Shiites."

My interviews with planners made me realize that planning and development in Beirut may be actually post-poverty, by which I mean that poverty seems to have receded as a prominent lens through which to understand, organize, and act upon space. For the most part, poverty has been rendered invisible as a public national discourse. Instead, territories of poverty have been delineated, zoned, labeled, and reinscribed as a sectarian issue left for the religious-political organizations to address. Planning as an exercise in attaining—or at least aiming to attain—socioeconomic equality along with spatial justice seems to be rarely discussed.[23] As a result, the importance of the peripheries as targets of national development has receded, taken over by conversations about the unequal sectarianized distribution of planning monies across areas affiliated with different religious-political organizations.

There are several local, regional, and global reasons for this shift in the governing logic toward peripheries as territories of poverty. One cannot ignore the spatiality of the civil war that resulted in expanded sectarian-homogenous neighborhoods. After the end of the war, many such homogenized areas came under the de facto rule of the corresponding former militias turned religious-political organizations. In this mapping, Beirut's southern peripheries, for example, came to be seen as zones inhabited by Shiites and serviced by Hezbollah and Haraket Amal, the two main Shiite religious-political organizations. Within this logic, the socioeconomic conditions of the "Shiite" peripheries are no longer relevant to the larger debate of development and planning—as Mr. I said: it is "none of [the planner's] business." This not only applies to Beirut's southern peripheries, but to all the other areas that are seen to be under the control of religious-political organizations.[24] Under these conditions, the questions of who is in need of development, what, where, and when are all under the discretion of the religious-political organizations that are in control of the areas, and are no longer up for debate in the expert circles, as illustrated by the withdrawal of Mr. I and Mr. H from making any claims about resource redistribution or spatial justice.

The current shift in focus from the spatiality of poverty to the spatiality of political and sectarian difference in Beirut has coincided with a global shift in the debate in discourses around planning, "community," "identity," and development. The global debate has moved from being about development, modernization, and the role of the welfare state in providing resources and distributive justice to a discussion on neoliberalization and postmodernism that has prevailed since the 1980s. Within the neoliberal and postmodern paradigm, the global production of architecture and planning knowledge shifted from designing for "large-scale, metropolitan-wide, technologically rational and efficient urban plans" to "a conception of the urban fabric as necessarily fragmented" (Harvey 1989: 66). The focus is now more on the well-being of self-defined "communities" that make their own "choices" about their lifestyles, leaving many of the disadvantaged and marginalized populations neglected in slums and squatter settlements. This has replaced to a certain extent the earlier obsession with overarching national, regional, and even urban social distributive schemes. This shift has major repercussions on access, marginalization, segregation, and urban citizenship that not only define the geography of Beirut as a city in conflict but urbanization across cities in the global North and global South.

In Beirut one can further argue that this shift in the logic of governing the peripheries has flipped the prewar "formula" on development and planning: the practice of planning has replaced the question of development as the overarching framework through which to approach the organization of territories. Planning nowadays delineates zones and territories that delegate socioeconomic development—within their boundaries—to religious-political organizations.

Conclusion

Beirut's geographies of the wars yet to come have transformed the city's southern and southeastern peripheries into contested frontiers characterized by feverish urban growth and violent sectarian conflict. These geographies do not produce territories of poverty per se. As a governing modality, the war yet to come instead yields patchworks of planned spaces that can provide affordable housing for low-income families but also have overlapping industrial and residential zones, towns where highways are never finished and playgrounds are never built. It is a governing logic that produces simultaneously poverty and lavishness, violence and marginality, profit and neglect.

The case of Sahra Choueifat illustrates the significant role of the practice of urban planning in shaping these contested geographies. Gutted of ideas and goals of development, urban planning in Beirut has become confined to the task of delineating zones. Within this spatial logic, religious-political organizations have used planning, infrastructure provision, real estate, and housing markets to configure Beirut's peripheries in their own interests through housing developments and service provision as well as through militarization, violence, and segregation formulated within their expected roles in the local and regional wars that are yet to come.

The spatial and temporal logics of the war yet to come has so far foreclosed the possibilities of urban politics outside the sectarian political order perpetuated by the religious-political organizations. The impossibility of proposing a different future has rendered many a planner as mere technicians of the spatial logic of the wars yet to come. Also, the governing logic of the war yet to come has rendered questions of poverty alleviation, spatial justice, resource distribution, and job creation mostly irrelevant, raising questions about whether Beirut is post-poverty as a discourse through which to understand spatial injustices and act upon them.

Yet, these geographies are constantly being negotiated, reconfigured, and reproduced, redefining in turn what poverty, peripheries, marginality, as well as "sectarianism" come to mean at each historical moment. It is within these unstable, continuously shifting spatial logics that one can locate hope in what are otherwise dystopic geographies of the war yet to come.

NOTES

1. Parts of this essay were published in Bou Akar 2012a.
2. Interview January 30, 2010.
3. Interview April 2010.

4. On May 5, 2008, an amputated Lebanese government (after Hezbollah and its allies had resigned) announced that it had "discovered" a private, parallel telecommunication network operated by Hezbollah. It deemed the network illegal and announced that it would be removed. Hezbollah's leader, Hassan Nasrallah, called the government's decision a "declaration of war" against Hezbollah's resistance to Israeli occupation. He claimed that the network was key to Hezbollah's success in its resistance effort, and it was therefore Hezbollah's "moral duty" to use its arms to defend the network to keep Lebanon protected from Israel's incursions. As a result, on May 7, 2008, Hezbollah and allied paramilitary groups took over Beirut's streets in a show of force, cordoning off the airport, the house of government, and the homes of major political leaders. Within a few hours, Hezbollah announced that they were in full control of the city. Over the next five days the fighting moved to Beirut's peripheries and adjacent mountain villages, where the battles were mostly fought between Hezbollah and the Druze PSP. The battles that took place in Sahra Choueifat and Choueifat were significant in the unfolding of these violent events, which came to be commonly known as the "May 7 events."

5. I conducted the first phase of this research in 2004–5 for my master's thesis on issues of war displacement and access to housing in postwar Beirut (Bou Akar 2005). After the May 2008 violence, Sahra Choueifat was one of three sites where I examined the spatial production of Beirut's peripheries as frontiers within the planned geographies of possible future local and regional conflicts (Bou Akar 2012b).

6. There are few official archives in Lebanon. Also, a national census has not been conducted since 1932. To compensate for that, in 1997 the Ministry of Social Affairs and the United Nations Development Programme published a study on mapping the living conditions in Lebanon.

7. Technically, the area now known as Hayy es-Selloum was also part of Sahra Choueifat.

8. The Druze are a minority religious group in the Middle East. They live mainly in Lebanon, Syria, and Palestine/Israel.

9. The relationship between the two Shiite militias (Haraket Amal and Hezbollah) and the Druze militia (the PSP), changed many times during the civil war as local and regional geopolitics alliances and fault lines shifted. These actors were allies at times, and enemies that fought notorious wars at many other times.

10. For a more in-depth discussion on these spatial processes, see Bou Akar 2012a.

11. For a more in-depth analysis, see Mona Fawaz's (2004, 2008) work on Hayy es-Selloum.

12. For further discussion, see Bou Akar 2012b.

13. After the end of the Lebanese civil war, militias' weapons were confiscated for the most part. The only entity that was able to keep its weapons was Hezbollah. Hezbollah had established itself as the primary armed resistance movement against the Israeli occupation, and its existence was deemed necessary at a time in which Israel was occupying South Lebanon. In 2000 Israel withdrew from the south. However, Israel kept a few villages occupied and has since frequently violated Lebanese airspace, which provided justification for Hezbollah to continue its resistance. Hezbollah argues that its resistance

tactics necessitate the ability to make military decisions without informing the Lebanese government and its army. Hezbollah's ability to decide matters of war and peace has been heavily debated in the country, especially since the 2006 Israeli war on Lebanon, which followed a Hezbollah military operation against the Israeli army along Lebanon's southern border.

14. The short-lived sovereign union between Egypt and Syria (1958–61) resulted in the United Arab Republic.

15. The fact that Lebanon was the only country in the Middle East with a Christian head of state positioned it as plausible destination.

16. The Church intervened in the debate on development in an effort to cool the boiling communist sentiments that were on the rise especially among the disadvantaged populations in developing countries. In 1966 Vatican II, in cooperation with the World Council of Churches, established the Committee on Society, Development, and Peace, which in turn organized the World Cooperation for Development conference in Beirut. The aim of the conference was to advise the churches on "economic and technical aspects of certain issues of grave interest to them and to the entire human family" (Mundy, Vatican Commission on Peace and Freedom, and World Council of Churches 1969, ix). At the time, the economic problem was central to the church's anxieties.

17. For a discussion on the slum clearance of Qarantina, see Verdeil 2008.

18. Although the plan came to be commonly known as the Ecochard Plan, what was ultimately approved was modified from Ecochard's proposal. He ended up distancing himself from it.

19. This is due to the eminent domain law that still holds many plots in this area hostage to the Ecochard plan. Previously, there was no time frame for action. As a result, plots that were affected by the Ecochard plan in 1964 remain frozen in time. The new eminent domain law that was revised in 2006 (law 58, revised on December 8, 2006) limits to three years the time between when the government orders land acquisition for public use and the date it starts executing the acquisition process. The new law also limits the period of time between land acquisition and the date of starting the project to ten years. After ten years, if the government does not start the project, the landowners can request to reacquire the plots. The new law might change this reality, but thus far, the law remains contested.

20. This is also related to the historians who have been writing from this historical point of view—basically leftist and socialist scholars—for whom uneven development has always been a central issue.

21. Many interviewees also mentioned the environment and issues of sustainability. These conversations might have been influenced by the current global moment where a significant amount of foreign aid money to developing countries like Lebanon is channeled toward NGOs or projects that deal with environmental concerns.

22. In the process of forming Lebanese governments, religious-political organizations always fight over what they call "service portfolios." This is not a fight over different visions of development but over ministries that are allocated large funds in the government budget or ones that could move large sums of money (such as the Ministry of Finance,

Energy and Water, Telecom, Public Works, etc.) that can be invested in certain areas to lure in voters (in contrast to the Ministry of Social Affairs, for example, which does not have such funding). The Ministry of Public Works is the umbrella entity for most of the planning work in Lebanon (besides the Council for Development and Reconstruction) and is considered a key service portfolio.

23. This shift in focus could be also be felt in the knowledge that is currently being produced about urbanism in Beirut (including this study). Besides a handful of urban scholars who still discuss poverty and informality in Beirut (such as Fawaz and Clerc), research on urban planning's approach to poverty, the poor, and their "informal" spaces in Lebanon seems to have taken a back seat dominated by debates that are more focused on secterianism, infratsructure, luxiourious developments, and so forth.

24. For example, the development and planning of Shouf is decided for the most part by the PSP, the development of Doha Aramoun is decided by the Sunni Future Movement, and the development of Jounieh is decided by the relevant Christian religious-political organizations.

REFERENCES

Al-Harithy, Howayda, ed. 2010. *Lessons in Post-war Reconstruction: Case Studies from Lebanon in the Aftermath of the 2006 War*. New York: Routledge.

Bou Akar, Hiba. 2005. "Displacement, Politics, and Governance: Access to Low-Income Housing in a Beirut Suburb." Master in City Planning thesis, MIT.

Bou Akar, Hiba. 2012a. "Contesting Beirut's Frontiers." *City and Society* 24:2, 150–72.

Bou Akar, Hiba. 2012b. "Planning Beirut: For the War Yet to Come." PhD diss., University of California, Berkeley.

Caldeira, Teresa P. R. 2000. *City of Walls: Crime, Segregation and Citizenship in Sao Paulo*. Berkeley: University of California Press.

Charafeddine, Wafa. 1991. "L'Habitat illégal dans la Banlieue Sud." PhD diss., Université de Paris VIII.

Clerc, Valerie. 2008. *Les Quartiers Irréguliers de Beyrouth: Une Histoire des Enjeux Fonciers et Urbanistiques de la Banlieue Sud*. Beirut: IFPO.

Dikec, Mustafa. 2007. *Badlands of the Republic: Space, Politics and Urban Policy*. Malden, Mass.: Wiley-Blackwell.

Elyachar, Julia. 2005. *Markets of Dispossession: NGOs, Economic Development, and the State in Cairo*. Durham: Duke University Press.

Fawaz, Mona. 2004. "Strategizing for Housing: An Investigation of the Production and Regulation of Low-Income Housing in the Suburbs of Beirut. PhD diss., MIT.

Fawaz, Mona. 2008. "An Unusual Clique of City-Makers: Social Networks in the Production of a Neighborhood in Beirut (1950–75)." *International Journal of Urban and Regional Research* 32:3, 565–85.

Fawaz, Mona. 2009. "Hezbollah as Urban Planner? Questions to and from Planning Theory." *Planning Theory* 8:4, 323.

Ghandour, Marwan, and Mona Fawaz. 2008. "The Politics of Space in Postwar Reconstruction Projects: Waʿd and SOLIDERE." Middle East Center Conference: Negotiation of Space: The Politics of Destruction and Reconstruction in Lebanon, St. Antony's College, University of Oxford, June 13–14, 2008.

Ghannam, Farha. 2002. *Remaking the Modern: Space, Relocation, and the Politics of Identity in a Global Cairo.* Berkeley: University of California Press.

Gregory, Derek. 2004. *The Colonial Present: Afghanistan, Palestine, Iraq.* Oxford: Blackwell.

Gupta, Akhil, and James Ferguson. 1992. "Space, Identity, and the Politics of Difference." *Cultural Anthropology* 7:1, 6–23.

Hamadeh, Shirine. 1987. "A Housing Proposal against All Odds: The Case of Squatter Settlements in Beirut. M. Arch. thesis ,Rice University

Harb, Mona. 2001. "Urban Governance in Post-War Beirut: Resources, Negotiations, and Contestations in the Elyssar Project." In *Capital Cities: Ethnographies of Urban Governance in the Middle East*, ed. S. K. Shami 111–33. Toronto: Toronto University Press.

Harb, Mona. 2008. "Faith-Based Organizations as Effective Development Partners? Hezbollah and Post-War Reconstruction in Lebanon." In *Development, Civil Society and Faith-Based Organizations: Bridging the Sacred and the Secular*, ed. G. Clarke and M. Jennings, 214–39. New York: Palgrave Macmillan.

Harvey, David. 1989. *The Condition of Postmodernity: An Enquiry into the Origins of Cultural Change.* Oxford: Blackwell.

Holston, James. 2009. "Insurgent Citizenship in an Era of Global Urban Peripheries." *City and Society* 21:2, 245–67.

Khalaf, Samir. 1983. "Some Sociological Reflections on the Urban Reconstruction of Beirut." In *Beirut of Tomorrow*, ed. F. Ragette, 18–24. Beirut: American University of Beirut.

Leitner, Helga, Jamie Peck, and Eric Sheppard, eds. 2007. *Contesting Neoliberalism: Urban Frontiers.* New York: Guilford Press.

Miraftab, Faranak. 2009. "Insurgent Planning: Situating Radical Planning in the Global South." *Planning Theory* 8, 32–50.

Mitchell, Don. 2003. *The Right to the City: Social Justice and the Fight for Public Space.* New York: Guilford Press.

Munby, Denys Lawrence, Vatican Commission on Peace and Freedom, and World Council of Churches. 1969. *World Development: Challenge to the Churches; The Official Report and the Papers.* Washington, D.C.: Corpus Books.

Pradeep, Jeganathan. 1998. "'In the Shadow of Violence': Tamilness and the Anthropology of Violence in Southern Sri Lanka." In *Buddhist Fundamentalism and Minority Identity in Sri Lanka*, ed. T. J. Bartholomuesz and C. R. d. Silva, 89–109. Albany: State University of New York Press.

Rowe, Peter, and Hashim Sarkis, eds. 1998. *Projecting Beirut: Episodes in the Construction and Reconstruction of a Modern City.* Munich: Prestel.

Roy, Ananya. 2003. *City Requiem, Calcutta: Gender and the Politics of Poverty.* Minneapolis: University of Minnesota Press.

Roy, Ananya. 2009. "Strangely Familiar: Planning and the Worlds of Insurgence and Informality." *Planning Theory* 8, 7–11.

Roy, Ananya, and Nezar AlSayyad, eds. 2004. *Urban Informality: Transnational Perspectives from the Middle East, Latin America, and South Asia*. Lanham, Md.: Lexington Books.

Sawalha, Aseel. 1998. "The Reconstruction of Beirut: Local Responses to Globalization." *City and Society* 10:1, 133–47.

Simone, AbdouMaliq. 2004. *For the City Yet to Come: Changing African Life in Four Cities*. Durham: Duke University Press.

Simone, AbdouMaliq. 2007. "At the Frontier of the Urban Periphery." In *Sarai Reader 07: Frontiers*, ed. Monica Narula, Shuddhabrata Sengupta, Jeebesh Bagchi and Ravi Sundaram, 462–70. Delhi: Centre for the Study of Developing Societies, 2007.

Simone, AbdouMaliq. 2010. *City Life from Jakarta to Dakar: Movements at the Crossroads*. New York: Routledge.

Smith, Neil. 1996. *The New Urban Frontier: Gentrification and the Revanchist City*. New York: Routledge.

Tabet, Jad. 1993. "From Colonial Style to Regional Revivalism: Modern Architecture in Lebanon and the Cultural Problem of Identity." In *Recovering Beirut: Urban Design and Post-war Reconstruction*, ed. S. Khalaf and P. S. Khoury, 83–105. Leiden: Brill.

Traboulsi, Fawwaz. 2007. *A History of Modern Lebanon*. London: Pluto.

Tsing, Anna Lowenhaupt. 1993. *In the Realm of the Diamond Queen: Marginality in an Out-Of-The-Way Place*. Princeton: Princeton University Press

United Nations. 1962. *Report: Conference on the Social Aspects of Development Planning in the Arab States. Organized by the United Nations in Co-Operation with the Government of Lebanon in 1961*. New York: United Nations.

Verdeil, Eric. 2008. "State Development Policy and Specialised Engineers: The Case of Urban Planners in Post-War Lebanon." *Knowledge Work Society* 5:1, 29–51.

Watson, Vanessa. 2009. "Seeing from the South: Refocusing Urban Planning on the Globe's Central Urban Issues." *Urban Studies* 46:11, 2259–75.

Weizman, Eyal. 2007. *Hollow Land: Israel's Architecture of Occupation*. New York: Verso.

Yiftachel, Oren. 2000. "Social Control, Urban Planning and Ethno Class Relations: Mizrahi Jews in Israel's 'Development Towns.'" *International Journal of Urban and Regional Research* 24:2, 418–38.

Yiftachel, Oren. 2006. *Ethnocracy: Land and Identity Politics in Israel/Palestine*. Philadelphia: University of Pennsylvania Press.

Gray Areas: The War on Poverty
at Home and Abroad

ANANYA ROY, STUART SCHRADER, AND EMMA SHAW CRANE

> Poverty abroad leads to unrest, to internal upheaval, to violence, and to
> the escalation of extremism. . . . It does the same within our own borders.
> —ROBERT S. MCNAMARA, August 23, 1966, Speech to the Veterans of
>   Foreign Wars

In 1961 John K. Galbraith, then U.S. Ambassador to India, published an essay in *Foreign Affairs* titled "A Positive Approach to Economic Aid." In it, he argued, "clearly, economic development can occur only in a context of law and order, where persons and property are reasonably secure." The statement is important on its own terms, but it is also significant because it appears as an epigraph on a 1961 summary of the Public Safety Program of the U.S. Agency for International Development (AID). The text begins: "In this simple statement Ambassador Galbraith has concisely identified a truism which is so fundamental, it is frequently overlooked or neglected. At the same time he has indicated the basic rationale and purpose of the AID Public Safety Program." In pencil at the top of the page, written by a high-ranking reviewer, it says "Summary wonderful" (No Author 1961). The Public Safety Program's template originated in occupied Japan; under President John F. Kennedy, it became the Office of Public Safety, as part of the newly organized AID, where it lasted until 1974. It extended training, logistical, and technical assistance to police and paramilitary forces in approximately forty countries across the global South for the prevention of subversion and revolution. It was, in essence, the key U.S. civilian organizer of counterinsurgency on a global scale.

This fragment from the archives of American government speaks to the central proposition of this essay: the yoking of economic development and security in the context of the turbulent 1960s. The mandate of security was of course not new to the mission of foreign aid and development. Under President Harry Truman's (1949) Point Four vision, American development interventions were described as "weaving a world fabric of international security and growing prosperity." But beginning in the early 1960s, this geopolitical concept had given way to a quite different territorialization of security, one fundamentally concerned with the fate of cities and ultimately with a territorial unit that was to be the locus of programs of government: the community.

In this essay we study the emergence of poverty as both a domestic and an international public policy issue in the 1960s. We are interested in how the theme of poverty came to be closely linked to widespread anxieties about racialized violence in American cities and wars of insurgency in the global South. In particular, we examine one program: Gray Areas, an ambitious Ford Foundation experiment of neighborhood intervention that was implemented in six metropolitan regions across the United States. Imagined as a comprehensive solution to juvenile delinquency and social disorder in urban neighborhoods of migration and racial transition, Gray Areas is a program of government, specifically designed to govern territories of poverty. We refer here to Rose and Miller's (2010: 279) analysis of government as a "problematizing activity," such that programs of government are elaborated around "difficulties and failures." Programs of government, which consist of the exercise of political power beyond the state, as Rose and Miller (2010: 280) note, "provide a kind of *intellectual machinery* for government." They render "the world thinkable." In this sense, Gray Areas must also be understood as a theory of poverty, of poverty's ongoing problematization for intervention, and thus as the precursor to the War on Poverty and the invention of community of development as a field of practice. As a theory of poverty, Gray Areas conjoined programs of government and "poor people's movements." We borrow the latter term from Piven and Cloward's (1977) classic text to indicate the social mobilizations that also shaped this historical conjuncture. From Alinsky's community organizing to the rise of the Black Panther Party (BPP), Gray Areas and programs like it were shaped by the possibilities of radical action, as they also shaped, in turn, the horizons and imaginations of radical movements.

This essay also intervenes in the methodologies of poverty studies and its geographic jurisdictions. We place the Gray Areas program in a global context to reveal important interconnections between the wars on poverty at home and abroad. As Goldstein (2012: 3) argues, "Cold War doctrines of international development and modernization—with their abiding faith in the transformative power of economic growth and political democratization, as well as their anxieties about anticolonial insurrections and socialist revolutions—were intimately and increasingly associated with U.S. policy on domestic poverty during the thirty years following the Second World War." Specifically, we demonstrate how American experiments with domestic pacification were related to American counterinsurgency efforts abroad, as they shared a focus on juvenile delinquency as an intractable impediment to broader community uplift, which could not be alleviated with strictly coercive means. Gray Areas was one such experiment, and it was a progenitor of Great Society programming. But it also found echoes in programs like Robert McNamara's Great Society program Project 100,000, aimed at young black men, many of whom would be sent to the battlefields of Vietnam. This program, like the ethos of "defensive modernization" later elaborated by McNamara at the World Bank (Ayres 1983), rearticulated foreign and domestic spheres, as well as security and development—with community at the vertex of these articulations.

These global interconnections are of profound importance because they reveal the fundamental contradictions of American liberalism, especially its encounters with racial difference, and its efforts to overcome the historical racial subjugation against which its conceptions of freedom and equality emerged. As O'Connor (2007: 2) notes on this project of liberalism, what was at stake was to "reconcile its incomplete commitments to racial justice and economic security with the global crusade against communism." Project 100,000 amplifies these struggles. Launched by McNamara under the auspices of the Department of Defense, this Great Society program was meant to resolve problems of racial disadvantage by inducting young black men otherwise rejected from the military draft. Thus, Daniel Patrick Moynihan (1966: 22), its key intellectual influence, described the program as the effort "to use the armed forces as a socializing experience for the poor—particularly the Southern poor—until somehow their environment begins turning out equal citizens." If Martin Luther King Jr. had argued that the Great Society had been "shot down on the battlefields of Vietnam" (Carter 2009: 163), then Project 100,000 demonstrates how the two wars were co-constitutive. Indeed, the global imagination of political struggle in the 1960s was crucially about finding a vocabulary to characterize such entanglements and a mode of political action adequate to the problem: "Saigon and Harlem" thus came to be seen as "two fronts of the same war" (Phillips 2012: 218).

It is instructive to hold Gray Areas and Project 100,000 simultaneously in view. Together they suggest that such poverty programs must be understood not to emphasize strategies of discipline but instead to hone an apparatus of security. In his lectures on "Security, Territory, Population," Foucault (2007: 20) argues that "whereas discipline structures a space . . . security will try to plan a milieu." For Foucault (2007: 65) the shift from "the safety of the Prince and his territory" to "the security of the population" is a shift from "fixing and demarcating the territory" to "allowing circulations to take place." As Elden (2006: 2) argues, "while discipline operates through the enclosure and circumscription of space, security requires the opening up and release of spaces, to enable circulation and passage." Above all, for Foucault (2007: 48), an "apparatus of security" pivots on the idea of freedom, a freedom that comprises "no longer the exemptions and privileges attached to a person, but the possibility of movement, change of place, and processes of circulation of both people and things." It is in this sense that the poverty programs of the 1960s, from Gray Areas to Project 100,000, must be seen not as strategies of containment and ghettoization but rather as projects of global liberalism concerned with the milieu of the times.

The term "milieu" is of course a recurring theme in Foucauldian thought. Osborne and Rose (1999: 740) present the modern city as a "milieu of liberal government"; the city is a "laboratory of conduct." Rabinow (1989: 77) defines modern urbanism as "a normative project for the ordering of the social milieu." But Rabinow is also attentive to the colonial practices implicated in the ordering of the social milieu. He notes how, in the late 19th century, the interlocutors of a science of milieu were also the interlocutors of a science of pacification in the French colonies, including Vietnam. Milieu was that which could be altered and improved by human beings; it was also "no longer a preordained place, but simply the 'between' of two places, mi-lieu, a relational system without metaphysical grounding" (Rabinow 1989: 128). But it was at sites of colonial experimentation, such as Tonkin, that these concepts were put into place. "The truest sign of pacification," Rabinow (1989: 149) notes, was "the peaceful animation of roads and markets." Several decades later, during the Vietnam War, the U.S. Department of Defense came to define pacification thus:

> Pacification is the military, political, economic, and social process of establishing or reestablishing local government responsive to and involving the participation of the people. It includes the provision of sustained, credible territorial security, the destruction of the enemy's underground government, the assertion or re-assertion of political control and involvement of the people in government, and the initiation of economic and social activity capable of self-sustenance and expansion. The economic element of pacification includes the opening of roads and waterways, and the maintenance of lines of communication important to economic and military activity. (United States Military Assistance Command, Vietnam 1968)

Put simply, it is not possible to understand Gray Areas or Project 100,000 without acknowledging the histories of colonialism that shaped the possibilities of their present.

"A Threat Which May Overshadow Vietnam"

In 1966, as cities across America were convulsed in what came to be known as "ghetto revolts" (Feagin and Hahn 1973; Sugrue 2008), the President's Task Force on the Cities (1966: vii), chaired by Paul N. Ylvisaker, met to discuss the "spectre of civil discontent and potential guerilla warfare . . . spreading over the land." In his letter to President Johnson accompanying the Task Force report, Ylvisaker argued that the urban crisis posed a "possible threat to our security which may too soon overshadow Vietnam." The diagnosis presented by this 1966 Task Force on Cities was unambiguous: that the "overriding problem" of American cities was "segregation by race and income"; to overcome such "apartheid," the report called for "integration" (President's Task Force on the Cities 1966: i, 4). The specific recommendations, which were directed at both the "majority who are relatively content with their urban lot" and "restive and outspoken minorities," were oriented toward education, manpower development, and community action. In addition, there was a recommendation to increase federal funding for law enforcement. "The Federal share of this cost," the Task Force estimated, "would be about $1.7 billion per year, or $30 per city resident (including poor and non-poor)." The Task Force (1966: 23) noted, "current expenditures in this area are effectively zero." The Office of Law Enforcement Assistance, a precursor to the Law Enforcement Assistance Administration that the 1968 Omnibus Crime Control and Safe Streets Act inaugurated, issued federal grants to state and municipal law-enforcement agencies totaling $20 million between 1966 and 1969. The successor organization spent $63 million in its first year of existence alone and in 1973 reached the annual expenditure level recommended by the Task Force.

But the concerns and recommendations of the 1966 Task Force on the Cities were not without precedent. By the time this task force convened, interventions in the urban crisis were already well underway. The Community Action Program, established by the Economic Opportunity Act of 1964, had instituted the Community Action Agency. Organized around the principle of "maximum feasible participation" of poor people, these agencies were meant to be vehicles for community organizing and social mobilization. The most significant precursor to such programs, and more generally to the field of ideas and practices that is community development, however, was the Gray Areas project of the Ford Foundation (see also O'Connor 1996). Conceptualized and led by Ylvisaker, the Gray Areas program was implemented through a series of community action grants to five cities—Oakland, Boston, Philadelphia, New Haven, and Washington, D.C.—as well as to the state of North Carolina. Lasting through the 1960s, the bulk of Gray Areas activities and funding disbursements took place between 1961 and 1967. By 1965 the Ford Foundation had committed $26.5 million to Gray Areas (Halpern 1995: 89). This program, what Marris and Rein (1967: 28), termed "experimental community action," was designed to preempt many of the urban problems that the 1966 Task Force set about to confront.

Gray Areas marks the confluence of several lines of interest and debate. Of these, five must be highlighted. First, in sharp contrast to the 1966 Task Force, which had explicitly pinpointed "segregation by race and income" as the "overriding problem of American cities," Gray Areas, as a theory of poverty, was haunted by what Halpern (1995: 90) has described as a "prohibition against dealing directly with race." Instead, the somewhat ambiguous concept of a "gray area" took the place of more explicit race talk, though the chromatic references were not difficult to parse:

> The most familiar pattern of the "Gray Areas" on the American scene is the decay noticed first in the near-downtown sections, centered usually around the railroad station or other main hubs of the old transportation systems, and spreading ring-like toward the boundaries of the central city and suburban fringe. Slums, skid-rows, etc. form a dark inner ring; from there out, the "gray" grows lighter but moves more swiftly as obsolescence of housing and industrial plant accelerates. (The Gray Areas 1963: 1)

Reminiscent of the Chicago School's conceptualization of the city as composed of concentric zones (Park and Burgess 1925), this Ford Foundation description is strangely devoid of people and human activity. However, as O'Connor (1996: 605) notes, a Gray Area was meant to be not only an urban zone between central business district and suburb but also a space of social transition, one in which the middle class was leaving and poor migrants were moving in rapidly. In Ylvisaker's urban imagination these migrants included "Negroes from the rural South; mountain folk from the Ozarks and Appalachians; Puerto Ricans from their island villages" (O'Connor 1996: 606). Gray Areas were to be the sites of racial and cultural assimilation. Thus, the 1964 President's Task Force on Metropolitan and Urban Problems (1964: 16) defined the task as: "to inject a new environment in the old gray areas, an environment in excess of some critical minimum mass, so as to the change the attitude of middle-income groups toward the area." In other words, Gray Areas were to be a milieu of social transformation.

Second, Gray Areas signaled a renovated approach to urban problems, a shift from "physical" to "human problems in the city." In particular, Ford Foundation staff conceptualized Gray Areas as "realistic and humane methods of handling the human problems involved" and thus as an alternative, and a response, to urban renewal programs (Public Affairs and Education 1961: 9, 11). A few years later, the 1964 President's Task Force on Metropolitan and Urban Problems echoed such ideas. The report acknowledged the failures of urban renewal, and it called for the "local preparation of social renewal plans" and the "recapture of large residential gray areas" in order to combat "social problems" (President's Task Force on Metropolitan and Urban Problems 1964: 8, 13–14). Norvel Smith, the coordinator of Oakland's Interagency Project, charged with the implementation of Gray Areas, described such an approach as "human engineering," the "renewal of people" rather than the "renewal of things" (*Oakland Tribune*, February 25, 1964).

Third, the "renewal of people" entailed specific methods of intervention. Indeed, Moynihan (1970: 39) argued that "Ylvisaker had no *program* for social reform, only a *method* whereby local communities could evolve their own . . . community action." Gray Areas was the first instance of the social technology of community action, and was described as a prototype in this regard. As conceptualized by the Ford Foundation, grants were to be directed to private nonprofit corporations that would implement community action. Working at the scale of the community, as Halpern (1995: 87) notes, was in keeping with Alinsky-style direct action strategies, which had created "optimism about neighborhood and community politics among professional reformers." But at the same time, as an "adjunct to government" (Magat 1979: 122), Gray Areas marked the effort to institutionalize community organizing, in particular by creating a set of mediating institutions that were meant to manage community action. A similar mandate guided the War on Poverty's community development efforts, such as the Community Action Program. Within only three years of opening their doors, these community action agencies, with their charge of "maximum feasible participation," were seen as threatening by conservatives and even some liberals. By 1967 community action had given way to community development and "political organizing goals" had given way to "economic development activities" (de Filipis 2012: 30). Reflecting on the War on Poverty, Alinsky (1965: 42) noted that poverty funds were "used to suffocate militant independent leadership and action organizations which have been arising to arm the poor with their share of power." The story of Gray Areas in cities like Oakland is more complex, for the program became a platform for new formations of black radicalism. We return to this point later in this essay. However, it is fair to say that, in general, Gray Areas makes evident the deep-seated contradictions of community action as a program of government. As noted by Moynihan (1970: 42), Gray Areas was an uneasy articulation of "shaggy, inexact communitarian anarchism" and "a shiny, no-nonsense city-as-system, Robert S. McNamara style."

Fourth, an important part of the method deployed by the Ford Foundation was that of experimentation: "There is considerable support for the notion of designing pilot communities and conducting grant and demonstration activities in these communities in order to achieve experiments of consistent and critical impact" (Public Affairs and Education, 1961: 3). Indeed, by 1964 the idea of "demonstration cities" had become a part of the national policy vocabulary. The President's Task Force on Metropolitan and Urban Problems (1964: vii) called for the creation of a demonstration city program in order to advance human development. Thus, an article on the War on Poverty in the *New Haven Register* presented Gray Areas as "pilot efforts in the wedding of human renewal to urban renewal—and in the blueprinting of the War on Poverty" (Byers 1966). Nowhere was this idea of experimentation stronger than in Oakland, the first of the Gray Areas cities. The Ford Foundation found there what Regal (1967: 6) described as a "laboratory to study various methods of social intervention." Ford Foundation staff rejoiced that within two months of the Gray Areas grant, "planners from around the country" were "flocking to Oakland to 'touch the elephant'" (Public Affairs and Education 1962: 2). We return to the laboratory that was Oakland below.

Finally, Gray Areas has its roots in the preoccupation of the Ford Foundation with the problem of juvenile delinquency. This problematization of juvenile delinquency is worth taking up in greater detail because it rather pointedly demonstrates the resonances and even connections between the wars on poverty at home and abroad.

The Milieu of Delinquency

By the mid-1950s the Ford Foundation's newly invigorated Public Affairs staff was broadly interested in issues of juvenile delinquency, inner-city school improvement, and urban governance. O'Connor (1996: 595) writes: "Informing these programs and linking them together was a sense that the city was in crisis, unable as a governing unit to cope with the twin threats of economic 'obsolescence' and neighborhood 'blight' brought on by industrial decentralization, middle-class suburbanization, and the in-migration of poor minorities." The foundation's long-standing interest in schools and a new interest in the "hot" issue of juvenile delinquency led to Gray Areas, after it became clear during the Great Cities School Improvement programs, which preceded Gray Areas, that a broader, more comprehensive approach was necessary to address urban poverty.

In the mid-1950s the Ford Foundation initially funded research that linked delinquency to dysfunctional family life, but the group later adopted a structural approach informed by the work of sociologists Richard Cloward and Lloyd Ohlin. Countering dominant ideas about the pathological and deviant individual in need of punishment and reform, Cloward and Ohlin (1960) argued that juvenile delinquency was the result of a lack of opportunity for the urban poor and should be addressed with comprehensive social programs. In 1961, the same year that Gray Areas began, the Ford Foundation gave $2 million to Mobilization for Youth, a project jointly run by the Henry Street Settlement and the Columbia School of Social Work and informed by Cloward and Ohlin's opportunity theory. Mobilization for Youth, like Gray Areas, included a mandate for participation from community members. But unlike Gray Areas, it went on to spark controversy as participants and an increasingly militant staff organized to challenge local bureaucracies and school officials.

At the same time that juvenile delinquency was emerging as a problematized object for programs of government domestically, it became folded into the new security calculus of counterinsurgency. Meant to pacify populations as well as to animate economic development, counterinsurgency was a descendant of the milieu of pacification that French colonialists sought to create in the late nineteenth century. The Kennedy administration in its first year bolstered efforts toward the investigation and development of remedies for insurgency in the Third World, as well as the expansion of ongoing police and paramilitary assistance in Southeast Asia. By 1962 counterinsurgency had become official U.S. policy across the civilian agencies with the issuance of a series of National Security Action Memoranda by the Kennedy administration, resulting in the formation of the Special Group (Counter-Insurgency) or SGCI and the promulgation of the Overseas Internal Defense Policy (OIDP). That year also saw the inauguration of Gray Areas as well as the passage of the Juvenile Delinquency and Youth Offenses Control Act. The first generation of scholars to study Kennedy-era community action noted the dovetail between such poverty alleviation and the legislation aimed at juveniles (Kravitz and Kolodner 1969). The framework employed here, which holds together the foreign and the domestic in a single multiscalar analytic unit, however, reveals how the mixture of punitive policy and community development at home resonated deeply with civic action as the key adjunct to police and paramilitary action for counterinsurgency overseas. Civic action consisted of "training and equipping of engineer units for public works type projects" and "assistance in the field of vocational training," plus "medical, public health or sanitation components" (Johnson 1963). In other words, at home and abroad, development was yoked to security. The threat to present and future security, the threat that even overshadowed Vietnam, was not just poverty; in the early 1960s, it was embodied in the figure of the youth as delinquent.

Attorney General Robert Kennedy chaired the President's Committee on Juvenile Delinquency and Youth Crime, which oversaw grants administered under the pilot program inaugurated by the 1961 Juvenile Delinquency and Youth Offenses Control Act. Lloyd Ohlin and David Hackett, a former schoolmate of the attorney general, envisioned the program as comprehensive community action—in the President's words "a total attack upon the prevention and control of youth offenses" (Kennedy 1961)—modeled in part on Mobilization for Youth. A series of bills in 1968, 1971, and 1974 would extend federal legislation on juvenile delinquency. But Attorney General Kennedy's determined stance toward the problem of juvenile delinquency was not to be hemmed in by the territorial borders of the United States, as evidenced in documents from the SGCI. Or, put another way, apparently unruly youth were found at home and abroad. Attending the counterinsurgency meetings at the behest of his brother, Robert Kennedy repeatedly, and with resolve and truculence, pushed the mandate of finding methods to manage juvenile delinquency. Youth and students were prominent subjects of discussion; "youth programs" were of "vital importance" to the "U.S. effort overseas" (Moody 1964: 2). The OIDP noted that among the causes of insurgency were "a frustrated but articulate segment of the youth and intelligentsia (often foreign-educated) which advocates radical solutions to speed modernization" (Department of State 1962: 7). In American cities, too, youth discontent was soon pinpointed as the cause of urban and suburban rioting (Feagin and Hahn 1973). In Oakland, the laboratory city of Gray Areas, the experiment with community development "grew out of the efforts of the police chief to bring some coherence to public agency responses to escalating gang violence and the broader problems of juvenile delinquency" (Halpern 1995: 97).

The Laboratory City of Oakland

Oakland in the 1950s and 1960s was deeply segregated, and most of the city's black population lived in the West Oakland ghetto (Self 2003: 51). The site of the first black union in the country, West Oakland was an important political base for a generation of civil-rights activists, black progressives, and community organizations. During and in the wake of World War II, black migrants from the South arrived to Oakland en masse, and though the overall population of Oakland decreased between 1950 and 1960, the black population nearly doubled (Self 2003: 160). Established racial boundaries were crossed and redrawn as black homeownership increased outside of West Oakland and white families moved to the suburbs. "In the 1960s," said a resident, "you had this mass migration out of West Oakland to East Oakland. The whites were giving it up out there" (Self 2003: 161). Racialized anxieties about urban decay, crisis, and blight were intimately tied to the trope of migration, and migrants were imagined as culturally deficient and as unassimilated into city life.

As neighborhoods and schools uneasily began to integrate, fear of juvenile delinquents—imagined as angry young black men—increased. In 1957 there was a "potentially explosive inter-racial conflict" at Castlemont High School in East Oakland, and public officials met and "agreed that individual agency efforts at youth control were inadequate" (Regal 1967: 3). That meeting established an association of agencies, including the city manager's office, the police department, and the Oakland school district, with a mandate to control "problem youth" through increased coordination and communication across social-welfare, schooling, and penal institutions.

Impressed with this multi-agency approach to juvenile delinquency, the Ford Foundation, led by Ylvisaker, selected Oakland as the first Gray Areas city. The Gray Areas program in Oakland built directly on these previous efforts to reform, manage, and punish delinquent youth. In December 1961 the Ford Foundation awarded the city a $2 million grant, distributed over a two-year period. The Gray Areas program in Oakland exemplified a twin concern with economic development and security, operationalized at the level of the community, and implemented through an array of programs that sought to engineer better citizens. The project in Oakland was led by a group of well-established local leaders, including black professionals who formed strategic alliances with progressive organizations and organized for black representation in local government. The grant stipulations called for a citizen's advisory board, which led City Manager Wayne Thompson to assemble a board of fifteen elites, mostly local businessmen (Hayes 1972: 146).

The neighborhood selected for the Gray Areas program was Castlemont in East Oakland. Officials chose Castlemont, according to the *San Francisco Examiner*, because "this is a neighborhood with a variety of social problems, but it's not a slum. Oakland officials see Castlemont as an ideal area for experiment — because without help it could easily sag into new slums" (*San Francisco Examiner*, December 28, 1961). Indeed, the Ford Foundation had specified that they preferred to work with "low income migrants rather than long-time slum dwellers" (*Oakland Tribune*, February 18, 1963). The first goal of Gray Areas in Castlemont was to "reverse the process of social disorganization now characteristic of many neighborhoods and which lies at the root of many pathological manifestations such as delinquent behavior, school failures, and neighborhood deterioration" (Regal 1967: 6). Gray Areas, named the Interagency Project in Oakland, sought to transform Castlemont and prevent further decay by fostering a milieu of integration, participation, and progress. The Gray Areas projects included educational and recreational programs (language arts classes, integrated summer camp, afterschool tutoring, a bike club for teenage boys, and new school librarians), increased coordination among penal institutions (including a pretrial release program and elementary school programs to preempt delinquent behavior), health and sanitation (visiting hygiene nurses, a study of breakfast eating habits, and a program for pregnant teenagers), and job training. "The primary unstated goal," wrote the project's principal evaluator, "was to create a new social awareness" (Regal 1967: 111).

The programming linked the influence of what it deemed positive, exogenous cultural influences, which had a middle- or upper-class and white valence, to the ability of those in the target areas to engage in industrious self-help and grab opportunity. Thus, an article in the *Oakland Tribune* about a Gray Areas project read: "25 MOTHERS JOIN QUEST FOR CULTURE. Where does one find culture? It might be most anywhere. At an airport, a museum, a rose garden. Perhaps even a television station. But how can parents who know so little about such things hope to help their children help themselves?" (*Oakland Tribune*, June 9, 1963). A nurse in one of the Gray Areas projects reflected, "Our main job is to motivate people to be responsible for their own care" (*Oakland Tribune*, February 22, 1963).

As it made a particular slice of the world "thinkable" within the terms of American liberalism, Gray Areas in Oakland aimed to manage difference; to map, and thus make visible and reformable, black social reproduction; and to police young black men. Arguments categorizing the black migrant as urban pathogen; young black men as violent and ungovernable delinquents; cultural deficiency as evidenced in the need for education, hygiene, job training; and built-environment blight intertwined to frame the issue of poverty as a dilemma of "culturally disadvantaged" problem families who lacked opportunities and skills. The project sought to prevent racialized violence and to reform or police delinquent youth, but it was also more ambitious, for it sought to deal with the problems of urban dislocation and transformation and to deploy the idea of community as an antidote to the cultural deficiencies of migration and juvenile delinquency. In particular, the project targeted unassimilated migrants. It was called "a special welcome mat for newcomers to the Castlemont section of the city" that sought to foster the "proper assimilation of new citizens into the community" (*Oakland Tribune*, December 28, 1961). Although the project was framed as an intervention specifically targeting new migrants, only 11 percent of the population in Castlemont were newcomers—defined by the Health Department as those who had moved within the previous ninety days. Newcomers were imagined as rural, southern, black, poorly educated, and unassimilated into city life, yet only 23 percent of the newcomers had arrived from outside of California. Less than half—43 percent—of newcomers were black, and they had a higher median income than white newcomers from within Alameda County (Regal 1967: 37).

A hopeful project, Gray Areas was ultimately founded on the belief that if people living in poverty in neighborhoods of transition could be given the skills to participate in middle-class life, they too could have access to boundless opportunity. But ultimately this required, as Galbraith (1961) had argued, that "persons and property are reasonably secure." And so, in Oakland's Gray Areas experiment, integration and punishment were essential elements of the same program of government; the Recreation Department and California Youth Authority (CYA) were intimate partners in this project of security. In this period, the CYA created a "revolving door between juvenile prisons and society at large" for black youth as well as "a direct conduit to the adult prison system" through which many future members of the Black Panther Party passed. This experience of multifaceted, state-sanctioned hostility crystallized the identity of "the lumpen" that came to be a focal point of the "new forms of politics and speech" the BPP developed to "counter the hostility" (Murch 2010: 67–68).

However, if Gray Areas in Oakland was a precursor to the federal War on Poverty and experimental community action, then it also exemplified the conjoining of programs of government and poor people's movements. The project was fraught with severe contradictions and generated intense contestation. Here is a glimpse of these struggles.

With the federal Economic Opportunity Act of 1964—the inauguration of the War on Poverty—the Gray Areas program in Oakland was converted into the Department of Human Resources. Oakland's conservative white mayor, John Houlihan, handpicked the members of the Oakland Economic Development Council (OEDC), the mandated citizen participation board. Houlihan included nine members of his "black kitchen cabinet" (Smith 2004: 165) on the twenty-five-person board: members of Oakland's powerful black middle class, attorneys, administrators, and civil-rights leaders. In only the second meeting of OEDC, black progressives leveraged the mandate for representation in the citizen participation board to lead a coup against Mayor Houlihan, replacing him as chairman with Judge Lionel Wilson, who in 1977 became the first black mayor of Oakland, with a campaign managed by Elaine Brown, then chair of the BPP.

In compliance with the national mandate of "maximum feasible participation," the OEDC established Target Area Advisory Committees made up of citizens from each of the four neighborhoods with community action programs. But by 1967, members of the Target Area Advisory Committees, mostly poor and black or Latino, became frustrated with middle-class professionals who "defended their leadership of the poverty programs, despite their high incomes and residence outside the target areas, by referring to their own personal origins and memories of growing up in the ghetto" (Rhomberg 1997: 226). By citing political authenticity and legitimacy based on their own experiences, activists claimed that middle-class OEDC board members did not represent poor people and could not speak for them. They bypassed city government and went directly to the regional Office of Economic Opportunity, leveraging the stipulation for "maximum feasible participation" to gain a 51 percent majority on the board. For a moment at least, the Great Society poverty bureaucracy was transformed into a platform for poor people's movements.

But the reclaimed OEDC also built on several of the central assumptions of the Gray Areas program. It called for citizen participation, neighborhood-level interventions, and community control of institutions. What marked a break with Gray Areas programming was the rejection of penality as a method of managing and regulating territories of poverty. Within a month of winning the majority on the OEDC, Target Area members outvoted governing and business elites to call for a police review board to investigate and address police violence. This vote represented a first victory for the new board, though the recently elected Republican mayor, John Reading, vetoed funding for the police review board (Hayes 1972: 154). The police review board battle, and contestation over a new executive director of the OEDC, led to a full rebellion from the poverty board. When the candidate for executive director endorsed by the Neighborhood Advisory Council activists and supported by the Oakland Black Caucus was passed over, the OEDC severed their formal relationship with the City Manager's Office to become the Oakland Economic Development Council Incorporated (OEDCI)—a separate, autonomous organization. Though the mayor still appointed twelve public officials to the thirty-nine-member council, the poverty board now functionally belonged to activist community members, was independent of local city council supervision, and was accountable only to the regional and national Office of Economic Opportunity. In 1971 the mayor of Oakland appealed to then-California governor Ronald Reagan to veto funding for the "renegade, black power–driven anathema" of the OEDCI. He did, and the national Office of Economic Opportunity upheld the veto, which eliminated the poverty board (Self 2000: 778).

The battles in Oakland reveal the paradoxes of community action during the turbulent 1960s. Participation by community members in the Gray Areas program in Oakland began with a small, handpicked group of city elites. However, once transformed into the national directive for community action, first middle-class professionals and later poor people's movements seized the mandate of "maximum feasible participation," thereby transforming the landscape of poverty politics in Oakland and leveraging poverty platforms to build political power (Self 2000: 776). In particular, neighborhood activists rejected the programs of penality that had been entwined with programs of social service. Most striking is how Oakland's poverty programs became platforms for diverse articulations of Black Power. First, progressive black leaders interested in integration crafted strategic alliances with local government to build middle-class black political organizations and increase black representation in poverty bureaucracies. Later, with the militant OEDCI and the parallel rise of the Black Panther Party, Oakland was more than an experiment in pacification; it was also a site of contestation and struggle. In 1967 two former poverty workers from the North Oakland Target Area Office, Huey P. Newton and Bobby Seale, founded the Black Panther Party for Self-Defense and organized black communities against brutal police. Like Ford Foundation officials, the Black Panther Party announced that Oakland would be their demonstration city (Self 2000: 769), the territory within which full control of community institutions could be assured.

A War on Two Fronts

In an account of the global reach of the Ford Foundation, Rosen (1985: 3) charts the transformation of the foundation from a "comparatively small local organization operating mainly in Michigan to the international organization it is today." An important benchmark in this transformation was the Gaither Report. Issued by the foundation in 1949, it was concerned with "the tide of communism." The foundation, the report argued, had to advance "the economic well-being of people everywhere" and had to do so because "their eventual well-being may prove essential to our security" (Rosen 1985: 3). Such ideas were further developed in projects and programs funded by the Ford Foundation. For example, at the Center for International Studies at MIT, Max Millikan and Walt Rostow called for "a long-term program to promote sustained economic growth in the Free World" (Millikan and Rostow 1957: 126). A strain of their vision of modernization would be implemented a decade or so later by Rostow's rival, Robert McNamara. Architect of U.S. warmaking in Vietnam, McNamara found a quite different role for himself as president of the World Bank. Redefining security as human development, McNamara reoriented the World Bank around issues of poverty alleviation. Ayres (1983: 12) presents the McNamara World Bank as an institution seeking to create "social change short of cataclysmic revolution," a phrase he borrows from Albert Hirschman. McNamara's philosophy of "defensive modernization," Ayres (1983: 226) notes, was thus meant to create "political stability" while implementing social and economic change.

In their Cold War vision of modernization and security, Millikan and Rostow (1957: 149) argued that "the United States is now within sight of solutions to the range of issues which have dominated its political life since 1865." For them, this included "social equity for the Negro, the provision of equal educational opportunity, the equitable distribution of income," and so forth. They warned: "If we continue to devote our attention in the same proportion to domestic issues as in the past we run the danger of becoming a bore to ourselves and the world." Needless to say, Millikan and Rostow were unduly sanguine about the state of social affairs in America. More important, their statement obscured a crucial fact: that the war on poverty at home was entangled with the war abroad. A poignant example of this articulation was the Great Society program McNamara oversaw, Project 100,000.

In a scathing critique of the emerging field of community development, from Gray Areas to Community Action Agencies, Moynihan (1970: lvii) contrasted two approaches to poverty alleviation: one concerned with youth employment and the other concerned with community action. Describing the latter as "maximum feasible misunderstanding," and thus expressing his disdain for the poverty bureaucracies of the Great Society, Moynihan clearly sided with the former. Moynihan's insistence on youth employment as the solution for black poverty signaled his distinctive problematization of racial difference. Concerned with the cultural deficiencies of the "Negro family," Moynihan saw work as a means to cultural uplift.

Whereas Gray Areas, and the related debates about human problems in American cities, foregrounded the question of juvenile delinquency, the matter of youth employment came up in a quite different arena of debate: that around military service. In a 1966 essay for the *New Republic* titled "Who Gets in the Army?" Moynihan (1966: 20) identified military service as an "immensely potent instrument for education and occupational mobility" but noted that "the least educated, least mobile young men," especially black men, were being excluded from the armed forces. Moynihan's essay was a recitation of the findings of the 1964 President's Task Force on Manpower Conservation. Titled "One-Third of a Nation," the report drew attention to both "the critical increase in the number of unemployed youth" and the statistical observation that "fully a third of the age group does not meet the required standards of health and education" for military service. In the report's cover letter to President Johnson, Secretary of Labor W. Willard Wirtz argued that these "young men have missed out on the American miracle." Of course, more was at stake than youth employment. Moynihan, in particular, saw the armed forces not only as a remedy for unemployment but also as the induction of the "down-and-out Negro boy" into "the male, American society" (Carter 2009: 136). Military service was to be a civil rights program, righting the wrongs of racial discrimination. It was also to be the pedagogy of heteronormative masculinity, a solution for the problem of cultural deficiency.

The surplus bodies who constituted "one-third of a nation" were a tangible reminder of the limits of the War on Poverty. Initially framed as an issue of labor, as a "human salvage program" (Starr 1973: 188), the problem was soon redefined as within the jurisdiction of the Department of Defense. In 1966, bypassing congressional approval, McNamara rolled out the ambitious Project 100,000, which was meant to induct previously rejected men into the military services (Drea 2011). Announced during a speech to the Veterans of Foreign Wars, McNamara framed Project 100,000 as a remedy for "America's subterranean poor" (Laurence and Ramsberger 1991: 18). In keeping with the "defensive modernization" philosophy he was to outline a few years later as World Bank president, McNamara presented poverty as that which "endangered national security" (Phillips 2012: 200). Between 1966 and 1972 more than 354,000 "New Standards Men," as they came to be called, were inducted into the military. They averaged twenty years of age; half came from the South; and 41 percent were "minorities" (Sellman 1990).

We do not intend here to undertake an evaluation of Project 100,000. Many have penned its indictments. A 1990 Congressional Hearing on the program posed the following questions: "Was Project 100,000 a legitimate Great Society social program? . . . Or was Project 100,000 a calculated, even cynical means to satisfy the manpower needs of the Armed Forces and, at the same time, lessen domestic opposition to the war in Vietnam?" (Evans 1990: 1–2). Stephen J. Smith, a former army draftee and later captain of the Savannah, Georgia, police force, declared: "We tried to fight a war on two fronts in the sixties—a war in Vietnam and a war on poverty—and we lost both" (Laurence and Ramsberger 1991: 139). Our work indicates that these framings fail to capture the logic of Project 100,000 as a program of liberal government. Project 100,000 was intended to create "equal citizens" and it did so by sending disproportionately large numbers of poor men, many of them black, to combat in Vietnam. Based on the premise that war could be the "first taste of integration into a white man's work" for African American men (Purnell 1967: 8), Project 100,000 relied on McNamara's promise of the armed forces as "the world's largest educator of skilled men" (Baskir and Strauss 1978: 1966). That such a promise was belied by what was later discovered to be the impoverished fate of veterans (Laurence 1990: 5) was irrelevant in the face of the Moynihan-led myth of cultural uplift for young black men.

Great Society programs, and precursors like Gray Areas, had failed to ameliorate racial subjugation. Project 100,000 was yet another experiment to tackle the question of racial difference, this time in a manner that explicitly linked the war at home with that abroad. Those whose neighborhoods represented a threat greater than Vietnam were now strangely tethered to the battlefields of Vietnam. But it was also impossible to ignore, as the bureaucrats of Gray Areas and elected officials of Oakland discovered, the no less international and multiscalar practices of freedom developed from racial subjugation. Antiwar petitions thus repeatedly drew attention to the struggle for freedom and equality in America: "We can write and ask our sons if they know what they are fighting for. If he answers Freedom, tell him that's what we are fighting for here in Mississippi. And if he says Democracy, tell him the truth—we don't know anything about Communism, Socialism, and all that, but we do know that Negroes have caught hell right here under this American Democracy" (Phillips 2012: 242). Soon, Martin Luther King Jr. was expressing opposition to the war. He lamented that young black men "crippled by our society" were sent thousands of miles "to guarantee liberties in Southeast Asia which they had not found in southwest Georgia and east Harlem" (in Phillips 2012: 248).

It is worth noting that these critiques emerged in tandem with, not as a response to, Project 100,000. Put another way, as Project 100,000 was unfolding, civil rights protesters sought to craft a different practice of integration and human freedoms, and in doing so they too connected the war abroad and oppression at home. Carter (2009: 138), for example, shows that the Student Nonviolent Coordinating Committee (SNCC) was "the first of the major civil rights organizations to come out against the war. The SNCC resolution called on all Americans to do civil rights work 'as an alternative to the draft.'" SNCC chairman John Lewis's statement read: "We believe that the United States Government has been deceptive in its claim of concern from the freedom of the Vietnamese people, just as the Government has been deceptive in claiming concern for the freedom of colored people. . . . We ask, where is the draft for the freedom fight in the United States?" Note the date: January 6, 1966. Project 100,000 launched later that year.

We are arguing then that political struggle in the face of, and against, programs of pacification also had a global imagination. Nikhil Pal Singh (2004) notes that the constitutive element of the black radical tradition in the twentieth century was its envisioning and practice of democratic equality, political universality, and freedom in excess of that available to racially subjugated peoples within the terms of liberal democracy. This practice generated universals that themselves were not bound by the territorial boundaries of the United States, but were both greater and smaller in scale than the nation. For example, the BPP articulated internationalism through a counterpublic sphere and travel abroad (including as exiles), as well as efforts toward relations with nations otherwise unrecognized by the United States, including North Vietnam. Many interpretations of the Panthers have remained bound by a methodological nationalism that was simply not operative for these historical actors. It is an artifact of historiography, as well as of the Cold War meliorist liberal project, of which Moynihan and McNamara were a part, to construct black freedom struggles as consonant with U.S. democratic but anticommunist yearnings and American exceptionalism (Dudziak 2000). It is instead important to recognize the global reach and universal ethos of Black Panther claims. Nik Heynen (2009: 416) thus discerns a specifically geographic set of practices in the Panthers' "revolutionary intercommunalism." If Gray Areas had territorialized poverty in a milieu of intervention operationalized as community, then Panther leaders such as Huey P.

Newton later saw "community to exist not just in the local contexts of Oakland or Chicago" but instead as "collectives of people living in colonized ghettos" (Heynen 2009: 416). Heynen's (2009: 419) analysis of the radical imagination that was the Black Panther Party's "utopian multiscalar imaginary" is especially instructive. He notes that Newton in particular was trying to fight a spatial logic whereby "oppressed people were scattered through a dispersed collection of communities, each with its own set of institutions geared toward serving the people and facilitating social reproduction." Gray Areas, as an expression of liberal government, was precisely such a spatial logic.

Provincializing the Great Society

In Ylvisaker's personal files is a letter from a correspondent named Lester W. Nelson. Dated 1965, the letter credits Ylvisaker for his efforts to deal with "people problems, particularly as they exist in urban life." Nelson hails Ylvisaker for a "precocious wisdom" and argues that Great Society programs were no more than "lineal descendants" of Ylvisaker's efforts. Of Gray Areas, Nelson argues: "Had these insights been adequately recognized and given timely support, as should have been the case, one must believe that such catastrophic events as Watts and others might not have occurred, or had they developed, might have been far less severe" (Nelson 1965: 1). Nelson's letter matches Ylvisaker's own aspirations. In an oral history conducted in 1973, Ylvisaker presents Gray Areas and other Ford Foundation interventions as "experimental programs that would go into governmental programs" (Ylvisaker 1973: 28).

How then should we view Gray Areas and its lineal descendants? Did Gray Areas fail because of a lack of adequate recognition and timely support, as Ylvisaker's correspondent claims? Could the widespread application of the Gray Areas method have preempted Watts and other black rebellions by creating a milieu of pacification and integration? In this essay, we have argued that Gray Areas must be understood not as success or failure but rather as a program of government fraught with the race and class anxieties of American liberalism. Ylvisaker presents the historical conjuncture at which Gray Areas was launched as being "right up against the confrontation of the old order and new" (Ylvisaker 1973: 24). In particular, Gray Areas was a delicate negotiation by liberal government of multiple power structures—from emergent formations of black radicalism in cities such as Oakland to the corporatized and militarized power that was an integral part of the apparatus of security.

But Gray Areas was more than neutral language: it was a spatial logic. Manifested in targets such as delinquent youth and urban migrants, Gray Areas sought to construct a milieu of intervention, of pacification, and, more boldly, of integration. The tumultuous 1960s were of course marked by these concerns about pacification and integration. In 1964, the last year of the Gray Areas program in Oakland before OEDC programming began to subsume and replace it, the President's Task Force on Metropolitan and Urban Problems (1964: 11) framed the urban problem of the day as that of "security," arguing that such security hinged on the capacity to "break up urban Negro ghettos that in their present form inevitably encourage a high rate of juvenile delinquency and adult crime." However, as both the story of community action in Oakland and that of the ambitions of Project 100,000 reveal, much more was at stake here than delinquent bodies to be redlined and quarantined. Each sought to remedy cultural deficiency with the liberal solution of opportunity; each sought to treat racial subjugation with the liberal solution of integration. That each sought to "neutralize" race rather than dismantle racial hierarchy speaks to the political openings and closures of the decade. The complexity of this historical moment, the anguish and incessant compromises of global liberals, are visible in this reflection provided by Ylvisaker as he describes his efforts to reconcile the interests of the Ford Foundation's trustees, including industrial magnate Stephen Bechtel, with the "militancy" of Black Power: "By this time militancy was beginning; the urban renewal projects which 'establishment' members (such as Bechtel and other Foundation trustees) were individually involved in, were being stopped because of the social veto that blacks and other urban minorities had imposed. So when we came in talking in terms that Bechtel and other trustees understood, we managed to duck the old embargoes" (Ylvisaker 1973: 23–24).

With such complexity in mind, we present, by way of conclusion, a coda to our reframing of the construction of community as a territorialized target for poverty alleviation. Specifically, we note an alternate genealogy of the term, "gray area." In his description of gray areas as a "neutral language," Ylvisaker credits the term to Raymond Vernon, who directed the Regional Planning Association's New York Metropolitan Regional Study, and his interest in "the gray area developing between downtown and suburb" (Ylvisaker 1973: 23, O'Connor 1996: 605). But we find that the genealogy of the term stretches beyond the Kennedy era. It goes back to an earlier Democratic administration and to foreign relations. A consummate Washington insider, Thomas K. Finletter, Secretary of the Air Force during President Truman's second term, elaborated this usage. Finletter's widely reviewed Cold War book, *Power and Policy: U.S. Foreign Policy and Military Power in the Hydrogen Age*, was published in 1954, just after the end of Truman's presidency. In it, he depicted the swath of territory along "the long frontier between Freedom and Communism from Turkey on the west, and leading eastward through Iran, Afghanistan, Pakistan, India, Burma, Thailand, Malaya, Indonesia, Formosa, Korea, and Japan to the Western limit of NATO in the Aleutian chain" (Finletter 1954: 84–85) as an area that was "still neither ours nor the Communists'" (Graff 1955: 137). These lands composed the "Gray Areas" (Finletter 1954). As one reviewer summarized: "The United States does not want to become involved again in local wars . . . Moreover, Russia and China are not likely to resort to direct attack in the 'Gray Areas,' but will use indirect aggression, infiltration, and subversion." The reviewer dryly remarked, "Finletter actually has no solution to this problem" (Vandenbosch 1956: 135).

Nor would the United States develop that solution in subsequent decades—other than the endlessly reinvented carrot-and-stick admixture of development-oriented enticements and coercive prevention of subversion and "indirect aggression." Two of Finletter's undersecretaries, John McCone and Roswell Gilpatric, would during the Kennedy administration become central figures in counterinsurgency planning, as CIA Director and Deputy Secretary of Defense, respectively, as the United States *did* again become involved in "local wars." It was the particular status of the "Gray Area" in the mind of policymakers that required counterinsurgency's combinatorial approach: loyalties and allegiances of the populations in these territories were up for grabs, so to speak, and the task was to prevent infiltration by those who would orient allegiances toward Beijing or Moscow *and* to provide evidence of how that allegiance to Washington, or to its proxy governments, was most beneficial to the target population. A "Gray Area" would be shaded more starkly in one direction or the other by the territorialization of loyalty to the nation. We suggest that the "Gray Areas" metaphor functioned in similar fashion in the hands of liberal domestic policymakers. The loyalties of delinquent youth—in territories of poverty, from Oakland to New Haven—were also in question. Our extended genealogy of the Gray Areas term is meant to "provincialize" the Great Society and its programs of government. Following Chakrabarty (2000), we hope to dislodge the War on Poverty from its securely American geographies and to make visible the global entanglements through which universals such as community and nation came to be articulated in the 1960s.

The historical sociologist Norbert Elias (1978: 48) described pacification as the process by which a range of discrepant types of habitus was eliminated in order for a distinctly European bearing and way of being in the world associated with "civilization" to emerge. Of note, he cites Voltaire, who wrote that Louis XIV "succeeded 'in making of a hitherto turbulent nation a peaceful people dangerous only to its enemies.'" For Elias, therefore, pacification is a nation-building process, in which operates a distinction between external enemies and internal misfits. The pacification of the internal misfits is crucial to the defeat of external enemies. When the French used this term to describe their efforts in Indochina, the distinction was between those who would be loyal to the colonial power and those who would not. The latter would be pacified until they became loyal. In the hands of U.S. officials, who were reluctant to adopt the term until 1966, the meaning shifted slightly, as the nation-building process had come into its own, and the United States did not deem *itself* to be fighting an external enemy. Instead, it was helping the South Vietnamese regime fight an external enemy, because the nation-building process in South Vietnam was to be the creation of a liberal republic on the Euro-American model. Those loyal to South Vietnam were not the object of pacification, nor were those considered hardcore loyalists of Ho Chi Minh, China, or the Soviet Union. The object was those who might be swayed—those in a Gray Area. As the course of the war shifted, as the nation-building project in South Vietnam became more and more difficult, and cities of the United States were aflame, writes Paul Starr (1973: 186), "To an Administration trying to fight both a ground war in Asia and a war on poverty at home, it must have seemed a stroke of genius to fight one war with the other." The internal misfits, made so through centuries of white supremacy, might be pacified through the fight against external enemies, as Project 100,000 would have it. In other words, pacification to build the South Vietnamese nation would be yoked, in vision, design, execution, and fate to the pacification needed to suture what was understood by 1968 as a fatally divided nation, or the "two societies, one black, one white," of the Kerner Commission's lapidary declaration (National Advisory Commission on Civil Disorders 1968).

As a glimpse of such projects of pacification, Gray Areas is both a program of government and a metaphor. We have repurposed the metaphor of Gray Areas to analyze key tropes and practices that traversed the North–South divide in the field of poverty, security, and development during the 1960s. Gray Areas, then, is a hinge of history, a moment of great ambivalence as questions of race and revolution were tackled in the interlude between the American New Deal and global neoliberalism.

REFERENCES

Alinsky, Saul D. 1965. "The War on Poverty: Political Pornography." *The Journal of Social Issues* 21:1, 40–47.

Ayres, Robert L. 1983. *Banking on the Poor: The World Bank and World Poverty.* Boston: MIT Press.

Baskir, Lawrence, and William Strauss. 1978. *Chance and Circumstance: The Draft, the War, and the Vietnam Generation.* New York: Knopf.

Byers, Donald C. 1966. "Overview' of War on Poverty." *New Haven Register*, April 3.

Carter, David C. 2009. *The Music Has Gone Out of the Movement: Civil Rights and the Johnson Administration, 1965–1968.* Chapel Hill: University of North Carolina Press.

Chakrabarty, Dipesh. 2000. *Provincializing Europe: Postcolonial Thought and Historical Difference*. Princeton: Princeton University Press.

Cloward, Richard A., and Lloyd E. Ohlin. 1960. *Delinquency and Opportunity: A Theory of Delinquent Gangs*. New York: The Free Press.

DeFilippis, James. 2012. "Community Control and Development: The Long View." In *The Community Development Reader*, ed. James DeFilippis and Susan Saegert, 28–35. 2nd ed. New York: Routledge.

Department of State. 1962. United States Overseas Internal Defense Policy, September; Office of Public Safety, Office of the Director, Numerical File, 1956–74, Entry 18; Box 5, IPS 7-2; Records of the Agency for International Development, Record Group 286; National Archives at College Park, Md.

Drea, Edward J. 2011. *McNamara, Clifford, and the Burdens of Vietnam 1965–1969*. Secretaries of Defense Historical Series VI. Washington, D.C.: Department of Defense.

Dudziak, Mary L. 2000. *Cold War Civil Rights: Race and the Image of American Democracy*. Princeton: Princeton University Press.

Elden, Stuart. 2006. "Rethinking Governmentality." *Political Geography* 26:1, 29–33.

Elias, Norbert. 1978. *The Civilizing Process: The History of Manners and State Formation and Civilization*. Cambridge, Mass.: Blackwell Publishers.

Feagin, Jo R., and Harlan Hahn. 1973. *Ghetto Revolts: Politics of Violence in American Cities*. New York: Macmillan.

Finletter, Thomas K. 1954. *Power and Policy: U.S. Foreign Policy and Military Power in the Hydrogen Age*. New York: Harcourt, Brace.

Foucault, Michel. 2007. *Security, Territory, Population: Lectures at the College de France, 1977–78*. Trans. Graham Burchell. New York: Picador.

Galbraith, John Kenneth. 1961. "A Positive Approach to Economic Aid." *Foreign Affairs* 39:3, 444–57.

Goldstein, Alyosha. 2012. *Poverty in Common: The Politics of Community Action during the American Century*. Durham: Duke University Press.

Graff, Henry F. 1955. Review of *Power and Policy: U.S. Foreign Policy and Military Power in the Hydrogen Age* by Thomas K. Finletter, *Political Science Quarterly* 70:1, 137–38.

Halpern, Robert. 1995. *Rebuilding the Inner City: A History of Neighborhood Initiatives to Address Poverty in the United States*. New York: Columbia University Press.

Hayes, Edward C. 1972. *Power Structure and Urban Policy: Who Rules in Oakland?* New York: McGraw-Hill.

Heynen, Nik. 2009. "Bending the Bars of Empire from Every Ghetto for Survival: The Black Panther Party's Radical Antihunger Politics of Social Reproduction and Scale." *Annals of the Association of American Geographers* 99:2, 406–22.

Johnson, U. Alexis. 1963. Memorandum for the President, March 7; Records of the Special Group (Counter Insurgency), 1962–1966, Entry 5206; Box 2, Special Group (CI) 1/17/63–3/7/63; General Records of the Department of State, Record Group 59; National Archives, College Park, Md.

Kennedy, John F. 1961. Letter to the Speaker of the House of Representatives Concerning Measures to Combat Juvenile Delinquency. May 11. Online by Gerhard Peters and John T. Woolley, The American Presidency Project. http://www.presidency .ucsb.edu/ws/?pid=8125.

Kravitz, Sanford, and Ferne K. Kolodner. 1969. "Community Action: Where Has It Been? Where Will It Go?" *Annals of the American Academy of Political and Social Science* 385:1, 30–40.

Laurence, Janice H. 1990. Statement at Hearing before the Subcommittee on Oversight & Investigations of the Committee on Veteran's Affairs, February 29. United States House of Representatives, Serial no. 101-38.

Laurence, Janice H., and Peter F. Ramsberger. 1991. *Low-Aptitude Men in the Military: Who Profits, Who Pays?* New York: Praeger Publishers.

Magat, Richard. 1979. *The Ford Foundation at Work: Philanthropic Choices, Methods and Styles.* New York: Plenum Press.

Marris, Peter, and Martin Rein. 1973. *Dilemmas of Social Reform: Poverty and Community Action in the United States.* London: Routledge and Kegan Paul.

Millikan, Max, and W. W. Rostow (with P. N. Rosenstein Rodan). 1957. *A Proposal: Key to an Effective Foreign Policy.* New York: Harper and Brothers.

Moody, C. G., Jr. 1964. Minutes of the Meeting of the Special Group (CI), July 16; Office of Public Safety, Office of the Director, Numerical File, 1956–74, Entry 18; Box 6, IPS 7–2; Records of the Agency for International Development, Record Group 286; National Archives, College Park, Md.

Moynihan, Daniel P. 1966. "Who Gets in the Army?" *New Republic,* November 5, 19–22.

Moynihan, Daniel P. 1970. *Maximum Feasible Misunderstanding.* New York. Free Press.

Murch, Donna Jean. 2010. *Living for the City: Migration, Education, and the Rise of the Black Panther Party in Oakland, California.* Chapel Hill: University of North Carolina Press.

National Advisory Commission on Civil Disorders. 1968. *Report of the National Advisory Commission on Civil Disorders.* New York: Bantam.

Nelson, Lester W. 1965. Letter to Paul N. Ylvisaker, February 3; Papers of Paul N. Ylvisaker, 1939–1992; Box 5, Personal Folder 4 of 4; Harvard University Archives, Cambridge, Mass.

No Author. 1961. The Public Safety Program, October; Office of Public Safety, Office of the Director, Numerical File, 1956–74, Entry 18; Box 3, IPS 2; Records of the Agency for International Development, Record Group 286; National Archives, College Park, Md.

O'Connor, Alice. 1996. "Community Action, Urban Reform, and the Fight against Poverty: The Ford Foundation's Gray Areas Program," *Journal of Urban History* 22:5, 586–625.

O'Connor, Alice. 2007. *Social Science for What? Philanthropy and the Social Question in a World Turned Rightside Up.* New York: Russell Sage Foundation.

Osborne, Thomas, and Nikolas Rose. 1999. "Governing Cities: Notes on the Spatialisation of Virtue." *Environment and Planning D: Society and Space* 17:6, 737–60.

Park, Robert E., and Ernest W. Burgess, eds. 1925. *The City*. Chicago: University of Chicago Press.

Phillips, Kimberley L. 2012. *War! What Is It Good For?: Black Freedom Struggles and the U.S. Military from World War II to Iraq*. Chapel Hill: University of North Carolina Press.

Piven, Frances Fox, and Richard A. Cloward. 1977. *Poor People's Movements: Why They Succeed, How They Fail*. New York: Pantheon Books.

President's Task Force on Manpower Conservation. 1964. *One-Third of a Nation: Report on Young Men Found Unqualified for Military Service*. http://www.eric.ed.gov /PDFS/ED021045.pdf.

President's Task Force on Metropolitan and Urban Problems. 1964. *Task Force Report*. Lyndon Baines Johnson Library, Austin, Tex.

President's Task Force on the Cities. 1966. *Task Force Report*. Lyndon Baines Johnson Library, Austin, Tex.

Public Affairs and Education: Gray Areas Program. 1961. Report on the Status of the Great Cities–Gray Areas Program, Enclosed with letter from Dyke Brown to Henry T. Heald, November 9; Papers of Paul N. Ylvisaker, 1939–1992; Box 5, Folder: Ford Foundation—Gray Areas—1961. Harvard University Archives, Cambridge, Mass.

Public Affairs and Education: Gray Areas Program. 1962. Request for an Extension of the Great Cities–Gray Areas Program, March; Papers of Paul N. Ylvisaker, 1939–1992; Box 5, Folder: Ford Foundation—Gray Areas—1962. Harvard University Archives, Cambridge, Mass.

Rabinow, Paul. 1989. *French Modern: Norms and Forms of the Social Environment*. Chicago: University of Chicago Press.

Regal, J. M. 1967. *Oakland's Partnership for Change*. Oakland, Calif.: Department of Human Resources.

Rhomberg, Chris. 1997. "Social Movements in a Fragmented Society: Ethnic, Class, and Racial Mobilization in Oakland, California, 1920–1970." PhD diss., University of California, Berkeley.

Rose, Nikolas, and Peter Miller. 2010. "Political Power beyond the State: Problematics of Government." *British Journal of Sociology* 61:s1, 271–303.

Rosen, George. 1985. *Western Economists and Eastern Societies: Agents of Change in South Asia, 1950–1970*. Baltimore: Johns Hopkins University Press.

Self, Robert O. 2000. "'To Plan Our Liberation': Black Power and the Politics of Place in Oakland, California, 1965–1977." *Journal of Urban History* 26:6, 759–92.

Self, Robert O. 2003. *American Babylon: Race and the Struggle for Postwar Oakland*. Princeton: Princeton University Press.

Sellman Wayne S. 1990. Statement at Hearing before the Subcommittee on Oversight & Investigations of the Committee on Veteran's Affairs, February 29. United States House of Representatives, Serial no. 101-38.

Singh, Nikhil Pal. 2004. *Black Is a Country: Race and the Unfinished Struggle for Democracy*. Cambridge, Mass.: Harvard University Press.

Smith, Norvel. 2004. "A Life in Education and Public Service." By Nadine Wilmot in 2002 and 2003, Regional Oral History Office, The Bancroft Library, University of California, Berkeley.

Starr, Paul. 1973. *The Discarded Army: Veterans after Vietnam. The Nader Report on Vietnam Veterans and the Veterans Administration.* New York: Charterhouse.

Sugrue, Thomas J. 2008. *Sweet Land of Liberty: The Forgotten Struggle for Civil Rights in the North.* New York: Random House.

The Gray Areas. 1963. Papers of Paul N. Ylvisaker, 1939–1992; Box 5, Ford Foundation—Gray Areas—1963 January–June and undated; Harvard University Archives, Cambridge, Mass.

Truman, Harry S. 1949. "Inaugural Address." January 20. Transcript. Harry S Truman Library and Museum, Independence, Mo. http://www.trumanlibrary.org/whistle stop/50yr_archive/inagural20jan1949.htm.

United States Military Assistance Command, Vietnam. 1968. *Handbook for Military Support of Pacification.* February, folder 14, box 05. United States Armed Forces Manuals Collection, The Vietnam Center and Archive, Texas Tech University. http://www.vietnam.ttu.edu/virtualarchive/items.php?item=1370514001.

Vandenbosch, Amry. 1956. Review of *Power and Policy: U.S. Foreign Policy and Military Power in the Hydrogen Age* (book) by Thomas K. Finletter, *The Journal of Politics* 18:1, 134–35.

Ylvisaker, Paul. 1973. Interview by Charles T. Morrissey. Ford Foundation Oral History Project. New York: Ford Foundation, September–October.

Spatializing Citizenship and the Informal Public

TEDDY CRUZ

Rethinking the Public: From a "Free" to an *Urgent* Imagination

It is obvious by now that the celebrated metropolitan explosion of the recent economic boom also produced a dramatic project of marginalization. This has resulted in the unprecedented growth of slums surrounding major urban centers, increasing the urban conflicts of an uneven development. This urban asymmetry at the center of today's socioeconomic crises also brought with it the incremental erosion of a public imagination, as many governments around the world enabled the encroachment of the private into the public.

Our conversation must begin then with the obvious: The *public* is collapsing as an ideal within a political climate still driven by inequality, institutional unaccountability, and economic austerity. This is true not only for the American context in which I write, but at countless sites across the world that have ascribed to and reproduced the neoliberal myth of a public-private schism. In other words, as the longevity of the top-down public welfare-state paradigm is in question today, we need urgently to search for alternatives, and seek a more functional manifestation of public thinking and action at "other" scales and within community-based dynamics: a bottom-up public? We must ask different questions if we want different answers. This is why one of most relevant and critical challenges in our time is the problem of how we are to restore the ethical imperative among individuals, collectives, and institutions to coproduce the city, as well as new models of cohabitation and coexistence in the anticipation of socioeconomic inclusion.

Rethinking the public cannot begin without exposing the controversies and conflicts that define the present moment's unprecedented socioeconomic inequality. In fact, decoupling the public from the imperative of socioeconomic equity only risks romanticizing our notions of the public, perpetuating the depoliticization of this urgent topic from our artistic fields and their practices. As a point of departure, this is a political project that contemporary architectural and artistic practices must engage. Today, as urban designers, we cannot begin any conversation about the future of the megacity without critically understanding the conditions that have produced the present crisis.

Since the early 1980s, with the ascendance of neoliberal economic policies based on the deregulation and privatization of public resources, we have witnessed how an unchecked culture of individual and corporate greed has yielded unprecedented income inequality and social disparity. This new period of institutional unaccountability and illegality has been framed politically by the erroneous idea that democracy is the "right to be left alone," a private dream devoid of social responsibility. But the mythology of this version of free-market "trickle down economics," assuring the public that if we forgive the wealthy their taxes all of us will benefit and one day become as rich, has been proven wrong by such undeniable evidence as political economists Saez and Piketty (2013: 1) have brought to light. They have noted that during both the Great Depression of 1929 and today's economic doldrums, we find both the *largest* socioeconomic inequality and the *lowest* marginal taxation of the wealthy. These are instances when the shift of resources from the many to the very few has exerted the greatest violence to our public institutions and our social economy. The polarization of wealth and poverty in the last decades has been a direct result of the polarization of public and private resources, and this has had dramatic implications in the construction of the contemporary city and the uneven growth that has radically increased territories of poverty.

This hijacking of the *public* by the private has in fact been mobilized by a powerful elite of individual and corporate wealth, who in the name of free-market economic policies has enjoyed the endorsement of federal and municipal governments to deregulate and privatize public resources and spaces of the city. This has prompted many planning and economic development offices to "unplug" from communities and neighborhoods at the margins of the predictable zones of economic investment, resulting in the uneven urban development that has characterized many cities in the world, from Istanbul to New York City. This retreat of the institutions of governance from public investment has resulted also in the erosion of public participation in the urban political process, as many communities affected by this public withdrawal have not been meaningfully involved in the planning processes behind these urban transformations, nor benefited from the municipal and private profits they engendered.

An argument can be made, however, that broad, structural political and social changes are possible. Such changes have occurred in certain moments in history, when the instruments of urban development were primarily driven by an investment in the public; two examples are the emergence of the New Deal in the United States after the 1929 economic crisis and the postwar Social Democratic

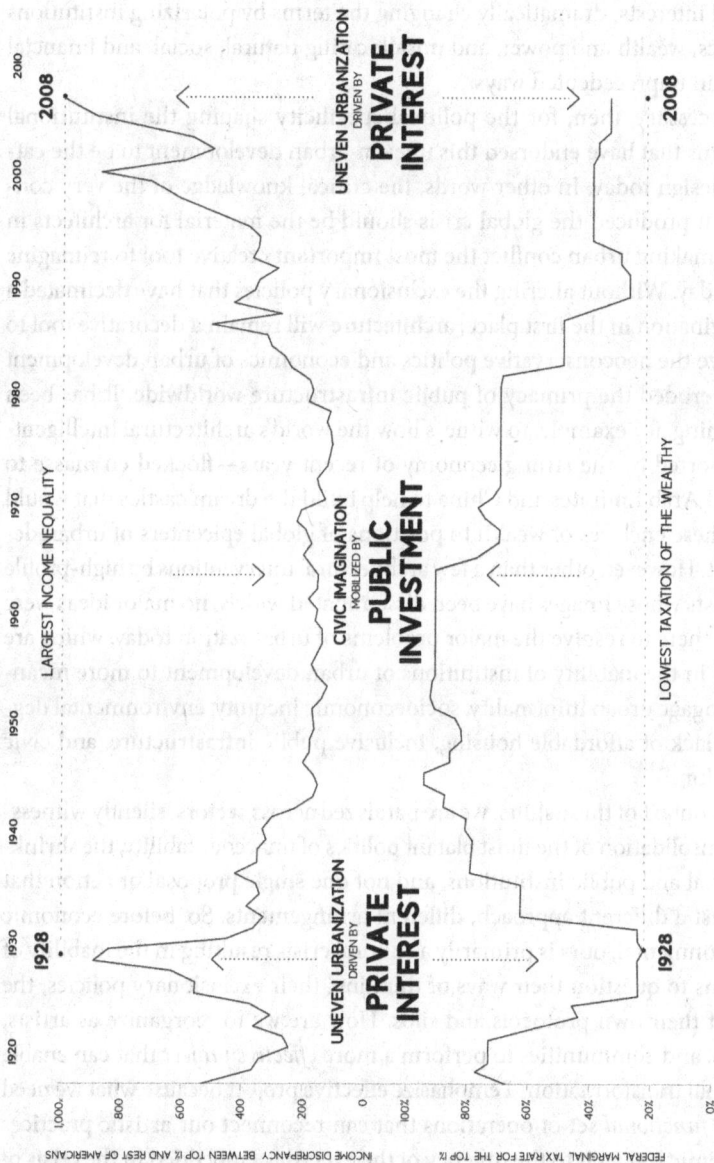

FIGURE 3. Diagram based on Saez and Piketty's study of American inequality, showing periods when privatization and income inequality dominate and periods when a public agenda enables a more equitable distribution of resources.

urban politics in Europe, and so forth. But today's crisis and its conditions are exponentially more complex, as the consolidation of exclusionary power is not only economic but also political, driven by one of the largest corporate lobbying machines in history, which has subordinated collective responsibility to serve individual interests, dramatically changing the terms by polarizing institutions and publics, wealth and power, and misallocating natural, social, and financial resources in unprecedented ways.

It is necessary, then, for the political specificity shaping the institutional mechanisms that have endorsed this uneven urban development to be the catalyst for design today. In other words, the critical knowledge of the very conditions that produced the global crisis should be the material for architects in our time, making urban conflict the most important creative tool to reimagine the city today. Without altering the exclusionary policies that have decimated a civic imagination in the first place, architecture will remain a decorative tool to camouflage the neoconservative politics and economics of urban development that have eroded the primacy of public infrastructure worldwide. It has been disheartening, for example, to witness how the world's architectural intelligentsia—supported by the strong economy of recent years—flocked en masse to the United Arab Emirates and China to help build the dream castles that would catapult these enclaves of wealth to positions of global epicenters of urban development. However, other than a few architectural interventions by high-profile protagonists whose images have been disseminated widely, no major ideas were advanced there to resolve the major problems of urbanization today, which are grounded in the inability of institutions of urban development to more meaningfully engage urban informality, socioeconomic inequity, environmental degradation, lack of affordable housing, inclusive public infrastructure, and civic participation.

In the context of these shifts, we are paralyzed across sectors, silently witnessing the consolidation of the most blatant politics of unaccountability, the shrinkage of social and public institutions, and not one single proposal or action that can suggest a different approach, different arrangements. So, before economic and environmental, ours is primarily a cultural crisis resulting in the inability of institutions to question their ways of thinking, their exclusionary policies, the rigidity of their own protocols and silos. How are we to reorganize as artists, architects, and communities to perform a more *effective project* that can enable institutional transformation? I emphasize effective project because what we need is a more *functional* set of operations that can reconnect our artistic practices and academic research to the urgency of the everyday embedded in the crisis of urbanization in order to produce new housing paradigms, other modes of socioeconomic sustainability, and conceptions of public space and infrastructure, as well as a new poverty scholarship and practice. At this moment this means that our work needs to complicate itself by infiltrating existing institutional protocols, negotiating modest alterations, and being persuasive enough to transform top-down urban policy and economy.

In fact, one primary site of artistic intervention today is in the widening gap between institutions of knowledge and the public. How to mobilize a new interface between the specialized knowledge of institutions and the community-based knowledge embedded in marginalized neighborhoods? It is through this meeting of knowledges that we can we instigate a new civic imagination. But this cannot occur without also intervening in our own practices and research protocols.

On one hand, we must question the role of architecture and urban planning, art and the humanities in engaging the major problems of urban development today, as well as the social and political sciences, and their obsession with quantified data as the only way to measure social inequity without giving us any qualitative way out of the problem. In other words, it is not enough only to reveal the socioeconomic histories and injustices that have produced these crises, but it is essential that theory and practice become instruments to construct specific strategies for transcending them; it is not enough for architecture and urban planning to camouflage, with hyper-aesthetics and forms of beautification, the exclusionary politics and economics of urban development; at this moment, it is not buildings but the fundamental reorganization of socioeconomic relations that must ground the expansion of democratization and urbanization. In the same manner, it is not enough for social and political sciences to only "measure" and expose the institutional mechanisms that have produced territories of poverty—important though that element is—but it is essential that they communicate these measurements to those who can make use of them, and work with communities to develop policy proposals and counter-urban development strategies, helping us to reimagine how the surplus value of urbanization can be redirected to sites of marginalization.

What this suggests is a double project, one that exposes the institutional mechanisms that have systematically and through often overtly racist and nationalist policies produced the stigmas, and the political and economic forces that perpetuate marginalization; it is also one that simultaneously intervenes in the gap between top-down resources and bottom-up agency, avoiding the trap of static victimization that has prevented the increase of capacity within marginalized communities for political agency.

But the formation of new platforms of engagement in our creative fields can only be made possible with a sense of urgency that pushes us to rethink our very procedures. The need for expanded modes of artistic practice, pedagogy, and research, which, connected to new sites of investigation and collaboration, can generate new conceptions of cultural and economic production, as well as the reorganization of social relations, seems more urgent than ever.

From Critical Distance to Critical Proximity: Radicalizing the Particular, from the Ambiguity of the Public to the Specificity of Rights

This double project of research and action must dwell within the specificity of these urban conflicts, exposing the particularity of hidden institutional histories, revealing the missing information that can enable us to think politically and piece together a more accurate, anticipatory urban research and design intervention. It is in fact at the collision between the top down and the bottom up where a new urban political economy can emerge.

It is at this juncture of abstraction and specificity where the revision of our own artistic procedures must take place. The same ideological divide that permeates politics is also found in art and architecture's ongoing debates. On one hand, we find those who continue to defend art and architecture as a self-referential project of apolitical formalism, made of hyper-aesthetics for the sake of aesthetics, which continues to press the notion of the avant-garde as an autonomous project, "needing" a *critical distance* from the institutions to operate critically in the research of experimental form. On the other hand, we find those who need to step out of this isolationism in order to engage the sociopolitical and economic domains that have remained peripheral to the specializations of art and architecture, questioning our professions' powerlessness in the context of the world's most pressing current crises.

These emerging latter practices seek, instead, for a project of *radical proximity* to the institutions, encroaching into them to transform them from the inside out. Such infiltration allows us to produce new aesthetic categories that can problematize the relationship of the social, the political, and the formal, questioning our own creative fields' unconditional love affair, in recent years, with a system of economic excess that was needed to legitimize artistic isolationism and irrelevance. How to reconnect artistic experimentation and social responsibility, a major aspiration of the historic avant-garde, must be the central question in today's debate.

What is being sought then are expanded modes of practice, engaging an equally expanded definition of the public, where architects are responsible for imagining counter spatial procedures, where architects are responsible for creating political and economic structures that can produce new modes of sociability and encounter. Without altering the exclusionary policies that have produced the current crises in the first place, our professions will continue to be subordinated to the visionless and homogeneous environments defined by the bottom-line urbanism of the developer's spreadsheet and the neoconservative politics and economics of a hyper-individualistic ownership society.

It has been said, for example, that the Civil Rights movement in the United States began on a bus. A small act trickling up into the collective's awareness: When Rosa Parks sat where she did not belong, the bus was public but it was not accessible to all. While public transport at that time was labeled PUBLIC it was hugely exclusionary, ridden with inequality. This resonates with the collision between our abstract notions of the "public" and the specific reality of economic inequality on the ground today. For this reason it is necessary to move from the neutrality of the term public in our political debate at this moment in order to arrive at the specificity of rights, the rights to the city, to the neighborhood.

What is needed is a more critical role for design to encroach into the fragmented and discriminatory policies and economics that have that have produced these collisions in the first place. Artists and architects have a role in conceptualizing of such new protocols. In other words, it is the construction of the political itself that is at stake here: not just political art or architecture. This opens up the idea that architects and artists, besides being researchers and designers of form, buildings and objects, can be designers of political processes, alternative economic models, and collaborations across institutions and jurisdictions to ensure accessibility and socioeconomic justice. This means we need to expand forms of practice, through which design takes a less protagonist role, via small, incremental acts of alteration of existing urban fabrics and regulation to mobilize counter propositions to the privatization of public domain and infrastructure. The most radical intervention in our time can emerge from specific, bottom-up urban and regulatory alterations, modest in nature, but with enough resolution and assurance to trickle up to transform top-down institutional structures. And this is the reason, I maintain, that this project of rethinking public space today is not primarily an architectural or artistic project but a political one, a project that architects and artists can mobilize.

This new political project must also mobilize cross-sector institutions to confront socioeconomic inequality, seeking to elevate marginalized communities not only as sites of stigmatization, alienation, and control, but primarily as sites of activism and praxis. In this context, the most relevant new urban practices and projects moving socioeconomic inclusion forward will emerge from sites of conflict and territories of poverty, where citizens themselves, pressed by socioeconomic injustice, are pushed to imagine alternative arrangements. It is on the periphery that conditions of social emergency are transforming our ways of thinking about urban matters and matters of concern about the city.

Cross-Border Neighborhoods as Sites of Cultural
Production: The Informal as Praxis, the Informal Public

These questions have framed my thinking during the years that I have been researching the Tijuana–San Diego border region. It is here where one can directly
witness how the incremental hardening of the border wall and the apparatus
of surveillance behind it has occurred in tandem with the hardening of urban
legislation toward the public, deepening the erosion of social institutions, bar-
ricading public space, and dividing communities. In other words, the protectionist strategies of the last decades, fueled by paranoia and greed, have defined
a radically conservative social agenda of exclusion that threatens to dominate
public legislation in the years to come. It is at this juncture, in the context of this
sociocultural closure and the incremental privatization and erosion of public
culture worldwide, where marginalization gets specific.

For more than a decade, I have been working and investigating critical issues
of housing and urbanism that emerge from the observation of the many communities that flank the U.S.-Mexico border. In contrast to the generic "global city,"
which in recent years became the focus of an urbanization of consumption, local
neighborhoods in the margins of such centers of economic power remained sites
of cultural production. These are peripheral communities where new economies
are emerging and new social, cultural, and environmental configurations are
taking place as catalysts to produce alternative urban policies aimed at a more
inclusive social sustainability, giving the local a more critical role in rethinking
global dynamics.

My research-based architecture practice has oscillated from the scale of the
global border to the border neighborhood. After 9/11, I devised the Political
Equator as a visual diagram, which considers the Tijuana–San Diego border
as a point of departure. The Political Equator traces an imaginary line along
the U.S.-Mexico border and extends it directly across the world atlas, forming
a corridor of global conflict between the latitudes of 30 and 36 degrees north.
Along this imaginary border encircling the globe lie some of the world's most
contested thresholds including the U.S.-Mexico border at Tijuana/San Diego,
the most intensified portal for immigration from Latin America to the United
States; the Strait of Gibraltar, where waves of migration flow from North Africa
into Europe; and the Israeli-Palestinian border that divides the Middle East.

This global border, forming a necklace through some of the most contested
checkpoints in the world and emblematic of hemispheric divisions between
wealth and poverty, is ultimately not a "flat line" but a critical threshold that
bends, fragments and stretches in order to reveal other sites of conflict worldwide. Across the world, invisible trans-hemispheric sociopolitical, economic,

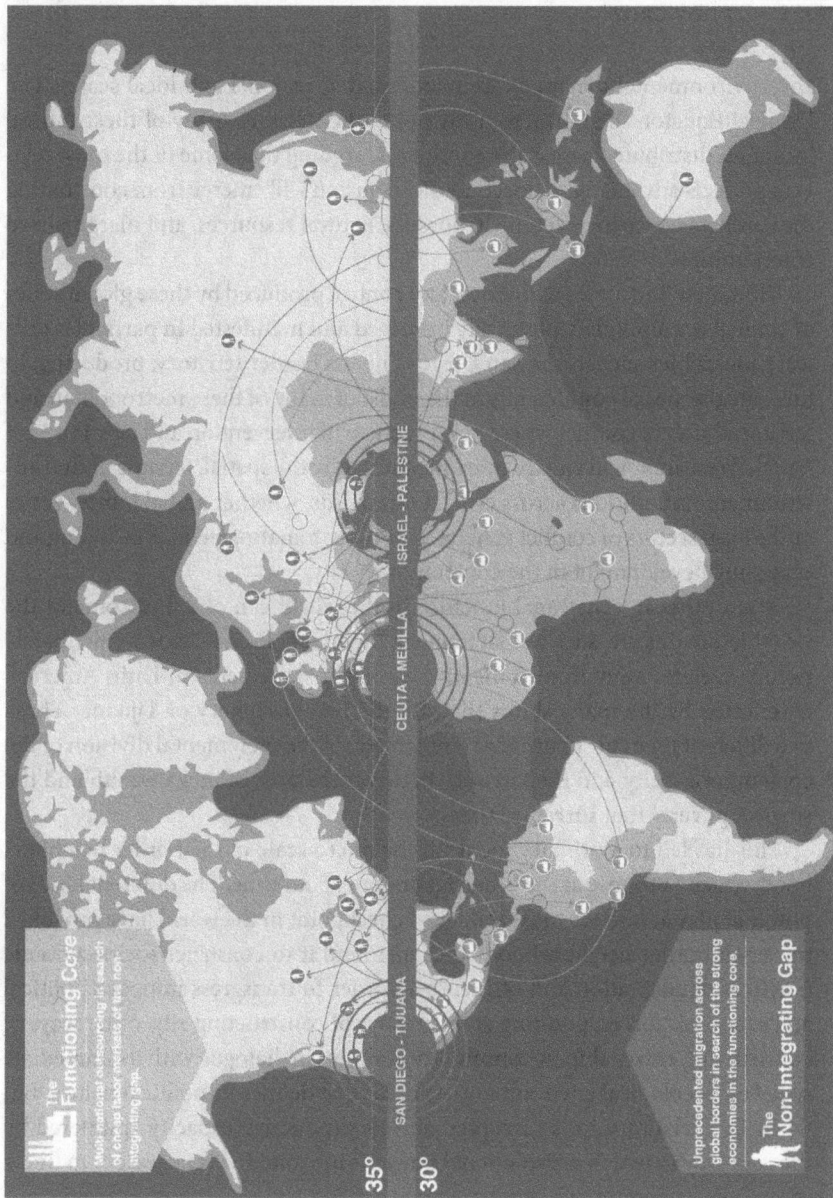

FIGURE 4.
The Political Equator traces an imaginary line along the U.S.-Mexico continental border and extends it directly around the world, forming a corridor of global conflict between the latitudes of 30 and 35 degrees north that connects some of the world's most contested border regions.

The Functioning Core
Multi-national outsourcing in search of cheap labor markets of the non-integrating gap.

The Non-Integrating Gap
Unprecedented migration across global borders in search of the strong economies in the functioning core.

SAN DIEGO · TIJUANA

CEUTA · MELILLA

ISRAEL · PALESTINE

35°

30°

and environmental dynamics are manifested at regional and local scales. The Political Equator, then, has been my point of entry into many of these radical localities, distributed across the continents, arguing that some of the most relevant projects advancing socioeconomic inclusion will emerge from confronting the conflicts between geopolitical borders, natural resources, and marginalized communities.

Ultimately, the forces of division and control produced by these global zones of conflict are amplified, physically inscribed and manifested in particular critical geographies such as the San Diego–Tijuana border territory, producing, in turn, local zones of conflict. It is in the midst of many of these metropolitan and territorial sites of conflict where new practices of intervention and new forms of "applied research" will engage more meaningfully the spatial, territorial, and environmental conditions across critical thresholds, whether global border zones or the local sectors of conflict generated by discriminating politics of zoning and economic development in the contemporary city.

At no other international juncture in the world can one find some of the wealthiest real estate, such as that found in the edges of San Diego's sprawl, barely twenty minutes away from some of the poorest settlements in Latin America, manifested by the many slums that dot the new periphery of Tijuana. These two different types of suburbs are emblematic of the incremental division of the contemporary city and the territory between enclaves of mega wealth and the rings of poverty that surround them.

This has led to a primary focus on the micro scale of the border neighborhood, which I propose as the urban laboratory of our time. The different kinds of power at play across the most trafficked checkpoint in the world have provoked the small border neighborhoods that surround it to construct socioeconomic practices of adaptation and resiliency in order to transgress imposed political and economic forces, pointing at other ways of constructing city, other ways of constructing citizenship. A community is always in dialogue with its immediate social and ecological environment—this is what defines its political nature. But when this relationship is disrupted and its productive capacity splintered by the very way in which jurisdictional power is instituted, it is necessary to find a means of recuperating its agency.

This agency and activism can be found in informal urbanization, which I see not only as an image of institutional alienation and poverty exploitation but as a set of practices, a set of every day procedures that enable communities to negotiate time, space, boundaries, and resources in conditions of emergency. We can learn from these urban processes in order to reimagine the meaning of public infrastructure in the official city and to mobilize new forms of accountability from the institutions of planning and private industry, as well to engage these communities as agents capable of challenging their exploitation by emergent models of financialization masqueraded as inclusive and ethical.

In this context, one of the most important issues underlying my research has been to produce new conceptions and interpretations of the informal. Instead of a fixed image, I see the informal as a functional set of urban operations that allow the transgression of imposed political boundaries and top-down economic models. I am interested in a practice of translation of the actual operative procedures behind informal settlements into new tactics of urban intervention. I see the informal not as a noun but as a verb that explodes traditional notions of site specificity and context into a more complex system of hidden socioeconomic exchanges. Primarily, because of my work in marginal neighborhoods in San Diego and Tijuana, I see the informal as the starting point of a new interpretation of community and citizenship, understanding the informal not as an aesthetic category but as praxis. This is the reason I am interested in the emergent urban configurations produced out of social emergency, and the performative role of individuals constructing their own spaces.

In recent years, I have been visualizing the many invisible informal trans-border flows, which are physically manifested by the informal land use patterns and economies produced by migrant workers flowing north from Tijuana into San Diego, and by "infrastructural waste" moving south to construct an insurgent, cross-border urbanism of emergency in Tijuana. This suggests a double urbanism of retrofit by which the recycling of fragments, resources, and situations from these two cities can allow new ways of conceptualizing housing and density.

SCENARIO 1.
NORTH TO SOUTH SUBURBS MADE OF WASTE:
SAN DIEGO'S LEVITTOWNS ARE RECYCLED INTO TIJUANA'S SLUMS

My research in this city has been studying the relationship of informal settlements, emergency housing, and the politics of cheap labor, as maquiladoras (NAFTA factories) settle in the midst of these slums. The periphery of Tijuana is dotted with slums, which build themselves with the urban waste of San Diego. This waste flows south-bound to construct an urbanism of emergency, as one city recycles the "leftover" of the other into a sort of "secondhand" urbanization.

I am referring to the postwar bungalows that have been part of the older rings of suburbanization in Southern California and are being recycled into the slums of Tijuana. These small houses are moved physically across the border as developers in the United States have recently begun to give them away to Mexican speculators in order to replace them with new and larger McMansions. So, not only people cross the border but entire chunks of one city move to the next.

Tactics of encroachment: as the Latin American Diaspora travels Northbound, it inevitably alters and transforms the fabric of San Diego's older subdivisions, generating non-conforming mixed uses and high densities that retrofit Levittown with difference.

Non-Conforming Buddha: a tiny post-war bungalow in a San Diego mid-city nieghborhood has been transformed from a single-family residence into a Buddhist temple.

An urbanism 70' deep: thirty some tunnels have been dug beneath Homeland Security in the last eight years. One of the largest ones was discovered last year. It had retaining walls, water and air extraction systems and electricity. It connected a house in Tijuana and a factory in San Diego.

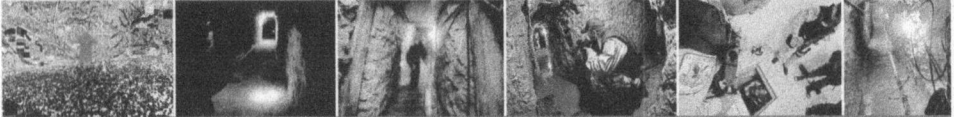

South to North: Neighborhoods made of non-conformity. Tijuana's informal land use patterns encroach into San Diego's sprawl.

North to South: Neighborhoods made of waste. San Diego's Housing waste is recycled into Tijuana's slums.

Migrant housing: Mexican builders recuperate post-war bungalows that are slated for demolition in San Diego, and bring them across the border. Once imported into Tijuana they are assembled above one story steel frames. These floating houses define a space of opportunity beneath them, that will be filled with other uses.

Housing urbanism made of waste: one city recycles the leftover of the other into a second hand urbanism. Used garage doors and wooden crates make wall systems.

Recycled rubber tires are cut and dismantled into folded loops, creating a system that threads a stable retaining wall.

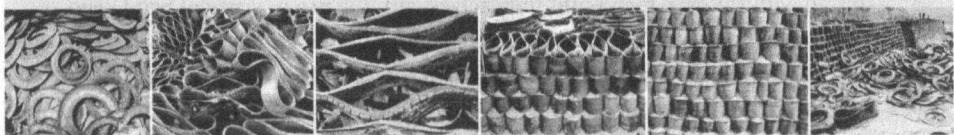

FIGURE 5. North-south/south-north invisible trans-border flows are physically manifested in one direction by an urbanization of adaptation, as informal densities and economies produced by migrant workers flowing north transform San Diego neighborhoods; and by "infrastructural waste," in the opposite direction, as Tijuana's slums recycle the urban "leftovers" of San Diego to construct emergency housing.

When these houses are moved into Mexico, they are put on top of steel frames, leaving the first floor open to be filled in time with a small business or an addition to the house, setting into motion an incremental layering of small-scale spaces and economies.

This recycling process does not only include houses, but a variety of small urban debris come into play—that is, standard framing, joists, connectors, plywood, aluminum windows, garage doors. Once in Tijuana's informal neighborhoods, these parts are reassembled by people into fresh scenarios, creating a housing urbanism made of fragments. Recycled rubber tires, for example, are used to construct retaining walls; but in the context of social emergency and housing shortage, people in these informal settlements have figured out how to strip the tires, how to thread them and interlock them to produce a more functional retaining wall. Also, the garage doors from the older subdivisions of Southern California are imported en masse into the slums of Tijuana, becoming the new structural walls for emergency housing in these informal settlements.

It is undeniable that these slums have erupted as the underbelly of exclusionary global neoliberal economic policies that have turned cities like Tijuana into tax-free manufacturing heavens. In other words, Tijuana is one of those global zones of exception where multinationals set up shop to take advantage of cheap labor, and where they can avoid any sort of regulation against human exploitation and environmental degradation. Yet, these slums are also intensive urbanizations of juxtaposition, emblematic of how Tijuana's informal communities are growing faster than the urban cores they surround, creating a different set of rules for development, and blurring the distinctions between the urban, suburban, and the rural. How to intervene in these environments and with their communities? Beyond the static logics of the institutions of charity that generally muddle the distinctions between resistance and complicity, the applied academic research only treats—at a distance—these communities as subjects to be "randomized" and "assessed," and the indifference of governments and private industries have allied themselves in the further marginalization of these neighborhoods.

Tijuana Project: Manufactured Sites

While for architects it is compelling to witness the creative intelligence and entrepreneurship embedded in these communities, we must ensure that by elevating this creativity, we do not simultaneously send a message to governments and other sources of economic support that because these communities are so "entrepreneurial" they are capable of sustaining themselves without public support and that institutions, across sectors, can ethically unplug from these precarious environments. Or, in more specific terms, that it is not enough to

FIGURE 6. A housing innovation made of waste: A maquiladora-made prefabricated frame performs as a hinge mechanism to connect a variety of recycled materials and systems brought from San Diego and reassembled in Tijuana's slums.

simply give property titles to slum dwellers to incorporate them into the official economy—as Peruvian economist Hernando de Soto (2000) pointed out years ago—without the social protection mechanisms that can guarantee environmental and social justice (2). Otherwise, we risk perpetuating these environments as laboratories of neoliberal economic tinkering, based on individuals improving and selling their own parcels as commodities, without any social protection mechanisms that can avoid exploitation by the generic financialization machine that does not take into account local communities and their social and economic well-being. In essence, I am also aware that this creative intelligence needs socioeconomic support systems, political representation, and a new approach to spatial and infrastructural design that can be inclusive of the temporal socioeconomic dynamics embedded in this stealth urbanization.

This is how, on the Tijuana side, I have been researching the alternative urbanisms of resilience and adaptation inscribed in informal urbanization in order to redefine urban density. Learning from these bottom-up forms of *local socioeconomic production* is essential to the rethinking of urban sustainability, focusing on neighborhoods as sites of environmental, cultural, and economic productivity. (I realize that when these two topics—neighborhood marginalization and economic productivity—are brought together, some academics get nervous, since this might suggest a complicity with the logics of top-down privatization and disinvestment, or that the language of entrepreneurship, resilience, and sustainability, resonates with neoliberal urban rhetoric. I want to retake

those terms and give them meaning through a more robust community-based engagement. What I mean here is that one of the most fundamental questions today is how to mobilize other economic pro formas of development that are neighborhood-led and whose profits benefit the community and not private developers only.)

This is how my urban research in Tijuana inserts itself in the midst of the conflict between factories and slums, opening alternative cross-sector processes for the production of social housing within informal settlements. We have observed that as NAFTA maquiladoras position themselves strategically adjacent to Tijuana's slums in order to have access to cheap labor, they do not give anything in return to these fragile communities. Our site of intervention is, then, the factory itself and the utilization of its own systems and material production and prefabrication in order to produce surplus micro-infrastructure for housing.

The Manufactured Sites project involves the production of a prefabricated frame (assembled with materials from the factories surrounding the slums) that can act as a hinge mechanism to connect a variety of recycled materials and systems brought from San Diego and reassembled in Tijuana. This small piece is also the first step in the construction of a larger, interwoven, and open-ended scaffold that helps shore up an otherwise precarious terrain without compromising the improvisational dynamics of these self-made environments. Conditions of social emergency ask for the reorganization of resources and the cross-institutional accountability and collaboration. The frame is produced by the Spanish company Maquiladora Mecalux and supported by Tijuana municipal subsidies, and it takes into account the hidden value of the sweat equity of people living in the informal settlement, a process that is coordinated and facilitated by community activists and agencies. The prefabricated parts emerge from the recombination of existing material systems inside the assembly line, and they become available for small cooperatives to collaboratively develop extra housing units with other residents. The design "intervention" here is a result of a process of negotiation with boundaries, resources, and people in a cross-sector curatorial project that critically approximates prefabrication industry, government subsidies, and communities organization.

SCENARIO 2.
SOUTH TO NORTH SUBURBS MADE OF NONCONFORMITY: TIJUANA'S ENCROACHMENT INTO SAN DIEGO'S SPRAWL

As waste flows south, people go north in search of dollars. The shifting of cultural demographics in American suburbs has transformed many poor immigrant neighborhoods into the site of investigation for my practice. My research in San Diego has focused on the impact of immigration in the transformation of the American neighborhood, projecting that the future of Southern California's urbanization will depend on the alteration of the large scale of exclusionary urban development by a small urbanization of adaptation: The micro-socioeconomic contingencies of informal urbanization will transform, through time, the homogeneous largeness of official urbanization of San Diego into more sustainable, plural, and complex environments.

Increasing waves of immigrants from Latin America have had a major impact on the urbanism of American cities. Already, Los Angeles, for example, is home to the second largest concentration of Latin Americans outside the capitals of Mexico, Guatemala, and El Salvador, among other countries. Current demographic studies have predicted that Latin Americans will compose the majority of California's population in the next decade. As populations travel north in search of new opportunities, they inevitably alter and transform the fabric of neighborhoods where they settle, including in San Diego and Los Angeles. In these older neighborhoods, multigenerational households of extended families shape their own programs of use, taking charge of their own informal economies in order to maintain a standard for the household.

It is not a coincidence, then, that these older mid-city neighborhoods compose the territory that continued to be marginalized in the process of urban redevelopment in the last decades of growth. Not able to afford the high-priced real estate of downtown or the McMansions of the new sprawl, waves of immigrant communities from Latin America, Asia, and Africa have settled into these first rings of suburbanization in many American cities in recent years, making these neighborhoods the service communities for the newly gentrified center and the expensive suburbs. The temporal, informal economies and patterns of density promoted by immigrants and their socioeconomic and economic dynamics have fundamentally altered what was the first ring of Levittown-type suburbanization of the 1950s, transforming it into a more complex network of socioeconomic relationships.

If we were to construct a binational land-use map between San Diego and Tijuana, for example, showing the different attitudes of these two border cities toward land use and density, we would notice the large blocks of color of an exclusionary zoning—a maximum space with minimum complexity—to the north, and to the south the high pixilation of more compacted uses in Tijuana, a minimum space with maximum complexity.

This confetti of alternative uses in Tijuana has been slipping into the largeness of Southern California land uses, and when it hits the ground it alters the mono-use monoculture of many parcels in San Diego's homogeneous suburbs. An informal economy is plugged into a garage; an illegal granny flat is built in the backyard to support an extended family. This is an urbanization of retrofit transforming the large with the small, with more sustainable and inclusive land uses.

Many stories of alteration and nonconformity can be found in these San Diego environments. The Informal Buddha is the story, for example, of a tiny postwar bungalow that transformed into a Buddhist temple in the last two decades, incrementally altering the small parcel it occupies into a micro socioeconomic infrastructure. These community-based agencies are able to organize and bundle the invisible socioeconomic entrepreneurship embedded in this community and translate it into new policies and economies.

San Diego Project: Casa Familiar Micro-Policy

My work on the San Diego border has focused on the translation of the sociocultural and economic intelligence embedded in many marginal immigrant neighborhoods in order to propose more inclusive land use and economic categories that can support new forms of socioeconomic sustainability. The hidden value (cultural, social, and economic) of these communities' informal transactions across bottom-up cultural activism, economies, and densities continues to be off the radar of conventional top-down planning institutions.

These bottom-up urban transformations ultimately show the need to expand existing categories of zoning, producing alternative densities and transitional uses that can directly respond to the emergent political and economic informalities at play in the contemporary city. It is, in fact, the political and cultural dimension of housing and density as tools for social integration in the city that has been the conceptual armature of my work as an architect. How to enable this urbanization beyond the property line—this micro-urbanism—to alter the rigidity of the discriminatory public policies of the American city? How can the human capacity and creative intelligence embedded in migrant communities be amplified as the main armature for rethinking sustainability?

The story of the nonconforming Buddha suggests the need for mediating neighborhood-based agencies that can curate the interface between institutions and communities, top-down resources and bottom intelligence. I have articulated this research not only as a form of discourse that has enabled new critical conversation and debate across different constituencies, from academics to activists and politicians, but as a tangible process of collaboration with community-based nonprofit organizations such as Casa Familiar, in the border neighborhood of San Ysidro, to codesign and manage physical interventions in neighborhoods on both sides of the border.

The main achievement through this process was the tactical design and organization of a series of community dialogues and workshops with Casa Familiar that in turn generated the idea of a micro-zoning policy for San Ysidro, providing fertile political ground from which alternative hybrid projects and their sources of funding could emerge. This process opened an alternative channel of relationship with the City of San Diego to demand a more robust partnership and interface with neighborhood-based local nonprofit organizations, to enable them to co-own the resources of development and become the long-term choreographers of social and cultural programming for housing.

In essence, the Casa Familiar Micro-Policy was the proposition to seek a new role for many NGOs in neighborhoods to develop housing. This included the mediation and translation of otherwise invisible neighborhood dynamics: These NGOs can connect tangible housing needs to specific community participants, and they can support and generate new economies that emerge from the community itself and enhance social service capabilities to be plugged into housing. Agencies like Casa Familiar can mobilize the internal entrepreneurial energies and social organization that characterizes these neighborhoods toward a more localized political economy latent in these migrant communities. These socioeconomic agendas can be framed by particular spatial organization.

The Casa Familiar Micro-Policy includes the documentation of all stealth illegal additions and small informal economies sprinkled through the neighborhood in order to legitimize their existence, enabling the approval of a new affordable housing overlay zone for the neighborhood. The second part of the policy included the partnership of Casa Familiar with property owners who cannot afford to maintain their own properties—the production of social contracts within the community to produce a new form of shared ownership and social protection mechanism is essential here. Then, Casa Familiar will be enabled by the city to officially prepackage and facilitate construction permits to

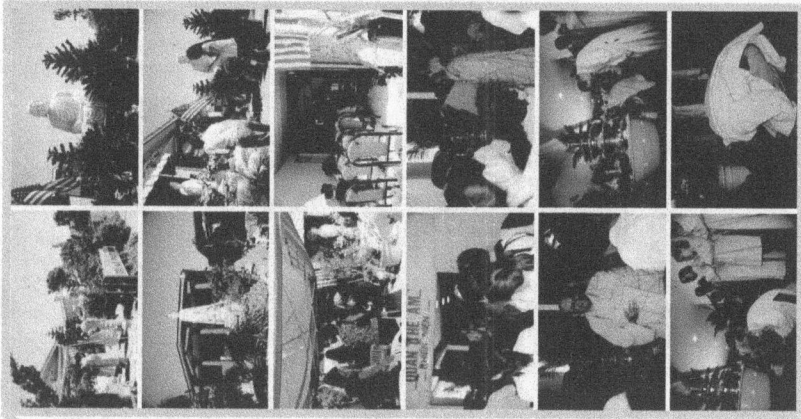

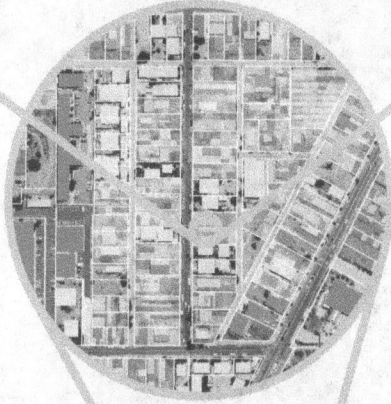

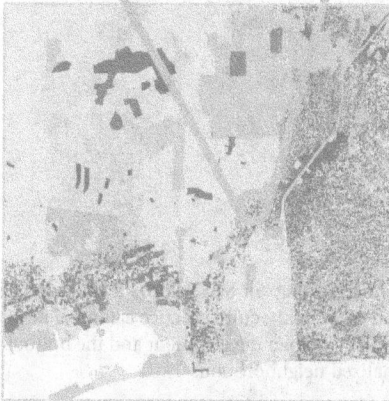

FIGURE 7. The alternative land-use pixelation of a migrant urbanization found in many older California neighborhoods where mono-use parcels are transformed into complex microeconomic systems and social networks.

Top Down Institution
Economic value as seed of development for the city.
Private developer sees...

Housing Development as market owned
Profit as an individual's right
Density as maximum amount of units and minimum investment in public infrastructure
Inhabitants as generic customers

the power of
Economic Capital

City Official
Financing
Designing Collaboration
Community Activist
Neighborhood Participant

the power of
Social Capital

Bottom Up Agency
Cultural and social value as economic engine for the neighborhood
Community Activist sees...

Housing Development as neighborhood owned
Profit as the community's right
Density as maximum social exchanges per acre embedded in public infrastructure
Inhabitants as participants

Casa Familiar Micro-Policy

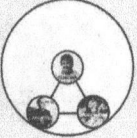

1 Translating the Informal
Casa Familiar coordinates mapping and documenting of all non-conforming additions and mixed uses.

2 New Zoning Categories
City Hall legalizes non-conforming units through a new affordable housing overlay zone and authorizes their reconstruction.

3 Casa Familiar: Informal City Hall
NGO facilitates the design and production of plug-in additions. City Hall prepackages new units' construction permits and allows NGO to manage process.

4 Casa Familiar: Facilitator of Micro Lending
NGO manages prepackaged tax credits and other subsidies and facilitates micro-credits by breaking large construction loans. Residents partner with NGO to co-own resources.

FIGURE 8. Housing micro-policy for San Ysidro, or the neighborhood as a political unit: expanded models of architecture practice can mediate between top-down politics and economics of urban development and the bottom-up social agency at the scale of marginalized neighborhoods

Tax credit subsidies do not support small development; existing land uses prohibit alternative mix uses and small lot housing densities.

No advances in housing design and affordability can be achieved without advances in housing policy and economy.

Youth

Education

Casa Familiar:
Community Based Non-Profit

nior Citizens

Sweat Equity

Arts and Culture

Micro Infrastructures for Coexistence

Small public rooms, a community garden and the retrofitting of a historic church serve as a social framework for housing.

Flexible units for young adults and single mothers + Artists live-work duplex + Casa Familiar Hub for social infrastructure + Extended families accessory buildings + Large families living with grandmothers.

The tactical distribution of diverse housing building types within a small infrastructure of collective spaces supports different housing economies and demographics.

Casa Familiar Programs		Informal Uses / Time Scenarios
Tues 3:30 PM	ARTS WORKSHOPS	
FARMER'S MARKET	Sun 9:30AM	
Sat 7:30 PM	QUINCEÑERA	
COLLECTIVE KITCHEN	Wed 6:00 PM	
Mon 10:30 AM	CATERING LEASE	
PUBLIC SYMPOSIUM	Sat 4:00 PM	
Sun 1:00 PM	GARDEN ORIENTATION	
GALLERY SHOW	Fri 8:00 PM	
Wed 7:30 PM	COMMUNITY MEETING	

A small frame, co-owned by residents, is conceived as a social service infrastructure threaded into housing. Plugged with electricity and collective kitchens, the frame is activated across time with specific social, cultural and economic programming tactically choreographed by Casa Familiar.

replace the precarious existing illegal dwelling units as well as tax credit subsidy–based pro formas to support their designation as affordable housing. Since
developer-driven tax credit subsidies do not support small development, Casa
Familiar would also be enabled to prebundle tax credit subsidies pertaining to
a large housing building, but breaking it apart into small loans and facilitating
them through the neighborhood, for which Casa Familiar would take liability.
The facilitation of entitlement and lending amplified the notion that marginal
communities need political and economic representation by agencies like Casa
Familiar. This micro-policy opened up a small-lot ordinance process in San
Diego, one seeking to infill transitional and suburban areas of the city while
enforcing an incremental densification and supporting community-led small
development. Most importantly, it presented a challenge: can communities become developers of their own housing stock and public infrastructure?

Toward an Urban Pedagogy: The Visualization of a New Civic Imagination

During the last two years, I have been collaborating with political theorist Fonna
Forman to further question the relationship between social justice, citizenship
culture, and the construction of the city: Can these marginalized communities
across the world and particularly those flanking the San Diego–Tijuana border
enable us to reimagine not only the meaning of public space, housing and infrastructure, but also the construction of new interpretations of citizenship? The
largest bi-national metropolitan region in the world has provoked the question:
Can a cross-border citizen exist whose idea of citizenship is organized around
the shared interests between these two divided cities?

We need to seek other conceptions of citizenship, beyond its inscription within the official protocols of the nation-state. As evidenced by these
under-represented border neighborhoods, citizenship is primarily a creative
act, enabling the transformation of institutional protocols and the spaces of
the city. It is within these marginalized communities of practice where a new
conception of civic culture can emerge, whose DNA is found in informal urbanization, and from which we can incrementally construct new interpretations of
community and praxis.

But as we return to these informal settlements for clues, their invisible urban
praxis also needs artistic interpretation and new tools and methodologies for
research. This should be the space of intervention for new forms of pedagogy
and scholarship. In this context, we must expand meanings of spatial and social
justice, understanding them not only through the redistribution of physical and
economic resources but as dependent also on the redistribution of knowledges.
An investment in an urban pedagogy—the transfer of knowledge across governments and communities—is the fundamental pursuit to construct a civic culture

as the basis for an inclusive urbanization and new conceptions of public space. Because of this, seeking new forms of urban pedagogy is one of the most critical areas for artistic investigation and practice today. The conventional structures and protocols of academic institutions and urban planning agencies may be seen to be at odds with activist practices, which are by their very nature organic and extra-academic and trans-institutional. Should activist practices challenge the nature/structure of pedagogy within the institution? Are new modes of teaching and learning called for?

These questions have inspired the construction of the Bi-national Citizenship Culture Survey, conducted by former Bogotá mayor Antanas Mockus and his nonprofit Corpovisionarios, in collaboration with political theorist Fonna Forman and me at the University of California, San Diego, and the municipalities of Tijuana and San Diego. The Bi-national Citizenship Culture Survey is an instrument that will measure and help visualize the shared values and norms, the common interests and sense of mutual responsibility around which a new bi-national conception of citizenship can be formed—beyond the arbitrary jurisdictional boundaries that too rigidly define cityhood, and beyond the identitarian politics of the nation-state. The results of the survey in the spring of 2015 will be stewarded by a cross-sector bi-national council that will develop a set of priorities and proposals in collaboration with the municipalities of San Diego and Tijuana and will usher in a new era of cooperation between them. By recognizing both Tijuana's and San Diego's urban policies and taking account of the assets, resources, and ideas that can be shared, the survey will facilitate the coproduction of bi-national vision and a process that derives its strength from cross-border synergies, inclusive of the most vulnerable communities on both sides of the border.

These are essential questions at a time when the hidden urban operations of the most compelling cases of informal urbanization across territories of poverty need to be translated into a new political language with particular spatial consequences from which to produce new interpretations of public infrastructure, property, and citizenship.

An Informal Public Manifesto:
- To challenge the autonomy of buildings, often conceived as self-referential systems, benefiting the one-dimensionality of the object and indifferent to socioeconomic temporalities embedded in the city. How to engage instead the complex temporalization of space found in informal urbanization's management of time, people, spaces, and resources?
- To question exclusionary recipes for *zoning*, understanding it not as a punitive tool that prevents socialization but instead as a generative

tool that organizes and anticipates local social and economic activity at the scale of neighborhoods.

- To politicize *density*, no longer measured as an abstract amount of objects per acre but as an amount of socioeconomic exchanges per acre.
- To retrofit the large with the small. The micro-socioeconomic contingencies of the informal will transform the homogeneous largeness of official urbanization into more sustainable, plural, and complex environments.
- To reimagine exclusionary logics that shape jurisdiction. Conventional government protocols give primacy to the abstraction of administrative boundaries over the social and environmental boundaries that informality negotiates as devices to construct community.
- To produce new forms of local governance, along with the social protection systems that can provide guarantees for marginalized communities to be in control of their own modes of production and share the profits of urbanization to prevent gentrification.
- To enable more inclusive and meaningful systems of political representation and civic engagement at the scale of neighborhoods, tactically recalibrating individual and collective interests.
- To rethink existing models of property by redefining affordability and the value of social participation, enhancing the role of communities in coproducing housing, and enabling a more inclusive idea of ownership.
- To elevate the incremental low-cost layering of urban development found in informal urbanization in order to generate new paradigms of public infrastructure beyond the dominance of private development alone and its exorbitant budgets.
- To mobilize social networks into new spatial and economic infrastructures that benefit local communities in the long term, beyond the short-term problem solving of private developers or charitable institutions.
- To sponsor mediating agencies that can curate the interface between top-down, government-led infrastructural support and the creative bottom-up intelligence and sweat equity of communities and activists.
- To close the gap between the abstraction of large-scale planning logics and the specificity of actual everyday practices.
- To challenge the idea of public space as an ambiguous and neutral place of beautification. We must move the discussion from the neutrality of the institutional public to the specificity of urban rights.
- To layer public space with protocols, designing not only physical sys-

tems but also the collaborative socioeconomic and cultural programming and management that ensure accessibility and sustainability over the long term.

- To enable communities to manage their own resources and modes of production while creating multiple points of access to share the profits of urbanization.

The *informal public* is the starting point from which to generate other ways of constructing the city, and its role today is to mediate between top-down and bottom-up dynamics: in one direction, how specific, bottom-up urban alterations by creative acts of citizenship can have enough resolution and political agency to trickle upward to transform top-down institutional structures; and, in the other direction, how top-down resources can reach sites of marginalization, transforming normative ideas of infrastructure by absorbing the creative intelligence embedded in informal dynamics. This critical interface between top-down and bottom-up resources and knowledges is essential at a time when the extreme left and the extreme right, bottom-up activism and top-down pro-development smart growth, as well as neoliberal urban agendas, all align in their mistrust of government. A fundamental role the informal public can take in shaping the agenda for the future of the city is pressing for new forms of governance, seeking a new role for progressive policy, a more efficient, transparent, inclusive, and collaborative form of government. For these reasons, one of the most important sites of intervention in our time is the opaque, exclusionary, and dysfunctional bureaucracy, and the restoration of the linkages between government, social networks, and cultural institutions to reorient the surplus value of urbanization to not only benefit the private but primarily a public imagination.

NOTE

I am grateful to the editors for inviting me to participate in this project; their comments and interventions have been very helpful to me. My thanks as well to Fonna Forman for her insightful comments on various drafts and for the many concepts which have emerged through our collaborations.

REFERENCES

de Soto, Hernando. 2000. *The Mystery of Capital: Why Capitalism Triumphs in the West and Fails Everywhere Else.* New York: Basic Books.

Saez, Emmanuel, and Thomas Piketty. 2013. "Top Incomes and the Great Recession: Recent Evolutions and Policy Implications." *International Monetary Fund Economic Review* 61:3, 456–78.

REPRESENTATION

The Bridge between Design and Poverty Action

SOMAYA ABDELGANY

As a student of architecture and urban planning equally passionate about poverty action as I am about design, I have met few classmates in the architecture program at UC Berkeley that share my desire to look at design as a potential tool to promote social justice within the urban fabric. At times, I feel very alone in my interest in the spatial manifestations of socioeconomic disparity in many of the world's cities, and even more so in my interest in developing strategies that seek to reverse the processes that have created these visible gaps. Perhaps this disconnect results from the nature of conventional design pedagogy and practice; in my experience, the ways in which architects are trained often lead them to ignore poverty, those who experience it, and the untapped creative genius of those who are poor. As a result, architecture is a profession of power, prestige, and money. Throughout history and in its modern practice, architecture has been an industry that serves the wealthy, carried out by those privileged enough to be able to afford a design education.

My deep interest in the visibility of poverty in the built environment stems from the fact that I grew up in a city that deliberately ignores poverty. I've spent most of my life in Irvine, California, a sterile and sheltered suburb that has earned a reputation as "The Bubble," ranking among the nation's wealthiest and safest cities. The city was designed with a master plan that set the stage for a very particular aesthetic standard: Irvine is divided into townships, called "villages," separated by wide thoroughfares, each containing single-family homes and apartments of similar design and accompanied by commercial centers, religious institutions, and schools. Today, this plan is manifested as a neatly compartmentalized agglomeration of low-density gated communities inhabited primarily by middle- and upper-middle-class residents. Its aesthetic of homogeneity, wealth, and exclusion has created a culture that ignores poverty. Because of the city's planning and policies, poverty is rarely given the opportunity to exist in Irvine, and if it does, it is made invisible to the city's general population. Without a single emergency shelter in the city, the Irvine police will promptly pick up homeless individuals that wander into town and drop them off in the less affluent neighboring city of Santa Ana, where services are available. Friends who live in the limited supply of subsidized housing tucked away in some of the Irvine villages have expressed that they feel the need to "keep up appearances," to hide their financial struggles among a vast majority of classmates and companions that simply can't relate.

My move to Berkeley was a culture shock, and a beautifully eye-opening one at that. I was met by a host of new experiences and interactions that suddenly made poverty visible to me. I encountered not just homeless individuals, but homeless communities on my daily walk to campus; I had the opportunity to sign up for classes dedicated specifically to the study of global poverty; I learned alongside classmates who, for the first time in my life, had not grown up with the same privileges and comforts that I had. Berkeley was an alternate universe in which I was given the opportunity to interact with and learn from people from many different walks of life, so a life of ignoring poverty became one that I was quite unwilling to return to. Now that I could see poverty, I wanted to see what poverty action looked like. I wanted to learn about the ways in which my academic and professional fields of interest could alleviate poverty instead of hiding it, and my design education was no exception to this new desire.

However, I found that even at Berkeley, architectural education tends to avoid issues of poverty because the practical implementation of design's social aspects more generally is rarely encouraged in a concrete way. The principles of "designing for a difference" and with greater consciousness of the social needs of user groups through ethnographic research and public participation are discussed at length in theory-based classes, but I have found that these principles are virtually lost when it comes to studio, the core of the architecture major and the laboratory in which students are given the opportunity to develop their own design sensibilities and priorities. In this laboratory, the cultural and social needs of human beings tend to be forgotten, as students are encouraged to "just give it a go" and design the most interesting structures and spaces they can conjure up. In my introductory classes, my instructors have gone as far as to tell me not to worry about how my buildings could ever work structurally or how expensive it would be to actually build them.

While instructors understandably do this early on to avoid limiting the creativity of their students, this type of pedagogy insinuates that the most beautiful and exciting designs are those that are not limited by reality or budget. Even as architecture students are forced to face the realities of the field in higher-level studios and professional practice, this mindset stays with them. The quintessential dream of many design students is to one day work on modernist monuments and big-budget projects funded by wealthy families and foundations, because they have come to understand that money allows one to build with the sky as the limit. This paradigm is aptly articulated in Ananya Roy's writing on praxis in the time of empire: "For professions like architecture and planning, the disavowal of [the] rule of beauty is difficult because empire presents a range of aesthetic opportunities—to experiment, build, construct, the Corbusian fantasy of colonialism" (Roy 2006: 19).

Poverty is understood to be a design limitation, but paradoxically, my instructors have made a point of reminding me time and again that design limitations should be treated as design opportunities. Architecture is a practice in problem-solving, and the most impressive architects are those who can create something beautiful despite the walls erected by design constraints. Why exclude poverty, with its complexities and opportunities for innovative thinking, from the list of "limitations" that can push the creativity of designers forward? And who better to consult for solutions to issues of poverty than the poor themselves, who exhibit creative genius every day in their struggles to make do? The thoughtful inclusion of poverty issues and poor people in the practice of architecture has the potential to play a significant role in both architecture and poverty action: it can make way not only for novel architectural projects that push the boundaries, but also for processes that legitimize poor people's knowledge.

As a designer interested in building for poor communities as a primary user group and with poor people as lead consultants, I take inspiration from exceptional architects working on affordable architecture both in the global North and the global South.

For example, David Baker + Partner Architects, an award-winning firm well-versed in affordable housing design in the Bay Area, has illustrated successful ways of building for lower-income residents as a user group. When I asked a principal from the firm about the design compromises that must be made in order to keep an affordable housing project within budget, I was told that making the form less aesthetically pleasing does not actually make the project any less expensive: architects can and should have the ability to create beautiful architecture for all audiences, including the poor. He also highlighted the intersectionalities between affordability and architectural ideals such as sustainability: the myth that green building relies on expensive technology is disproved by the energy-saving qualities of simple considerations like proper daylighting and site location. In addition, taking these inexpensive steps to make a building more energy-efficient further contributes to its affordability by reducing long-term energy costs.

When it comes to meaningful engagement of the poor in the design process, the architectural work of Estudio Teddy Cruz in Tijuana is a model for the field and my own aspirations. Cruz's projects revolve around the story of how designers, planners, factories, and poor communities can work side by side to make sense of recycled environments and ultimately create new programmatic paradigms through the translation of bottom-up productivity and informality into the built environment. It is unique in that it calls for a complete reversal of conventional allocations of knowledge between the poor and institutions of power and professional expertise. By redistributing knowledge production about affordable housing and neighborhood development to the poor, planners and designers allow the poor to become co-developers, and thus they are more capable of creating inclusive neighborhoods and housing that is both culturally relevant and useful to poor populations.

These approaches to architecture and planning are extremely important to design as a field as well as for my career. They prove that design and poverty action are not completely disparate practices in the way that my studio classes seem to suggest—that they can complement one another to create inventive advancements in both architecture and knowledge production. An understanding and consideration of poverty in architecture is an important first step, and if the socially conscious designers of the world are to create architecture and urban conditions that are both beautiful and beneficial to the poor, they must engage these communities as active participants and leaders in both design and knowledge production. Through this work, I hope for the emergence of a new genre of truly universal design that is both accessible to the poor and that can be appreciated by all sectors of society.

REFERENCES

Roy, Ananya. 2006. "Praxis in the Time of Empire." *Planning Theory* 5:1, 7–29.

CONCLUSION

Theory Should Ride the Bus

EMMA SHAW CRANE

This is not a book about poor people. It is about the politics of poverty. A collective, interdisciplinary project, *Territories of Poverty* hopes to unsettle dominant poverty discourse, dislocating the subjects and sites of inquiry. Instead of studying the often-pathologized bodies, behaviors, and places of "the poor," these chapters instead ask questions about how poverty is produced, defined, and governed. This is crucial work because how we think and act on poverty informs how we imagine what is possible, and what is just. As a participant in and scholar of movements for economic and social justice, I am particularly interested in questions of praxis in what Roy (2010: 40) calls "that impossible space between the hubris of optimism and the paralysis of cynicism." In the long, rich, and varied tradition of militant, engaged, and activist scholarship, critical poverty studies engages this impossible space. American poet Ruth Forman writes (1993: 10):

> poetry should ride the bus
> in a fat woman's Safeway bag
> between the greens n chicken wings
> to be served with tuesday's dinner
>
> poetry should drop by a sweet potato pie
> ask about the grandchildren
> n sit through a whole photo album
> on an orange plastic covered lazyboy with no place to go
>
> . . . poetry should bring hope to your blood
> when you think you're too old to fight.

Theory must also ride the bus. The final wager of *Territories of Poverty* is that critical poverty studies should be useful, not just for scholars but for anyone interested in thinking critically about power. We believe theory can have meaning beyond the policed boundaries of academic community and must be useful as a strategy for representing and engaging complex realities. As radical scholars have long suggested, theory should be something we construct with others and carry with us to make sense of our worlds. Like poetry, theory is representational work; it tells stories. It is never neutral, always tangled up with and implicated in projects of power. What stories are celebrated and what stories are silenced tells us a great deal about the present moment and reminds us that the audience is never innocent. The stakes are high because, as Katz and Flores remind us, poverty knowledge is also and always an exercise in social and political power, historically unaccountable to those it theorizes and represents. In "poetry should ride the bus," Forman offers us the possibility of another poetry: attentive to the racial politics of representation and also sustaining, hope in the blood. As a conclusion to this book, I offer here three moments from my work as a millennial poverty worker: dilemmas that haunt me and that force me to engage theory—always partial, appropriated, forgotten, invented—in intimate spaces of encounter.

After college my undergraduate peers went to rural Kenya, inner city schools, Peruvian slums, and San Francisco nonprofits. I joined a small media collective, building and supporting indigenous and peasant community radio stations in Mexico, Guatemala, and Honduras. As agents of international development, paid to deliver both infrastructure (radios) and empowerment (workshops), we spent weeks at a time in rural villages facilitating popular education workshops and providing technical training and support. Committed to radical solidarity and informed by antiglobalization struggles of the 1990s, my colleagues, like me, were young and foreign—Adams's (2013) underpaid laborers, participants in an affect economy that transformed our convictions and political commitments into labor. We were, I joked, the opposite of the World Bank.

One of the villages in which we worked was in the Guatemalan highlands, a place I will call Las Altas. It took us a full day picking our way along washed-out hillsides to get into the valley during landslide season. Part of a national organization of communities in peaceful resistance to the government, Las Altas was a village of Ixil and Ki'che indigenous people displaced by Guatemala's forty-year civil war. Most were refugees who had organized during the long genocide and won a land grant, successfully building a local, autonomous village council and a primary school. Up the hill, there was an abandoned health clinic, a crumbling cement ghost of some past development project. There was a muddy crossroads at the bottom of the village, a daily bus that left in the still-dark mornings, and a slat-board town store that sold rubber boots, potato chips, bundles of rope, shovels, cigarettes, and soda. On this trip we planned to install a new radio tower and offer workshops for women in radio production.

We were, it turned out, not the only international development workers in Las Altas. There was a South African who flew in and out of the remote valley in a helicopter. Our hosts told us he worked for a transnational Christian evangelical aid organization, directing a small business development and microfinance program. There was a widely believed rumor that he was a former mercenary who had worked for the apartheid government in South Africa. Families that enrolled in the Christian aid microloan program were given a pig, and their children went to a separate school staffed by foreign volunteers, who stayed in a dormitory with a generator and running water. Las Altas had been divided for several years between villagers participating in the aid program (many of whom had by now killed and eaten the pigs) and families involved in the national peasant movement. The two groups had separate churches (one evangelical, one Catholic), separate schools (one with English instruction and Bible Study led by the volunteers, the other without), and separate political bodies. The radio we were to build was for half the village.

Most villagers had lived in Las Altas since long before the arrival of foreign aid of any kind, and the homes of the two groups were interspersed. Some shared backyards. On my way back to the house where I stayed each evening, some families would wave and say hello, while others averted their eyes. People we worked with at the radio stations in other places left keys in unlocked doors or left windows open—but in Las Altas the radio was a cinderblock bunker with shutters that bolted from the inside. After several attempts at sabotage or theft, the radio team brought in the solar panels from the roof at night. The evangelicals planned to construct their own radio station.

Like many rural indigenous communities in the highlands, the land on which the village is built was collectively owned—held in a legal arrangement similar to a land trust—and could not be divided or sold. The Christian aid organization asked to buy a parcel of land (for a project, according to our hosts, affiliated with the World Bank), but the village council voted against dissolving collective ownership. Eventually, after enrolling half the village in the microfinance program, the scales tipped in favor of allowing the purchase of a small parcel. Now, in the wake of the dissolving land trust, it was rumored that a Guatemalan mining company, a subsidiary of the international weapons manufacturer Lockheed Martin, had sent surveyors to the village, and there was talk of lucrative metal deposits below the riverbed.

At stake in the battle between the new evangelicals and members of the national peasant organization was a theory of poverty: what causes it, who or what is responsible, and how it can be addressed. The evangelical aid organization claimed to lift families out of poverty by incorporating them into markets, markets that would reward entrepreneurial hard work. Economic growth would foster peace and stability. Members of the national peasant and indigenous movement saw the evangelical program as an attempt to financialize the village-based cooperative economy, put collectively held resources to work as potential sources of profit, and destabilize their struggle for political representation in the wake of genocide, cultural recognition, and autonomy. Aid workers were part of these debates, as signifiers, participants, gatekeepers of money and other resources, and sources of legitimacy with local and national government. I met another foreign volunteer at the village store. He was a college student from England who smiled at us as we eyed his raingear jealously. He spoke very little Spanish, and I wondered if he knew about the conflicting development agendas in Las Altas or if, like me, he had simply shown up to help, motivated too by a sense of justice.

Much of hegemonic poverty knowledge theorizes impoverishment as a problem to be solved: a lack of resources, services, or gadgets—a need for a radio or a pig, for example. Poverty is often framed as a deficiency of people or of place, or incomplete inclusion into prosperous and benign global markets (see, in this volume, Katz, Gupta, and Han). In these stories, the poor are entrepreneurial heroes or deviant, self-defeating failures. The non-poor disappear entirely or are present only as benevolent helpers or potential victims of poverty's dangerous contagions: disease, violence, disaster (Gupta, in this volume). This obscures the work they—we—do as we construct and legitimate theories of poverty. The story of invisible, neutral poverty workers persists even in a radical iteration of poverty action: as an ally, I imagined myself as outsider-beyond, a quiet assistant in a story of heroic peasant organizing. Yet in Las Altas, we were anything but outside or beyond. We were political subjects implicated in an unresolved struggle of ideas. As Adams and Han remind us in their essays here, the affect economy is irrevocably linked to projects of power. The theory I had learned in university classrooms and which I carried with me into the field was revealed to be utterly inadequate: I was prepared for the metapolitics of international development, armed with histories of international financial institutions and the tattered paperback classics of political economy, but I was unprepared for the small battles and their troubling questions.

I had hoped for a simple story, and I had hoped for a simple place within it. I could not refuse to engage with the strange constellation of multilateral development institutions shaping the field of millennial development, or with my own participation in that contested and fractured project. I was forced instead, following Maurer (this volume), to replace cleanness with complexity. In Las Altas, poor people's movements were imagined and produced in relationship to bureaucracies of power (see Roy and Kohl-Arenas). Effective engagement in these movements demanded a careful, critical understanding of poverty knowledge and institutions. Above all, Las Altas demanded a shift from thinking about places of poverty to territories of poverty. To understand a village not only as place but as territory offers a different kind of theory, one attentive to the awkward complicities and intimacies of poverty work, of imperfect engagement, and of poverty politics. Above all, praxis demanded that I take sides. In Las Altas there was—quite literally—no neutral ground on which to stand.

The project of international development is hopeful, and its poor subjects are so often celebrated: entrepreneurial women, or smiling children available for sponsorship online. There were different subjects of development that I encountered as a youth worker at a continuation high school in the San Francisco Bay Area. The specter of poverty elsewhere is shared tragedy, and ending this poverty a collective, millennial ambition. This millennial optimism is troubled by poverty in the North Atlantic: it does not inspire colored wristbands or concerts, tangled up instead with racialized hatred and fear. It is millennial development's sharp edge.

The young people at the high school were poor students of color expelled from mainstream schooling, for infractions from a fistfight between classes to stealing a bag of chips from the high school cafeteria. At the upper boundaries of childhood, aging out of the waning welfare infrastructure available to them as children, the students were—for many of their teachers, social workers, and security guards—unruly, marginal, and problematic. They were victims of poverty but also and always potentially dangerous. They were to be educated and they were to be policed: the school had a free lunch program and locked the gates during the day. It looked and felt like county jail.

I came to the high school to lead poetry workshops through a Department of African American Studies project. We had seed money from the university, an attempt to improve fraught "community relations" and offer college students marketable volunteer opportunities. Our project competed with other college student organizations for small grants, which usually included just enough for bus fare, copies, juice, and pizza. We were one of three groups of college students at the high school, and we diligently kept track of how many students attended each poetry workshop and how many volunteers we brought to the school. I photocopied students' poems and asked them for written feedback about the workshops. It would all go into next year's grant proposal, a translation of poor lives and teenage brilliance into readily accessible three-page summaries for administrators.

I had only been at the high school for a few weeks the first time a wealthy donor to a local foundation asked me about what we should do about low-achieving urban youth. Were there any innovative models for solving urban underachievement being piloted at my school? I was, suddenly, an expert on "urban problems." It did not seem to matter that I had grown up in a small rural town, or that I was a twenty-one-year-old white college student. The askers of such questions were also quick to congratulate me. Those teenagers were so lucky. I was a young success story, a hard worker: I was just what students *like that* needed. It was assumed that I was a tutor because most of the college students working at the high school were tutors in afterschool programs. Like me, they were paid below minimum wage, or they were volunteers. Our presence wasn't just about the material we tutored or taught. Poverty work is also affective labor. We were middle class or rising middle class, and as the school health worker said, we knew how to *talk* correctly. We knew how to *read*.

One day in our poetry classroom we read the letter a group of students in June Jordan's (1985) classroom wrote to the police officers who had recently murdered Reggie Jordan, the unarmed, twenty-five-year-old brother of student Willie Jordan. Students at B-Tech choose to write a letter to the tutors. They titled it "Guidelines for White Tutors":

> We are not bad people or bad Black kids . . . we are not stupid. Do not talk to us like we are monkeys. We are smart, intelligent, and brilliant people. This school is not a war zone. We are not failures. We are not dropouts. We are not convicts. This is not juvie. We are not all Special Education and we do not lack education. We do not need white people to save us. Our relationships with tutors must be reciprocal . . . we know what you think of us.

Both message and critique (directed not just to the tutors, but to us, the poets, perhaps not so separate a category as we imagined), the letter was an interruption of the class performance of tutoring, challenging the assumptions of the visiting college students but also the very conditions that produce such relationships, so often characterized as charitable, inspired by middle-class goodwill. The students demanded a shift in accountability: from the grant-making institution (the university) to them, the objects of such interventions. In this unlikely space of encounter (Valentine 2008), the tutors (and poets) were forced to reckon with poverty as a racialized relationship of power.

The guidelines sparked a conversation about what Goldstein in this volume calls this "unseemly presence in the present." As Goldstein observes, there is great interest in white America to foreclose on the past, to close it off as a strategy for security. We, the tutors, expected a fresh start. We were willing participants in multiculturalist blamelessness. The students were not so eager to engage uncritically with the post-racialism of millennial development discourse, which perhaps for this very reason operates more smoothly across national difference, the question of intimate inequality left unexamined. The letter was a momentary rupture of a representative deadlock. Imperfect and incomplete and temporary, it was a moment of speaking back, an interruption of the established script of benevolent tutors and delinquent black kids.

There are, of course, all of the obvious and searing observations to make about this: the white college student learns about privilege and power in a crucible of black poverty; the classrooms of poor students become sites of experimentation to sensitize and educate future middle-class professionals. But right alongside those truths: the awkward and earnest attempts of both tutors and students to build relationships across difference. We wanted, as visitors, both to help and to demonstrate humility. Simultaneously, we were eager, uninformed participants in a punitive program of government (the continuation high school) and an assimilationist cultural project (tutoring). We were in many ways conjuring our own successful futures and cementing professional credibility with a short sojourn to a risky frontier. And yet: the poems we wrote, the stories we told, the questions that arose, and the awkward beginnings of accountability taught us something about race in our country, about legacies of whiteness and the will to improve, about the unseemly past in the present. We were making theory, each of us: a theory of our own realities more honest and critical than what we had before.

Three weeks after the students wrote the letter, they came on a field trip to UC Berkeley to lead a seminar for college students considering volunteering in high school classrooms. Campus police stopped the students to check their IDs and detained them until I came to confirm that they were, in fact, invited guests.

During the weeks that I worked on this conclusion, two people were murdered on my block in West Oakland. Both were killed on the street, midday. The first time, I was around the corner, writing about millennial development in Guatemala. Through my headphones, the shots sounded very far away.

A few weeks before the murders, the City of Oakland hired "super cop" William Bratton as a consultant to the embattled Oakland Police Department, under the oversight of a federal judge after losing a series of police brutality cases. A former police chief in New York, Boston, and Los Angeles, Bratton pioneered the mutating, traveling model of "stop and frisk" policing, a practice that enables police to detain and search anyone suspected of involvement in a past, present, or imminent crime. We are promised that Oakland, the "robbery capital of America" (*Artz* 2013) will be the frontier of a new policing, an amalgam of global best practices. This Oakland of the future may also be one of the first cities in California to fly local law enforcement drones. Though the Alameda County sherriff initially reassured county lawmakers that the drone would be used as a search-and-rescue tool, the grant application submitted to the Department of Homeland Security stated the drone would be used for "surveillance (investigative and tactical) . . . intelligence gathering . . . suspicious persons, large crowd control disturbances, etc." (Harkinson 2013). A model manufactured by

Lockheed Martin's Skunk Works was suggested and displayed during the meeting (Woodall 2013). If Beirut is planned for the war yet to come (Bou Akar, this volume), Oakland too is calculated for violence to come, manhunts yet to begin. If the celebrated, model antipoverty programs are of the global South (Peck and Theodore, this volume), then perhaps the future of policing and surveillance is here in Oakland, demonstration city of the 1960s (Roy, Schrader, and Crane, this volume), and still laboratory of the future. Such modes of governance are strategies for managing territories of poverty and are, not unlike many interventions in the vast industry that is global poverty, primarily concerned with the security of non-poor subjects (Gupta, this volume). We are reminded that questions of poverty are also questions of death: of who lives and who dies, of what lives count and what lives are a threat.

In 2012, as a member of my local neighborhood association, I went door-to-door reminding my neighbors of an upcoming meeting to discuss neighborhood safety and a recent surge in foreclosures and evictions. I went with three teenagers from our block: two bored fifteen-year-old boys who shyly knocked on doors, sighing deeply, and Sarah, fourteen, in her final year of middle school. A confident and engaging doorknocker, Sarah rushed through the invitation to the meeting and the survey of neighborhood concerns and moved quickly on to what she urgently wanted to discuss: Kony 2012. Sparked by a viral video from the nonprofit Invisible Children, the Kony 2012 movement calls for the capture and trial of Joseph Kony, Ugandan war criminal and leader of the Lord's Resistance Army. That an Oakland teenager was moved by Kony 2012 is a testament to a global imagination of what it means to be a citizen, to an expanded sense of self, affected by the suffering of those a world away and concerned with justice and accountability. This is the reconfigured landscape of millennial poverty: boundaries between global North and South tangled and uncertain, a strict division, as highlighted by much of the work in this volume (in particular, Adams, Gupta, Han, and Peck and Theodore) no longer analytically useful. This landscape demands that we take seriously the work of African Christian aid workers in Guatemala and white American evangelical filmmakers in Africa; that we are attentive to the volunteers in classrooms and villages and knocking on doors.

My city reminds me that some violences are viral, spectacular, visible, and other violences are disappeared, so everyday common they don't make the local paper. When I tell my neighbors what I do for a living—poverty research—they often chuckle and ask wryly how that's going. Then, always, they congratulate me. It's a good job, and I am grateful to make a living. But this is work sharply marked by absences. I leave West Oakland in order to write about poverty from an office on a carefully policed university campus; I witness from a safe distance the deaths of my neighbors. Do I betray their memory when I write about them in a book that the people who loved them will likely never read? Who owns theory, anyway? Is it possible to make theory that is accountable beyond academic community? As Roy asks in her introduction to this volume, "What are the limits of truth at these limits of life?" And who decides what counts as theory and what is dismissed as anecdote? These questions are open, unresolved, unsettling.

When theory rides the bus it is made and remade by these devastating questions, these impossibilities and borders, these passages refused. Perhaps they serve not as a roadmap for getting it right but to alert us to the terrible contradictions and complicities of both academic work and poverty action, and indicate a receding horizon toward which we might move. Perhaps the primary purpose of poverty scholarship is not to generate solutions but to remind us that poverty is not a topic or a place or a behavior, something to which we apply theory, a series of problems waiting to be solved, but a problematizing frame for understanding power, for questioning what is intimately familiar and accepted. Critical poverty scholarship makes impossible the imagination of poverty researchers and poverty workers as somehow separate from the relationships of power we study, as beyond or outside of the places we work. It is against framings of poverty that depoliticize, threaten to render both scholarship and praxis irrelevant to the intimacies, dilemmas, and possibilities of poverty action. Critical poverty studies complicates our optimism but demands engagement with the contradictions. It has pushed me to untangle overlapping development agendas in which I am irrevocably implicated, to historicize the fraught intimacies of poverty action, to render strange the normalized deaths of my neighbors, and to unsettle old understandings of center and periphery, present and past.

Katz (this volume) writes, "the gap between theory and implementation is filled by power." Perhaps theory can build power by giving us tools to make sense of the past and see the present differently, and in doing so, forge alliances—always fragile, imperfect—across difference. Perhaps scholarship like the ethnographic and historical work in this volume can reveal potential openings, ruptures, and exploitable contradictions that enable what Cruz calls practices of "collective imagination" or what Abdelgany calls "the redistribution of knowledge production" (both in this volume). When theory rides the bus it invites us to critically engage our lives and to make theory out of our understandings of them. As scholars, educators, cultural workers, and organizers have insisted for a long time, theory can be part of a larger project to remake our collective common sense of poverty. When theory rides the bus it is made in and through praxis, the things we've been taught are undone by doing. What seems inevitable becomes contingent, unstable: this is the hope in the blood that Forman (1993) writes. This is a book about futures: the multiplicity of these futures, and the ways in which we may yet intervene in and shape them.

NOTE

I am grateful to Hannah Birnbaum, Mukul Kumar, Aurora Masum-Javed, Chris Mizes, Stuart Schrader, Ethan Watters, and, always, Ananya Roy for their thoughtful comments on this essay. Their generous help was invaluable. I am of course responsible for the final product.

REFERENCES

Adams, Vincanne. 2013. *Markets of Sorrow, Labors of Faith: New Orleans in the Wake of Katrina*. Durham: Duke University Press.
Artz, Matthew. 2013. "Oakland: robbery capital of America." *Contra Costa Times*, May 7, 2013, http://www.contracostatimes.com/ci_23191897/oakland-robbery -capital-america.
Forman, Ruth. 1993. *We Are the Young Magicians*. Boston: Beacon Press.
Harkinson, Josh. 2010. "Can Police Be Trusted with Drones?" *Mother Jones Magazine*, February 19, 2013, http://www.motherjones.com/mojo/2013/02/meet-california -sheriff-who-wants-use-drones.
Jordan, June. 1986. *On Call: Political Essays*. Boston: South End Press.
Roy, Ananya. 2010. *Poverty Capital: Microfinance and the Making of Development*. New Brunswick: Routledge.
Valentine, Gill. 2008. "Living with Difference: Reflections on Geographies of Encounter." *Progress in Human Geography* 32:3, 323–37.
Woodall, Angela. 2013. "Alameda County: Drone Meeting Ends with No Resolution." February 15, 2013, http://www.mercurynews.com/ci_22593768/alameda-county -drone-meeting-ends-no-resolution.

CONTRIBUTORS

VINCANNE ADAMS is Professor of Medical Anthropology in the Department of Anthropology, History and Social Medicine at the University of California, San Francisco. For the past seven years, she has been studying conditions of neoliberal governance and the role of faith-based institutions in processes of disaster recovery in New Orleans. Her previous work and publications have focused on medical pluralism, international health and development, modernity, women's health, and political change in Nepal, Tibet, and China. Her book *Markets of Sorrow, Labors of Faith: New Orleans in the Wake of Katrina* was published in 2013.

HIBA BOU AKAR is an Assistant Professor of Middle Eastern Studies and Urban Planning in the School of Critical Social Inquiry at Hampshire College. For 2014–15, Bou Akar is a Mellon postdoctoral fellow at the Mahindra Humanities Center at Harvard University. Bou Akar received her PhD in City and Regional Planning with a designated emphasis in Global Metropolitan Studies from the University of California, Berkeley. She holds a Bachelor of Architecture degree from the American University of Beirut and Master in City Planning from the Massachusetts Institute of Technology. She has published on the geographies of planning and war, on the question of urban security and violence, and on the role of religious political organizations in the making of the city. She is the coeditor of *Narrating Beirut from Its Borderlines* (2011) and the special issue "Security in/of the City" in the journal *City & Society* (2012). She is finalizing her book manuscript, titled "For the War Yet to Come: Planning Beirut's Peripheries." Bou Akar is the coeditor of *Jadaliyya Cities*, an online electronic journal on urban issues in the Middle East. She has also worked as an architect and planner, and as a research consultant with local NGOs and international UN organizations in the Middle East.

TEDDY CRUZ is Professor in Public Culture and Urbanism in the Visual Arts Department and co-director of the Center for Urban Ecologies at the University of California, San Diego. He is an architect and founder of Estudio Teddy Cruz, and he has been recognized for his urban research on the Tijuana–San Diego border, forwarding border neighborhoods as sites of cultural production from which to rethink urban policy, affordable housing, and civic infrastructure. He was recently featured in the exhibition *Small Scale Big Change: New Architectures of Social Engagement* at the Museum of Modern Art in New York, selected as one of twelve Social Change Visionaries by the Ford Foundation, and awarded the 2013 Architecture Award from the U.S. Academy of Arts and Letters.

ALYOSHA GOLDSTEIN is Associate Professor of American Studies at the University of New Mexico. He is the author of *Poverty in Common: The Politics of Community Action during the American Century* (Duke University Press, 2012), the coeditor (with Alex Lubin) of "Settler Colonialism," a special issue of *South Atlantic Quarterly* (2008), and the editor of *Formations of United States Colonialism* (2014). His essays have been published in such journals as *American Quarterly*, *Comparative Studies in Society and History*, *J19: The Journal of Nineteenth-Century Americanists*, *Radical History Review*, and *South Atlantic Quarterly*. His current book project is a study of the entanglements of U.S. colonialism, racial capitalism, and economies of dispossession and conciliation in the historical present.

AKHIL GUPTA is Professor of Anthropology at the University of California, Los Angeles, and Director of the Center for India and South Asia at UCLA. Professor Gupta's research interests include development and the state, ethnography of information technology, environmental anthropology, and India and South Asia. He is the author of *Postcolonial Developments: Agriculture in the Making of Modern India* (1998), and coeditor of *The Anthropology of the State* (2006) and *The State in India after Liberalization* (2010). His recent book *Red Tape: Bureaucracy, Structural Violence and Poverty in India* was published in 2012.

JU HUI JUDY HAN is Assistant Professor in Geography at the University of Toronto Scarborough. Her research interests include missionary mobilities, evangelical capitalism, contentious religious politics, the transnational production of racial and sexual difference, and Korea and the Korean diaspora. Her current projects focus on church growth and urban poverty in Seoul, religious property and church financing, and cultivation of religious-political homophobia. Her publications to date have discussed custodial politics of missionary rescue, intersubjectivity and ethnography, evangelical developmentalism, and missionary geoscience of racial difference and cultural distance. She is completing a book manuscript titled "Reaching for the World: Missionary Aspirations and Korean/American Evangelical Christianity," which concerns evangelical missionaries engaged in religious, humanitarian, and development projects throughout the world.

MICHAEL B. KATZ was Walter H. Annenberg Professor of History at the University of Pennsylvania and co-director of the graduate certificate program in Urban Studies. A pioneering scholar in poverty studies and the history of social welfare, Katz's vast repertoire of published work includes *In the Shadow of the Poorhouse: A Social History of Welfare in America* (1986, 1996) and *Why Don't American Cities Burn?* (2012), as well as earlier important works on the history of American education and the history of urban social structure and family organization. A new edition of his classic book *The Undeserving Poor* (2013), first published in 1990, tackles "America's enduring confrontation with poverty." On the sad occasion of Professor Katz's passing in August 2014, the *New York Times* paid tribute to this extraordinary social scientist whose work "challenged the prevailing view . . . that poverty stemmed from the bad habits of the poor, marshaling the case that its deeper roots lay in the actions of the powerful."

ERICA KOHL-ARENAS is Assistant Professor at the Milano School of International Affairs, Management, and Urban Policy at The New School. Professor Kohl-Arenas's book *The Self-Help Myth*, on the history of philanthropic investments in addressing migrant poverty across California's Central Valley is forthcoming with the Poverty Interrupted Series of the University of California Press. Her primary research areas include critical studies of philanthropy and the nonprofit sector, participatory community development, and the intersection of American and global poverty studies. She earned her PhD from the Social and Cultural Studies in Education program at the University of California, Berkeley. Her article "Governing Poverty amidst Plenty: Participatory Development and Private Philanthropy" was published in *Geography Compass* (2011), and she has also published articles in the *Journal of Poverty* and *Social Movement Studies*. Prior to her graduate studies Kohl-Arenas worked as a popular education and community development practitioner and stays engaged in the field through partnerships with community-based organizations in New York City.

BILL MAURER is Dean of Social Sciences, Professor of Anthropology and Law at the University of California, Irvine, and director of the Institute for Money, Technology, and Financial Inclusion. His research focuses on the anthropology of money and finance, including offshore finance, alternative and Islamic banking, and the use of mobile phones for money transfer. He is the author of many books and articles, including *Mutual Life, Limited: Islamic Banking, Alternative Currencies, Lateral Reason* (2005).

JAMIE PECK is Professor of Geography and the Canada Research Chair in Urban and Regional Political Economy at the University of British Columbia. His research interests are urban and regional restructuring, theories of economic regulation and transformation, statecraft and policymaking, neoliberalization, and governance. His current research focuses on contingent labor markets, austerity governance, and the globalization of policymaking processes and practices. He is the author of *Constructions of Neoliberal Reason* (2010), the coauthor of *Fast Policy: Experimental Statecraft at the Thresholds of Neoliberalism* (2015), and coeditor of *The Wiley-Blackwell Companion to Economic Geography* (2012).

ANANYA ROY is Professor of Urban Planning and Social Welfare at the University of California, Los Angeles, where she is also the inaugural director of the Institute on Inequality and Democracy at UCLA Luskin. Roy is the author of *Poverty Capital: Microfinance and the Making of Development* (2010) and *City Requiem, Calcutta: Gender and the Politics of Poverty* (2003). She is coeditor of *Urban Informality: Transnational Perspectives from the Middle East, South Asia, and Latin America* (2004), *The Practice of International Health* (2008), and *Worlding Cities: Asian Experiments and the Art of Being Global* (2011). Her new research is concerned with paradigms of "inclusive growth" in the global South.

STUART SCHRADER is a PhD Candidate in the Program in American Studies, Department of Social and Cultural Analysis, New York University. His dissertation is titled "American Streets, Foreign Territory: How Counterinsurgent Knowledge Militarized Policing and Criminalized Color." He is the recipient of a Mellon/American Council of Learned Societies Dissertation Completion Fellowship, as well as numerous other research grants and fellowships. His writing has appeared in *American Quarterly*, *City: Analysis of Urban Trends*, *The Brooklyn Rail*, *Maximum Rocknroll*, and *NACLA Report on the Americas*.

EMMA SHAW CRANE is a graduate student in the Program in American Studies, Department of Social and Cultural Analysis, New York University. In 2012 and 2013 she was a Global Poverty and Practice Research Fellow at the Blum Center for Developing Economies at the University of California, Berkeley. She was a Fulbright Scholar at the National University of Colombia, Bogotá, in 2010–11, where she conducted a yearlong ethnography exploring access to health care for former combatants living with HIV. She graduated from the University of California, Berkeley, with a Bachelor of Arts degree in Interdisciplinary Studies and a minor in Global Poverty and Practice. She was a Student Teacher Poet with June Jordan's Poetry for the People in the Department of African American Studies, and the 2009 University Medalist.

NIK THEODORE is Professor of Urban Planning and Policy, and Associate Dean for Faculty Affairs and Research in the College of Urban Planning and Public Affairs at the University of Illinois at Chicago. He is the editor, with Neil Brenner, of *Spaces of Neoliberalism: Urban Restructuring in North America and Western Europe* (2003). Theodore is coauthor, with Neil Brenner and Jamie Peck, of *Afterlives of Neoliberalism* (2012), and coauthor, with Jamie Peck, of *Fast Policy: Experimental Statecraft at the Thresholds of Neoliberalism* (2015).

LOÏC WACQUANT is Professor of Sociology at the University of California, Berkeley, and Researcher at the Centre européen de sociologie et de science politique, Paris. A MacArthur Foundation Fellow and recipient of the 2008 Lewis Coser Award of the American Sociological Association, his research spans urban relegation, ethnoracial domination, the penal state, embodiment, and social theory and the politics of reason. His books have been translated into twenty languages and include the trilogy *Urban Outcasts: A Comparative Sociology of Advanced Marginality* (2008), *Punishing the Poor: The Neoliberal Government of Social Insecurity* (2009), *Deadly Symbiosis: Race and the Rise of the Penal State* (2015), as well as *The Two Faces of the Ghetto* (2015). For more information, see http://www.loicwacquant.net.

Student Bios

SOMAYA ABDELGANY received a Bachelor of Arts in Architecture from the University of California, Berkeley, with minors in City and Regional Planning, Environmental Design and Urbanism in Developing Countries, and the Social and Cultural Factors of Environmental Design. As an undergraduate, she researched community development and antidisplacement policies with the Institute of Urban and Regional Development, and assisted the City of Emeryville with its affordable housing program. Abdelgany currently works with the City of Anaheim's planning department to make local policies and resources more accessible to the public. She is pursuing a Masters Degree in Urban Planning, and her areas of interest include social equity, affordable housing, public transit, economic development, and community engagement.

LUIS FLORES JR. was raised along the U.S.-Mexico barrier, where the transnational ironies of U.S. economic power are a visible part of everyday life. He graduated from the University of California, Berkeley, in 2012 with dual degrees in History and Political Economy. As an undergraduate, he worked at the Blum Center for Developing Economies and served as national politics editor for the *Berkeley Political Review*. A 2013–14 recipient of the Judith Lee Stronach Baccalaureate prize, Flores worked in Oakland and San Francisco on issues of housing vulnerability, credit dependency, and property investments, and collaborated with local tenant rights' organization Causa Justa: Just Cause. He is currently a doctoral student in sociology at the University of Michigan at Ann Arbor.

CHRISTINA GOSSMANN holds a Master of City Planning degree from the University of California, Berkeley, and an undergraduate degree in Economics and Psychology from Wellesley College. Before returning to graduate school, she worked as a freelance journalist and researcher, investigating media and technologies as tools of economic development in informal settlements in the global South. Following three months with the United Nations Human Settlements Program and field research on Nairobi's and San Francisco's technology industries, she wrote her master's thesis about job creation through technology for slum dwellers. She continues to explore the potential of technology and media in the urban space.

ANH-THI LE graduated from the University of California, Berkeley, in 2013 with a Bachelor of Arts degree in Political Science with a minor in Global Poverty and Practice. She currently serves as a Program Coordinator at the Blum Center for Developing Economies, supporting its Development Impact Lab. Before working at the Blum Center, she volunteered with a wide range of community development organizations in the Bay Area, Washington, D.C., Philadelphia, New Orleans, and India. She is most passionate about women and gender issues, the role of technology in global development, and political development in Southeast Asia.

REBECCA PETERS fostered an interest in community-led water resources management from an early age and graduated from the University of California, Berkeley, with degrees in Society and Environment and Interdisciplinary Studies in 2014 as the University Medalist. She examined peri-urban water access in Bolivia as a Berkeley Law Human Rights Fellow, researched the role of international institutions in shaping water policy in the global South, and taught a student-led course on water and social justice. She is pursuing graduate degrees in International Development and Public Law in the United Kingdom as a Marshall Scholar.

STEPHANIE ULLRICH is a consultant with the United Nations Development Programme where she works on results management and impact evaluations for environment and energy projects. She was a 2013–14 John Gardner Public Service Fellow after she graduated from the University of California, Berkeley, with a double major in Peace and Conflict Studies and Media Studies and a minor in Global Poverty and Practice. Her academic and practitioner interests surround the water-energy-food security nexus. Before working with the UNDP, she investigated electronic waste labor patterns in Ghana, and served as an Americorps volunteer with the Magnolia Project, a student initiative to help rebuild post-Katrina New Orleans.

INDEX

Page references in italics refer to figures and tables.

GEOGRAPHIES OF JUSTICE AND SOCIAL TRANSFORMATION